L.M. Montgomery's Complete Journals

The Ontario Years, 1918–1921

Edited by Jen Rubio

Introduction by Elizabeth Rollins Epperly

Rock's Mills Press

PUBLISHED BY

Rock's Mills Press

For information, visit us online at www.rocksmillspress.com or email us at customer.servicerocksmillspress.com.

Contents

Introduction

by Elizabeth Rollins Epperly

This is the journal of a consummate story teller. War, death, madness, fury, despair, sheer grit, laughter, love, and exquisitely realized beauty and joy: all are rendered through the eye and "I" of an artist for whom her journal was not so much a place as an act of engaging—a companioning of and questioning of herself. I suggest that this volume, covering 1918 to 1921, is one of the most important works in Montgomery's entire writing career. Here we see her personal world shattered, and we see her consciously remaking it.

Having been a reader of Montgomery's life story for many years and in many forms[1]—letters, scrapbooks, photographs, diaries, fiction, others' scholarship—do I find anything of special merit in reading the "complete" journals and in reading this grouping of years together? Yes, I do. Not only do I think these four years together create a pivotal juncture in Montgomery's life, but I see them differently as I read them without excisions. Many details that had to be deleted by Rubio and Waterston in the "selected" journals, in order to keep to their allotted space, are here supplied and now so seamlessly, of course, that I don't remember exactly what is new and only know the whole is more impressive, richer than before. There are so many tender moments with the children—and telling glimpses into Chester's beloved but worrisome complexity.

As in the complete journals of her Island years and the first volume of her Ontario years,[2] here, too, from 1918 to 1921 in Leaskdale, Ontario, Montgomery used her journal to vent private feelings and to record and to question her perceptions of life and meaning. War news and household and parish duties continued to occupy her. Yet there is, I think, a significant difference in quality and kind between the journals of these four years and those that come before and after because in 1919 she was shaken at the core of her being, not once but twice. The death of Frederica Campbell MacFarlane was a blow she knew she would never fully recover from, even as she was experiencing it; and that grief was then assaulted four months later by the first appearance in her marriage of her husband's recurrent mental illness. Seldom again would her journals be so intimately revealing of her struggles to identify and to reclaim herself as she faced and lived with the consequences of these two incalculably bleak events.

For me, these four years stand out as a turning place in Montgomery's manner and in her material. The events themselves shaped and shadowed everything afterwards: the loss of Frede; the horrible recurrences of Ewan's illness; the Page lawsuits that seemed to develop a life of their own; her worry about the boys' health and prospects with only one parent as guide and disciplinarian; and even the car accident in 1921, late in these pages, that led to an unfair lawsuit and a hounding of the Macdonalds for money she would refuse to pay—a hounding that would follow them even into the next parish and years away. But by that time, I think, and because of her determination to re-establish her life and to ground herself, Montgomery had found numerous ways to cope, not all of which are registered intimately in the pages of her journals. The November 18–28, 1921, entries describing the celebration of Canadian Book Week may suggest how the journals will be a place (again) to record and to rehearse for an audience that will eventually become as much public as private.

Montgomery's anguish in recounting Frede's death makes heart-rending reading. The writing seems as vivid to me now as it did forty years ago when Dr. F.W.P. Bolger and I first read a shorter version of the February 7, 1919, entry she copied into a letter to her Scottish pen pal, George Boyd MacMillan.[3] Perhaps, as she said (for different reasons) of Byron: "passion is always immortal" (May 9, 1920), and these thirty printed pages capture something elemental and profound about grief and love.

Figuring out how to live without Frede, determined to ground herself again for the sake of her dear children, she then was shocked to discover what she considered the shaming and horrifying taint of "religious melancholia" in Ewan—horrifying for a minister who in its throes saw himself as having committed the "unpardonable sin" and thus as damned for eternity and unfit to hold a pulpit. Rock-solid-seeming Ewan Macdonald, whose "india-rubber optimism" (March 31, 1918) Montgomery had taken for granted, was alternately paralyzed by despair or goaded to impatient restlessness. Montgomery believed it was her duty, and her best means of survival for all of them as a family, to hide Ewan's illness from the world. The pressures of coping and hiding were almost unbearable. Without Frede, her dearest friend and confidant, she knew her journal was the only "being" to whom she could pour out all of her immediate feelings and questions.

Hers is masterly writing; we have the privilege of (over)hearing some of the thinking that informed her creativity. She drew from a richly stocked memory, both for literary works and for minute details of her own past experiences. She was fascinated by what she seemed to perceive as the spectacle of human drama. She did not just keep up with the daily (war) news and avidly read current literature and scientific discoveries, she also read (actually re-read) such massive historical works as the six volumes of Edward Gibbon's *Decline and Fall of the Roman Empire* and the twelve volumes of George Grote's *A History of Greece, from the Earliest Period to the Close of the Generation Contemporary with Alexander the Great*,[4] so that while she was fully experiencing the uncertainty and sometimes agony of current life she was also conscious of a much longer view in which war and loss are mercilessly recurrent. This longer view strengthened her artistic focus on the domestic and particular, I think. History may give us perspective, she seemed to say, but we make sense of life and peace with it through the intimate moments that touch us. Her life writing, including what Elizabeth Waterston calls Montgomery's many "fictions,"[5] reflects what Montgomery thought changed lives and what could not be changed in them because we are human.

As she had since war was declared in 1914, Montgomery focused on war for much of 1918. Always a teller of stories, she framed and wove narrative from the news. As though apologizing for the monotony of her tale, and despite its genuine pain, she said, for example, on March 31, 1918, "One day of anguish was becoming much the same as another." The October 6, 1918, entry announcing the end of war is as satisfying to read as the climax of a novel—"at last, at last," we feel with her, the long war was over and glorious peace could return. She described calling all over the village to spread the news and excitedly walking the floor in sheer delight. And then, as in her fiction, the most touching part of her description about the end of war is captured in an intimate, domestic moment with Ewan: "I flew out in the rain and met him at the gate. 'Have you heard the news?' I cried, hoping like a child that he hadn't, so that I would be 'the first' to tell him. He *hadn't* so I had the fun of being the first. Then we had supper and a gay, merry, happy circle we were" (p. 67). We can see her child-like eagerness and his responding dimpled pleasure. Such details and scene painting are legion in the journal.

In Montgomery's experience and certainly in her telling (and our reading), there is seldom one story happening at a time. Complicating strands overlap so that moments of joy seem just that—moments suspended in a larger, often darker, story. Her time on Prince Edward Island with the children in the summer of 1918 seems like a warm, golden bubble. The story teller makes me feel her reprieve from the customary pain of war worry, but also keeps me conscious that these moments are vulnerable in their suspension. She had not been home in three years and was surprised to find almost everything a pleasure. She even laughed at her own seeming inability to describe this pleasure: "Very lovely days and very pleasant weather—very delightsome meetings with old friends—very unwriteable walks in my so-beautiful old lane. I am very happy. It is good to be here" (June 29, 1918). Later, after Frede's death and during Ewan's illness, Maud would say "It is easier to write out pain than joy" (September 21, 1919). Yet in this golden bubble of a summer she did describe many of those walks in Lover's Lane. Twice she pretended she was back in her old life and going home to the Macneill house at night. Once she even entered the tumble-down house and moved in the dark from room to boarded-up room, picturing everything exactly as it was. The experienced Montgomery reader knows that every second of this bitter-sweet re-living of the past is material for her writing and will appear in the autobiographical Emily novels. Cousin Jimmy's garden, the fairies, the "so" blue sea and the red roads and green fields: she experienced all these just as Emily would experience them: "A certain well-spring of fancy which I thought had gone dry in me bubbled up as freshly as of old. I was again a poet" (July 3, 1918).

Yet even this golden time was touched by an ominous chill. Montgomery visited Lizzie (Stewart) Laird, a childhood friend who had suffered insanity and was a shell of her former self. Montgomery said of Lizzie exactly what she would later experience with her own husband: "Bodily illness is bad enough but illness of the mind is incomparably worse. It is as if your friend's dead body moved and spoke before you in a horrible imitation of a life that had fled" (July 14, 1918). For only one moment did Lizzie seem like her old self and spoke directly to Maud in the old way. The master story teller experienced and told about this moment with an image that would later become, I think, the "disappointed house" of the Emily series and may already have been anticipated as Leslie Moore's grey house in *Anne's House of Dreams*.[6] Here, the house held Lizzie's former spirit: "Only once, just as I was leaving did she reappear for a moment, as a face might peer briefly from the window of a deserted house." Maud tried to engage this spirit, "But 'Lizzie' had gone. The creature who had usurped her faded body answered in the strange stilted unnatural tone she had used all the evening. . . . I came away saddened." Readers may recall this "deserted house" image when Maud dreams prophetically of Frede's death, imagining workers have torn her house to pieces (February 7, 1919, p. 94); readers will certainly recall Montgomery's response to Lizzie later when Ewan Macdonald stares into hell fire and Maud cannot reach him.

Many scholars have noted Montgomery's increasing interest, during and after the war, in the Gothic and uncanny, the seemingly darker strands of a Romanticism that had also shaped her love of nature. Montgomery believed some of her war dreams were prophesies, and she gave an eerie, mystic quality to Gertrude Oliver's dreams (versions of Montgomery's own dreams) and pronouncements in *Rilla of Ingleside*, written during 1919 and 1920 (and dedicated to the memory of Frede).[7] On January 25, 1919, just as Frede was dying, Montgomery reminded her of their old promise to get in touch from beyond the grave if that were possible. Table rapping and Ouija boards had been a (perhaps wistful) play-version of Montgomery's abiding interest in psychic connections. During the 1918 summer visit, as though presciently preparing for what was to happen to Frede and to their connection, Montgomery revived her interest in table rapping. Neuroscientific research in our own times could support her speculations about the mysterious powers of the mind:

> Nothing I have ever seen or read has convinced me for a moment that any communication from the dead is possible by such means [table rapping]. But I *do* believe that the phenomena thus produced is produced by some strange power existent in ourselves—in that mysterious part of it known as the subconscious mind—a power of which the law is utterly unknown to us. But that there is a law which governs it and that the operations produced by that law are perfectly natural could we but obtain the key to them I am firmly convinced (July 19, 1918).

She would appeal to this "perfectly natural" unknown law a few months after Frede died and when Maud badly wanted and needed to know Frede was somehow present, aware of her suffering and there to comfort. The May 21, 1919 entry about Montgomery's experience with Daffy the cat is worth reading not only for its own sake but for what it suggests about Montgomery's post-Frede, post-war pre-occupation with psychic possibilities. The Emily books reflect this preoccupation.

The Emily books as opposed to the Anne books: this is a change the journals directly and indirectly reveal. Famously, and only half facetiously, Montgomery said on August 24, 1920, when she finished *Rilla of Ingleside*: "I am done with *Anne* forever—I swear it as a dark and deadly vow.[8] I want to create a new heroine now . . . . Her name is 'Emily.'" Montgomery later said that she had been thinking about

Emily for ten years and it was time to tell her story, and we see traces of Emily in the journals well before Montgomery's declared intention to write the series. I suggest Frede inspired the Emily series far more than she inspired the *Rilla of Ingleside* that is dedicated to her. I think the Emily series owes its flavour and quality to Montgomery's having lived through the agony of Frede's death and having fully realized how irreplaceable she was in Maud's life. At the end of the long February 7, 1919, entry recounting Frede's life and death, Montgomery said: "I have lived one life in those seemingly far-off years before the war. Now there is another to be lived, in a totally new world where I think I shall never feel quite at home. I shall always feel as if I belonged 'back there'—back there with Frede and laughter and years of peace." She had experienced the golden summer visit of 1918, too, with the happy knowledge that Frede was waiting for her in Park Corner when she left Cavendish. I read, now, the October 6, 1918, entry about the end of war as an extended part of that golden summer. After it came blow after blow. Maud questioned what her life could now be; the Emily books register some answers.

From 1918 to 1921 Montgomery got reviews of *Anne's House of Dreams* and wrote *Rainbow Valley*, *Rilla of Ingleside,* the proposal for the Emily series, and *Emily of New Moon*. Probably as writing therapy after Frede's death, she had begun re-copying her old journals into uniform-sized ledgers. In copying those scenes—as in walking in the gloom through the ruins of the Macneill farmhouse—she was intensely reliving her earlier life. Note this: she was *reliving* the scenes; she was fully experiencing them, not just intellectually acknowledging them. This is part of Montgomery's great gift as a story teller—she actually relived moments as her pen traced them on the page. She had to wrestle the experiences into a livable shape and she had to exorcise them from her consciousness. When they were fixed, on the page, she could re-enter them, at her will. It would be a mistake to underestimate the importance of the journals as living text. Her life is literally in these pages and in the pages of her novels. We cannot ever[9] enter the day-dream world she also created and conjured so that she would have a parallel, positive existence alongside the daily one she lived as Maud Montgomery Macdonald (see January 31, 1920), but we are invited to enter the texts she published and wanted published after her death.

In 1919, 1920, and the first part of 1921 especially, Montgomery was talking to the journal as though to a friend, a friend she no longer had anywhere in the flesh.

The January 31, 1920 entry is essential reading for anyone who wants to try to understand Montgomery's complex personality. Mary

Rubio took the title of her biography, *A Gift of Wings*,[10] from this long entry. In it, Montgomery described her long-time habit of going on "imaginary adventures"—where she could "thrill and glow and delight and exult." Using treasured quotations from their works, she engaged with writers she admired, such as George Eliot, Kipling, Oliver Wendell Holmes, J.M. Barrie, Olive Schreiner, among others. She talked about three different kinds of love ("friendship, passion, worship")—a passage that is often quoted by scholars—and remembered again the scorching heat of her stolen hours with Herman Leard on PEI. She even gave a rather light-hearted sounding but still revealing list of things she "likes" as her response to Ruskin's invitation: "'Tell me what you *like* and I'll tell you what you *are.*'" It is certainly funny, and perhaps deliberately provocative, that she registered "I like my husband" almost at the end of the list, situating that tepid sentence between "I like good spruce gum" and "I like people to like me." If this list is light, other parts of the entry are not—and the rhythm of the whole is like a conversation with a confidant, switching tone and moods as one does when thinking out loud with a trusted friend.

The journal cannot be Frede, but it can be an engagement of the kind she shared with Frede. She speculates about re-incarnation and the guidance of a few grand teachers:

> We may exist in numberless new incarnations; but those new personalities will have no remembrance of the old. For *us* then it seems to me there is nothing but to make the best of it and fight against our night with the little fires and tapers of hopes and creeds and dreams and visions. They are as a flickering lantern to the sun. But a lantern keeps us from stumbling hopelessly in the darkness and gives one enough light to travel by with a fair degree of safety (January 31, 1920).

Her writing is the light she offers others.

After a bracing, brief trip to PEI, she wrote (another) long entry of self-analysis (December 13, 1920), this one prompted by reading Lady Asquith's autobiography. Lady Asquith claimed to be objective in her self-portraiture, and Montgomery thought she, too, was capable of objectivity. She ended the long self-portrait (physical as well as emotional) with characteristic humour and her signature combination of forthrightness and evasion: "I am physically a great coward, intellectually quite fearless; morally about half and half." Oh, what a world is revealed and hidden in that deceptively glib "morally about half and half"! Just because she is capable of objectivity does not mean she is going to exercise full disclosure, even for an imagined, kindred other.

Readers of the journals may "overhear" many forms of living engagement, but the long entry about Frederica Campbell MacFarlane is still, I think, the most deeply felt and unreservedly expressed—and thus the most revealing—of anything in the journals.

This volume is studded with gems—funny moments (such as her response to courtroom antics: "French is acting in a fashion that would aggravate a bronze Buddha!"—June 11, 1920), resigned comment on her reduced emotional life ("I think and it seems it is not permitted to anyone to have sunshine from first to last. In some way or another we have to pay"—January 23, 1921), wisdom about a chosen life's work ("Our best reward is the joy in the struggle"—February 3, 1920), her signature nostalgia and love of beauty ("to taste the inimitable flavor of the wild fruit, to lie amid the sun-warm grasses, to hear the robins whistling, to tiptoe through the lanes of greenery and fragrance in the mornings of those faraway years"—September 3, 1919), recognition of her own cinematic way of experiencing ("My drive home was a seven-mile-film of brilliant adventures of fancy"—December 22, 1919). And throughout, so many references and spontaneous quotations from literature, so many uses of her own favourite images such as the "bend in the road" to characterize her philosophy of life, despite torment: "What happiness I have had has been far out balanced by suffering. Yet I have always found life interesting and I have never wished to stop living, save in temporary moments of torture. There is always the lure of something further on—something in hiding just around the next bend—to lend a spice to it. It may be only a trick—it has always seemed to be a trick hitherto—but it serves" (July 10, 1919).

L.M. Montgomery's journals make compelling reading because she was so interested not only in what she saw but how. She needed to capture just the right words or she was not satisfied. She gave this desire to Emily, just as she gave Emily her love of reading, clan, PEI landscapes, poetry, cats, star-gazing, rapture, houses, home-making, and dream vision. She also gave Emily the acerbity, fierceness, pride, and passion we find in these journals. In the pages of these four years, Montgomery became the person who was able to write *Rilla* and the Emily series. She never again belonged fully to the idyllic green land she imagined before the war, and re-created in the early Anne books, conjure it though she would, but she became, I think, self-reliant in a way that allowed her to reveal in her novels and in her journals more about the depth and intricacy of her creative imagination as it worked.

Endnotes

1   For an overview of Montgomery scholarship since 1992, see Elizabeth Rollins Epperly, "Preface to the 2014 Edition" in *The Fragrance of Sweet-Grass: L.M. Montgomery's Heroines and the Pursuit of Romance* (1992) Toronto: University of Toronto Press, 2014: ix–xlii.

2   *The Complete Journals of L.M. Montgomery: The PEI Years, 1889–1900,* edited by Mary Henley Rubio and Elizabeth Hillman Waterston, Toronto: Oxford University Press, 2012; *the Complete Journals of L.M. Montgomery: The PEI Years, 1901–1911,* edited by Mary Henley Rubio and Elizabeth Hillman Waterston, Toronto: Oxford University Press, 2013; and *L.M. Montgomery's Complete Journals: The Ontario Years, 1911–1917,* ed. Jen Rubio, Ontario: Rock's Mills Press, 2016.

3   See F.W.P. Bolger and Elizabeth R. Epperly, eds. *My Dear Mr. M.: Letters to G.B. MacMillan.* (1980) Toronto: Oxford University Press, 1992. Mary Beth Cavert is preparing the complete letters of Montgomery to MacMillan.

4   Not to mention that she also reads the five volumes of Justin McCarthy's contemporary *History of Our Own Times, 1830–1912* in 1921.

5   Elizabeth Waterston, *Magic Island: The Fictions of L.M. Montgomery,* Toronto: Oxford University Press, 2008.

6   In *Anne's House of Dreams,* the windows of the grey house are "incarnadined" by the setting sun like the "blood-red thoughts" of an imprisoned soul (Oakville, Ontario: Rock's Mills Press 2016, p. 45).

7   See the helpful annotations in two different editions of *Rilla*: one edited and introduced by Benjamin Lefebvre and Andrea McKenzie, Toronto: Viking, 2010; and the other edited by Jen Rubio, Ontario: Rock's Mills Press, 2015. For a fascinating study of the writing of the manuscript, see Elizabeth Waterston and Kate Waterston, editors, *Readying Rilla: L.M. Montgomery's Reworking of Rilla of Ingleside,* Ontario: Rock's Mills Press, 2016.

8   Though, of course she was not finished with Anne, publishing *Anne of Windy Poplars* (1936), *Anne of Ingleside* (1939), and posthumously *The Blythes Are Quoted* (2009).

9   Except, perhaps, in reading the delightful *The Blue Castle* (1926), which is really a day-dream worked up as a fairy-tale novel.

10   Mary Rubio, *Lucy Maud Montgomery: The Gift of Wings,* Toronto: Doubleday, 2008.

The Ontario Years, 1918–1921

1918

Saturday, Jan. 5, 1918[1]
The Manse, Leaskdale, Ont.

We have had a terrible week of bitter cold—28 and 32 below zero. Our coal is very poor and we cannot keep the house even half comfortable. We have to all herd in the dining room—the only warm room in the house. I can get no writing done of course.

I am very tired, as we have been "on the go" all the week—out "to tea" every evening and this means no bed until twelve and sometimes later. Tonight we were home and it was heavenly. I've had what I've been starving for—a "good read."

The war news from Italy is better. The Huns are again checked and snow is blocking the mountains.[2] Then, too, the peace negotiations between Germany and Russia seem to have struck a snag and to be off—for the time at least.[3]

Friday, Jan. 18, 1918
Leaskdale, Ont.

I have not passed through such a week as this last since that terrible winter of long ago down home.

---

1   This entry begins in LMM's handwritten volume 4, covering the dates March 21, 1916, to December 19, 1919.

2   The Italian army had suffered huge losses at the end of 1917 in the battle of Caporetto. From October 24 to November 19, 1917, fighting had continued in what is now north-western Slovenia. The Austrian army, reinforced with German units, had launched a surprise attack, breaking through Italian lines along the Isonzo river, resulting in some 300,000 Italian casualties (many taken as prisoners). Austro-German forces advanced quickly but soon outran their own supply lines, and the advance held at the Piave River. Also, German commanders recalled many soldiers from the Italian front to prepare for the Spring Offensive (see also note on page 10). Meanwhile, French and British reinforcements soon arrived to help.

3   After the two Russian Revolutions of 1917, the new Bolshevik government wanted to withdraw Russia from the conflict. This involved putting in place a ceasefire between Russia and Germany, followed by the establishment of a "separate peace" between Russia and the Central Powers (this would come to be the Treaty of Brest-Litovsk; see note 11, page 4). Negotiations for such a separate peace deal were fraught, however. The demands of the Central Powers included the annexation of large portions of Eastern Europe, including territory held by Russia. Another problem was that members of the Russian delegation charged with negotiating the peace were not of one mind: Leon Trotsky, a theorist and leader of the Red Army, believed that the Germans would offer unreasonable demands, and, as a result, workers in both Germany and Russia would rise up—possibly even sparking a worldwide socialist revolution—and this uprising should be encouraged; Vladimir Lenin, on the other hand, wanted peace with Germany at any cost to stabilize politics within Russia. Russian negotiators sought to prolong negotiations in hopes of Germany being destabilized by unrest at home. The German delegation grew impatient and demanded big territorial annexations. On January 18, 1918, Trotsky called for a recess in order to establish some kind of consensus among Russian negotiators.

1

For a week after my last entry it was rough and cold. Various things, including a flare-up in the Red Cross Society were irritating. As to the Red Cross trouble it is the first of the kind to come up since we organized two years ago and was caused by some petty personal malice and spite among some of the members. I think I have nipped it in the bud. I told them plainly that if any trouble was made I would resign. This seemed to bring them into a more reasonable frame of mind for none of them want the bother and responsibility of being president. It is disgusting to think that while our boys are fighting and dying at the front our women cannot work for them at home without quarrelling. And the woman against whom all this outburst of spite has been directed has had a son killed at the front.[4] None of those who organized the cabal against her has anyone there. Gods, are such women worth fighting for?

However, the various alarms and excursions of the meeting were over and on Friday evening we drove over to Zephyr to visit a family. It was a mild evening with a brooding sky when we went and the roads were passable. When we left for home at eleven the worst storm I have ever known was just beginning. It was snowing thickly, blowing wildly, and turning bitterly cold. We were three hours covering the nine miles. Once we got stuck, and had to get out, unhitch Queen,[5] turn the cutter, and seek another road. We managed to get home at last and it was well we did. All Saturday and Sunday the storm raged, with a gale blowing sixty miles an hour and the mercury 36 below zero. I have been in many barns that were more comfortable than this house during those two days. My plants froze in the parlor at mid-day around the open radiator. Stuart *cried* with the cold. I wore my overboots and a fur coat and then was cold.

We had no mail for a whole week—but some came through today. No train got through to Uxbridge until today. The tracks are blocked everywhere. We drove to Uxbridge on Thursday and the roads were unthinkable.

Thursday, Jan. 31, 1918
The Manse, Leaskdale

I think no one will ever forget this January. The cold lately has been terrible—when the mercury goes up to zero we think it mild. Every

---

4   LMM explains this situation in more detail in her entry of January 3, 1919.

5   Queen was the horse the Macdonald family kept to pull their carriage; in this case they are travelling in a "cutter," a sled that travels over the snow.

other day we have a storm which at once blocks mails and trains, for an hour's snow fills the deep cuts now. A mail is a rarity. And oh, the house is so cold!

There is little war news. Germany and Austria seemed to be troubled by strikes and internal disturbances.[6] Rumors and forebodings increase of a coming German offensive on the Western front made possible by the disorganization of Russia.[7] So we are forbidden to hope for spring, hard as the winter is.

Friday, Feb. 1, 1918
Leaskdale, Ont.

The Red Cross met at a house two miles from here today and passed off serenely. But the roads were so terrible with bumps and pitches that I was exhausted when I got home and have neither courage nor strength to go on. I wish it were possible to take some magic draught and go to sleep for the next three months—to wake and find it May, with spring here and Armageddon over.

Sunday, Feb. 10, 1918

Last Monday and Tuesday were the coldest days so far this winter—which is saying much. Surely we are over the top now. But it has snowed more or less every day this week and the roads are a problem. We had just one mail this week—and it brought word that Hindenburg says that he will be in Paris by April first![8]

Hindenburg has made good his boasts on the eastern front. Can he make them good on the west? In the answer to that question lies the future of humanity and of civilization.

I was alone in the evening, tired, ill and nervous, when I read it. I walked the floor unable to reason off my dread. In my misery I resorted desperately to the old superstition—perhaps?—of opening the Bible at

---

6   Labour unrest in Germany and Austria, from 1918, were a sign of the population's changing attitude toward the war. Up to 250,000 workers were affected across Germany; in Berlin strikes in the early months of the year even threatened arms production. Labour unrest would continue until armistice in November of that year.

7   The Germans would launch the Spring Offensive in March 1918, hoping to gain ground before the United States deployed its full resources.

8   Paul von Hindenburg was Chief of the General Staff of the German Army from 1916. Hindenburg was planning a large multi-pronged attack along the Western Front in hopes of defeating the British Army and forcing France to surrender.

random and reading the first verse my eyes fell upon. With a passionate prayer I opened the book; and I read this verse in the first chapter of Jeremiah.

"And they shall fight against thee; but they shall not prevail against thee; for I am with thee, saith the Lord of Hosts to deliver thee."[9]

Coincidence? Very likely. We shall see.

I believe that there is a great battle coming on the Western front— the greatest battle of the war—the greatest battle the world has ever seen—perhaps the last great battle it ever will see—

"the day of Armageddon, the last great fight of all."[10]

That battle will end the war whichever way it goes. Oh God, give us strength to bide it for we are weak and sorely tried!

Sunday, Feb. 24, 1918
The Manse, Leaskdale, Ont.

The blow has not yet fallen—and we wait, cringing. There are moments when I feel that I *cannot* bear the suspense any longer. In the forenoons, when I am busy and the sun shines I can force it to the background of my mind where it growls like a cornered dog. But when the day wanes and the shadows deepen and I grow tired, it comes out of its den and preys on me. The news from Russia has been very bad—Russia has quit the war and the Germans are sweeping over her undefended territory.[11] And on the west—the ominous hush before the storm. One despatch lately says that Hindenburg has stipulated that he will take Paris if he is left free to expend a million lives. At such a price he *must* purchase some successes and how can we live through them, even if he be baffled[12] in the end?

---

9   Jeremiah 1:19.

10   LMM knew this line (originally from Revelation 16:14) from a 1918 collection by Rudyard Kipling. "England's Answer": "So long as The Blood endures, / I shall know that your good is mine; ye shall feel that my strength is yours: In the day of Armageddon, at the last great fight of all, / That Our House stand together and the pillars do not fall."

11   A complicated scenario lies behind LMM's comments here. Following an armistice between Russia and the Central Powers on December 15, 1917, the Russian army ceased fighting Germany. The two sides entered into peace negotiations, which culminated with the Treaty of Brest-Litovsk on March 3, 1918. Negotiations between Russian (represented by the Bolsheviks) and Germany did not go well, however, with many demands being made by Germany, particularly for ever more territory. Russia withdrew from negotiations. The Central Powers renounced the armistice on February 18, 1918; over the following weeks, seized most of Ukraine, Belarus, and the Baltic countries. See also the note on page 1.

12   That is, confounded or unsuccessful.

I wish there were no such hour as three o'clock in the morning. I generally waken then and I cannot sleep again because I see Hindenburg in Paris and Germany victorious. I never see her so at any other than that accursed hour, no matter what Hindenburg may do. But then I see civilization swallowed up in barbarism.

The only gleam of light has been the British advance in Palestine. They have Jericho now.[13] But if Hindenburg smashes through on the west!

We have had milder weather lately and some thaws.

Monday, Feb. 25, 1918
Leaskdale, Ont.

There was no very "new" war news today. Russia is seemingly in a hopeless plight and for the rest the papers were filled up with gloomy predictions by the war correspondents concerning the lowering offensive in the west. I suppose they have to fill their columns with something—but it is hard on our *morale*.

A letter from McClelland today says they have sold 15,341 copies of *House of Dreams* in Canada.[14] That is pretty good.

Tonight I finished re-reading MacCaulay's History.[15] My mind has been a good deal harrowed during the process by the war but it was calmness personified compared to my condition the last time I read it in the winter of 1910. There were a couple of weeks that winter in which I tasted all the bitterness of death—and a dreadful and lingering death. It induced a nervous breakdown to which I made reference in my journal of the time. But I did not explain the *cause* of it—I could not. The agony had been so awful that for years I could not bear even to think of it.

One Friday night in the January of 1910 I was lying awake in my old

---

13   At the end of October 1917, the Egyptian Expeditionary Force (a multi-national army led by British General Edmund Allenby) broke the Ottoman lines at the town of Be'er Sheva, entered Southern Palestine and fought their way north and later to the east. About six weeks later they moved into Jerusalem as the Ottoman army retreated. British success in Southern Palestine had been an important moral booster to Allied forces.

14   LMM had written *Anne's House of Dreams* in 1916, and it was published the following year. In her private journal, she wrote that she had never written a book "in so short a time and amid so much strain of mind and body" (October 5, 1916). The novel explores suffering, unhappy marriage, and the redeeming power of friendship. Anne's first baby lives only for one day; in 1914, shortly after the outbreak of war, LMM herself had delivered a second baby that had been a stillbirth. "McClelland" was John McClelland of her Toronto publisher, McClelland & Stewart.

15   Thomas Babington Macaulay, *The History of England from the Accession of James the Second* (1848).

My Old Room

room in Cavendish. I was drowsy and comfortable and on the point of falling asleep when I happened to put my hand on my left breast. To my intense horror I felt in it a small "kernel" seemingly about the size of a pea.

All my life I had had a dread of *cancer*. I don't know exactly why for no one in my connection on either side had ever had it. But Grandfather Macneill had a morbid dread of it and was always imagining any little wart or mole which appeared on him to be cancer. His talk about it made an ineffaceable impression on my childish mind and I grew up with a deeply rooted horror of the disease and a conviction that it was the most horrible of deaths.

And now I had discovered a developing cancer in my breast. I had not the slightest doubt of that. Nor do I exactly wonder at my terror. I never slept for a moment that night. I got up in the cold and hunted out all the "doctor's books" in the house and read what they had to say on the subject. I found nothing to encourage me.

A dreadful fortnight followed. I thought I would go mad with fear and dread. I could say no word to anyone—there was no one I could say anything to. Sleepless night succeeded sleepless night—agonized day followed agonized day. I could not work—it was impossible to concentrate thought on anything. I tried to read—I had just begun on MacCaulay's History.[16] But though my eyes followed line after line and page after page my mind took in hardly anything of what I saw. I would read for a few minutes, then fling down the book and pace the floor in restless misery. Sometimes at night I got a little sleep by dosing myself with "hop" tea.[17] I had no drugs that might have given a temporary oblivion and no chance of getting them and the hop tea was not strong enough to overcome for any length of time my terrible unrest or soothe my tortured nerves. And the hardest thing was that I had to go about

---

16   On February 7, 1910, LMM wrote, "I have had a month of nervous prostration--an utter breakdown of body, soul, and spirit. ... It came on very suddenly after my last entry. A new and dreadful worry which preyed on me for a week or two, precipitated the crisis I suppose. At all events I broke down completely."

17   Hop tea is a kind of herbal medicine brewed from the flower of the hop plant, believed to provide relief from anxiety and insomnia.

and perform certain church and social duties and affect calm and composure. I would not let anyone suspect my trouble and I ascribed my unconcealable nervousness and general haggardness of appearance to facial neuralgia.[18] I could not think of the future. What could I do? I would have no one—no one to help me or stand by me. Marriage was not to be thought of with such a thing hanging over me. I decided that I would have to break my engagement. Everything in the world seemed to have become far away and indifferent to me. I moved among shadows. I remember one evening of choir practice in especial when under my surface calm I endured such agony that I made up my mind that rather than face my future I would kill myself in some way. Of course worry and sleeplessness soon produced utter nervous prostration and one thing reacted on another until I was almost insane. I could not sleep or eat or think or work. Monday, Jan. 17, 1910, eleven days after my finding of the kernel, was the most dreadful day I ever experienced in my life. I walked the floor all day in hideous restlessness. My misery reached its climax that day and that evening a reaction set in. Suddenly my restlessness departed, as if some evil spirit had rent and left me; and I felt quite calm but so physically weak I could hardly stand. For the rest of that week I suffered no more from restlessness but I felt broken—sad—helpless—a dreadful weariness of spirit. The next week I had several returns of the restlessness but none lasted so long as the first—the reactive calm generally coming after one day of agony.

I could not think of consulting the local doctor. He had a gossipy wife who told everything. My horrible secret would soon be known everywhere—a thought I could not tolerate. I could not get to town to consult a doctor there. So, soon after I discovered the kernel, I wrote the doctor in charge of the medical column in a Montreal paper asking if the kernel were likely to prove a cancer and what I had better do. Eighteen days later his letter came—I had sent the fee for a private reply. I did not dare open it just then. I had to go out to tea and spend the evening and I was afraid the contents would upset me too much. I must keep it until the day's duties were over and I could be alone with the night to face the worst. So at bedtime I opened the letter. It was very brief and I remember every line of it—I can never forget it. It shut the gates of death upon my tortured soul and opened the gates of life.

"Dear Madam," it read, "the little kernel in your
breast is not a cancer and my advice is to leave it completely alone."

---

18   "Neuralgia" was a term used for pain associated with nerves. In this case, LMM is likely referring to a condition now known as trigeminal neuralgia, pain in the face often caused by a blood vessel pressing on a nerve near the brain.

I felt as if I had returned from the grave. Life was possible once more—hope was not excluded. But the physical effects of that hideous fortnight lasted all winter. I was tired, depressed, sleepless and nervous for many months. Not till summer did I feel like myself. As for the little kernel, it remained as it was for a couple of years and disappeared altogether after Chester was born. What caused it I do not know but I doubt if anything can ever again make me so utterly miserable—not even the discovery of a real cancer!

I have never read MacCaulay since until recently. As I read it, enjoying it hugely, now and then a poignant memory of those weeks would flash over my mind—I would see myself huddled in the old kitchen, dully reading a few paragraphs, then throwing the book down and walking the floor—repeating the alternate performance until the dull gray winter's day had worn itself out and darkness came down over the old homestead and I went upstairs alone, with death grinning at my side, to toss sleeplessly until another dreaded dawn.

Not a living soul ever knew or suspected. I got a dozen "sure" remedies for neuralgia and much sympathy on the score of it. But not one ever guessed that among them moved that fortnight a soul in torment.

Friday, March 1, 1918
The Manse, Leaskdale

Edith was married here last Wednesday and Lily Meyers reigns in her stead. It is too soon to decide whether the change is for the better or worse but I am inclined to think the former.

I had a curious dream last night. I dreamed I held a newspaper in my hand and across it in huge letters ran the words, "There are thirty evil days coming." Then I woke. I have had so many strange and true dreams since the war broke out that I have an abiding faith in them. And what is to come after the thirty evil days? My dream did not tell me that.

Lily Meyers

Saturday, March 2, 1918
Leaskdale, Ont.

Last night I dreamed again. [19] I stood on a plain in France. It was sunset and the red light streamed over the plain. I held in my arms a man whom I knew, in some inexplicable way, to be dying. He leaned against me, his back and head against my breast. I could not see his face. Then he died, slipped from my grasp, and fell to the ground. I saw his face and recognized it—it was the face of the Kaiser's father—the man who, all through my girlhood, was known to me as the Crown Prince of Germany and whose pictured face, owing to his long and tragic illness, was very familiar to me.[20]

Strange? Will the thirty evil days be followed by some disaster to the present Crown Prince—or to that Hohenzollern dynasty of which the dead Frederick was the only worthy representative?[21] The next three months will answer that question—and we wait—and wait—and Germany masses her legions and guns on the Western front—and the world holds its breath in this awful and ominous calm.

19　A similar dream forms part of the narrative in LMM's novel about the war, *Rilla of Ingleside* (1919). Gertrude Oliver recounts two dreams; in the second, she recalls that in her dream she was "standing again on the veranda steps—just as I stood in that dream on the night before the lighthouse dance, and in the sky a huge black, menacing thunder cloud rolled up from the east. … I turned in panic and tried to run for shelter, and as I did so a man—a soldier in the uniform of a French army officer—dashed up the steps and stood beside me on the threshold of the door. His clothes were soaked with blood from a wound in his breast, he seemed spent and exhausted; but his white face was set and his eyes blazed in his hollow face. 'They shall not pass,' he said, in low, passionate tones which I heard distinctly amid all the turmoil of the storm" (Chapter 19, "They Shall not Pass").

20　Frederick III (1831–88), the only son of Wilhelm I, was Crown Prince of Germany for 17 years (and Crown Prince of Prussia for 27 years). He had been raised in the military tradition and also educated at University of Bonn; he was widely seen to be intelligent, insightful, and peace-loving. When he came to the throne in 1888 following the death of his father Wilhelm I, he had been suffering from cancer of the larynx; a botched surgical procedure to remove the trachea had almost killed him. He died 99 days after becoming German Emperor and King of Prussia. (1888 is known as the "Year of the Three Emperors": Wilhelm I; Wilhelm's son, Frederick III; and Frederick's son, Wilhelm II, who would lead the country into World War I). See also note 21, below.

21　The "House of Hohenzollern" was a dynastic family that traced its roots back to the Roman Empire, reigning over large parts of Europe for centuries. When the German Empire was formed in 1871, it was ruled by hereditary members of the royal House of Hohenzollern. Frederick III (see note 20 above), a Hohenzollern descendant, was the only son of Emperor Wilhelm I (Wilhelm I had ruled the German Empire until his death in March 1888). Frederick III, who LMM is referring to here, had been widely considered to be a fine and humane leader who eschewed war.

Saturday, March 16, 1918
The Manse, Leaskdale

Still no especial war news, but the same old forebodings of the coming German offensive. For a month now we have been crouching, waiting for the blow to fall. And war correspondents and generals alike unite in protesting and assuring muchly that the western front cannot be broken. I believe—and yet I tremble. For Hindenburg has said that he will be in Paris on April 1—and hitherto Hindenburg has kept his word.[22]

Spring is coming. We have had huge thaws and sunshine. I am glad that the dreadful winter is over but I cannot rejoice in the spring. What will it bring the world.

I have gone my round of duty—and duties—as faithfully and unflaggingly as possible—the usual routine work of the parish which I dislike and the routine work of the household which I love. And I wake at three o'clock o'night and wonder if the Iron Legions have struck at last.

Friday, Mar. 22, 1918
The Manse, Leaskdale

Armageddon has begun! The Great offensive opened yesterday.[23] They have attacked the British army. Haig reports that the enemy failed to reach their objectives but says they penetrated to the British battle positions and that severe fighting continues.[24] I do not like the sound of that last phrase but I am calm. At least, the dreadful suspense is over and a short time must decide the issue. But it will seem very long. God defend the right!

Saturday, March 23, 1918
Leaskdale, Ont.

Again a morning of dread, watching for the mail. The British report the situation unchanged, but the Germans claim 16,000 prisoners and

---

22   Germany's Chief of the General Staff, Paul von Hindenburg, who was preparing a big offensive on the Western Front in spring 1918.

23   On March 21, 1918, the German army, reinforced by German units that had been relocated to the Western Front following the surrender of Russia, launched a four-pronged attack along the Western Front; this would become known as the Spring Offensive.

24   British Forces suffered heavy losses in the first day—nearly 20,000 dead and 35,000 wounded—and Germans penetrated their front lines at several points. Douglas Haig, Field Marshal (1861–1928), commanded the British Expeditionary Force for most of World War 1.

200 guns. This sounds rather badly, but the line still holds, and American experts think the offensive will fail, judged by the opening two days. I try to think so. But I find I cannot write or do any work that requires concentration of thought.

We went to Mr. Bushby's tonight to tea. It was very atrocious—supper, company, roads, everything. The people are comparatively new comers and hopelessly vulgar. One has to descend to their level and joke commonly or no conversation is possible at all. Always after such an evening I feel that I want to come home and take a bath. I feel physically contaminated and cheap, as if I were shopworn goods in a very dusty and cluttered country store window.

Sunday, Mar. 31, 1918
The Manse, Leaskdale, Ont.

I wonder if there has ever been a week in the history of the world before into which so much of searing agony has been crammed. I feel sure that there was not. And in this week there was one day when all humanity was nailed to the cross. On that day the whole planet must have been agroan with universal convulsion. That day was last Sunday, March 24, 1918.[25]

The morning was fine and cold. I went to church anxious but calm. As I sat in church I wondered what I would feel like next Sunday. It would be Easter—but would it herald death or life. After the service I came home and, Lily being away, was busily preparing dinner when I heard Ewan say "Do you want to hear the latest news from the front?"

He had been reading a note handed to him after service by one of his elders. Something in his question or the tone of it filled me with dread. I snatched the letter. It was from Jas. Mustard[26] who had come out from Toronto the night before. It said, simply and boldly, that the latest despatches had stated that the British line was broken and that the German shells were raining on Paris.

---

25 "Operation Michael" was the beginning of the German Spring Offensive (see note 23, page 10). The attacking German divisions were spread along a 69-kilometre (43 mile) front, with Arras in the north, past St. Quentin, to La Fère in the south. The Operation began at dawn on March 21, 1918. In the ensuing days, the Germans did break through Allied lines in places, penetrating some 65 km (40 miles) in French territory; on March 24, the date LMM notes above, the village of Bapaume (some 160 km/100 miles north of Paris) was evacuated. Casualties were high on both sides; German troops in particular had become exhausted, and had trouble defending their gains. Ultimately—although LMM did not know this when she wrote this entry—the Operation failed to achieve its objectives: the strategic cities of Amiens and Arras had not been captured, and the territory gained by German was of little value and hard to defend.

26 The Mustards were a prominent local family, with whom LMM and Ewan were friends.

"It *can't* be true! It *can't* be true," I gasped again and again. I went all to pieces—I was nothing but a heap of quivering misery. If the Germans were shelling Paris they must have crashed through everywhere and be at its very gates! Paris was lost—France was lost—the war was lost!

Somehow or other I finished getting dinner for the rest but I never ate or thought of eating. Ewan, who is of a very phlegmatic temperament and never goes to pieces as I do, was calm though depressed and tried to encourage me, but it was a hard task even for his india-rubber optimism. As for me I writhed physically in my intolerable suffering. Oh, what an afternoon I passed! Ewan was away. I was alone, save for the children who were not old enough to realize the catastrophe that had befallen the world. I took a dose of lavender[27] and that restored to me a small measure of self-control but that whole afternoon I walked the parlor floor, wrung my hands and prayed—"Oh God—Oh God—Oh God"—nothing else—no other words—I could utter nothing but that age-old plea—that age-old moan of supreme anguish.

If only the news had not come until Monday, I thought piteously. It would not have been so hard to endure—one could have gone somewhere—done something. So I thought then. But now I am thankful that I learned it when I did and bore my share in the world's great pain. Everywhere that day humanity was in its supreme agony—everywhere the hearts of men were failing them for fear. I would feel shame if I had spent that day in painless ignorance reading or dreaming calmly. It was better to share the pain of my fellow beings.

Ewan came home from Zephyr at five and brought with him a Saturday night *Star*. I found that the news was not *quite* so awful as it had seemed in Mr. Mustard's letter. The line *had* been broken in *one* place, before St. Quentin, but the British forces seem to be retreating in fairly good order. There was as yet no rout and the guns that were shelling Paris were seventy miles away from it—monsters hitherto unknown, spectacular enough, but rather negligible from a military point of view.[28] But the truth was sufficiently awful. Mr. Harwood telephoned up the latest despatches that evening and they were far from reassuring. Furious fighting was still continuing. The German losses were said

---

27   Lavender has been used for a variety of applications for at least 3,000 years. In LMM's case it would have been taken to ease stress and relieve depression.

28   German long-range guns—known as the "Paris gun"—began shelling Paris on March 21 from a forest near Aisne in northern France, some 120 km/75 miles away. The Paris Gun was not a great military success, with its small payload and poor accuracy; it was rather used as a psychological weapon, to terrorize the city. In total around 320 to 367 shells were fired, with 91 people killed and 68 injured.

to be enormous—probably were. But that old sop of comfort has been served up to us too often when reverses came to be of any power now. What boots it how many they lose if they smash through?

That night I took a veronal tablet and so slept loggishly.[29] Worked feverishly all the morning at some routine tasks requiring no thought. The mail came. The headline of the *Globe* was, "Battered but not Broken." The British had retreated to the Somme losing the territory captured in its last summer's campaign at the cost of half a million lives. The despatches were terrible. The Kaiser boasted himself of victory and the Germans had taken 30,000 prisoners.[30]

I felt miserably depressed. Ewan and I went to Uxbridge and then to tea at Herbert Pearson's. Nice place—nice people—but they seemed as shadows to me in my maze of pain. Lizzie told me of an incredible story of a despatch that had just come through saying that the British had captured 100,000 Germans. I knew this could not possibly be true. I feared that it had been twisted in transmission and that they had *lost* a hundred thousand. This added to my distraction. But that night I slept from exhaustion. And the evening and the morning was the fifth day.

Tuesday morning I paced the floor waiting for the mail. Again the news was bad. The German advance continued and though the British line was not again broken it was pressed back and back. Back much further it could not go without irretrievable disaster. They were very close to Amiens—and the loss of Amiens would mean that a wedge had been driven between the French and British armies.[31]

I could do nothing that afternoon and evening. I don't remember much about it. One day of anguish was becoming much the same as another. Again I took veronal that night and obtained a little merciful oblivion. All the forenoon I worked at routine tasks.

Hitherto, when I have had reason to dread the news I never would go to the store for the mail myself. I have always felt that I could not endure reading bad news, with those men who infest country stores sitting around on boxes and counters and looking at me with curious eyes. If the news was bad I must read it at home. But on this day this hitherto strong feeling was drowned out by another yet stronger. I could *not*

---

29   Veronal is the trade name for the barbiturate barbital or barbitone. It was brought to market by the Bayer company and remained a widely used sleeping aid until the 1950s.

30   The first part of the German Spring Offensive, "Operation Michael," did cause heavy losses to Britain and France, including some territory. However in the long run, losses to Germany where probably higher, and mostly in exchange for territory that was not ultimately of great strategic significance, led to the failure of the Offensive.

31   It was known that part of the German strategy was to separate the French and British armies, enabling them to force the British "into the sea."

wait here while Ewan went down for the mail—I had borne so many of those agonies of suspense that I could not bear just that particular kind again. The "drop of water" must fall on a new place—a new kind of torture would be more bearable so I went down with Ewan to the office. It was a dull, bitter, *hard* day. All the snow was gone but the gray,

The Store, Leaskdale

lifeless ground was frozen hard. A biting wind was blowing. The whole landscape was ugly and repellent. It weighed on my soul—it seemed typical of the world in which the German hell-hounds were to be our masters. I went into the store, feeling, "Oh, if it were only over—if I had just seen the news and knew the worst." Mrs. Cook[32] was just leaning over the counter, reading a *Globe*. The headline hung down over the counter, big and black. It was upside down to me but I read it at a glance, without even the slight effort we usually make to read letters upside down. It was,

"British and French check the Germans."

The relief was almost awful. I felt like a prisoner on the rack when they stopped turning it. But I was not off the rack. The torture might begin anytime. The situation was still critical—the danger still horribly great and imminent. But at least the onrush of Germans had been halted—there was still a chance. I was able to work that afternoon and sleep at night. The next day's news was again reassuring but still the danger had not passed. Friday's news was bad again. Montdidier and Rosiere were taken—two important points.[33] If the Huns advanced much beyond Montdidier Amiens must fall—and if Amiens fell the Channel ports or Paris—or both—must be given up. I was worried and upset all day. Yesterday I again went for the mail and the headline was, "Even Berlin admits the offensive checked." I exclaimed aloud "Oh, Thank God," not caring if all the loafers in Scott[34] heard me.

---

32   The Cook family was well established in Leaskdale, having come from England in the late 1860s and settled as farmers.

33   Montdidier, an important communication centre, was lost on March 27; the town (or commune) of Rosière was lost the following day.

34   That is, Scott Township. By "loafers" LMM presumably is referring to men who have not enlisted or men who hung around the general store to talk and smoke.

And so it stands. Today was Easter and I went to church. I did not, as I had hoped last Sunday, feel rejoicing in the thought that the German offensive had failed. Alas, it had had too great a measure of success. But at least I went feeling thankful that so far it had failed of decisive success. Armageddon is not over—it has but begun. But though I doubted God last Sunday I do not doubt Him today. The evil cannot win. My dream will come true!

There has come out of this catastrophe one good—one supremely good thing. At last there is a generalissimo of the Allied forces and that man is Foch, the great French leader. It has taken this disaster to break the stubborn British repugnance to this. I believe that if Foch had been generalissimo long ago the war would have been over.[35] May it not be too late!

On such evenings of the past week as I could read I re-read a history of Ancient Egypt by Rawlinson[36] and found, as in all previous readings, that even the dryest details were as interesting to me as a letter from home. Always I read with the feeling of reading of a life *I* had once lived. I wonder if Egypt weaves this same sorcery over others who read of her. There is a certain couplet in *Ben Hur* which always makes me incredibly *homesick*.

"No more does the Nile in the moonlight calm
Moan past the Memphian shore."[37]

Gods! There comes the ache! I *see* that moonlit shore, with the palm trees on the banks. I yearn for it—I could weep with very longing to see it *again*. I *must* have seen it once.

Monday, April 1, 1918
The Manse, Leaskdale, Ont.

This was the day Hindenburg was to have been in Paris. He is not there yet. But he would have been if the Huns had smashed through

---

35   General Ferdinand Jean Marie Foch (1851–1929), a brilliant and experienced military theorist who became the Supreme Allied Commander in March 1918. LMM uses the popular Italian term here of "Generalissimo," meaning the military rank of the highest degree.

36   Historian George Rawlinson's (1812–1902) *History of Ancient Egypt* (1881).

37   A "Lament" sung by an unknown woman in Lew Wallace's (1827–1905) *Ben Hur: A Tale of the Christ* (1880): "The play with plumes of the whispering palm / For me, alas! No more; / Nor more does the Nile in the moonlit calm / Moan past the Memphian shore." Incidentally, Anne was caught reading *Ben Hur* in *Anne of Green Gables* (1908); Anne knows it is a "religious" book but admits that she enjoys it also because it is an exciting story.

utterly as they expected last week. It is a big "if"—which may yet lose the subjunctive.

To-day was a dismal blend of fog and rain and mud. The news was reassuring. The enemy has made no further progress. But most of the "critics" think there is another tremendous effort coming. This may be. I dreamed that strange dream on March first. Did the "30 evil days" mean thirty days from my dream? If so, they were out yesterday and the worst is over. But somehow I do not think so—I do not *feel* so. I think it meant thirty days from the opening of the offensive. And if this be so there is a long endurance of the rack before us yet.

In the *British Weekly* that came to-day was a very kind review of *Anne's House of Dreams* by a critic whose opinion I value highly.[38]

Saturday, April 6, 1918
Leaskdale, Ont.

This week there has been no disquieting war news. Yesterday the Germans attacked heavily again but so far have made no important gains. I was in Toronto one day to give a reading at an art club and had an enjoyable time.

Sunday, April 14, 1918

This has been another week of worry and suspense. Monday and Tuesday the news was not bad but on Wednesday came word that the Germans had attacked successfully at Armentieres.[39] In the evening I drove down to meet Ewan who was coming out from Toronto and got the evening papers. They were far from reassuring. Thursday and Friday were non-committal but yesterday the word was bad. The Germans are pressing on and Bailleul is in danger.[40] Haig has sent out a message which sounds almost like a cry of desperation. He tells his men that they are fighting with their backs to the wall—that they "must not give

---

38 *The British Weekly: A Journal of Social and Christian Progress* was published in London by Hodder and Stoughton from 1886 to 1961.

39 The Lys Offensive was part of the larger Spring Offensive (see note 23, page 10) in Flanders, Belgium, designed as a surprise attack with the goal of capturing Ypres and ultimately forcing the British out of the war. By launching an assault on the salient in April 1918 the Germans hoped to cut off British positions from their supply line in France. They captured Armentières in northern France on April 10. The Lys Offensive did capture some ground, notably the Messines Ridge, but on balance cost Germany many casualties for limited gains.

40 Bailleul, a village (or commune) in northern France 12 km/7.5 miles west of Armentières, was captured by the Germans on April 15.

up another yard of ground."[41] Well, that is where the British always fight best. But what news will tomorrow bring?

Monday, April 15, 1918
The Manse, Leaskdale

To-day was like summer. We drove down to Uxbridge and I did all my business before I ventured into Willis' drugstore to ask for a paper. The headline was "British Lines Hold at Every Point" and I shook with the re-action of relief.

Uxbridge Viewed from Aeroplane

Saturday, April 20, 1918

This has been a hellish week of ups-and-downs. Tuesday's news was fair. The British line held but Neuve Eglise, an important point, was lost.[42] Still, I felt encouraged and worked with good heart. Wednesday morning just after Ewan had left the house to go down for the mail the telephone bell rang sharply. I felt that there was something ominous in its sound. It sounded like Mrs. Alex Leask's[43] ring. They get their mail before we do, owing to their having a mailbox. I ran to the 'phone with a chill of fear. "Oh, Mrs. Macdonald," came Mrs. Leask's agitated voice, "have you seen the paper today?" "Not yet," I said, "Why?" "Oh, there is terrible news—terrible news."

I saw the British line broken at last—entirely and hopelessly broken. "What is it?" I gasped.

"Oh, you'll see—it's terrible—it's dreadful."

She raved on like this and I could not get one word of sense out of her as to what had really happened. So I hung up the receiver and waited for Ewan. He came and the news was that Messines Ridge

---

41   Douglas Haig (1861–1928), Field Marshal who commanded the British Expeditionary Force for most of the war, had issued a now-famous order on April 11, 1918: his men must carry on fighting "With Our Backs to the Wall and believing in the Justice of our Cause" to protect "The safety of our homes and the Freedom of mankind."

42   The Belgian village of Neuve Eglise (also known as "Nieuwkerke"), east of Bailleul in Western Flanders (Belgium), was captured, but the British and French did contain the main offensive, limiting its success.

43   The Leasks were a prominent, founding family of Leaskdale, having emigrated from England in the 1859s.

was lost.[44] This was bad enough. But the line was only pushed back, not broken. As for Mrs. Leask's hysterics, I discovered that they were caused, not by the indisputably bad news of the loss of the ridge but by the Governmental announcement that all young men of military age were to be called up at once, regardless as to whose sons they were, farmers or otherwise. Mrs. Leask has two strapping slackers of military age. Hence *her* upset.

All day I was worried and depressed. In the evening we drove down to Uxbridge and got an evening paper. Again bad news—the British had retreated from the Ypres salient.[45] That they had retreated "successfully" did not gild the pill much. Thursday the news continued bad. Friday I went to the office and waited in my usual horrible suspense. It seemed to me that I could *not* open a paper to look at the headlines and I dreaded the moment the *Globe* would be passed out to me. I was spared this. When the mailman came in he said, "The war news is better today." So I opened the paper more calmly. It *was* better. The Germans had not make any further progress and the British were holding firmly against fierce attacks. Today the *Star* reviewer thinks that the crisis of this attack is over.

Yesterday the thirty days since the opening of the offensive were out.

Saturday, April 27, 1918

I fear my dream meant nothing. All this week up to yesterday there was no especial war news. Yesterday we read that the Germans had struck again. Today the news is that Kemmel Hill has been taken.[46] I do feel "downhearted." I had not realized how much my belief in that foolish dream had upheld me until it was wrenched away. But perhaps it was well I had it to keep me over that first week of the offensive.

We have been housecleaning. But I cannot put heart into anything.

---

44   On the overall strategic value of the Messines Ridge, see note 39, page 16.

45   A continuation of the Lys Offensive (see note 23, page 10). The Ypres salient had already been the scene of much fighting in World War I (a "salient" is a military term for a feature within a combat zone that pushes into enemy territory). The Battle of Passchendaele in October 1917 had been a costly series of operations on the Western Front in this region, culminating in four Divisions of the Canadian Corps under Canadian General Arthur Currie successfully gaining control of the ridge. The cost was high, however: 15,600 casualties. The Germans did capture some ground in this offensive, but on the whole, as with the rest of the Offensive, it was costly and ultimately of limited strategic value.

46   The Germans carried out a surprise attack on Kemmel Hill, also known as Kimmelberg, a hill formation overlooking the area between Armentières and Ypres in Beligum. The Germans had been repulsed in an attempt to capture it a few days earlier (April 17 to 19) but did successfully take it on 25 and 26 April.

Tuesday, April 30, 1918

The war news which has been vacillating was emphatically good today. Yesterday heavy German attacks all along the line were repulsed with fearful losses. I cleaned house all day and in the evening I went to Zephyr with Ewan to help him with a lantern talk. I am just back and woefully tired.

Tuesday, May 7, 1918
Leaskdale, Ont.

Since last entry the war news has been neutral, but it is evident another attack is impending. The British have advanced in Palestine and there are warnings of another Austrian offensive on the Piave.[47] I have been housecleaning hard all week.

To-day was something of an "epoch." Ivor Law brought our automobile home tonight.[48] It really gave me quite a thrill. It is only very lately that I had begin to think we might have one. Seven years ago I would have laughed at the supposition.

Our New Car

I remember the first time I ever rode in an auto—that morning when Stella and I arrived in Boston and Mr. Nernay took us out to Roslindale in a taxi. I had several rides while there and when Ewan and I went to England we had several. We liked them immensely; but when I said jokingly to Ewan "What will your congregation say if we set up an auto," he replied, "My session would likely ask me to resign."

---

47   See note 13, page 5; Britain continued to consolidate its territorial gains in Palestine. Piave River: See note 2, page 1 on the battle of Caporetto. The Central Powers had broken through Italian lines, and inflicted heavy losses on the Italian army, forcing its retreat to the Piave River. A new Austro-German offensive would take place in June 1918.

48   Between 1915 and 1919 in Canada, car ownership increased hugely, as automobile production expanded in the US and Canada. Ivan Law (LMM refers to him incorrectly here as "Ivor"), had opened a car dealership in Zephyr.

When I came here cars were still so much of a novelty that we ran to the window to see one going by. Now half our people have them and there are almost as many cars as buggies at our church Sunday mornings. Our old buggy was ready to scrap so we decided to get a car. It is a Chevrolet five passenger.

I don't know that I am wholly pleased. Personally, I prefer a buggy with a nice lovable horse like dear little "Queen." But I realize a car's good points also, as time and distance-savers. And one must "keep up with the procession." But I think I shall occasionally remember with regret the old days—and moonlit nights—of buggy driving. A moonlit night loses its charm in a car with its glaring lights.

Anyhow, I'm glad my courting days were over before the cars came. There is no romance whatever in a car. A man can't safely drive it with one arm! And loitering is impossible.

Saturday, May 11, 1918
The Manse, Leaskdale, Ont.

On Thursday the word was that the Germans had attacked in the Lys sector and won some success.[49] Since then there has been little news. We are still housecleaning. Tonight I had my first ride in our car.

Friday, May 17, 1918

A hard week of housecleaning. I have also been miserable physically with an attack of cystitis.[50] Sometimes the heart goes clean out of me. There has been no more bad war news however—only threats and suspense. This is our third "tortured spring. "How long, oh Lord, how long?"

Tuesday, May 28, 1918
Leaskdale, Ont.

Very bad news! The Germans have opened a new offensive, this time against the French, and have re-captured the Chemin-des-dames.[51] This is bad—bad!

---

49   Toward the end of April the Germans made a final assault in the Lys region, capturing Sherpenberg, a hill northwest of Kemmel Hill (see note 23, page 10).

50   Inflammation of the urinary tract and/or bladder, usually caused by a bacterial infection.

51   In late May 1918, the Germans launched the third prong of the German Spring Offensive, known as Blücher–Yorck, continuing with the goal of splitting the French and the British. The attack took place in Northern France, between Soissons and Reims. On the morning of May 27, the Germans launched what would become known as the Third Battle of the Aisne, capturing the strategic Chemin-des-Dames ridge.

Wednesday, May 29, 1918

Worse news—the Germans are sweeping on to the Aisne. We went to Uxbridge this afternoon to see a military funeral. Colonel Sam Sharpe, for whom I voted last December was buried.[52] He came home from the front quite recently, insane from shell-shock and jumped from a window in the Royal Victoria at Montreal. Thousands of people attended the funeral.

Thursday, May 30, 1918

To work all the morning in anguish and then get bad news is again the normal order of things. Bad, very bad, news. Soissons has fallen, Rheims is in great danger. I am cold and sick with the horror of it all.[53]

Friday, May 31, 1918

Couldn't sleep last night. But the news to-day was not quite so bad. The Huns' advance seems to be checked for the time being but the situation is very critical. And now we have to wait till tomorrow.

Saturday, June 1, 1918
The Manse, Leaskdale, Ont.

I spent the forenoon of this warm and windy day preserving rhubarb with my body and waiting for the war news with my soul. And it was bad! The Germans have reached the Marne again—the *Marne*! They have got Chateau Thierry—an outpost of Paris, so to speak.[54] The afternoon was haunted for me. But in the evening Ewan motored down to Uxbridge and got an evening paper. The news was a little better—the French are counter-attacking in the Chateau Thierry region. Perhaps I shall sleep tonight after that—and perhaps I won't.

---

52   Samuel Simpson Sharpe, originally a lawyer in Uxbridge, had been elected MP in 1908. In November 1915, Sharpe raised a new battalion, the 116th from Ontario County; Sharpe recruited many of its soldiers personally. Shortly after he served with distinction in Vimy Ridge in 1917, he was re-elected to his seat in Parliament. In early 1918, Sharpe was hospitalized in England. In May of that year he returned to Canada and was treated for nervous shock at the Royal Victoria Hospital in Montreal. On May 25 he jumped to his death from a hospital window.

53   By May 30, 1918, the Germans had continued pursuit following the capture of Chemin-des-Dames, taking over 50,000 Allied soldiers and considerable territory, advancing on the Marne River and ultimately threatening to advance—always LMM's great fear—on Paris.

54   At this point, the German capture of the French capital of Paris was a real possibility; there was much panic in Paris, with officials were preparing plans for an evacuation.

Saturday, June 8, 1918

All this week the war news has been negatively good. The Germans have made no further advance. They are quiet—preparing I suppose for a final leap on Paris.

I went into Toronto on Tuesday and stayed till last night. Had a pleasant time but always with an ache of dread in the background. I wonder if there will ever again come a time when life will be free from *fear*. For nearly four years now we have lain down with fear and risen up with it. It has been the unwelcome sharer in every meal, the unbidden guest at every gathering.

Saturday, June 15, 1918
Leaskdale, Ont.

Another week of suspense and ding-dong fighting. The news to-day was that the Germans have again been "fought to a standstill."[55] But they are a *little* nearer Paris. Just one more spring! And what then?

June is half gone. It and May have been nightmares of months. The world is beautiful now—but the spring means nothing to me. I shall never forget May and June of 1918.

I am preparing to go "down home." It is three years since I was there. I have no feeling that I want to go—partly, I suppose, because of the war, partly because the impression made on my subconscious mind by my physically uncomfortable visit last time is still so strong. Then—I *hate* to leave home. I *like* my home so well—I am so interested in my garden and all my household doings. Last night I saw the "new star" over which the astronom-

[The Manse, Leaskdale]

ical world is vastly excited just now.[56] It is very brilliant. The general

---

55	By June 3, 1918, Germans forces had advanced to within 56 km (35 miles) of Paris, but were suffering from supply shortages, fatigue, lack of reserves, and heavy casualties. Allied forces continued to launch counter-attacks; finally on June 6, the German advance halted.

56	A bright nova that became known as Nova Aquilae was first seen in in the night sky in June 1918. A nova is now understood to be the result of a nuclear explosion on a white dwarf, a very

theory is that it is the product of a collision which occurred some-time in the reign of good Queen Bess.[57] News of this disaster, signalled across space on the wings of light, has just reached us. It is curious to look at that star and realize that you are looking at something that happened over three hundred years ago. But even this event cannot dwarf into what may be the proper perspective in star systems the fact that the Germans are again but one leap from Paris.

I have never had time to resume the studies in astronomy which so fascinated me a year or two before my marriage. I wish I might have but I suppose I never shall. The memory of them is most fascinating. They gave me such a strange, *spiritual* pleasure—an *unearthly* pleasure in more senses than one. I should have liked to be an astronomer—failing that to have an astronomer among my friends. Fancy talking the gossip of the hosts of heaven! I wonder if astronomers feel as much interest in earthly affairs as other folk do. Perhaps a student of the canals in Mars would not be so keenly awake to the significance of a few yards or so of trenches lost and won on the Western front. I have read somewhere that Ernest Renan wrote one of his books during the siege of Paris in 1870 and "enjoyed doing so very much." I suppose one could call him a philosopher. I have also read that just before his death he said that his only regret was that he "had to die before he had seen what that extremely interesting young man, the German Emperor, would do in his life." If Ernest Renan "walked" today and saw what "that interesting young man" had done to his beloved France, not to speak of the world I wonder if his mental detachment would be as complete as it was in 1870.

Monday, June 17, 1918
The Manse, Leaskdale, Ont.

We are in for another period of suspense—but the scene has been temporarily shifted. The Austrians, quiet since last fall, have struck in the Italian sector. Their success so far has been very meagre, but they have

---

dense "stellar remnant"; in other words, a collapsed star in its final evolutionary state. In the case of a nova, a white dwarf is in a binary system with a normal star, and its gravity pulls material—almost all hydrogen—off the surface of the other star. This material is added to the white dwarf's own surface. As the pressure increases, the hydrogen starts nuclear fusion, becoming helium, in an uncontrolled reaction. In the case of Nova Aquilae the nuclear explosion made the nova appear "brilliant" to observers on earth.

57   That is, Elizabeth I of England (1533–1603). However astronomers now think Nova Aquilae is some 812 light years away, which suggests that the nuclear explosion—and the resulting "brilliant new star" that LMM and others were witnessing in 1918—took place between 1080 and 1132 AD, in roughly the time of Henry I of England (1068–1135).

won a toe-hold across the Piave.[58] Is Venice to be lost after all? I cannot believe it.

Wednesday, June 19, 1918

The news is good—the Italians are holding splendidly. I am thankful that I will not have to leave home in the shadow of another disaster.

I am all packed up and we leave in an hour. I wish the journey were over. It is bound to be rather strenuous with two children. And I really don't want to go. I *wouldn't* go, if it weren't for the probability that if I go I can induce Aunt Annie to come back with me for a visit.[59] She needs a change and a rest so badly but she cannot face the thought of starting out alone.

Thursday, June 20, 1918

We have just left Montreal. I am pretty tired but the boys are as bright as buttons. We spent last evening at Laura's and the four children had a large time.[60] Ralph and I went out to a military hospital to see Carl who is just recovering from an operation for appendicitis.[61] We left this morning and reached Montreal at 6.30. Saw Frede for a few moments. She goes soon to Park Corner and we are hoping for one more happy vacation in the dear old spot.

Saturday Noon, June 22, 1918
Victoria Hotel,
Charlottetown, P.E. Island

Glory be, here we are. Last night we reached Sackville,[62] three hours late. I had been worried lest the boat train wouldn't wait for us, but it did. We had a most tedious ride to Tormentine in the dark. This was the first time I had travelled over the new car-ferry route. Perhaps I shall like it when I get used to it but I found it horrible last night. There

---

58   On the war front in Italy see note 2, page 1, and note 47, page 19.

59   Aunt Annie was the daughter of LMM's maternal grandparents, Alexander and Lucy Woolner Macneill, married to Uncle John Campbell. The Campbells lived in Park Corner, across from LMM's late Grandfather Montgomery

60   Laura, along with Jim, Cuthbert, Harry, Lewis, and Beatrice ("Bertie") were the children of aunt Mary Montgomery McIntyre (LMM's father's sister) and Duncan McIntyre. LMM had become close to the family in 1893 while a student at Charlottetown's Prince of Wales College. Laura McIntyre Aylesworth lived in Toronto.

61   Hugh Carlyle Montgomery, LMM's half brother, son of her father and his second wife.

62   Sackville, New Brunswick, is a town near the border with Quebec; from here they could travel to Cape Tormentine, across the Northumberland Strait to Borden, Prince Edward Island.

seemed to be no end to the shifts and changes, and with a heavy grip and two tired children these were not exhilarating. And amid all the men around me not one ever offered to carry that grip for me or lift a child. Certainly chivalry is not among the virtues of the majority of our Canadian men, whatever else they may possess! It was 20 to eleven the boat left Tormentine

[Victoria Row, Queen's Square, Charlottetown, P.E.I.]

and twenty to one when our train left Borden. Luckily both lads went to sleep as soon as we got in it and slept the whole way to Ch'town where we arrived at the agreeable hour of 2.30. It was past three when we finally got to bed at the hotel.

To-day was fine and distinctly cool. The Island *flavor* is excellent. But I feel very much like a stranger in Ch'town now. It does not seem to be the town of my girlhood in any respect. I took a walk round "The Square" and tried to "think myself back" but couldn't.

The war news *seems* good but is so wretchedly mixed up and inadequate in the Island papers. At least, the Italians are still holding.[63]

Tuesday, June 25, 1918
Kinross, P.E. Island

Saturday afternoon we went out to Bellevue and stayed till this afternoon with Rod and his new wife—who is—or was—a widow, older than himself with three children.[64] Ewan's mother has lost her memory completely—did not know us at all—does not know anybody. It is very pitiful. I have known so many cases like this. It makes one dread the thought of growing old.

Most of Sunday was a cold driving rainstorm. Yet I liked it. It was so thoroughly "down-eastern." We have nothing like it in Ontario. The

---

63   The Italian army had suffered heavy losses in the war. But in spring 1918 the tide was turning. Allied countries were providing new resources, Germany pulled out its troops in advance of the Spring Offensive, and Austro-Hungarian generals could not agree on the next step.

64   Roderick C. Macdonald (1879–1969), Ewan's youngest brother, who ran the family farm in Bellevue, south-eastern Prince Edward Island.

Ontario rains have no "bite" to them—no such fine real fury and swoop. Then in the evening it cleared up suddenly and goldenly and Rod took Stuart and me to Valleyfield church where the minister preached as if he were scolding the people. But we had supper at the manse afterwards and he is good company of a sort. He is a Scotchman with a tang to his conversation which is not—exactly—wholly spiritual!

Monday afternoon Rod drove me over to Montague to see a family of my second cousins over there—Dr. MacIntyre's.[65] The drive was delightful. Never did I smell more delicious odors of ferns and fir along the road. Yesterday's storm was an alchemist of power.

The doctor's mother was a Park Corner Montgomery—one of "Little Donald's" daughters—and a long-ago friend of my mother. She told me the dearest little story of her—a story that *revealed* her to me as nothing else has ever done—that made her *real* to me—that made me understand clearly what a gulf of difference there must have been between my mother and her two sisters. It made me feel, too, that if mother had lived she and I would have been *chums*—we would have understood each other.

"One day when I was in Clifton," said the old lady, "I went up to see your mother. She opened the door for me and exclaimed, 'Oh, I am *so* glad to see you. I am all alone and I just felt I *couldn't* endure it if somebody didn't come.'"

House where mother lived in Clifton, P.E.I.

"Well, I'm here now and I'll help you out," I said. "What is your trouble?" "Oh," Clara said, "little Lucy Maud is *so* sweet and lovely to-day and Hugh John is away and I've *no one* to help me enjoy her!"[66]

I felt as rich as a multi-millionaire when this old old lady fished up

65　　John Donald MacIntyre, MD (1864–1925), who had studied at McGill University.

66　　LMM's mother, Clara Woolner Macneill Montgomery (1853–76), and father, Hugh John Montgomery (1841–1900). In the final entry in this volume (December 29, 1921), LMM reflects on her mother's life.

out of the deeps of her memory, so soon to be dust, this pearl for me. How easily I might never have possessed it! My girlish mother—only 21—exulting in the charm of her baby. I have so often felt this over my own and missed Frede for nothing more than our mutual raptures of adoration over chubby little Chester and angel-eyed Stuart.

We went out for a ride in the Doctor's big "Overland" in the evening. For the motor car is on the Island at last—to stay. To be sure, there are yet two closed days—Tuesday and Friday—and some complicated Sunday regulations.[67] But soon these will cease to exist.

In one way I'm rather pleased. I hate to hear the Island made fun of for its prejudice against cars. On the other hand I resent their presence in this haunt of ancient peace.[68] I wanted it kept sacred to the gods of the old time. I wanted to think that there was one place in the world where the strident honk-honk of a car-horn could never jar on the scented air.

But I enjoyed my drive in the doctor's car for all that—even if we did get ingloriously ditched at the end, owing to a certain grim old dame who *wouldn't* rein her horse out to let us pass. The others were furious. But in my heart I believe I sympathized with the old girl. Had I been a spinster lady, driving along with my own nag, in maiden meditation fancy free, I believe *I* wouldn't have stirred a finger when an obstreperous car honked behind me. No, I should just have sat up as dourly as she did and said "Take the ditch or the devil for all of me!"[69]

It all depends on the point of view!

Rod brought me up to Christy's[70] this evening and tomorrow we go to Cavendish.

---

67 Overland automobiles were American "runabouts"—a light, inexpensive, uncovered car—produced from 1903 until 1926. Automobiles had been banned in Prince Edward Island from 1908 until 1913, when they were allowed on the road (but only for several days each week). Communities had the right to vote on whether to lift restrictions on their local stretch of road; in 1919, the last "closed" road was voted open.

68 "A haunt of ancient peace" was a line originally used by Alfred Tennyson in "Gunby Hall," a poem first published in 1832 to describe Gunby Hall in Lincolnshire, England: "And one, an English home—gray twilight pour'd / On dewy pastures, dewy trees, / Softer than sleep—all things in order stored, / A haunt of ancient Peace."

69 A similar tale can be found in Chapter 27 of *Rilla of Ingleside*: "We were all—except Susan—out for a trial ride in father's new automobile tonight. A very good one we had, too, though we did get ingloriously ditched at the end, owing to a certain grim old dame—to wit, Miss Elizabeth Carr of the Upper Glen—who wouldn't rein her horse out to let us pass, honk as we might. Father was quite furious; but in my heart I believe I sympathized with Miss Elizabeth. If I had been a spinster lady, driving along behind my own old nag, in maiden meditation fancy free, I wouldn't have lifted a rein when an obstreperous car hooted blatantly behind me. I should just have sat up as dourly as she did and said 'Take the ditch if you are determined to pass.'"

70 Ewan's oldest sister, Christie Macdonald MacLeod (1866—1908), who lived in Kinross.

Wednesday, June 26, 1918
Cavendish, P.E. Island

It seems just as natural as ever to write that heading. Yesterday morning we came to town and had dinner with Fannie Wise. Whom should I meet there but Ida McEachern whom I have never seen since we parted in Ch'town station over twenty four years ago.[71] Yet she had not greatly changed—a little older looking but I would have known her anywhere. She is Mrs. George Sutherland and is living in Ch'town.

We came out to Hunter River on the afternoon train and started from there with McGuigan's team as of old, on a beautiful evening. On the Mayfield hills we were overtaken by a motor load of H.R. folks who knew me and they offered transportation to Cavendish. So we crawled down and up and in, and speedily reached Cavendish— where even yet it causes a sensation when anyone arrives in an auto.

As we spun down over Laird's Hill I got a blow in the face![72]

On the Road, North Shore to Hunter River, Prince Edward Island

Three years ago I had been horrified on reaching that same hill to discover that the beautiful living wall of spruces on the western side had been cut down. Nature has done her kindly best in those

---

71   Fannie Wise Mutch (1876—1956) and Ida McEachern Sutherland (1874—1973), two friends from LMM's days at Prince of Wales College.

72   On her previous trip, LMM had followed a similar route to Cavendish: "Chester and I are at Ernest Webb's. We left Kinross yesterday morning. I had dinner with Fannie Wise Mutch in town and got to Hunter River in the evening. Ernest met us and we had a pleasant drive down, as the weather had suddenly turned warmer. But there was one heart-breaking feature about our drive. When we came over the crest of 'Laird's Hill' I gazed about me in dismay. For years that hill road has been so beautiful, with the thick velvet growth of young firs standing up on either side like a green wall. Some vandal road master—may jackals sit on his grandmother's grave!—has caused all those beautiful trees to be cut down leaving a most unsightly hillside of stumps and brush. Gods, how blind some people are! The sacrilege hurt me as if I had seen some beloved temple profaned. It was a temple of my soul—that once beautiful hill" (June 9, 1915).

three years to repair the wrong. The wonderful beauty of that wooded slope she could not replace; but she had cured the hideousness. The piles of unsightly brush and unsightlier stumps were hidden under a lush growth of ferns and shrubs. The hill was once more beautiful in a much humbler way.

But this blow was far worse. The old school woods had been cut down!! That once green, wide, beautiful hill was an abomination of desolation of stumps. The school-house sat on its crest wanton-ly, indecently naked. The whole sight was obscene. If I had had the power I would have spitted Garfield Stewart—the author of the outrage—on a bayonet with-out pity and without remorse.

It hurt me horribly—not only then, but every time I passed it. A thousand little pitiful ghosts were robbed of their habitations and haunts by the felling of those trees. Scores of tender memo-ries were outraged and banished.

A nook in the old school woods.

That spot I had loved so much since the first day I had followed shyly my older schoolmates into its green shadows to be so desecrated!

Oh, Cavendish, I think I had better not come back to you evermore!

But here I am and half-drunken with the old charm of it. Yonder in the twilight is Lover's Lane. I shall go to it tomorrow. They tell me no wickedness has been worked there. It is well.

Saturday, June 29, 1918
Cavendish, P.E.I.

Very lovely days and very pleasant weath-er—very delightsome meetings with old friends—very unwriteable walks in my so-beautiful old lane. I am very happy. It is good to be here.

The war news, too, has been good. The Italians have routed the Austrians entirely and chased them back over the

Lover's Lane

Piave.[73] But, the western front still awaits the next decisive blow. I long for a *Globe* somewhat—but my hungry soul is being fed with divine manna and other longings are numbed. I had not really remembered that the sea here was *so* blue and the roads so red and the wood nooks so wild and green and fairy haunted. Yes, the fairies still abide here. Even the motor cars cannot scare them away. Do not scores of them live in the white and pink bells of the columbines growing wild just over the fence in the old orchard?[74]

"So wild and green and fairy haunted"

Sunday Evening, June 30, 1918
Cavendish, P.E.I.

To-day was a warm, golden-cloudy, lovable day. Myrtle,[75] Chester and I went to the Baptist church in the morning. Verily, I have to write

[New Baptist Church]

of a greater miracle than the motor car. The minister, Mr. Piper, asked all members of any church to sit at the communion table with the others there! That, with the Cavendish hard-shells, is miraculous. Verily, the world do move!! And even Deacon Arthur Simpson has to be dragged along with it. Had anyone, twenty years ago, predicted that one day Arthur Simpson and I should sit at the same communion table I would have laughed in graceless disbelief and Arthur would likely have died of heart failure caused by shock on the spot. Yet it has come to pass.

---

73   On the war front in Italy, see note 2, page 1, and note 47, p. 19.

74   LMM uses this idea in *Emily of New Moon* (1923): "'Are there any fairies there?' asked Emily, wistfully. 'The woods are full of 'em,' said Cousin Jimmy. 'And so are the columbines in the old orchard. We grow columbines there on purpose for the fairies.'"

75   Myrtle Macneill Webb had been born in 1883 out of wedlock to a schoolteacher named Ada Macneill. From 1894, Ada and Myrtle lived with Ada's uncle and aunt, David Macneill and his sister Margaret (David was a distant relative of LMM.) In 1905 Myrtle married Ernest Webb, and the two bought David and Margaret Macneill's farm, now the site of the "Green Gables" house.

However, if Deacon Arthur felt any qualms over the un-immersed "communing" with him, he was doubtless consoled by the sermon which preceded it, preached, not by Mr. Piper, but by a certain Rev. Wallace, an evangelist of the old type, who has been holding "revival" meetings here for a fortnight. It was the rankest "Baptist" discourse I ever listened to—utterly unsuited to the occasion and utterly uncalled for in a Baptist church, where everyone—presumably—was a Baptist. Otherwise, it was a deliberate insult to those of another denomination. But I think I had a bit of revenge.

After the service I was speaking to people outside. Presently old Mrs. Arthur dragged me up to Rev. Wallace to be introduced. Poor old Mrs. Arthur S. always hated me as she hated my mother before me and all through my girlhood pursued me with petty malice and invective. But even she couldn't resist the temptation to sun herself in a bit of reflected glory emanating from a real live author.

She presented me to Rev. Wallace as "Mrs. Macdonald." Rev. Wallace nodded in a bored way and extended an indifferent hand as if to say, "Woman, what is your Mrs. Macdonald to *ME*?" Poor Mrs. Arthur, seeing her fireworks fall thus flat, hastily added, "The author of *Anne of Green Gables*, you know."

The most laughable change came over that man's face. First he looked surprised and delighted; then—I swear, he thought of that awful sermon—he turned a dull red. His manner was the most ludicrous mixture of embarrassment and adulation. He seized my hand again—he exclaimed fulsomely, "Did I ever think I would live to see this day?"—he piled compliment on compliment—and all the while I could see him thinking, in the back of his mind, "Oh Lord, what an ass I have made of myself! Why did I say those things? Let me get away and kick myself."

But I did not pity him a bit. He had made statements which were false—which he must have known were false but which he thought would impose on an audience of uncritical country hearers—and he deserved what he got. May a like confusion fall on all of his kidney.[76]

After dinner while Stuart was asleep Ernest rowed Chester, Marion, Keith[77] and me down the pond

"Come on in, the water's fine."

---

76 Expression meaning "all of his ilk."

77 Marion and Keith were Myrtle and Ernest Webb's children.

"No so bad as it's painted."

to the shore and we had a delightful afternoon. Chester had his first experience of paddling and, though he hung back very suspiciously at first, he enjoyed it after being thoroughly initiated. Not only did the minister's son go paddling but the

[LMM, Chester, Marion, and Keith]

minister's wife went too. In the snap Ernest took of us I fondly believed I had hidden my legs—but there is an odd number, as anyone can see!

But my greatest delight was to climb to the top of the old "Watch-Tower" and repeat, as I always did when standing on it.

"Could I but climb where Moses stood
And view the landscape o'er."[78]

The Watch-Tower is the largest and highest dune of the range

The Watch Tower

and the view from it is, I believe, when all points are considered, the most beautiful and *satisfying* that I ever beheld. I gazed at it, not only with physical eyes, seeing material beauty, but with the eyes of memory which saw all that in the past had filled it with charm for me. I could see

---

78   From Isaac Watts' (1674–1748) poem, "There is a Land of Pure Delight": "Could we but climb where Moses stood, / And view the landscape o'er, / Not Jordan's stream nor death's cold flood / Could fright us from the shore."

from it almost every-
thing in Cavendish
that I ever loved—the
old church hill and
graveyard, the school,
the woods that held
Lover's Lane, the
old red road, Mollie's
home, the two ponds,
the "Big Lane," my
own old home site,
the lovely New Lon-
don Harbor and New

Sliding down the Watch Tower

London Point, the shining sandshore, the red rock-shore, the sweep of
azure sea.

In the evening I went to the Presbyterian church. It was a little depressing. There were so few there—and of those few still fewer of those
I knew and some of them much changed. I recalled old evenings when
the church would be filled. But there are not the people to go now.

Wednesday, July 3, 1918
Cavendish, P.E.I.

Lover's Lane

I have had some
beautiful walks in
Lover's Lane—
some with my
little lads, some

Lover's Lane

delightfully alone.
the "deep hollow." I
summer. Such a
cal well-being make.
to the manse.

My little lads.

Today I went back to
enjoy everything this
difference does physi-
Tomorrow I am going

Wednesday, July 10, 1918
Cavendish, P.E.I.

I had a delightful sojourn at
the manse. I rather dreaded
going, because my last visit
there, for several reasons was
not at all pleasant, though
nobody was to blame. But this
time it was wholly delightful. It poured rain the night I
went over—the first bad rain

The Manse

I've had in Cavendish, but that did not matter. Margaret and I settled
down to a good, soul-satisfying gossip.[79]

The next day was fine. Some old friends called. In the evening Stuart and I had a walk in the graveyard. I felt again acutely the peculiar

charm of the Island. A certain well-
spring of fancy which I thought had
gone dry in me bubbled up as freshly as
of old. I was again a poet.

Moreover, there was one little thing
which made it seem like old times.
Years ago, whenever I walked there in
the evening, the clear calm air was always threaded by the distant sound of
children's voices and laughter at Uncle John's.[80] In recent years when no
children were there, there has been
silence. But on that evening the olden
music sounded again—this time from
the manse where Doris and Chester
and Ian were playing and calling.[81]

All very good friends

"So generations in their course decay,
So flourish these when those have passed away."[82]

---

79   Margaret Ross Stirling was a Cavendish friend, wife of the Reverend John Stirling.

80   John Franklin Macneill (1851–1936) was brother to LMM's mother, Clara Woolner Macneill
(1853–1876); his children were Lucy (1877–1974), Prescott (1879–1910), Frank (1882–1963),
Katie (1884–1904), Ernest (1884–1969), and Annie (1889–1970).

81   Doris and Ian were the children of Margaret Ross and Reverend John Stirling, who lived at
the Manse.

82   From Alexander Pope's (1688–1744) translation of Homer's *Iliad*: "Like leaves on trees

Sunday afternoon I took the four children for a walk down the school road, up Laird's Hill, across the fields and down Lover's Lane. It gave me strange sweet thrills to see Chester and Stuart careering down that lane joyously, with

Mud Pies

Chester, Doris, Ian, and Stewart

their little squeals of laughter.

Tuesday morning my visit to the manse had to end, for Margaret was going to S'side that day and next day I was due at Alec's.[83] I felt especially sad at going. For it will, in all human probability be my last visit there. Margaret and John are leaving Cavendish and going to Breadalbane. It makes me ache to think of it—to think that if I ever come back to C. I will not be a guest in this old manse where we have had so many good times.

_____

the race of man is found, / Now green in youth, now with'ring on the ground; / Another race the following spring supplies; / They fall successive, and successive rise: / So generations in their course decay; / So flourish these, then those are passed away" (Book IV, lines 181–86).

83   Alexander Charles ("Alec") MacNeill (1870–1951) was the son of Mary Buntain and Charles MacNeill, and the brother of LMM's childhood friend and cousin, Pensie MacNeill. (Alec's family spelled, and continue to spell, their name as MacNeill.) A second cousin to LMM and also an early romantic interest, Alec was married to May Hooper and lived in Cavendish.

At George R's

Geo R's House

In olden days the manse stood for nothing very pleasant to me. I was not especially fond of the Archibalds. I did not dislike them but they were certainly not of the race of Joseph.[84] We young fry never connected the manse with any thought of good times. I was never there much, save for brief calls and during them I always felt rather bored and uncomfortable. After the Archibalds left came the Robertsons. In their dynasty no one visited at the manse. A succession of young bachelor ministers followed during which it was tenantless. A new era came in with the Stirlings. Margaret was there for only a year before I left but we had lots of good times in that year. I so often ran through the bush to the manse. Evening after evening we sat around the table in the dining room and nibbled goodies and laughed and told stories. These memories have overlaid the older, less agreeable ones, until Cavendish manse has come to mean one of my shrines of friendship. But henceforth it will be another forsaken one.

Tuesday was an abominable day. Oh, the weather was beautiful. But the boys and I had to go through and spend it with Amanda.[85] I was so thankful when it was over. We came out to George R's where we stayed all night and spent today. George and Eva are alone there now. Poor old Aunt Jane ended her troubled life last year. [86] To be frank, it is

---

84   A favourite expression of LMM that she learned from Frede, which reverses the description found in Exodus 1:8: "Now there arose up a new King over Egypt, which knew not Joseph."

85   Amanda Macneill, LMM's third cousin, was slightly older than LMM and had been her closest friend around age nine.

86   "George R." is LMM's friend and cousin George Raglan Macneill, the son of Jane and

rather a pleasanter place to visit without her. One never felt very safe with her. She was insane for many years, queer and uncertain all the rest of her life. She took a very gloomy view of existence and resented anyone taking a cheerful one. I was dreadfully afraid of her when I was a little girl, and I never really felt quite comfortable in her presence, though she has always been very kind to me of late years. But she was one of the "old stock" and there are so few of them now—that "race of yore" who were the great people of our infancy.

The school road

When I had tucked my two tired babies away in their bed I gave myself a little secret pleasure. Away I went alone in the twilight. I was going *home*. I walked down to the corner, whence I could see the New London light flashing against the misty sky. Then I went along the school road and climbed the fence into what used to be our old lane. I shut my eyes as I walked up along the fence through the hay. I imagined the old lane was there just as it used to be—and that the homelight was shining through the trees. But when I found myself

As it used to be

again in the old "front orchard" it was hard for imagination to do more.

There was no transforming moonlight as when I was there last. The gray twilight revealed the woeful desolation of everything. Uncle John

Jimmie Macneill. "Eva" is his sister, the oldest child of Jane and Jimmie, is described by LMM this way: "The oldest bore the—to her—singularly inappropriate name of Evangeline. ... Evie Macneill is one of the most hopelessly plain women I have ever seen—but she possesses a most beautiful disposition and soul, sweet, unselfish, patient loyal uncomplaining, through a life that can have held very little sunshine for her. ... She has never married and has been a slave to her mother's imperious whims all her life" (January 28, 1912). In the same entry, LMM describes "Aunt Jane": "Across the road from the manse used to be the little low-roofed white house where 'Uncle Jimmy' and 'Aunt Jane' lived. Uncle Jimmie was an older brother of grandfather's and a most eccentric individual—a curious compound of child and genius. ... He married Jane Harker. She was his inferior; his family considered her so; Jane knew that they considered her so and bitterly resented it. When I was a child I had the most deeply-rooted terror of 'Aunt Jane.' She had been out of her mind several times and was always of a most ungovernable temper."

The old front orchard

had been murdering more trees in the grove. The old maple was gone and all the dear white birches. Through the broken window panes torn strips of the old white blinds were fluttering. The poor old home, how sad, how forlorn, how reproachful it looked!

I slipped around to the back and saw that the door was secured only by a wire easily unfastened. I did what I had never expected to do again—I opened the door and once more crossed the old threshold. I stood in the old kitchen. It was quite clearly visible. A damp odor of decaying plaster hung heavily on the air. I went through the sitting room and the parlor. In each I shut my eyes and *thought myself back* into the past. Everything was around me as of old—each picture, each chair in its place. I went up the stairs in the dark. I stood on the threshold of my old room—my old small illimitable kingdom. But I did not go in. The window was boarded up and the room was as dark as midnight. Somehow, I could not enter it. It was too full of ghosts—lonely, hungry ghosts. They would have pulled me in among them and kept me. I would have disappeared from the realm of mortals and nobody would ever know what had become of me. I was quite possessed by this absurd conviction.

But I went through the "lookout" and the north room. And I went down again and out and away. These pilgrimages to shadow land are eerie things with an uncanny sweetness. I will make no more of them.

We came to Alec's tonight.

Saturday, July 14, 1918
Cavendish, P.E.I.

We are having such a good time. The weather has been lovely, the boys good. Alec and May and I are out for fun. Our pleasantest times are after nine o'clock at night. Chores are done— the lads in bed. Then we

Alec Macneill's

three get into the dining room and sit around the table for a couple of hours, eating, talking and laughing. May is one of the best cooks in the world and there is no flavor like memories of old times—the preserved essence of the best of the past. The last time I was here I had a poor sort of visit, through nobody's fault, and was secretly glad to go. But this time I shall be very very sorry.

To-day was idyllic as to weather. After dinner I took the boys to the shore, stripped their legs and let them splash and wade at will, while I sat on the sand and read a novel, or dreamed dreams I thought I had forgotten the secret of.

When we got back the Stirlings came along in a friend's auto and we all went for a spin to the harbor.

This evening Alec took me in to Lizzie (Stewart) Laird's and left me there while he went on an errand.[87] That was a rather gruesome experience. I have never seen poor Lizzie since my marriage. We used to be good friends. But about six years ago she became insane—was in the asylum for a year—and has never been her old self since. She looks so old—and is so quiet and strange. She seemed glad to

"The barefoot boy"

"Two of a kind"

see me but would not or could not talk. I don't know what I should have done if Everett hadn't been there. *He* could and did talk enough for four. I don't greatly relish his type of conversation but I was thankful for anything to tide over my ghastly predicament. Bodily illness is bad enough but illness of the mind is incomparably worse. It is as if your friend's dead body moved and spoke before you in a horrible imitation of a life that had fled. *Where was the Lizzie I used to have such pleasant hours with? She* was not there, wherever she was. Only once, just as I was leaving did she reappear for a moment, as a face might peer briefly from the window of a deserted house.

---

87   Lizzie Stewart was an old Cavendish friend who had married Everett Laird (of the match LMM had written in an entry of January 28, 1912, "He married Lizzie Stewart two years ago after a long and—seemingly—a by no means ardent courtship. 'Twas a curious match, Lizzie was much older than Everett but far too good for him.")

"You look just the same, Maud," she said in her old tone. "You haven't changed at all."

It was the only thing she had said without being spoken to. I answered laughing.

"Oh, you can't see that I've some gray hairs in this light, Lizzie."

But "Lizzie" had gone. The creature who had usurped her faded body answered in the strange stilted unnatural tone she had used all the evening.

"Well, they are honorable."

I came away saddened.

Tuesday, July 16th, 1918
Cavendish, P.E.I.

So far my holiday has not been spoiled, as it was three years ago, by bad war news. But it was not good today. A new German drive has begun and again they are *across the Marne*—where we had hoped they would never be again.[88] It is impossible to size up the situation from the *Guardian's* meagre despatches but, except for this crossing of the Marne, the Huns do not seem to have gained the smashing success of their former drives. But the situation contains elements of great danger. They are *so* near Paris.

I had to go to a meeting of the W.M.S. and tea at Mrs. McCoubrey's today. They live at the old William Laird place. I have never been there since the Lairds moved away and I felt homesick. Besides, it was a nightmare of an afternoon in the crowded rooms and the heat. I was thankful to get back to the quiet of Alec's.

Wednesday, July 17, 1918
Cavendish, P.E.I.

I opened the *Guardian* with trembling fingers. But the news was reassuring. The drive seems already checked. So I went off to my afternoon at Hammond's in good cheer and had a very nice time. I missed Toff who died two years ago. But Aunt Margaret is still there, an old miracle of 95, able to do the finest and daintiest fancy work.[89] I could see no change, save that she seemed a little thinner and more shrunken.

---

88   German forces did cross the Marne south-west of Rheims in July; the territorial gain was short-lived, however, as the French launched a major offensive further west.

89   "Aunt Margaret" (actually LMM's great-aunt) was Margaret Woolner Mackenzie, the sister of LMM's grandmother (Lucy Ann Woolner Macneill) and mother of Toff and Tillie Mackenzie (Houston).

Chester eyed her with great curiosity and after we left said to me, "Mother, did you say she was 95?" "Yes," I replied. "Oh, she *couldn't* be, mother," he said. "That bed was very small and if she was 95 she would never be able to get into it." I suppose the poor laddie thought you went on growing as long as you live and that a person of 95 must be a giant!

In the evening Alec came for us and took us for a drive round the "shore road" to the harbor. It was delightful.

Thursday, July 18, 1918
Cavendish, P.E.I.

I had tea at Bob Mckenzie's today. Then I came home, put the kiddies to bed, and slipped away in the twilight for a solitary walk up Cavendish. Alec wanted to drive me but I refused. I told him and May I wanted that walk alone for the sake of old times and they were kind enough to let me have it. I said to myself, as I started "Now, I've just been down to Alec's for an afternoon's visit and I'm going *home*." And in this mood I walked slowly up that old beautiful road. I went to the graveyard and said good-bye to my dead. I went over to Myrtle's and had a chat. Then I came back to the manse and had a last long talk with Margaret in her old parlor—possibly the last time I shall ever be in it. Future minister's wives *may* ask me to call but who knows if I shall want to?

Then I walked back in the soft, dim night—slowly, to taste every atom of the sweetness of it. I was alone again with the stars and the sea—rarest of companions. I felt curiously *young* again—as if life had suddenly *folded back* twenty years. I was sorry when I got back to Alec's.

I go to Park Corner tomorrow. Of course I look forward to that with pleasure—but I hate to leave Cavendish. My whole three weeks here have been so perfect. There has been nothing to mar them in any way. So delightful has it been that I have a queer foreboding that I will not visit Cavendish again—or if I do that I will never again enjoy it so much. But at least I have had these three lovely weeks—they are mine forever. And I came almost with reluctance!

Thursday Night, July 19, 1918
Park Corner

Last night, after I had got back from my walk, I said to May, "Let's call up Jane for a bit of fun tonight."

Thereby hangs a tale—or what is worse, an explanation!

Park Corner, PEI

It is twenty eight years since I first learned to "make a table rap."[90] We used to do it out in Prince Albert for an evening's fun. When I returned home I introduced it among the Cavendish young fry and it was the fashionable amusement of the winter. Then we grew tired of it and dropped it. About ten years ago something started it up again and one winter we had lots of fun over it. I remember some rather remarkable evenings at Will Houston's,[91] where we got a great many rather strange answers. But I soon gave up this form of amusement— at least in public—for two reasons. In the first place, it annoyed me to have people say that "I pushed the table"; in the second place ignorant gossip got busy and circulated weird tales of dealings with devils.

I have never for one moment believed in what is called "spiritualism." Nothing I have ever seen or read has convinced me for a moment that any communication from the dead is possible by such means. But I *do* believe that the phenomena thus produced is produced by some strange power existent in ourselves—in that mysterious part of it known as the subconscious mind—a power of which the law is utterly unknown to us. But that there is a law which governs it and that the operations produced by that law are perfectly natural could we but obtain the key to them I am firmly convinced.

Although I gave up making tables rap in public May and I kept it up in private for our own amusement—and we had many an afternoon's fun out of it. We both held our tongues religiously and it never leaked out, so that ignorance and malice did not get any chance to flesh their tongues on us.[92]

---

90   Spiritualism had become increasingly popular in the late nineteenth- and early twentieth-centuries, with some investigative scientists becoming believers. Séances of one kind and another were common, particularly among middle- and upper-class women across the western world. In "table rapping," participants place their hands upon the surface of a small, lightweight (usually round) table, and concentrate on communicating with a departed spirit. Eventually the table should begin to move. (Nowadays the phenomenon would likely fall under the "ideomotor effect," a process in which a mental image brings about an apparently automatic muscular action).

91   Will Houston of North Rustico had married LMM's friend and cousin Tillie Mackenzie.

92   That is, gossip about us.

We used a little square "fancy" table in May's parlor and for con-venience sake we called the power that made it move "Jane." We also assumed, for the fun of it, that spirits *were* present and wanted to com-municate with us. We got no end of messages from this source—and some of them I must admit were strange enough. For one thing, they always were true to type—quite characteristic of the people as we knew them in life, or as we conceived them to be, for we did not limit our-selves in time or space and the "spirit" of "Roaring Ack" Stewart talked to us through "Jane" as freely as that of Queen Elizabeth[93] and St. Paul[94]—the latter always couching his message in Biblical style! I do not pretend to understand or explain it. There was one message in par-ticular which I could never explain and which gave me a queer chill. There was a circle of us around the table that night and "Jane" was rapping out a message from Alec's father—old "Mr. Charles." It began "See to our Pensie's—", at this juncture I, who was spelling out the message, felt quite sure that the next word would be "son" or "child." The others at the table all told me afterwards that they thought the same. But the next word was "grave"—"See to our Pensie's grave."[95]

After the others had gone May and Alec told me what I had never before heard—that Pensie's husband had never put a headstone up for her and that the grave was so overgrown with briar bushes that they could not be sure just where it was. Nobody at the table but Alec and May knew this and they had not thought of it. Nevertheless, I suppose the knowledge was in their subconscious minds.

I remember we once got a somewhat characteristic message from "Bloody Mary," the unhappy English Queen.[96] She was "among those present," as "Jane" declared, but refused to give a message. We insisted however, and kept on insisting. All at once "Jane" began to rap out, not in her usual gentle way but with a perfectly savage fury, as if something were being fairly hissed through her,

"No more. Mary Regina," came in such imperious thumps that we promptly "no-mored" as far as Mary was concerned.

We could never get a message from King David.[97] "Jane" informed us that it was because he could not talk English. But that had not floored St. Paul who couldn't have known it either—unless he has learned it in

93   Elizabeth I of England (1533–1603).

94   That is, St Paul the Apostle, c. 5–c. 67

95   Pensie MacNeill was Alec's sister, who had married Will Bulman of New Glasgow.

96   Mary I (1516–58), Queen of England and Ireland (1553–58). Mary, a Catholic, was respon-sible for the death of some 280 religious dissenters during her five-year reign, and became known as "Bloody Mary" after her death.

97   David (c. 1010–970 BCE), King of Israel and Judah.

the realm of spirits, being probably of a more democratic nature than King D.

May and I had never "called up "Jane" since my marriage. As we got out to the table I said, "It is so long since we talked to Jane that I expect it will be a long time before she will respond tonight."

It is a curious fact that when there are in the circle one or more people, who have never seen a table rap, even if they are not incredu-

Stuart, Alec and I

lous, it is a long time before it will begin. I have often sat for as long as three or four hours with a "green" circle before it would move. But once it has moved then ever after, if that same "circle" sit down the table will rap very quickly. In our old afternoons "Jane" would respond as soon as May and I laid our hands on the table; but

it had been so long since we had tried it that I thought likely it would be proportionately long before the raps would begin. To my surprise, the

minute we placed our hands in position the table almost *leapt up*—the impression made on both of us was that *something* was so amazingly glad to see us that it fairly bounded out in its joy.

We had an hour's fun out of "Jane." We did not call up any spirits from the vasty deep but contented our-selves with asking comical

Ham and Chester

questions and putting "Jane" through all her old stunts—such as walking around the room on two legs exactly like a human being, bowing, dancing, keeping time to music etc. etc. When we finished Alec got up off the sofa where he had been lying, said "Well, there's something in you, Maud, that isn't in other people" and went to bed.

This morning Stuart and I drove over to Park Corner with Alec, and Ham Macneill[98] brought Chester and my trunk. As we drove up under the birches Frede was at the well, fat as a seal and looking like the spirit of laughter incarnate. We've been talking ever since and our tongues are not quite worn out yet. There is enough to talk of, goodness knows—if talking would do any good. Matters here are bad and complicated enough. I see no way out and am rather sick at heart over it all. But then I'm very tired.

In spite of all, though, it is good to be here again. To adapt Alec, "There's something about Park Corner that isn't in other places."

I am rather worried over the war news. Rheims seems almost lost.[99] Yet there was a despatch in an obscure corner of the *Guardian* today that seems hopeful. I think the *Globe* would have headlined it. The allies have attacked on the German flank and captured several villages.

Saturday, July 20, 1918
Park Corner, P.E.I.

Good war news! Almost incredibly good! The allies are close to Soissons and have captured 20,000 Germans.[100] They seem to have broken clean through. Can the tide have turned at last? Shall Paris again be saved?

Monday, July 22, 1918

The miracle of the Marne has been repeated. It seems like a dream far too wonderful to be true. Again the Germans are hurled back across the Marne. It *is* the beginning of the end—I feel it—I feel it! I am *sure* the long agony is over. Frede remains somewhat pessimistic but I am suddenly borne aloft on the crest of a rosy wave of optimism.

Yesterday Life Howatt[101] came up with his motor and took us up to Princetown—"us," being Frede, Aunt Annie, myself, Amy[102] and Stuart. It was Aunt Annie's first trip in an auto. It was very pleasant—the day was fine and the sea beautiful. Aunt Emily is not very well—she has some heart trouble that is obscure and may be serious.[103] We had a

---

98   Hamilton Macneill, brother of LMM's childhood friend Amanda Macneill (Robertson).

99   The attack on Rheims—one of the final campaigns of the German Spring Offensive—was not successful and although threatened, the city was not captured.

100   French counter-offensives initiated by Marshal Ferdinand Foch began to take back the territory gained by the German army.

101   Eliphalet Howatt, a Park Corner neighbour and, incidentally, the brother of Irving (see for example note 218, page 138).

102   Amy Campbell, daughter of LMM's cousin George and Ella Campbell.

103   Emily Macneill Montgomery, daughter of LMM's maternal grandparents, married John

pleasant visit until the evening when we got into a foolish wrangle over conscription—Frede and I against Aunt E. We all got rather excited and some bitter things were said.

It was foolish—it is always foolish to argue with a woman of Aunt Emily's type. She is as narrow-minded and merciless as her mother before her. We should have laughed at her and let it pass—even if she did give Frede several nasty digs all along the afternoon. We combed her down well—and were remorseful all the way home about it. "Maudie," Frede remarked to me, as we swooped in under the old trees at the gate, "if Aunt Emily dies of heart failure tonight I shall always feel that we murdered her." "The gods forfend,"[104] I said, and repented me quakingly. It wasn't worth while to have tormented Aunt Emily. But she always did continue to set my teeth on edge every time I fell in with her. And yet she can be awfully nice at times and quite jolly. Only, she has poor grandfather's fatal love of "giving digs," as he called it. He could not refrain from it—neither can she. I wonder if the satisfaction of a "dig" balances the loss of affection and friendship it entails. Aunt Emily has always felt and resented the fact that people do not give her the love and confidence they give Aunt Annie. It never seems to occur to her that the reason is in herself. I recall some things that Aunt Emily said to me when I was a young

"Off for a first ride in a car"

Aunt Emily's

girl that I can never forget—little poisoned arrows that have rankled ever since. Yet I have no doubt she forgets she ever said them and would be amazed if she were told of them.

Malcolm Montgomery, one of LMM's father's cousins; the relationship between LMM and Aunt Emily had long been strained. Aunt Emily lived in Princetown, Prince Edward Island.

104   An archaic version of "God forbid."

I suppose conscription is a sore point with Aunt Emily because she has a son who is a slacker. Jack Montgomery never tried to enlist and juggled out of the draft someway.[105] She *must* feel it but she will not show it. Jack is a miserable specimen and I fancy his goings on are at the bottom of his mother's illness. He has a taste for low company and seems quite devoid of ambition. Yes, Frede and I were too hard on Aunt Emily—but in the dusk tonight as we sat on the north veranda we howled over some of the things we

The old trees at the gate

said and she said. We have not heard today that she died last night so we feel free to laugh in spite of our repentance. Frede and I can always laugh, thanks be! It is one of the strongest cords of the bond between us. If there is a lurking joke in anything Frede and I can always drag it out, hide it never so slyly. And if there isn't a joke we can make one. Aunt Annie looks at us occasionally as if to say, "Oh, when you're as old as I am you won't see much to laugh at." Well, I daresay that is true; and yet I can't conceive of Frede and I foregathering, even at seventy, and not being able to laugh— not being able to perceive that sly, lurking humor that is forever peeping round the corner of things. I am forty three and she is

x The north veranda

thirty five—old enough to be sobered. And God knows, the lives of neither of us have been devoid of sobering experiences. But when we are together we can laugh with the abandonment of sixteen.

---

105 In a long entry on family history dated June 2, 1931, LMM wrote of Aunt Emily's other son, James: "Aunt Emily's son James lives at Fox Point, a queer odd mortal with no children. So the old homestead of Hugh Montgomery will pass into other hands with this generation." In fact James Montgomery had adopted three children.

Saturday, July 27, 1918
Park Corner, P.E.I.

Still the war news continues good—still Foch is driving the German army back. Even Frede is growing enthusiastic. The mail comes about three in the afternoon and then she and I squat on the north veranda, with our feet hanging over the edge, and eat up the news. We study the maps and nip the whole Hun army by a few well directed moves!

I, myself, have no doubt of the outcome. When the news that Foch had broken through the flank of the Crown Prince's army came I remembered that odd dream I had last March—that thirty evil days were coming—followed by one in which I saw the Crown Prince Frederick die. I had lost faith in it when thirty days had passed since the opening of the offensive and still the German advance continued. But the other day I got out my daily notebook and counted up the whole number of days since the 21st of March on which the news had been positively bad—when the Germans had made significant advances. I counted in no days when the news had been good or indifferent.

There were just thirty days!

As for my dream of the old Crown Prince—well, it was the Crown Prince's army that has met with this great reverse. But I do not believe it was that—or that alone—which the dream foretold—I believe it meant some great disaster to the House of Hohenzollern—perhaps its total over throw.[106] We shall see.

I had another curious dream a few days before the news of the turning of the tide came. I dreamed I saw Marshall Foch[107] and he said, "October 3rd." I imagined that this meant that on October 3rd the tide would turn. But if it has turned already there must be another meaning. In this, too, we shall see.

Frede and I were up to tea at Wm. Ramsay's this afternoon.[108] Aunt Mary Cuthbert was there, too, and we had such a nice time—"like old times," as Frede said. In the evening we walked home together by way of the old short cut over the field and up through the maple grove. A thunderstorm was passing blackly out to sea and the night came down in a sweeping flood of rain.

---

106   See notes 20 and 21, page 9.

107   That is, General Ferdinand Jean Marie Foch (1851–1929), then Supreme Allied Commander; his title had long been "Marshal," a French military distinction awarded to Generals for exceptional leadership.

108   The Ramsays were long-time friends and neighbours.

Sunday, July 28, 1918

A beautiful day. This afternoon Aunt Annie and Dan and I drove through to Long River church. When we came back Life Howatt came up and motored us down to Mr. Howatt's for tea. We had one of those wonderful "spreads" which only Island people can—or do—get up, and which they still continue to get up despite the howls of the Food Board.[109] In my own house we haven't had cake for a year, but since I've been on the Island I've seen heaps of it—and eaten heaps of it, too, I must admit. We motored home under the stars and Frede and I, before we went to bed, sat down and talked everything over de gustibus.[110]

The Maple Grove

Monday, July 29, 1918
Park Corner, P.E.I.

Tonight Frede and I took Dan, Jim, Amy, Chester and Stuart to the shore.[111] We all went in bathing and had a glorious old plunge. Stuart is a regular little fish—loved to go in up to his neck. Then Frede and I wandered home in the twilight, talking everlastingly of course, while the kiddies frolicked around us like puppies, and the pond dreamed in the afterlight.

Saturday, July 30, 1918

Margaret Stirling came over yesterday evening and she and Frede and I had a delightful little supper together by our three selves and a good pow-wow of gossip and reminiscence.

An odd thing happened today.

I never like to sit down thirteen at a table. My reason tells me that it is only an absurd superstition. Something more primitive than reason

---

109   The government had created a Food Board to help manage food production and other essentials as part of the war effort. The Board had drawn attention to certain "wasteful cooking practices" to manage shortages.

110   Latin: "In matters of taste."

111   Donald (LMM and Frede called him "Dan"), Amy, and Jim were children of George and Ella Campbell (as were "Georgie" and "Maudie," mentioned in the next entry).

insists on being uneasy. Sixteen or seventeen years ago I was at a party one night and sat thirteen at table. Will Stewart, one of my school-mates was there, and he died before six weeks had passed. I have never happened to sit with thirteen from that time until today.

There is such a gang of us here, especially of children, that, since I came, we have never all sat down to any meal at once. Aunt Annie, Frede, or Ella would wait on the table and eat afterwards. Today at dinner time, however, it so happened that everyone sat down and I began to count them just out of curiosity to see how many there really were—George, Ella, Aunt Annie, John Cole (the hired man), myself, Frede, Dan, Amy, Jim, Georgie, Maudie, Chester and Stuart—thirteen!

More as a joke than anything else I said "Why there are thirteen of us at the table."

The next moment I thought, "Well, what an asinine thing of me to say! Here is Ella, expecting a baby and depressed and pessimistic as it is. If she believes in the superstition of thirteen it may prey on her mind and have a disastrous effect."

To erase any such impression from Ella's mind I laughed and said to Frede,

"Frede, you were the thirteenth to sit down—the omen must be for you."

Frede had, however, jumped up and declared she would not sit at the table. I laughed again and said, "Oh, you did sit and you had begun to eat. No use in getting up now—your doom is sealed. May as well sit down and eat resignedly."

But Frede vowed she wouldn't and made off to the porch. George who, it seems, had never heard of the superstition, burst into one of his howls of laughter at us and called Frede and me fools, etc. No doubt we were. Yet somehow the trivial incident has left a disagreeable impres-sion on my mind. What if Ella—but nonsense! I won't allow myself to think such silly things.

After we got everybody off to bed tonight Frede and I broiled our-selves a snack of beef ham and devoured it with sounds of riot and mirth.[112] We are at one in our love of beef ham. I wonder if the spirits of the departed ever eat spirit-beef-ham.

Sunday, August 4, 1918
Park Corner, P.E. Island

It won't be Park Corner much longer. We go tomorrow—Frede, Aunt Annie, my two lads and I.

---

112   Beef ham is a way of preparing high-quality cuts of beef, shaped like a traditional pork ham.

I can hardly say I'm sorry. In one way I've had a jolly time here—Frede and I together could make jollity in the realms of Pluto I verily believe. But in another way it has been rather hard. Seven children all under ten are something of a houseful. This does not mean that Chester and Stuart did not agree with their cousins—on the contrary they agreed remarkably well. But the better they agreed the more ear-splitting was the racket they made and the more fearful and unheard-of the scrapes they got into out of doors. One day Aunt Annie found them all out behind the barn thrashing a big mud puddle furiously with boughs. They were mud from head to foot. They were "fighting Germans," they told her, and the puddle was a trench!! In truth, the only times that were at all peaceful were when they had an occasional tiff and sulked for an hour or so before they made up.

A barrow-full. Jim, Chester, Stuart, Amy and Georgie

Chester and Jim were especial cronies but this did not prevent them from having bitter rows on *politics*—generally after they went to bed at night. Frede and I used to sit on the stairs in the dark outside their door listening to them, doubling up with suppressed laughter over their incredible speeches.

John Cole, the hired man, an eccentric old chap, has a great admiration for Chester. Frede delights to his speech to her when he first saw Chester,

"Never saw such legs—never saw such legs since I saw the strong old sea-captains down at Pinette. I would not be the man that crosses his path when he grows up—that would not I!"

Frede is always tickled when a compliment is paid Chester. He is her favorite. Most people are more taken with Stuart. *He* has a sunny little face, a ringing infectious laugh and an engaging personality which win him affection very readily and which will probably constitute one of his pitfalls in afterlife. Chester, on the contrary, is a rather reserved and distant little mortal and does not make so favorable an impression at first. But he has always been Frede's white-haired lad—they are both "cats that walk by themselves" and care little if other Toms and Tabbies are indifferent.

But I have wandered afar and must return to my mutton—my reasons for being rather glad to be leaving Park Corner. The real reason is the truly terrible and unhappy state of affairs that obtains here now—a state of affairs that has been gradually growing worse year by year until at last it has reached a pitch that seems to me utterly intolerable for those who live here. It seems to me that things *can't* go on like this any longer without some disaster. God himself must be tired of the situation.

In my childhood and girlhood Park Corner was one of the happiest, gayest spots in the world. Aunt Annie married Uncle John Campbell when she was 28 and he 42. I do not know that there was any romantic love on either side—certainly not on Aunt Annie's. But they were very happy together.

Uncle John's farm at Park Corner was—and is—one of the finest farm properties on P.E. Island. Two hundred acres of fertile soil, acres of fine woodland, shore rights, pond rights of mud and fishing, water on every field of the farm, a splendid orchard and a large beautiful house. The Campbells were a good old family. The original Campbell—Captain Campbell—who emigrated to Canada was a member of the Breadalbane Campbells. There is an old family tradition that he was really the heir to the earldom of Breadalbane. But he made an unhappy marriage in the old land, eventually left his wife and came to Canada, where he passed as an unmarried man and married a Miss Townsend—a cousin of Great Grandmother Macneill's. If the story were true she was certainly not his legal wife. But her right was never questioned in those days when there was little communication between P.E. Island and Scotland, even when it was desired. There may have been nothing in the tale. It sprang, I believe, from the fact that a stranger from Scotland had one day appeared and asked to see Captain Campbell, averring that he brought him news of his wife and family in the old land. Captain Campbell hustled him away and denied the story. So it rests.

His son, James Campbell, settled on the Park Corner farm. His first wife was Elizabeth Montgomery, a sister of "Little Donald" Montgomery, who died after she had borne him two or three sons. He then married her cousin, Elizabeth Montgomery, sister of "Big Donald" Montgomery, my grandfather. (It seems as if the Montgomeries must have been rather short of names in those days). It must be a rather odd sensation to have two wives of the same name. I think it would seem ghostly to me. They had a large family—seventeen children! Fancy one woman bearing seventeen children. And yet, when Aunt Elizabeth was over seventy, she told Aunt Annie one day that "she felt a strange feeling. I think it must be what you call *tired*."

Aunt Elizabeth, as we all called her, was living at Park Corner when

Aunt Annie went there and I remember her very well. She lived until I was quite a big girl. She was a very sweet old lady, with remarkably large, deep-set eyes. She had been a great beauty in her youth but her life had its tragedies. When the cholera plague swept over the Island long ago she was ill in bed after the birth of one of her children. When she was able to be up it was to learn that four of her children had died in one week of the cholera! Later on two of her sons were drowned in the prime of young manhood. Finally, her husband who had lived the average decent life until he was fifty, suddenly and unaccountably took to drinking and drank himself into the grave.

Some of his sons were by no means models but Uncle John Campbell was one of the best men that ever lived—kind, generous, open-hearted, moral, abstinent, and honest. I always loved him and always found in him a firm friend. Naturally, he had some faults. Intellect was not his strong point. He cared nothing for reading; emotionally he was very unbalanced, though fortunately his temper was of the best. I never saw anything like his agony of grief at the funeral of little Jacky, the oldest born of George and Ella, who died of pneumonia. Uncle John had idolized him and Frede and I had almost to drag him away from the casket by force when the undertaker went to close it. When he was about fifty or fifty-five he became "converted" at some meetings held by an emotional evangelist. Really, I think he was a little out of his head about that time. He could talk of nothing but "religion" and for two or three years bored everybody to death who went to the house. Then the wave passed as suddenly as it came and Uncle John reverted to his former self. He had always been a good man and a good man he remained to the end; but of his frantic religious spasm nothing remained save his newly acquired habit of saying grace, always prefacing it with such an unearthly groan that we graceless youngsters used to have much ado to keep from snickering outright. Uncle John's father became a dipsomaniac at fifty;[113] Uncle John's psychical upheaval took a religious form. That was all the difference. Although he was one of the hardest working men in the world he was absolutely devoid of any business instinct. He could never in all his life save a cent. Money ran through his fingers like water with nothing to show for it. Possessing a property on which, working as he did, he should have grown rich, while living as well as need be, he not only saved nothing in his long life, but died slightly in debt, though this was George's fault, not his.

Aunt Annie has been—and is—a wonderful woman in some ways.

---

113   Dipsomania is a term that is no longer in use that describes the symptoms of alcohol misuse.

A hard worker, a supreme cook, a splendid housekeeper. But she, too, had qualities that in the end were to make for tragedy. She had no "vision" of any sort. No ideals were ever set before her family save the most material ones. And, on the lower plane, she, as well as Uncle John, lacked thrift and business capacity. She made a great deal of money every year with her butter and eggs and poultry and never saved a cent of it. Everything was lavished on hospitality. This might have been pardonable where their own kin were concerned. But they really kept "open house" for the whole Island. They had continual shoals of visitors who cared nothing for them and simply made Park Corner a convenient house of call. It was rare that a summer day or a winter evening passed without "company." Aunt Annie was really quite proud of this, though she often complained of the hard work it involved. Uncle John revelled in playing the host. He was never happier than when seated at a long table carving up joints of meat and platters of geese and turkey. Uncle John Campbell could carve and serve after a fashion rarely seen—not seen at all nowadays. He was an artist at it—could dissect the most complicated old gobbler, give everyone a choice portion, and carry on an easy conversation all the time.

This was all very well in the hey-day. But when Uncle John and Aunt Annie grew old there was no money to fall back on. Everything had been lavished in some way. They had four children—Clara, Stella, George and Frede. Frede was the only one who was any comfort to them. Clara, the oldest, was a nice girl and rather pretty. She was good-tempered and full of fun. But her intellectual capacity was small and she had no ambition, save to be finely dressed and entertain her friends lavishly. Yet there was something very lovable about her and she and I were very dear to each other in our girlhood.

When Clara was seventeen her parents did something I have never been able to understand. They allowed that young girl, at the formative age, to go up to Boston and become a domestic servant. Many of the French River and Park Corner girls did this; it was all right for them; but for Clara it was, or should have been, unthinkable. Clara remained there until she married. She made her friends in a low class, she married in that class. What Uncle John and Aunt Annie were thinking of I cannot imagine. They both came of excellent families, with traditions of birth and breeding. One would have thought they would have been horrified at the idea. On the contrary they rather encouraged it.

Stella was clever, capable and jolly. At first her spasms of temper were not so frequent or so frantic as they afterwards became. But her parents never made any serious or intelligent effort to check it. The things Stella flew into rages over were the things Aunt Annie disliked also and therefore she found it easy to tolerate or pardon Stella's outbursts.

George Campbell was, from babyhood, a person I never had any use for. For his mother's and sisters' sake I have always taken care to "keep on his good side"—flattering his vanity and ignoring his drawbacks. As a result George has always liked me, treated me as decently as he could treat anybody, called one of his children after me—and borrowed money of me! I have considerable influence over him, as also has Frede. His mother and his wife have absolutely none.

George seemed to inherit the worst qualities of both parents, with none of their good ones. He has his father's lack of business ability without his father's industry, his father's lack of emotional control without his father's decency of emotion, he has his father's lack of taste for things of the intellect without his father's liking for society and conversation. He has his mother's intolerance of anything outside the narrow range of her experience without her kindly tolerance of things *in* it, he has her utter disregard for other people's feelings without her real regard for their material welfare, he has her lack of vision and ideals without her homely pleasure in everyday life, and her lack of any ability to judge character, without the innate dislike of taking suggestions from anybody that stood her in fairly good stead. In addition George inherited from a remoter source a taste for liquor, eventually resulting in drunkenness and immorality, a distaste for steady effort, and the temper of a fiend.

George was indulged all his life. The only son, born after two girls, he was petted and spoiled as a child. His sisters were expected to wait on him and his father never had any control over him. He matured early—used to be out half the night, driving girls about and "sitting up" with them when he was no more than twelve or thirteen. He soon began to drink. For years his mother refused to believe this and never forgave anyone who told it of him. She has learned it too well since, poor woman.

When he was twenty-one George married Ella Johnston. Out of all the world *she* was the last person he should have married. Out of all the world *he* was the last person she should have chosen. It was a marriage nobody could ever understand. It was impossible to see any reason why either of them should have been attracted to the other. Ella was six or seven years older than George—a pretty, delicate little doll who had been brought up in cotton wool all her life because her father and three of her sisters had died of consumption. If she had married a professional or businessman she might have been an average wife. As the wife of a farmer, and especially of big, roistering George Campbell—well, she was a joke. She was well warned that she was marrying a drunkard. He was well warned that he was marrying a useless little doll. In spite of this—or because of it!—marry they did.

"What do you think of her, Maud?" Uncle John Campbell asked me, during the festivities attendant on the wedding.

"I think she looks like a baby astray," I replied.

Uncle John laughed.

"You've just about hit it," he said.

The inevitable happened. In six months George was tired of his wife. In a year he hated her—and she him. For fourteen years they have lived together and things have gone from bad to worse. George is a notorious drunkard, with several unsavory adventures and several illegitimate children to his credit. His mother is broken-hearted, his health is wrecked. At thirty six he looks fifty—red-nosed, bald, bloated. He is in debt—he has a big family to provide for—he is discouraged—his temper is an awesome thing. He uses his wife abominably—oh, it is all utterly heart-sickening.

Ella, too, is a weakling. I pity her—I try to help her—but what is the use? All the little spunk she ever had has been crushed out of her by disappointment and child-bearing. She has had eight children—three of whom have died—and expects another. I am so sorry for the poor thing that it wrings my heart. She appeals to me constantly for advice, sympathy, and help. And I can do so little to help her.

Aunt Annie is perfectly well satisfied with herself as a mother-in-law. Yet she has been a hard one—not in deeds but in words. She has never spared Ella's feelings in any way—she has been unjust and unfair—she blames all George's bad habits and shortcomings on Ella, stubbornly shutting her eyes to the fact that George drank long before his marriage. As a result, there is not only no sympathy between these two women who have to live together but there is thinly veiled resentment and antagonism. Aunt Annie has all that strange animosity and injustice towards "outsiders" that was so conspicuous in her mother's character. It never occurs to her that she has failed in any respect towards Ella.

But there it is. What an unhappy household, compact of bitterness and hatred and discontent! I feel all the time I am in it as if I walked on the edge of a volcano. I do not *see* the worst—I am only told of it.

Since I have been here George has been outwardly decent. He *can* be quite good-humored and pleasant when he likes. George Campbell has a superficial popularity over the country—"a good, open-hearted fellow"—"his own worst enemy" etc.

The evening after I came Frede and I were in the kitchen and George came in. He sat for awhile, laughed and joked, told some funny stories, then went off to bed. Frede said to me,

"Maud, I wonder if you realize the influence you have over George? He is a different creature when you are here. I have been home for three weeks and in all that time I haven't seen him laugh or heard him tell a joke. He has just gone about in black silence, varied by outbursts of demoniacal temper."

"I think," I said, "that when I come here George feels that something of the atmosphere of old times comes back with me—those good old times when we were all young and gay and carefree together."

If George had married the right sort of a woman—a woman something like his own sister Stella—jolly, capable, strong-willed, not over-refined, with a dash of his own temper, I believe he might have developed into a passably decent citizen. As it is, things are simply dreadful here. Frede and I have talked matters over until we are black in the face—but what good does it do? We get nowhere. We seem to be in a blind alley. It seems to me that a catastrophe of some kind is about due. George will be brought home some night killed in a drunken row—as he almost was one night last winter—or he will kill Ella in some of his furies—or she will leave him—or—but there, I'll stop. I can't do anything—and so I will be glad to get away from a tragedy I cannot lighten or avert.

The only bright spot in this is George's family. They are as nice a brood of smart, handsome agreeable kiddies as you could find anywhere. They are not like either their father or mother. If they get half a chance they will, I believe, restore Park Corner to its old status. I am very fond of them all and so is Frede. We rather feel as if the responsibility of them rests on us—that we must put our shoulders to the wheel and see that they get a chance. They are fond of us and do not resent our guidance and preachments.

Tonight, as I sat for a moment on the veranda I childishly wished that some good fairy would appear and grant me a wish. I would have said,

"Give me back the old Park Corner for an hour—just an hour. Bring Uncle John back—restore Aunt Annie to her smiling, bustling prime— let Clara and Stella be here, gay girls in their teens—let George be the little chubby, innocent boy again. For just an hour give me that olden gladness and beauty back again."

But no good fairy appeared. The clock is never turned back. I cannot have that hour out of the past. The Park Corner of today, still beautiful, still almost the same outwardly, is a terribly different place from the Park Corner of twenty years ago. And so I am not sorry that I go tomorrow.

The Manse, Leaskdale, Ont.
Thursday, Aug. 8, 1918

Last Monday morning the House of Campbell bestirred itself at a very early hour. Everybody was more or less excited—for it was an uncanny thing for Aunt Annie to be going away for a visit. Aunt Annie never gets visibly excited. That is an excellent quality no doubt—but think of all the fun you miss if you are non-excitable. There's nothing quite so wonderful as dancing around a blazing fire. What matter if it end only in gray ashes? And while walking is a sure and safe mode of locomotion it isn't half as exhilarating as flying, even if you do come down with a thud.

It was quite dark when I got up. When I went out into the hall and looked out of the big hall window I saw an exquisite sight. Out to the east, over the birches and maples was a silvery red sky and floating in it what seemed like a new moon—but it was the old one in its last hours. I do not recollect ever seeing the old moon at that stage before. The colorings were so exquisite and the whole effect so fairylike and elusive that I called Frede and we watched it together delightedly, until the picture etched itself unforgettably on my brain. I have only to think of it to see it again. It continued beautiful for half an hour, the moon fading out to a wraith as the daylight deepened, and then just disappearing.

The big hall window

Life Howatt motored us to the station. As we left I suddenly burst into tears and cried until we reached the top of the hill. Why? I do not know. I never cried on leaving Park Corner before, though I have left it, feeling more sorrowful than I felt that morning. I was glad to be going home—I was taking with me the only people of it that I cared muchly for. And yet I sobbed uncontrollably as if I never expected to see Park Corner again.

When we got on the train the *Guardian* announced the capture of *Soissons* and all the way home every stop was punctuated with a fresh victory. The French were sweeping all before them. Very different from my last trip home three years ago to the tune of the Russian disaster. We had a very pleasant trip up to Montreal. As the car-ferry steamer was laid up for repairs we crossed by the old Summerside and Pointe-du-Chene route—which I must say I prefer.

Frede and I used to go into carefully secreted spasms of laughter over her mother's face. Aunt Annie had evidently started out with a firm determination not to betray the fact that she was not an accustomed globe trotter. No surprise or admiration or doubt or curiosity would she allow herself to betray. Her expression said plainly, "You need not suppose I am green or provincial. I know just as much as you or anybody." But she was a game old dame and enjoyed herself.

We missed the Toronto train so had to stay in Montreal all day. Left at night. Frede and Aunt A. got off at St. Anne's, as Aunt Annie was to stay a week there. The boys and I reached Toronto Wednesday morning and were met by Ewan and Mr. Fraser.[114] We motored home—52 miles—and got here at noon. My heart was in my mouth when Ewan attempted to negotiate Yonge St. but we got on very well. It has been fairly hot since we came back and I am yet very tired.

Wednesday, Aug. 14, 1918
The Manse, Leaskdale

Yesterday morning Ewan and I rose at four and left at five to motor into Toronto to meet the Montreal train. It was dark as far as Uxbridge and we saw no living creature until we reached Stouffville. It was very delightful to fly along in the cool morning air. We got to Toronto Station at eight and Aunt Annie was on hand. We spent the day showing her Eaton's and Simpson's. I also took her to a moving picture show.[115] I know she considered it an invention of the devil. The day was a record-breaker for heat—102 in the shade.[116] We left for home at five and had a very

114 James R. Fraser (b. 1867), minister at Chalmers Presbyterian Church in Uxbridge, may have played a role in bringing the Macdonalds to Leaskdale as the local presbytery's interim moderator in 1910. See also LMM's entry for August 8, 1918, and April 12, 1921.

115 A silent movie. During the war film-making in the US flourished (sound recordings were not included until the 1920s; silent films were often accompanied by live piano music).

116 Canada used the Fahrenheit temperature until March 31, 1975, when, as part of an overall

pleasant drive until about two miles from home when a terrific storm of thunder, rain and wind struck us with all the force and suddenness of a tornado. In a moment we were wrapped in darkness. In Parrish's hollow a tree had fallen across the road. Ewan turned out to avoid it, the car skidded and over we went into the ditch. I screamed as we took the plunge—I felt sure we were going over the culvert. If we had we would all have been killed but fortunately we were a few feet further on, where the ditch was shallower. We crashed into a mailbox post and stopped. Out we scrambled in the downpour. I thought the car was ruined. One wheel was lying on the ground. But at least our lives were spared. Then we had to walk up that long hill lane of Parrish's in the torrents of rain and the pitch darkness lighted only by wild flashes. We stayed there until the storm abated, wet to the skin, for there was no woman in the house to get us a change of clothes. I thought Aunt Annie would catch her death. We drove home after the storm ceased and today neither of us is any the worse. The car, too, is not seriously damaged. Mr. Warner has fixed it up all right. But it has broken my nerve. It will be a long time before I feel comfortable in "Daisy" again.

Monday, August 19, 1918
The Manse, Leaskdale

I resumed work on my book today. I am not as far ahead with it as I could wish. Still, I ought to be able to finish it by the last of October. We have been having a pleasant time. Aunt Annie seems to be enjoying herself thoroughly. The war news is good. Haig's army is advancing now. They go further in a day than in a year before.[117]

Ella has a daughter and is doing well. I feel relieved. I have been vaguely uneasy ever since that table of thirteen—which was very foolish and absurd of me certainly. But reason and feeling are two entirely different things.

"metrication" program, the Celsius scale came into use. 102°F is the equivalent of 39°C.

117   Following the failure of the German Spring Offensive, the Allies began the final military push that would ultimately end the war with Armistice on November 11. On August 8, 1918, a surprise attack was launched that included ten Allied divisions that included Australian, Canadian, British, and French forces, and over 500 tanks. (This would mark the beginning of the Hundred Days Offensive, in which Canadian forces played a key role.) Over the following days, German forces suffered heavy losses of men and territory. Field Marshal Douglas Haig (1861–1928), Commander of the British Expeditionary Force, had been instrumental in planning the attack.

Thursday, Aug. 22, 1918
The Manse, Leaskdale, Ont.

To-day we had a picnic up at the Lake. It was all very pleasant and I think Aunt Annie enjoyed it enormously. When we left to come home our steering gear broke—having, it turned out, been cracked the night of our accident. Fortunately we were going slowly in a level place so nothing dreadful happened. We had to sit on the side of the road for two hours however till we got it fixed. A sample of the joys of motoring.

Friday, Aug. 30, 1918

The war news has been increasingly good and culminated today in the announcement of the capture of Bapaume, Noyon and Perouse. It all seems rather difficult to believe.[118]

Carl has been visiting us for a couple of days.

Thursday, Sept. 5, 1918

Yesterday Aunt Annie and I got home after having taken in the Toronto Exhibition. Aunt Annie has had the time of her life and has admitted it. We went in Tuesday morning by train and in the afternoon went to see "Hearts of The World."[119] It is a wonderful thing. I wanted to see it especially because a battle that Carl took part in was featured in it—the battle of Courcelette.[120] He had told us he recognized one scene in particular by a big round hole in a brick wall. So all through the play Aunt Annie and

Carl

118   Haig launched a new offensive on August 21, pushing German forces back some 55 km (34 miles); in the following days key targets were captured, including the towns of Noyon, Arras, and Bapaume.

119   *Hearts of the World* was a 1918 film set in the trenches of World War one, directed by D.W. Griffith.

120   Canadian troops had claimed success for one of the few victories during the Somme Offensive, at the battle of Courcelette in September 1916. They used the new technique of "creeping barrage," which consisted of slowly advancing artillery bombardment of enemy lines, followed at a safe distance by infantry advance. Seven armoured tanks—another new tactical innovation—had accompanied the Canadian advance.

I watched for that hole. Holes there were without number, some of them fairly round, but none seemed exactly to measure up to our expectations. Near the end came the hole—unmistakably *the* hole; and we both exclaimed aloud "There's the hole!," much to the amusement of a row of young men in front of us.

This reminds me of a funny thing Frede told me. She went to see the film in Montreal. In one scene, a girl, locked in her room, secretes a knife in her stocking or some such place to defend herself. Enters a brutal German. In the ensuing struggle Frede got so excited by the realism of the thing that she suddenly stood up and shrieked at the top of her voice, "The knife is in your stocking! The knife is in your stocking!" She said afterwards that the only thought in her mind was that the girl must have forgotten the knife was there! To add to the effect, just after Frede shrieked this, the girl pulled out the knife and stabbed the German!!

In the evening, after dinner at the Walker House Aunt Annie and I went to another movie with the hectic title "To Hell with the Kaiser."[121] It was not so lurid as its name—very good, in fact, though not in the same class as "Hearts of the World."

Yesterday morning we went out to the Exhibition grounds. Of course the cars[122] were horribly crowded and it was funny to see Aunt Annie's face when after a breathless sprint to get on a car she found herself hanging to a strap in a jammed car aisle. It said, as plainly as words, "Has all the world gone mad?"

I think she enjoyed the Exhibition thoroughly, though, and it did her a tremendous amount of good to discover that there wasn't an apple in the fruit exhibit that was as good as what her own orchard at Park Corner could produce. I did not mar her joy by telling her that the season is late this year and very few apples as yet available. That would have been needless cruelty. I let her think Park Corner orchard could beat Canada.

And can it not, in a sense?

The other day I found an interesting thing in an old copy of *The Westminster Gazette* which Mr. MacMillan sent me. This weekly runs a "problem" page in which it offers prizes for various literary stunts. Recently it offered a prize for the best essay on "Wallpapers I have known" and in this especial copy the Prize essay was printed, signed by *Quincunx*. One sentence in it struck me—"wallpapers that came

---

121   This now-lost American comedy/propaganda film was directed by George Irving.

122   Electric street-cars had started to replace horse-drawn equivalents in 1861. A line ran directly to the Exhibition Grounds.

out or retreated when you looked at them with the right kind of eyes."

When I was a very small child—how small I do not know but it was as long ago as I can remember. It was before Aunt Emily was married, therefore before I was seven at least—I made a certain discovery.[123] This was that if I looked at the paper on the walls of a room in a certain way I could cause that paper to appear in miniature before me, as if on a transparent screen floating in the air between me and the real wall. As for the said "certain way of looking" I don't know what it was like, not being able to see my eyes in the process. But it seemed to me that I made a certain contraction of the muscles of the eye which produced the mirage. Once the appearance was produced the sense of contraction vanished and I seemed to be looking at it normally with no sense of effort. I could see the mirage thus as long as I looked at it but if I glanced away it vanished. I could also cause it to vanish by another little movement of my eyes which did not seem strong enough to call a contraction—more of a *letting-go*, so to speak. I could cause the mirage to appear at any distance from the wall I liked—a foot out—half way across the room—a foot or so from my eyes. The harder the contraction the nearer it came. But I could also bring it near gradually, by a series of easy contractions. That is, I would cause it to appear a foot from the wall. Then, by looking at this mirage itself, not at the paper, and making the movement of my eyes I could bring it a foot or so nearer, and so on until I had brought it as near as possible. The first mirage would be only a trifle smaller in pattern than the real paper. But with every shift it became smaller until the last one hung before my eyes the tiniest reproduction imaginable. These mirages were transparent—that is, the real wall could be seen through them and yet they seemed perfectly real and tangible.

All through my childhood this was a favorite amusement of mine. I loved to produce those aerial wallpapers—tiny roses and wreaths, like fairy screens. Whenever I found myself in a strange room I promptly "looked" at the paper. The prettier the pattern the prettier the result of course. Pictures and anything hanging on the wall were reproduced along with the paper; but I could not reproduce a picture by itself.

When I grew up I dropped the practice, only trying it now and again at long intervals when something recalled it to my mind. I haven't tried it for—why, it must be fifteen years. But when I read this essay in the

---

123   A similar description is found in chapter six of *Emily of New Moon*: "Emily had discovered that she possessed this odd knack when she was six. By a certain movement of the muscles of her eyes, which she could never describe, she could produce a tiny replica of the wallpaper in the air before her—could hold it there and look at it as long as she liked—could shift it back and forth, to any distance she chose, making it larger or smaller as it went farther away or came nearer."

Gazette I tried again and found that I still possessed the power though I fancied it was a trifle less easy to exert.

I have never come across any person who could do this or who seemed to have the faintest understanding of what I was talking about if I mentioned it. But I am inclined to believe that this *Quincunx* possesses or possessed it. That must be what his—or her—sentence means. I would like to be sure. I think if I can get the time I will write to *Quincunx* in care of the *Gazette* and see if I can find out for the mere curiosity of the thing.

Tuesday, Sept. 19, 1918
Leaskdale, Ont.

We are having a phenomenally wet September—and cold also. But we are contriving to give Auntie a good time for all. The war news continues good—the Serbs have the Bulgars on the run in Macedonia[124] and today came the news that the British have smashed the Hindenburg line on a front of twenty-two miles.[125] That *must* mean the beginning of the end for the Germans. Is the long nightmare nearly over? Will spring come in 1919—as springs of old came—as springs should come, free from dread and pain?

Saturday, September 28, 1918
The Manse, Leaskdale

To-day came the news that Bulgaria has asked for peace terms—the first of the enemy nations to throw up the sponge. The end must be very near. All the week the news has been good from every quarter. It has been a busy

Aunt Annie and I on the
Anderson lawn

---

124   Serbia suffered heavily in World War I, losing almost 30 percent of its overall population and 60 percent of its men (see note 128, page 65). With help from France, Serbia defeated the Bulgarians at the Battle of Dobro Pole (September 15–18). Days later, the Bulgarian army would defeat Allied forces at the Battle of Doiran. Following an Allied breakthrough, however, Bulgaria capitulated on September 29, 1918.

125   German defences were anchored along the famous "Hindenburg Line"—a fortified line designed as a fallback position in the event of a German retreat. The Allied strategy was to break through, cut German communications and supply, and push the entire front line back. On September 12, several key territorial features (known as "salients"—defensive enemy positions projecting into Allied territory) were captured. Although Allied forces were successfully consolidating their positions along the line, it was not broken until October 17.

and pleasant week. On Tuesday Alec Leask's and we motored to Whit-by and spent a very pleasant day with the Andersons. Thursday night Ewan and I went to Uxbridge, had tea with the Willises and then went to a W.C.T.U. Medal contest in the Methodist church where I was one of the judges. I spent most of Friday at the church helping to pack Christmas boxes for the Scott boys at the front and today I spent help-ing Mrs. Cook address them. I am all tired out—but Bulgaria has asked for peace terms!

Monday, Sept. 30, 1918
The Manse, Leaskdale, Ont.

The Hindenburg line smashed in several places—the whole western front ablaze with victory. That was the news the mail brought at noon. I wonder if we have all dreamed it.

Spent another afternoon doing up Red Cross boxes and then we all went down to Edith's to tea. After tea the telephone rang—our ring.[126] Ewan went to the 'phone and the word was, "Bulgaria has surrendered unconditionally and fighting on the Macedonian front ceased at noon today."

There was something dramatic in it as Ewan turned from the 'phone and told us the message.

And the first Allied triumph comes on the front that witnessed their darkest defeat in that terrible autumn of 1915. How vividly I recall the despairs and agonies of that October and November when Mackensen led his Central hordes over doomed Serbia.[127] And now Serbia is once more free—or will be in a very short time.

Thursday, October 3, 1918
Leaskdale, Ont.

On Tuesday came word of the death of Morley Shier, a fine young fel-low from our church who went overseas in the flying corps.[128]

---

126   In the days before wireless communication, telephony operated very differently than it does now. Up until a few decades ago in some rural regions, a neighbourhood would be connected to a single telephone cable, with specific rings to identify each house. Curious neighbours could easily pick up the phone and listen, even if they knew a given call was not for them.

127   Field Marshal August von Mackensen (1849–1945) led an Austro-Hungarian and German attack on Serbia on October 7, 1915, taking the capital Belgrade on October 9. On October 14 the Bulgarian army attacked from the north. The Serbian army, along with thousands of civilians, was forced to retreat to the Adriatic Sea. Serbian military and civilian loss of life was huge.

128   Morley Shier (1894–1918) had been a school teacher when he enlisted, becoming a Flight Lieutenant in the Air Force.

St. Quentin was taken yesterday—St. Quentin, that name of evil omen in the terrible retreat last spring.

And to-day is October 3rd—the day of my dream. Has it any significance? Today the *Globe* said "The big retreat has begun." The *Mail and Empire* said, "It may now be said that the battle of Hindenburg line has ended in favor of the allies."[129] Is this enough to justify my dream? One would almost think so—I would have thought so three months ago. But now I do not know. We shall see—we shall see.

SUNDAY, OCTOBER 6, 1918

It should be written in capitals—in letters of gold. Yet it dawned in gloom and drizzle and gloomed and drizzled all day outside. The afternoon

was dull. Aunty and I felt rather lonesome—at least I did. She is leaving for home tomorrow. I shall miss her dreadfully. But I think she has had a real good time. She looks ever so much better than when she came and will go home with a store of pleasant memories to refresh her. I wish she could have stayed until the end of October but I have been afraid to urge it lest she get cold travelling so late.

We were sitting in the parlor reading when the telephone rang. I went—but—could hardly believe my ears when I heard the message

Aunt Annie

The parlor

Mr. Harwood was phoning up. I dashed into the parlor. "Aunt Annie," I exclaimed, "Germany and Austria are suing for peace on President Wilson's terms."[130]

Then I flew back to the 'phone and rung up everybody in the village to tell them the great news. In a few minutes our small burg

---

129　By October 5, Allied forces had pushed well forward, breaking through the length of the Hindenburg defences over a front of 31 km/19 miles.

130　By the end of September, German military commanders realized the situation was hopeless; Kaiser Wilhelm II was informed that an immediate ceasefire was needed. Following internal debate, on October 5, 1918, the German government sent a message to US President Woodrow Wilson that they were ready to negotiate terms of peace.

was a thrill with the excitement that was agitating the whole world. The telephone rang constantly. Men ran up and down the street. I got out the flag and ran it up. Then I walked up and down the parlor in my excitement. It was impossible to sit still.

"Sit down, child," said Aunt Annie—who never gets excited over anything and so has missed a tremendous amount of trouble and delight in her journey through life.

"Oh, Aunty," I said, "I have walked this floor for hours in despair and anxiety during these past four years. Now let me walk it in joy."

Mrs. Alec Leask came down and we talked it all over. Ewan came home from Zephyr and I flew out in the rain and met him at the gate.

"Have you heard the news?" I cried, hoping like a child that he hadn't, so that I would be "the first" to tell him. He *hadn't* so I had the fun of being the first. Then we had supper and a gay, merry, happy circle we were.

Of course, the war isn't ended *yet*. There may be and probably will be several weeks of dickering, during which the fighting must go on. But Germany has *asked* for peace—the haughty nation which set out to conquer the world is suing humbly to the Entente. That means that she is down and out. If a ray of hope were left her she would not do it. Yes, the great, the stupendous drama of hell is drawing to a close. The curtain has gone up on the final act. At last—at last—at last! And oh God, at what a price!

Tomorrow is little Stuart's birthday—he is three years old. It has been a long, hard, woeful three years for the world, but for him carefree happiness. He is getting to be quite a companion for Chester. I am glad of this. It is one thing I regret that there are no boys in Leaskdale that are really desirable companions for Chester. He has some little boy chums but they are rather unclassifiable. They come from respectable homes but they do not use very good language at times and I am suspicious that they are smutty little rascals when no grown up is

Stuart.

Chester and two chums.

about. But Chester can't be shut away from them. I will be glad when Stuart is old enough to be a real companion. He will "catch up" more or less every year now.

Sunday, December 1, 1918
The Manse, Leaskdale, Ont.

The war is over! Many things are over. It is "a far cry" since my last entry in October. I feel as if I had lived many years in it. Huge, epoch-making world-events have jostled each other in it. And in my own little world has been upheaval and sorrow—and the shadow of death.

On the day following that wonderful Sunday Aunt Annie and I went in to Toronto. We spent the night at Laura's and had a very pleasant time for Carl was up to dinner and stayed for the evening. The next morning I saw poor Aunty off on the Montreal train and then, feeling lonely and sad, went uptown and put in a busy day shopping.

Toronto was then beginning to be panic stricken over the outbreak of the terrible "Spanish flu."[131] The drug counters were besieged with frantic people seeking remedies and safeguards. I didn't think much about it—really had no fear of taking it. Wednesday evening I began to sneeze and I kept that up all day Thursday. However, I felt quite well and would not believe I could be taking the flu. Ewan came in for me and we motored home that night. It was really perfect—the evening was so warm and bright, the autumnal world so beautiful. The fact that the day was warm probably saved my life. If it had been cold and I had got chilled I would probably never have got over it. For that night I took ill with flu—the deadly pestilence of which thousands have died—are dying.

At first it did not occur to me that I had the flu. Friday morning I had a cold in the head and felt sleepy and stupid but not sick. I decided to stay in bed and "sleep it off." Friday passed—Friday night—Saturday morning it was the same. I passed the day in what was really a semi-stupor. I just wanted to lie quiet and "sleep." Yet I never really slept. I was vaguely conscious all the time; but I had no feeling of

---

131   The Centre for Disease Control estimates that one third of the world's population (some 500 million persons) were infected during the 1918–19 influenza pandemic, with total deaths estimated between 20 and 50 million; the World Health Organization puts total estimated deaths at around 40 million. Some estimates are far higher; at any rate it is clear that the pandemic caused far greater loss of life than the war. The name "Spanish flu" arose from circumstances of censorship when the disease first struck. Wartime censors played down early reports of high mortality rates in Germany, Britain, France, and the United States. The news media, however, could report on the effects of the epidemic in Spain—a neutral country—creating the inaccurate belief that Spain suffered disproportionate mortality. The name "Spanish flu" stuck.

illness or discomfort. Nevertheless at dusk the idea suddenly dawned on my stupid mind that something was wrong. Two days was too long to be in this condition. I asked Ewan to phone for Shier.[132]

Dr. Shier came. He found me with a ridiculous temperature and a heart that was almost out of business. I would not—probably—have lived till morning. He gave me medicine for my heart and then tablets to induce perspiration—and went away. Later on he said that out of the 75 cases of flu he had I was the worst save one—and that one died!

I certainly don't think it was any merit of Dr. Shier's that I didn't die too. I think he did a perfectly dreadful thing in going away as he did and leaving me with no skilled attendance. I was too stupid to ask for a trained nurse but he should have suggested it. He did not—and I was left alone.

I lay there under piles of clothing—and presently sweating began. Rather! Rivers—literally—of water ran down my body. In no time my night dress and sheets were saturated. They grew cool and I was "demned moist and unpleasant."[133] I could not face the prospect of lying like that all night. But by this time the fever had gone down and my power of thinking returned. I knew it would be an exceedingly dangerous thing to change clothing and sheets in that chilly room. Still, it had to be done. Ewan was asleep in the spare room but I got Lily up and got her to light the oil heater and warm dry sheets and nightdress by it. Then I told her just what to do, as I remembered my nurse's doing it and eventually we managed it. But once or twice I shivered with cold and—knowing what I now know of flu—I wonder that I escaped pneumonia.

I was in bed for ten days. I never felt so sick or weak in my life. The first time I went downstairs I collapsed and Ewan had to carry me up. I am still taking strychnine[134] for my heart, my nerves are bad yet—for a month after I got up I would cry if a door slammed or if I couldn't find a hairpin when I was doing my hair!—and I have not yet been able wholly to shake off the depression and languor that is the worst legacy of the plague.

During my illness I had a letter from Aunt Annie saying that she had got home safely and that two days after she had reached Park Corner George had come down with flu. I feel anxious for I knew what George

---

132   Dr. Walter Columbus Shier was a medical doctor in Leaskdale and Uxbridge. He was an uncle of Morley Shier.

133   From *Nicholas Nickelby* by Charles Dickens (1838–39). The London-based characters of Mr and Mrs Mantalini are arguing, when Mr Mantalini threatens to throw himself in the Thames and become "a demd, damp, moist, unpleasant body!" (ch. 34).

134   Strychnine, although highly toxic, was used in very low doses as a stimulant.

Campbell was. There would be no keeping him in bed once he felt a little better. A week later, just after I was able to come downstairs, a telegram came from Aunt Annie, saying George had died from pneumonia.

I felt very badly. Not so much because of George's death—although it was curious considering my opinion of George how much I did regret him—these family ties of blood and association are curious things—as because of my sympathy for poor Aunt Annie. He was her only son and though he was far from being what a son should be his death would be a terrible blow to her. And then, with all his shortcomings, he kept things going after a fashion. What on earth would Aunt Annie do, a woman of 70, left alone with that poor, incapable Ella and six small children under eleven. It was a black prospect and I worried greatly over it, being in a condition of body and nerve eminently conducive to worry.

I wired Stell that I would pay her expenses if she would go home but Stell wrote back a fat epistle of excuses and said she was trying to get Clara and her husband to go. What use they would be under the circumstances I could not see.

I had a wire from Frede the next day after receiving Aunt Annie's saying that she was leaving for the Island, and had no further word until Nov. 2. In this interval I slowly grew stronger, in spite of Stella's terrible hysterical letters in which she raved and ramped as if insane. Great war news also came—Turkey's unconditional surrender and the complete smashing of Austria-Hungary by the Italians. Finally, when I was sleepless over lack of word from Park Corner, came a letter from Frede. They were all sick at Park Corner, Aunt Annie and Ella from shock, the children from flu. Little Georgie had died and Maudie and Jim were very low. Frede was alone in that house to do all the work and wait on the sick. I knew her strength was not equal to it. I felt I *must* go to her assistance. Her letter came at noon. I packed a grip and caught the evening train to Toronto. I had a tedious journey, for the connections after leaving Sackville were dreadful. Tuesday evening I got to Kensington and hired a rig to take me to Park Corner through the black, cloudy night and over vile roads. Never shall I forget the stones on those Irishtown hills. But at 9.30 I reached the old house. Frede and Aunt Annie were so thankful to see me. I found the children were on the mend. All were in bed but Frede and she and I sat huddled over the stove in the dining room till midnight and talked the whole tragedy over. Like myself, Frede did not regard poor George's death as an unmixed evil. Who did? Even his mother and wife, she told me, had said they were thankful he had died a respectable death in his bed, instead of being brought home killed in some drunken row as had nearly happened several times. It is a dreadful thing when that is how a man's nearest and dearest look upon his death.

Frede and I found it comforting to talk over all the problems with each other. It lightened and clarified them. They had got a middle-aged hired man and the prospect was not so bad—if Frede and I put our shoulders to the wheel, helped Aunt Annie with advice, decided things for poor Ella and appointed our-selves guardians and mentors of those poor children. Finally we went to bed and slept.

The old house

Follow the entries made during my stay in Park Corner in a note-book.

++*Saturday, Nov. 9, 1918*
Park Corner

Frede, Aunt Annie and I had a business seance tonight and tried to straighten out George's business affairs. They are in a terrible tangle I fear. George borrowed $2300 from me five years ago on a joint note. He always paid the interest but none of the principal. He frittered the money away—part in worthless fox stock, part God knows how—there is no record of it. Aunt Annie will give me a mortgage on the farm for it and I will never take a cent more interest from her. It won't hurt Danny when he grows up to pay the prin-cipal off that fine farm. My hope for Park Corner lies in Dan. He is a fine smart lad, industrious and thrifty—which is a new streak in the Campbells! So much his mother gave him. His worst fault is a quick temper. But he soon gets over it. He is warm hearted and loyal. Yes, I have hopes of Dan—if his mother doesn't drive him to ruin with her foolishness. She is a bigger baby than her own children. But I am sorry for her.

The sitting room.

Frede and I work all day cleaning and disinfecting the house; then at night, when Aunt Annie and Ella are

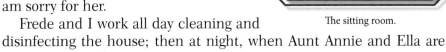

safe in bed out of hearing, we shut ourselves up in the cosy sitting room devour snacks, and talk and laugh at our pleasure, canvassing all things in the heavens above and the earth beneath and the waters under the earth. As for our "snacks"—well, we are good foragers. Frede and I have, neither of us, ever been indifferent to the charms of a "good bite"—though just now it is very unfashionable to confess such a thing. One would run the risk of being called a German. Nevertheless, it is a fact and we both shamelessly plead guilty. The Park Corner chicken-bones and ham-slices have lost none of their old-time flavor and savor and delight.

++*Sunday, Nov. 10, 1918*
Park Corner, P.E.I.

Today was wet and windy. But I found a charm in it. It is eight years since I was on the Island in November and I am enjoying it. Even its dourness and gloom have a charm.

This evening we all got in the sitting room and had a little singing of hymns while Ella played. It seemed like a pale reflection of old times. Frede and I both felt it. As we have often said to each other, there is now a strange peace about this house such as we have not felt in it since those old days. A restless disturbing presence has gone—we have a feeling as if a curse had been lifted—as if a malign influence had passed away.

All today I have found myself "thinking back" into the past, and so perfect has been the illusion that, as I lay on the sofa listening to the music, I *was* back, twenty years ago. I was a girl of seventeen at Park Corner. Stella and Clara were about. Our beaux came driving up outside with ghostly horses. All the ties of 1918 were wraith-like. Chester and Stuart in that strange mood meant nothing to me. I did not even love them—I, who normally love them so much that I fear the jealous gods. But it was not possible to love children who would not be born for nearly twenty years yet! When I told my feeling to Frede I found she felt the same. She, too, was a ghost! We sat alone and talked until midnight—and we were strangely, perfectly, weirdly happy. It will be a jolt to wake up tomorrow morning and find ourselves middle-aged women with husbands and endless responsibilities!"

++*Monday, Nov. 11, 1918*
Park Corner, P.E.I.

Today came the official announcement of the signing of the armistice! The Great War is over—the world's agony has ended. What has been born? The next generation may be able to answer that. We can never know fully.

I picked gum on the old spruces down by the road today while I waited for the mail—and dreamed *young* dreams—just the dreams I dreamed at seventeen. They are possible to me only at Park Corner—and only in certain moods here. The lingering spell of last night is still upon me.

To-night Frede and I went out in the darkness and walked down the lane and across the pond. It was so dark we could see nothing—only feel the planks beneath our feet

The old spruces down by the road

Across the pond

and sense the rippling waters below. How often have we walked together over that bridge—but never before I think on a grim, inky November night. We spoke of the armistice but without any exultation. Frede, I fancied, was dull and a little depressed.

I have never been able to picture Frede as a wife, living a domestic existence in a home of her own. I have tried. But always my imagination has met a blank wall. I have thought this was because of the uncertainty of Cam's return. But peace has come and his return is as certain as anything in the world can be certain. So I should be able to picture their life together now. I *cannot*: the paralysis of imagination still persists. I cannot rid myself of the odd, haunting feeling that Frede is not for calm domestic joys and tame house-mothering. In my thought she still "waves her wild tail and walks by her wild lone," like Kipling's cat.[135] That has always been her way of describing herself. It is a true one. Frede always gives the impression of one walking her chosen way alone and independent—not as Cam MacFarlane's[136] housekeeper and

---

135   This is an expression recalling Rudyard Kipling's story, "The Cat That Walked by Himself," from his *Just So Stories for Little Children* (1902). LMM uses it elsewhere in the pages below, particularly to describe Frede (see also LMM's journal entry and note on page 116).

136   On May 24, 1917, LMM learned, much to her surprise, that Frede suddenly married a col-

sock-mender—though capable, well-trained Frede can darn socks and run a house admirably. Only—it is not of the essence of her.

She said to me one day last summer—laughing, yet with an under-current of earnest, too—"I wish I could have both the 'job' and the husband." Even yet, I seem to feel that the "job" really means more to her than the husband. She loves her work and has been devoted to it. I know she dreads leaving it. I fear she will not be happy or contented after the novelty of her own home wears away. This worries me. But—perhaps motherhood will come to her and make everything worth while. Oh Freddie-girl, I want you to be happy! You have had so little happiness in your uneasy life.

++Tuesday, Nov. 12, 1918
Park Corner, P.E.I.

Frede and I crawled out in the cold and dark this morning and went to Summerside where we spent a weary day thrashing out business with a lawyer. At sunset we left. As we walked up and down the station platform while waiting for our train we saw a most wonderful sunset on Summerside Harbor. And I—I looked away across to the dim, twilit shore of Lower Bedeque. I saw the old warehouse at the wharf and up beyond it the spruce grove behind, which was the house where Herman Leard lived and where I suffered hell—and heaven.[137] Dead memories stirred in their shrouds as I gazed at it—memories whose ghosts have not walked for many a year. That winter of love and agony seems like a dream now—a dream that some one else dreamed. I have been free from its thraldom this many a year. If Herman Leard were living now and I were to meet him my heart would not beat one iota the faster. And yet—the old memories did stir uneasily as I looked across the purple harbor to that shadowy shore. Frede did not notice my silence or my long gaze. She knows that I once loved and that the love was a tragedy. She does not know who the man was nor where he lived. Not even to Frede have I ever named his name. Once it would have hurt too much—and now it never comes into my thoughts when we are together. It was half in my mind to point across to Lower Bedeque and

league, Nathaniel Cameron McFarlane (LMM spelled his last name "MacFarlane"). Both Frede and Cameron were hired in 1913 by Macdonald College, part of McGill University. McFarlane, a chemistry instructor, enlisted in 1915 in the Princess Patricia's Light Infantry and also served with the so-called "New Brunswick Kilties," the 236th Battalion of the Canadian Expeditionary Force.

137   LMM had become entangled in a romantic involvement with Herman Leard while working as a teacher in Bedeque, PEI, in 1897.

say, "See yonder, Frede. That was where the sweetest bitterest months of my life were passed." But somehow it did not seem worth while to say it—or I was too tired to make the explanation involved—or Dan interrupted us with questions. Anyway, I said nothing. Let the dead past bury its dead.

We drove home from Kensington through the cold, frosty moonlit night. As we drove up a long Irishtown hill I was suddenly impressed with the weird, striking beauty of the moonlight falling through the spruce trees along the road—alternate bars of shadow and silver. It was a road peculiar to P.E. Island. Just as the thought crossed my mind Frede said, "Maud, have you ever seen anything more beautiful than that road before us? One never sees a road like that anywhere else."

We got home tired and chilled. But Aunty had a good fire and a corking supper for us—and we concluded that perhaps after all things were not so much "managed better up in Mars." We went to bed and slept. No dream of long-dead Herman Leard disturbed my slumbers. I dreamed only of my chubby darlings in Leaskdale Manse.

I decided that I must leave for home on Friday Nov. 15. The day before was a wild November storm of rain and wind. Frede and I revelled in it. We longed to start off for the shore where the billows were rolling wildly in—and would have gone had it not been for a dread of catching cold and being laid up.

That night was not a quiet one in the old house. We were all tired and hoped for a good sleep. But it was written otherwise in the stars. Jim set up a toothache after going to bed and wailed and howled most dismally the greater part of the night. As both Aunt Annie and his mother were up waiting on him Frede and I decided we could do no good by getting up. So we cuddled down under our blankets and, as we could not sleep, began to wile away the hours by seeing which of us could say the wittiest things about poor Jim's weird noises and their probable effect on Mr. Jack, who occupied the next room. We succeeded, at all events, in amusing ourselves hugely and laughed until the bed shook.

Frede and I have never been in any predicament or situation yet where we could not beguile the tedium or lighten the gloom by mutual jokes. We both seem to possess the knack of saying things that, at the time and under the circumstances, seem excruciatingly funny, though if they were written down or repeated in different surroundings they would not be at all mirth-provoking. At least, we turned what would otherwise have been a long and dreary night into a perfect orgy of fun.

Friday was fine and Danny drove me to the station in the afternoon. Poor Aunt Annie put her arms about me when I said good-bye and sobbed.

"Thank you for coming to me, Maudie. I could never have plucked up spirit again if you hadn't."

But it was Frede it worried me to leave. I am not easy about Frede. Her heart is not acting right. It has never been strong since the typhoid. I wish she would give up working now and rest till Cam came home.

I came away sadly: yet I did not feel as I had felt when I left in the summer. The foretokened valley of the shadow had been passed. Two of the thirteen who sat at the ill-omened table that day were gone. Superstitious or not, never again will I, if I can avoid it, sit thirteen at a table!

I stayed all night in Summerside and left at six the next morning, through the gloom and chill of the first snowfall. My journey home was uneventful. I reached Uxbridge Tuesday night and Ewan met me with the car. It was wet and dark. As we drove into the yard Stuart and Chester came tearing out, flung themselves into the car and devoured me with kisses, shouting wildly, "My *dear* little mother—my *dear* little mother." It was good to be back in their love again. And it was good to be home. But I miss Frede so much—more than ever this time, I think. In Frede I find both emotional and intellectual companionship. Very rarely is that found in one person. Apart from Frede, and in a lesser degree, Bertie MacIntyre, I know it not. The people I have loved best have not measured up to my standard of intellectual comradeship.

I settled down to work at my book as soon as I could. It *must* be finished by New Years. I hate a despotic date like that. It takes all the pleasure out of the writing.

Stella writes that Clara has had flu-pneumonia and nearly died; but is recovering now. I am coming to feel a physical cringe whenever I hear the name of "Spanish flu." It has been worse than the "Black Plague" of old time. Ewan has had another bad attack of neuritis[138] this past week but seems to be improving now.

It has been a hard, dreary fall enough. But the war is over! And that means so much that we have not yet grasped what it *does* mean. We don't realize it. The sudden cessation seems uncanny—as if one had gone to sleep in one planet and wakened up in another.

I am sure no one could feel more profoundly thankful that the war is over than I—I am sure that no one, except the mothers and wives, could have felt it more keenly. And yet the truth is that everything seems flat and *insipid* now, after being fed for four years on fears and

---

138   That is, unidentified pain, here associated with nerves.

horrors, terrible reverses, amazing victories, all news now seems tame and uninteresting. I feel as if I had been living for years in the midst of hell; and then suddenly found myself lying on a quiet green meadow stretching levelly and peacefully to the horizon. One is thankful—and bored!

It is strange and blessed—and *dull* not to dread the coming of the mail every day—not to open the papers tremblingly and after a quaking glance at the headlines turn greedily to the "War Reviewed" column. Somehow, there is a blank in life. I suppose it will gradually fill up.

The Kaiser has abdicated and fled to Holland. Likewise Son Willy.[139] Germany is a republic. What a downfall for the man who, four years ago set out to conquer the world—to succeed where Napoleon failed. Byron's lines, written on Napoleon a hundred years ago, read to-day as if written for William Hohenzollern, especially the following verses.

'Tis done. But yesterday a king,
And armed with kings to strive,
And now thou art a nameless thing
So abject—yet alive!
Is this the man of thousand thrones
Who strewed our earth with hostile bones
And can he thus survive?
Since he, miscalled the Morning Star,
Nor man nor fiend has fallen so far.

*

The triumph and the vanity,
The rapture of the strife—
The earthquake voice of victory
To thee the breath of life,
The sword, the sceptre, and the sway,
Which man seemed made but to obey
Wherewith renown was rife—
All quelled! Dark spirit, what must be
The madness of thy memory!"[140]

139　Kaiser Wilhelm did not at first wish to abdicate, but anti-royal feeling in Germany was running high. His abdication was announced by the Chancellor on November 9, 1918, leaving Wilhelm no choice but to depart. Similarly, his eldest son, Crown Prince Wilhelm, wanted to lead the German armies back home, but this was deemed equally unwise by the government. He followed his father to exile in Holland.

140　From Lord Byron's (1788–1824) poem, "Ode to Napoleon" (1814).

Has there ever been a man so universally hated as William of Germany? Has any one man before in the history of the world been the ultimate cause of so much agony, heartbreak and death? Well, as I heard an old lady say once,

"If the devil doesn't catch a man like that what's the use of having a devil?"

Sunday, Dec. 8, 1918
Leaskdale, Ont.

To-day was Sunday and for once I flunked. I was simply too tired to go out. The responsibility of training the S.S. children for the annual Christmas concert has been mainly shuffled over on me this year. It is an imposition. I have more than enough to do as it is. I am president of the Red Cross, President of the Mission Band, President of the Social Dept. of the Guild both in Leaskdale and Zephyr and secretary of the W.M. Society. That is not enough forsooth but the work of training for the concert must be imposed on me, too! I was over at the church with the children all yesterday afternoon and came home at the point of tears. I have not been strong since I had the flu and any strain or over-exertion seems to play me right out. So I stayed home today and rested—and thereby, I believe, glorified God.

Tuesday, Dec. 17th, 1918
The Manse, Leaskdale, Ont.

The S.S. concert has been called off, owing to another outbreak of flu in the vicinity. I am glad for I dreaded it all. I haven't the strength for it. But I grudge the wasted afternoons I have already put in at the practices. If I had just had that time to rest! Oh, I want a *rest*! I've been really happy and contented during these past seven years but I have worked very hard and ceaselessly all the time. I bore three children in four years and there has been the four-year strain of the war. It has worn me out. I feel tired *all* the time—I *never* feel rested. I know what I would do if I could—go to bed and stay there for a fortnight, seeing nobody, talking to nobody, doing nothing but just lying flat!

But even this small boon is not to be compassed just now. And there is more worry ahead. Yesterday I got a letter from Mr. Rollins,[141] my Boston attorney, saying that my case against Page Co. was to come up

---

141   Weld Allan Rollins (1874–1952) was a lawyer specializing in corporate law.

in January.[142] I have to go down for it. This thing has been dragging on for two years and it is going to be settled at last. But even if I succeed I shall just have to file another suit;[143] and I anticipate nothing but legal conflict with the Pages the rest of my life. It is not a pleasant prospect, truly.

I must make arrangements to go to Boston "on business." The parish must not suspect that "the minister's wife" is mixed up in lawsuits against her publishers. They wouldn't think I was fit to run the mission band if they knew! Seriously, it wouldn't do for them to know. It would excite no end of gossip, even if most of them didn't think that all the parties in a lawsuit are tarred with the same brush.

Thursday, Dec. 26th, 1918
Leaskdale, Ont.

I am glad Christmas is over. It seemed such a *disappointing* day. I had hoped early in the autumn to have Frede here for Christmas once more but George's death made that impossible. For me it was a poor sort of day. I have been nervous, depressed, and headachy for a week and it culminated last night in a blinding, old-time sick headache. But the boys had a good time and that is the main thing now—that the children should be happy and enjoy the day. We had their tree for them and they were wild with delight, dear little souls.

I finished my ninth book, *Rainbow Valley*,[144] the day before Christmas. I am so thankful it is done. Everything has dragged so since I had the flu. It isn't as good as "Anne's House of Dreams"—in my opinion— but still averages up pretty well of its kind. But I'm tired of the kind. I've outgrown it. I want to do something different. But my publishers keep me at this sort of stuff because it sells and because they claim that the public, having become used to this from my pen, would not tolerate a change.

Nevertheless, if I ever get a little more leisure and a little renewed physical and nervous strength I mean to try my hand at something different.

Louis Page is a queer mortal. Before my break with his firm they always sent me a parcel of books at Xmas. After the break they sent no

---

142   LMM was suing her publisher, L.C. Page & Co., for withholding full royalties on *Anne of Green Gables*.

143   A separate suit was to be filed over Page's proposal to bring out *Further Chronicles of Avonlea*.

144   Published in 1919 by Frederick A. Stokes and the seventh in the *Anne of Green Gables* series, *Rainbow Valley* is dedicated to three men from Scott township who died in the war: Goldwin Lapp, Robert Brookes, and Morley Shier. (LMM misspelled Brooks's name, perhaps thinking of poet Rupert Brookes.)

more as was to be expected, and I certainly did not think they would ever do it again. Yet today came a copy of "Sunset Canada," an expensive travel book, and with it, not the firm's card as aforetime but L.P.'s personal one and written across it in his own fair hand "Merry Christmas and Happy New Year. L.C.P."[145] Quite free and easy! Especially for the man I'm suing in the Mass. Court of Equity for cheating and defrauding me! Wonder if he is trying to heap coals of fire on my ungrateful head!

Friday, Dec. 27, 1918
The Manse, Leaskdale

Had a letter from Frede today. She has just got back to Macdonald and seems very glad to be there. She had a hard time of it with that poor Ella, whose mind really seems to be unhinged to a certain extent by her troubles. I don't know what we are going to do with or for her. She is one dire problem and poor Stell is another—and Frede and I can find no solution for either. Frede writes that Cam hopes to be home by Easter. I hope to see Frede for a few hours on my way home from Boston. I'm *hungry* to see her again, even if it isn't so very long since I saw her in Park Corner.

---

145   This book by Archie M. Bell, published in the Page series *See America First*, was subtitled *British Columbia and Beyond*.

1919

Friday, Jan. 3, 1919
Leaskdale, Ont.

Today our Red Cross Society disbanded. This indecent haste to close down has a reason behind it. Normally we should have carried on our work all winter at least. But for over a year trouble has been brewing in that society. I have felt that I was walking on the edge of a volcano which might erupt at any moment and cause, not merely a Red Cross row, but a congregational one. The trouble was over our treasurer, who is suspected by some—quite unjustly, I feel certain—of diverting some of the money collected to her own purse. It started brewing last winter but I headed it off then and have been sitting on the lid ever since. But I knew that there was bound to be an explosion at the Annual Business meeting and I have been looking forward to it with dread for many moons. But when the armistice[146] was signed I saw my way clear and I worked out a little scheme which resulted in the disbanding today. If we tried to keep up the society there would be a venomous quarrel and no good work would be done—for the treasurer would be offended and leave and without her I know not what we could have done. She is the only woman in the place with any executive ability and she has worked like a slave cutting and planning. Not one of the women who have criticized and slandered her could, or would try to, take her place. In view of all this I felt it was better to disband the society peacefully and in good repute "before the smouldering scandal broke and blazed."[147] So it came about as I desired; and those very women who have gossiped about Mrs. Lapp[148] and said they would leave the society had she been retained as an officer voted her the thanks of the society for the good work she had done! For the love of Allah, what is human nature made of? Is there any sincerity anywhere?

One day last summer Frede, after telling me of some intimate friend at Macdonald who had betrayed her confidence, exclaimed passionately,

---

146   I.e., the armistice ending the war, signed on November 11, 1918.

147   From Tennyson's *Idylls of the King* (1859–1885); Guinevere is terrified that "some evil chance / Will make the smouldering scandal break and blaze / Before the people, and our lord the King." The scandal is Guinevere's relationship with Lancelot.

148   The Lapp family—Effie Loretta and George Washington Lapp—were, as LMM had written, "especial friends of ours" (January 22, 1917). Their son Goldwin Dimma Lapp (1893–1917) had been the first boy from Scott township to be killed at the front; Montgomery would dedicate *Rainbow Valley* (1919) to Goldwin as well as two other men from her local community who were killed in the war.

81

"Maud, upon my word there's *nobody* true—except *you*. You are the only person I've ever found whom I could trust absolutely."

Alas, there *are* very few people whom we can absolutely trust. In youth we fondly believe most friends are true; but after we suffer repeated disillusions and betrayals we grow wiser and more cynical.

Saturday, Jan. 4, 1919
Leaskdale, Ont.

We had a nice pleasant evening of reading at home tonight. This is by no means a frequent occurrence. One or both of us must very often be away in the evenings—or we have company here—or work to do which cannot be set aside for the best of books. So we heartily enjoy an evening when we can settle down easily and read, with a plate of russet apples or a box of chocolates within easy reaching distance. We generally sit in the parlor. It is the pleasantest room in the house. Frede always called it "a summer room"—I think because its good lighting and green carpet and pale yellow walls, and the pink touches in the decorations give it a woodsy, gardeny aspect. Our big china dogs[149] sit gravely on either side of the bookstand and Daffy generally wanders in, too, and goes sedately to sleep on the coyote skin rug or a rocking chair. Daffy will be thirteen years old in April, yet his eye is not dim nor the pluminess of his tail abated. The only sign of old age that I perceive in Daffy is that before he jumps up to his favorite basking place on the kitchen window-sill he sits a little longer than formerly

Corner of Parlor.

[Daffy]

---

149   In her entry of August 27, 1911, LMM describes purchasing china dogs while on honeymoon in England. See *L.M. Montgomery's Complete Journals: The Ontario Years, 1911–1917*.

gazing somewhat wistfully up at it before he makes his spring. I expect Daff-o-dil "feels in his bones" that all is not as it used to be. Ah, Daffins, it is not—neither with you nor me. Much water has flowed under the bridges of the world since that spring evening thirteen years ago when I carried you home from Alec Macneill's in a little covered basket.[150] You howled every step of the way and everybody who met me on the way smiled broadly.

Daffy and Frede's old "Maggie" have been the longest-lived cats I ever knew. "Maggie" died about ten years ago, being then seventeen. She was like one of the family at Park Corner and Frede adored her. The two grew up together. Frede and I always loved cats. Where we got the liking is a mystery for our fathers and mothers and our grandfathers and grandmothers on both sides detested them. There was a fine breed of cats at Park Corner—they were always so big and fat and furry. Maggie was gray and white, and had more brains, emotion, and personality than quite a few humans have. She had an enormous number of kittens in her lifetime. Maggie certainly replenished the earth with kittens and fine little bastes[151] they were too. Maggie finally got caught in a rabbit trap and was injured so badly that she had to be killed. I wrote some "In Memoriam" verses for her and Frede had them printed on a card with Maggie's picture. I have it framed in the library. Frede took Maggie's sad death very keenly to heart. It was hard that she should have died in such a way but I don't think she would have lived much longer in any case. During that last year she had got very deaf and had shrunk almost to nothing—a tiny handful of bones in her faded fur. I remember that I was up at Park Corner one autumn day before the winter of her death. Frede was away teaching school and I think Maggie, though well fed and cared for did not get much petting—Aunt Annie having no real liking for cats. I looked down to see her sitting at my feet looking up with imploring eyes. At once I took her up on my knee, cuddled and stroked her, talked to her and made much of her. She sat on my knee purring loudly and looking up into my face. Her eyes were absolutely uncanny. They haunt me to this day. They were not the eyes of an animal—they were *human* eyes. In them was exactly the expression I have sometimes seen in those of some poor old woman who has been neglected and overlooked when somebody sat down beside her and talked to her as if it were a pleasure or showed her some little attention such as younger women receive as a matter of course.

---

150 In a long entry dated October 24, 1911, Montgomery details how she arranged for her cat Daffy to be sent from Park Corner.

151 That is, "beasts."

Verily, it is hard *not* to believe that Maggie had a soul. Who knows? Perhaps long and intimate association with a loving human companion may, and sometimes does, develop a soul in an animal. Perhaps over beyond the dark valley Frede and I will find old Maggie again, plump and furry and kind in eternal youth. I don't think we would either of us feel perfectly at home in heaven if there were no adorable kittens frisking about the little grassy alleys leading down off the golden streets or snoozing on the window sills of the many mansions.

But I can't quite believe that Daff will go to heaven. He is such a weird, uncanny creature in many ways—absolutely diabolic.[152] He *may* go on living—he has got so in the habit of it—but not in heaven. Yet he can't be banished to hell either. There must be some nice shadowy limbo where gray ghost cats can prowl and "walk by themselves."[153]

Grandma, who never liked cats, grew quite fond of Daffy in her old age and was very good to him. But she would never tolerate his staying in the house at night. Only on the very coldest stormiest nights of winter would she connive at letting him go down cellar for the night. Most

[My old room]

nights out he must go. But on fine summer nights Daff used to outwit her. One moonlit night long ago I remember waking up in my old room, with a nightmare-like feeling that persisted after waking. Seeing a round blot of darkness on the white spread I put out my hand and touched a warm, breathing body. Daff was curled comfortably up on my stomach sound asleep. He had evidently climbed up on the kitchen roof, found the window of the north room open, and came straight over to mine. After that I always left the north window open at night as long as it was possible at all and Daff never missed his tryst but always spent the wee sma's[154] curled up on the bed at my feet. The "front passage" door being always securely shut no one was ever

---

152   This is an interesting echo of the Ingleside cat, "Doctor Jekyll and Mr Hyde," in *Rilla of Ingleside*.

153   A favourite expression of LMM, from Kipling's *Just So Stories for Little Children* (1903).

154   The early hours of the morning (from Scots the "wee small hours").

any the wiser. I got a dreadful scare one night, which no doubt served me right for hoodwinking grandmamma. I was wakened from a sound sleep by the most hideous and blood-curdling shrieks from the north room. I thought Daff was being torn in pieces and I also thought such a hellish concert would surely awaken grandma. So I sprang out of bed and hurried to the north room. It was in dense darkness and also—by this time—silence. But just under the window were two large blazing eyes. I thought they were Daff's and approached, calling him. Instantly I was greeted with a volley of profanity and a cat leaped to the window sill, his body with its distended tail seeming as huge as a dog against the pale gleam of the sky through the open space behind him. He tore madly away over the roof and disappeared. Whether 'twas the deil himsel' or merely some marauding Tom who had found himself cooped up in the room with Daff looking at him from outside I do not know. Next day I believed the latter—but just at the time I was of two minds. Then in slipped Daff, demure and crouse,[155] not a hair out of place and I was rather glad. He would surely protect me of cat demons here out on the roofs.

Daff has his own odd ways. He does not like—never has liked—petting. He seems to resent it, even from me. Once in a while he does me the honor of jumping up on my knees and going to sleep—of late years I think he has done it a little more frequently. He never purrs, except when he is very hungry. *Then* he will come and sit by me and purr loudly. So he *can* do it and it is provoking that he will not because I love to hear a cat purr. It is the most utterly satisfied and comfortable sound in nature.

In the late twilight is Daff's unchanciest time. I have been afraid of him then with good reason. Several times when I have been standing beside him in the dusk, admiring him—for he is always incredibly handsome then—when, without any warning, he would give one tigerish spring at me, striving to bury teeth and claws in my leg or arm and not giving over until I batted him soundly over the head. At such moments he seemed possessed. Again, he would be most kind and companionable then. Many a night long ago, when I would be coming home on my lonely way after dark and had just turned in at the old lane Daff would spring down from the fence where he seemed to have been waiting for me and frisk around my feet up the lane. He was my familiar in many twilight rambles. We hunted Halley's comet[156] together,

---

155   Confident or lively.

156   Halley's Comet is a short-period comet (a comet that has an orbital period of less than 200 years) that is visible from Earth every 75–76 years. The comet had been visible in April 1910,

I remember—at least, I hunted the comet. Daff, I suspect, was more interested in field mice, as evidenced by his sudden eager springs into the big fat clover "buttons" in the hayfields.

It was the funniest thing in the world to see Daff chase his tail—a habit that he kept up till he was quite old—four or five years. He would go around after it so fast that he seemed to be a mere revolving ball, growing madder and madder as it escaped him until when he did succeed in catching it he would bite it so furi-

[Lover's Lane]

ously that he shrieked with pain, and then pursue it with more vicious rage than ever, biting and squealing and snarling, till he became too enraged to go on.

The first winter and spring we were here Daff always slept at the foot of our bed. But he never would come near the room after Chester was born and never has to this day. Daff knew his nose was out of joint and he was not going to play second fiddle to anyone.

Daff and Frede are very fond of each other, but he does not stand any nonsense from her either. One day, the last Christmas she was here, she was sitting in the kitchen, her legs crossed and her feet stuck out, displaying a pair of very nice new silk stockings. She was dressed to go somewhere. Daff was sitting on the kitchen window sill, and Daff was looking very cross because Stuart had been teasing him. Daff can *look* cross in every muscle and stripe and whisker. Frede and I began to make fun of him and he knew it and got crosser than ever. At last Frede said, "Daff, I firmly believe that you are a German spy."

Daff—this is an actual fact—deliberately got down from the window, deliberately walked across the floor to Frede, deliberately turned his tail to her, *and* deliberately sent a *shower-bath* over her fine silk stockings! Madam Frede had to go upstairs and dress from the skin out. We simply shrieked with laughter. I never saw Daff, or any cat, do such a trick before. And he did it with such devilish coolness and malice with an expression that said plainly, "I will teach you to call *me* names, my lady!"

---

when LMM was 36 (shortly before she left Prince Edward Island for Ontario), and again in February 1986.

Tuesday, Jan. 7, 1919
The Manse, Leaskdale, Ont.

Sat up till one last night arranging the correspondence I have to take to Boston as evidence in the trial.[157] Went to W.M.S. in afternoon and then we went out to tea and spent the usual evening of boredom. To-morrow I must spend getting ready for my pleasure excursion. I wish it were all well over—but wishes boot not. The only thing to do is to set my teeth and go on with it to the bitter end. I have *not* informed the parish that I am going to Boston on litigation. They would probably think I had been doing something dreadful. Lizzie Oxtoby would take a new lease of life in gossip. So I have lavishly informed everyone that I am going down on "business connected with my old book contracts." Could anything be a more definite statement of fact? There is really no way of hood-winking people like telling them the plain truth!

Friday, Jan. 10, 1919

I am flying through the night on the Boston express. Yesterday I left home in a snowstorm and reached Toronto at ten. I had planned to stay there until morning but reports of trains belated by snow made me feel that it might be better to go right on to Montreal that night and take no risk of losing my connections next day. So I tore madly around, got a berth and left on the eleven o'clock train. We pulled into Montreal this morning. Frede was to meet me in the evening and we expected to have a precious half hour between trains. I 'phoned Macdonald and Miss Hill[158] said Frede had gone to Ottawa for the day but would be back at night and asked me out to spend the day. I went and had a delightful visit with her and Miss Philp.[159] In the evening I returned to Montreal. Frede's train was due an hour before mine started but it was delayed by the storm and so I never saw her at all. A few minutes ago at Rouse's point[160] I got a wire from her explaining the cause of her delay. I am disappointed at not seeing her. But I may be able to stop off a day on my way back.

---

157   That is, the continuation of her lawsuit against L.C. Page & Co.

158   Anita Hill was Head of the School of Household Science at Macdonald College from 1917 to 1920.

159   Bessie M. Philp was a lecturer in Household Science, who became head of the department in 1920.

160   Rouses Point is in New York, just across the border from Canada, on the western shore of the northern end of Lake Champlain.

Sunday, Jan. 12, 1919
East Braintree, Mass.

I arrived in Boston yesterday morning and spent the day with my attorney, going over evidence, etc. We are bringing suit upon two points. (I) That the Pages owe me a thousand dollars on the reprint edition of Green Gables and (II) that the selling of the reprint rights to Grosset and Dunlap[161] without my consent was a fraud on my interests.

We are certain that we won't win this point because I practically endorsed the reprint by accepting the checks for it. But it will give the judge something to give Page, if he wants to be impartial and he will then be the more likely to interpret clause (I) in my favor. Moreover, we will gain a good idea

The bungalow at Braintree

of where we stand when the *Avonlea* suit comes on, because in the case of the Avonlea reprint I have *not* accepted any checks and so have not endorsed it. I shall be perfectly satisfied if I win the first point.

I like Mr. Rollins.[162] He is nice and seems a shrewd, level-headed fellow.

Last evening I came out to Braintree and am here in Amos and Flora's[163] cosy little bungalow. There is something very fascinating to me in this little house on this New England hill-top. Their "den" is especially cosy.

Monday, Jan. 13, 1919
East Braintree, Mass.

Had my first experience in a court of law today. It was very interesting. Judge Jenny is on the case.[164] The Pages were in court but gave me a

---

161   Grosset and Dunlap was the main reprint publishing house in the United States; the company also published of juvenile fiction such as *The Bobbsey Twins* and *Tom Swift*.

162   Weld Allan Rollins (1874–1952), a lawyer specializing in corporate law.

163   Flora Macdonald Eagles was Ewan's half-sister. She and her husband Amos Eagles lived outside of Boston.

164   The Honourable Charles Francis Jenney (1860–1923) was Associate Justice to the

wide berth. I was shocked at Louis'[165] appearance. It is 8 years since I saw him and I had expected to see him 8 years older. He looks sixteen years older. He was formerly a handsome man. His good looks have almost vanished. Well, one can't live the life he has lived and escape the penalty. George Page[166] hasn't changed at all, as far as I could see. Louis was examined and swore to at least three deliberate lies.

The Page lawyer is a Mr. Nay who is an elderly man and very nice, too.[167] After the Pages had gone out he came up and smiled amiably "I hope, Mrs. Macdonald, that you realize that my opposition is purely professional. You wrote a wonderful book etc."

But this won't prevent him from grilling me in his best style in the witness box tomorrow morning.

Tuesday, Jan. 14, 1919
East Braintree, Mass.

A very hard day. Mr. Rollins and I went up to the court and Louis Page was again in the box. Swore to two more lies. He was very nervous all the time—kept moistening his lips and fiddling with his watch chain. After him, my turn came. I was in the stand about half an hour and swore to the very opposite of Louis P. It remains to be seen whom the judge will believe. I left the witness box, feeling as if I had made every possible kind of an ass of myself. But Mr. Rollins said to me as I went out, "You should be on the witness stand all the time if you enjoy it. You made a capital witness."

Perhaps the judge thought so, too. At any rate he made it rather clear in what he said after I was through that he meant to give me the first point. Evidently the Pages realized this, too, for before we left the courtroom their lawyer came across with an offer to compromise the suit by buying out my entire rights in the books of mine they publish.

I had thought of this as a possible solution of my troubles and a good way out. But I had not expected the Pages would offer it. They certainly would not have done so if they had not at last realized that I had a legal grip on them and was not to be bluffed or frightened into foregoing it. They offered me $10,000. I smiled at this but said I would

---

Supreme Judicial Court of Massachusetts.

165   Lewis Coues Page (1869–1956; LMM spells his name "Louis"); his Boston publishing firm, L.C. Page & Co., had been founded in 1891. He also published Bliss Carman, Charles G.D. Roberts, and Marshall Saunders.

166   George A. Page, Lewis' brother, had also started working at his father-in-law's firm, Estes and Lauriat.

167   Lawyer Frank Nelson Nay (1966–1942).

talk it over with Mr. Rollins. I did some mental figuring and decided that if the Pages would give me $18,000 I would sell out to them. It is nothing like the value of my books—or what would be their value in a different firm. But with a pair of scoundrels like the Pages, a bird in the hand is worth half a dozen in the bush. I can invest this money and the yearly interest will amount to as much as the yearly royalties would. So I said $18,000. Their lawyer smiled in turn. Oh, no, they would never do that. *Might* come up to $13,000—not a cent more. I smiled last and came away. I will not budge an inch. But non-budging is hard on the nerves. I was wretchedly tired when I got home. A reaction has set in and I am all in small pieces. But I'll gather up the fragments and face the Pages with restored morale tomorrow. Amen and amen! I shall win because I can afford to lose and the Pages can't. They are as desperately anxious to be rid of me as I am to be rid of them. *I* have discovered them to be conscienceless and reputationless rogues whom I cannot trust; *they* have discovered *me* to be a woman whom they cannot bluff, bully, or cajole. They know if I win this suit I will at once file another with still better chances of winning.

Thursday Night, Jan. 16, 1919
East Braintree, Mass.

I am in pieces again—but nevertheless I have fought a good fight—and won! Yesterday morning Mr. Rollins and I again hied us to the Equity court. Mr. Nay came suavely up and told us that the Pages would give me $17,000 for a settlement. I smiled once more and said "Eighteen." "Then the case must go on," he said. "They will not give it." "So be it," said I. It went on; the lawyers made their pleas and the judge announced, not exactly his formal decision but what his decision would be. As we expected, he gave the second point to Page on the ground that I had authorized the G. and D.[168] transaction by accepting the checks; *and* he gave me point one—the original point on which I had gone to law. The disputed thousand was mine—and all the other thousands which might hinge upon that phrase in the contract in future.

Nay came up and talked aside to Rollins. When we left the court Rollins said, "We've got them good and scared. Nay says their $17,000 offer still stands." "Eighteen," said I. Mr. Rollins laughed. "I think you'll get it," he said.

I left him and went to meet Alma Macneill.[169] We had lunch in a

---

168   That is, Grosset and Dunlap.

169   Alma Macneill was a cousin and childhood friend from Cavendish. In her retrospective entry of January 28, 1912, LMM describes the large family of "Arty" Macneill from Cavendish: "Alma

Chinese restaurant for the fun of it, then went to a movie. I stayed all night with Alma and then went up to Mr. Rollins' office this morning. He had a grin on.

"They have come up to the eighteen thousand," he said.

Vici![170]

The formal agreement is to be drawn up tomorrow. I went to a movie and then came home. I am so tired I don't know if I can pick up the pieces once more or not.

Sunday Night, Jan. 19, 1919
East Braintree, Mass.

I spent Friday and yesterday dickering with the Pages—or rather with George Page, for Louis, evidently, will not face me. George not having told me so many direct lies is not so shamefaced. But Louis pulls the wires behind the scenes and makes all the trouble he possibly can for me.

When my volume of short stories "Chronicles of Avonlea" was mooted, I sent Louis Page all my short stories up to date. He made a selection from them for the "Chronicles" and returned the rest to me. But now it appears, from Nay's letter on the subject, that, with characteristic thievery he kept copies of them. These old "culls" he now proposes to publish and I'm afraid he can—and will—publish them whether I agree or not, because the most of them were not copyrighted in the U.S. Among them, however, are two or three—and these the best— which were copyrighted and which he therefore cannot use without my consent. In order to obtain that consent he is willing to bind himself not to publish the book in a year during which I am to bring out a new volume. If I do not bind him thus he is quite capable of publishing those stories this spring and cutting the market for my new Stokes book which comes out in August. He must be prevented from doing this and I am the more willing to consent from the fact that I would never want any other publisher to publish those stories for they are poor stuff. Consequently I give up nothing of value to myself and I tie a pair of scoundrels down so that they can do me the least possible harm whereas if I left them loose they could—and I feel certain would—do me a good deal.

So I have consented but I have made them agree to several minor

---

was the flower of the family and universally popular. She was a very pretty girl, bright, clever, of pleasing manner. She went to Boston when she grew up but came home almost every summer and we always kept up our intimacy."

170   From the Latin "I conquered."

[Christie Montgomery Viles and cousins at Braintree]

details which made them grit their teeth. The consequent agreement is rather a curiosity in the way of legal agreements I think. It is not yet signed however, as one or two more points have to be settled but surely tomorrow will see the end of it.

We have had a very pleasant Sunday. Mr. and Mrs. Viles have been here—cousins of mine. Christie Viles was a daughter of Uncle Charles Crosby.[171] I never even met her until the last time she was here and she is so much my senior that she seems more like an aunt than a cousin. I feel absurdly disrespectful when I call her "Christie." She is a very fine looking woman—a feminine edition of the old Senator, resembling him much more strongly than any of his daughters. Her mother, Aunt Jane, did not resemble him at all. These family likenesses are very curious things. For instance, Chester, who is really very much like his father, has the eyes and brows of my mother, while Stuart has my father's eyes absolutely. There are times when Chester's expression gives me an absolutely *ghostly* sensation, as if eyes long closed in death were looking at me.

My dear little boys, how I long to see them tonight! How glad I shall be when all this vexatious law business is disposed of and, free at last, I hope forever, from the incubus of the Pages, I shall hasten back to my own dear home.

[Chester and Stuart]

I had a letter from Frede Friday night, regretting having missed me and urging me to stop off on my way back for a day or so. I must try to arrange it and have wired her to that effect.

---

171 A distant relation. Uncle Charles Crosby (b. 1823) was married to "Aunt Jane" Montgomery (b. 1835), a sister of LMM's grandfather. Christie (Crobsy) Viles had been born in 1863, so was 11 years older than LMM.

Friday, Feb. 7, 1919
Leaskdale, Ont. The Manse

On Saturday, January 25th, at seven o'clock in the morning Frederica Campbell MacFarlane died of flu-pneumonia in the infirmary of Macdonald College at St. Anne de Bellevue, Quebec.

——————————— ———————————

There, it is written! And I feel a strange relief. I have so dreaded the writing of it.

Oh, my God, can it be true? It is unbelievable—impossible! It is too hideous to be true!

It is true! And my heart is broken! Oh, how can I go on living?

——————————— ———————————

On the morning of Monday, January 20, I went into Boston again and spent most of the day wrangling with Geo. Page and Mr. Nay over the details of our agreement. Another characteristic bit of *Pageism* came to light. I discovered that the Page Co. has *not* got the copies of those stories. I suppose they wanted me to think they had lest, if I knew the truth, I would not have let them publish them. Nor would I; but having consented I will not be shyster enough to with-

[Frede]

draw now. They said they wanted me to send them the copies they had sent me back. I told them this was impossible as I had destroyed them but I would send copies of the original magazine stories. (The copies I had sent them had been changed somewhat to fit into the Avonlea atmosphere). They said this would be satisfactory but we could not get all the resulting details worked out that day, so I finally left and went out to Wakefield to spend the night with my old namesake and correspondent of long years, Lucy Lincoln Montgomery.[172] I had a very enjoyable eve-

————————————

172   In a long entry dated November 29, 1910, LMM described her first visit to Boston to negotiate with the Pages. She also also gave a description of her first meeting with Lucy Lincoln Montgomery: "Thursday morning I went out to Wakefield where I had promised to lunch with Lucy Lincoln Montgomery, my unseen literary correspondent. As soon as I left the train I saw her, recognizing her from her photograph. She seems to be a very sweet woman, of about 60 years of age. Her sister and brother-in-law, General and Mrs. Goodale, live with her and they have a nice

ning but shortly before bedtime Flora rung me up on the phone saying that a wire had come from Frede—to whom I had written, asking if such-and-such a day would suit her plans for me to call at St. Anne's. The wire said that she had "flu" but had two good nurses and was "very comfortable," and wanted me to stop off on my way home whatever day it was.

I did not feel the least alarm over this news. I was possessed with the idea that "flu" was only really dangerous if there was carelessness or lack of attention and I knew there was no fear of either in Frede's case. So I went to bed and I slept soundly and well—the last good sleep I was to have for many a dreadful night.

But I dreamed a strange dream. I thought I had arrived home. In my absence workmen seemed to have torn the whole inside of my house to pieces and to be making it over. Everything in the way of furniture and household gods seemed to have utterly disappeared. I ran upstairs to my room. It was likewise empty and had been made over to half its old size. This seemed to me a terrible blow. I felt broken-hearted. My dear home was all bare and changed. My own room had narrowed down to a mere closet. And where were all my treasured possessions? With a bitter sinking of spirit I said to myself, "Everything has gone and now I have to set to work to furnish my house all over again." And as I stood, gazing blankly at the new bare unpainted rooms around me I awoke.

I never thought of connecting the dream with Frede. Instead, I thought if it meant anything, it referred to the fact that Ewan had been asked if he would accept a call to a certain congregation. Possibly the dream meant that we would go—and so life be changed.

But now I know that it meant Frede's death. And has it not come true? Is not my house of life left unto me desolate—is not the inmost shrine of my heart narrowed down? Does not everything seem gone from me? Am I not left to furnish forth my soul's habitation afresh—if I can!

Tuesday morning I spent again with the lawyers and Friend George and got things so far along that it remained only to draw up the agreement formally and sign it. After lunch I went with Lucy Montgomery to Cambridge where we attended a meeting of some literary club and I gave a reading from "The Golden Road"[173] and had a very enjoyable time. Professor Dallas Sharpe motored me home and I arrived at Flo-

---

home called 'Gladhill.' Another sister of hers, Mrs. Slocum, the wife of a college president, was also there. I spent a very delightful day. They were nice, refined, cultured people, not so aggressively 'smart' as the Page set and consequently much more restful."

173   Published by L.C. Page in 1913, this is a series of interconnected stories.

ra's very tired out—but—oh!—very happy. The Page matter was virtually settled. The next night I would leave for home, spend a day or two at Macdonald with convalescent Frede, then hie me happily home to my own dear boys. I spent a pleasant, cosy evening in the "den" and at eleven o'clock I was ready for bed.

Suddenly the telephone rang. Flora answered it—it was a call for me.

Sick of soul I went to the 'phone. I knew it must be bad news. The message was delivered—briefly—mercilessly. Miss Hill sent it—Frede was seriously ill with pneumonia. They wanted me to come at once.

It fell on my heart like a knell of doom. "She will die—she will die," I moaned. I paced the floor in anguish—I went to my room wondering how the night was to be put in—and the next day. For I could not get into Boston early enough to catch the early morning train to Montreal. Oh, that night! The torment of my suspense was so hellish that when, about five, I felt myself dropping into the slumber of exhaustion, I *willed*, with a fierce intensity that I should *dream the truth* about the termination of Frede's illness. I had a queer forbidding idea that I was *doing wrong* in this—laying violent hands on the future—a different thing from a dream that came as an unsought gift or warning from the Keepers of the Gate. But my pain was so great that I did it—and I *dreamed*.

In my dream I had arrived at the outside of the Apartment at Macdonald and the only way to get up to it was to climb up the steep wall by iron spikes which were driven into it, after the fashion of the spikes on telegraph poles. I began to climb with frantic energy. Half way up my toilsome ascent I heard a terrible cry above me and I thought "Frede is dead." I redoubled my efforts—I reached a sort of open casement and looked in. I beheld a long hall. In the centre on a kind of bier lay Frede, with nurses and doctors standing around. "She *isn't* dead," I shrieked in agony. I rushed forward and flung myself over her. She *was* dead—I wakened.

From that moment I had no *real* hope of Frede's recovery. I *knew*. I had willed to tear aside the veil that hides the future and my punishment was the torture of the vision.

Flora and I went into Boston after breakfast and I went to Rollins' office and with him to Nay's. I was resolved that neither Nay nor George Page should see my suffering—so I preserved outward calmness. While we sat in Nay's office awaiting Page, Nay began to talk of Kipling and spoke of a poem of his in "The Brushwood Boy"[174] which he said had

---

174 "The Brushwood Boy" is a short story by Rudyard Kipling, first published in his collection,

always appealed strongly to him. He took out a notebook and read it. I bit my lip and clenched my hands under cover of the table to keep from screaming. It was "The City of Sleep" and the first time I had ever heard it had been when Frede had recited it to me one evening in my old room in Cavendish over ten years ago. I could see her sitting in my rocking chair—I could hear her voice lingering caressingly on the lines.

> "We must come back with Policeman Day
> Back from the city of sleep."[175]

Nay read the poem all through and I listened—and kept my calm and my senses! George Page came—the agreement was signed—my twenty thousand dollar check (including the royalties due) was in my hand. How gladly would I have torn it into bits and scattered it to the winds if only by so doing I could buy Frede's life! Pshaw! Frede could *not* die! Scores of people had recovered from pneumonia—even flu-pneumonia. I would go to Macdonald—I would find her better—we would yet be talking laughingly over my fright, as we had done after her typhoid.

But underneath—I knew—I *knew*!

I went back with Rollins, settled up, and said good-bye. "You have been a good client," he said. "You knew your mind. There was no wobbling with you." Yes, I had known my mind—I had matched my wits against roguery and won—but my victory was bitter in my mouth. What did it matter—what did anything matter? Oh, if with that twenty thousand dollars I could buy instant transportation to Macdonald College! How could I live until the next morning!

I rejoined Flora and we went to visit friends as we had promised. The afternoon dragged intolerably away. But even the tortures of the rack ended at last for the martyrs—and at last I found myself on the Montreal train. I prayed for just one thing—that I might see Frede *once* more—speak to her *once* more. I *must* have that or I should die, too. If I could just reach St. Anne's before it was too late!

I took veronal and so had a few hours of heavy drugged sleep. I arrived in Montreal just in time to catch the St. Anne's train. When I got off at the station at St. Anne's Miss Kirby—Frede's assistant—met me.

The Day's Work, in 1898. The story recounts the young life of a now-grown British army officer.

175   From Kipling's poem, "The City of Sleep" (in his 1898 collection, noted above, *The Day's Work*) in which a narrative voice likens waking up to being escorted out of "the Merciful Town" of sleep by a policeman, away from the restful mental realm that is "hard by the Sea of Dreams — / Where the poor may lay their wrongs away, / And the sick may forget to weep."

I forced myself to utter, "How is Frede?" and even as I spoke I knew that Frede must be living still or Miss Kirby would not be smiling.

"She had quite a comfortable night and the nurses think she is a little better this morning," was her reply.

Frede was still alive! In my reaction from my sickening terror I trembled so that I could hardly stand. We walked up the street and turned in at the big entrance gates, where Frede had so many times gone in. I was suddenly hopeful and in good spirits—on the surface. After all, had that dream meant anything? Had I not dreamed it because my mind was so full of the matter and my dread so great?

The entrance gates with Boys' Building beyond,

I had breakfast in the apartment with Miss Hill, who was or seemed to be, quite hopeful. She has always been a close friend of Frede's and is a very sweet woman. I can never forget her exceeding kindness and thoughtfulness to me in all those terrible days. Miss Phelp was there, too—another remarkably fine and sweet and clever woman whom Frede had loved and whom I had met several times before.

Miss Hill

After breakfast I went over to the college infirmary and, shrouded in mask and overall, was admitted to the ward and then taken to Frede's room. I found her very ill and again my heart sank. This was not typhoid, where the tide of life, however low it ran, might be turned by some sudden exhilaration or pleasure that stimulated Nature to another and supreme effort. Frede always had said that I saved her life in typhoid. Perhaps I did. Dr. Gordon said she began to improve from the moment I arrived. Perhaps it gave her just the fillip needed to start her on the upgrade. But I had no such power now. This was a grislier foe.

But she was very glad to see me, poor darling! She was no longer alone among strangers, even though they were kind and attentive strangers. Once more those brave, kindly, clever eyes lighted up with welcome as they met mine—as they had done hundreds of times in the past—as they would never do again. She did not know she had pneumonia—she thought it was only the flu. The doctor would not allow her to be told, fearing she would give up utterly. I think this was a mistake—I think she should have been told. But so it was.

I sat beside her and tried to soothe and encourage her. She had been delirious all night but she was perfectly sensible then. I found her terribly worked up and worried over some unkind, abusive letter that wretched Stell had written her a short time before. When I wrote Stell that afternoon I told her plainly that I should never feel the same to her again if Frede died. But to Frede I made light of it. "Don't worry, you foolish dear. You know perfectly well what Stell is. She is not worth a second thought."

She was worried over many things—her mother, the situation at Park Corner, Cam's prospects etc. I tried to calm and encourage her—I think I succeeded. As of old she turned to me for advice and assistance—and thank God I did not fail her—I never failed her—we never failed each other!

————————   ————————

I take up my pen again, after a wild outbreak of tears. I must go on with this—must get it over. If I "write it out" perhaps I will be better able to endure my pain.

X. Infirmary of Macdonald College.

I was permitted to sit by her and talk to her on condition that I did not let her talk very much. I told her all my news—that I had won my suit with Page and so on. I told her a little joke—one of Stuart's funny sayings over which we had laughed at the manse supper table the last evening I had been at home. We had pancakes and maple syrup and the edge of the one Stuart was eating had been crisped in the frying. He tried vainly to cut it with the spoon. "Mother," he said plaintively, "*how* do you cut pancake bones?"

Frede gave her little characteristic laugh when she heard it. That was the last time I was ever to hear Frede laugh. Never, never again! Oh, Frede, heaven must have needed some laughter and so you were taken.

She took off her wedding and engagement rings and gave them to me. "Keep them for me till I get better," she said. Her poor finger had grown so thin that they worried her, for fear they might drop off. I remembered how she had proudly shown me her engagement ring that morning I arrived at Macdonald after her marriage. Cam had given it to her just a few hours before their marriage.

I spent most of the afternoon with her. Went over to the apartment for dinner and returned. We talked over "the problem of Stella" and as usual arrived nowhere. Dr. Gordon arrived from Montreal. I had sent for him. He told me that she was very ill—that he was gravely anxious about her, but that he thought she had "an equal chance." It was scant food for hope but I fed avidly on it. I know now that, although I had asked him to tell

THE MAIN BUILDING, MACDONALD COLLEGE.

X. The Apartment.

me the exact truth, he had not quite done so. He had spoken more hopefully than he felt. I heard later that his parting words to Dr. Helso had been those old ones of doom—"Well, while there's life there's hope."

I said good-night to Frede and went over to the apartment, the nurse having promised to send for me if any change for the worse set in.

I was very tired after two bad nights and I fell into a heavy sleep almost at once. It seemed but a few minutes—although it was about two o'clock—when I became conscious that Miss Hill was bending over me saying that the nurses had phoned, asking me to come over—that there was a change for the worse.

I got up and dressed. I never hoped again. Miss Hill and I left the apartment, went down and down and down those interminable flights of stairs through the echoing, ghostly corridors, passed through the long "covered way" whose icy chill struck to my heart like a waft of death, and through the long corridor of the Women's Residence to the Infirmary. Frede was lying in the stupor-like sleep induced by an injection of morphine. Her breathing had grown heavy and stertorous.[176] The nurse feared that she was already in the coma that precedes death.

All the rest of the night I walked up and down the corridor outside Frede's room in the grip of hellish torment. Frede dying! I could *not* believe it—and yet I *did* believe it—I knew it was so. *How* can human beings live, or keep sanity, through what I endured that night? Why should they *have* to live through it? Why does God send us the blessing of great love and then send it away? *Is* it God—or some malignant Power of Evil who hates love and happiness and is mighty enough to destroy it in spite of the Power of God? Vain questions! I did not ask them that night—one question only I asked, over and over in my ceaseless pacing, "Oh God, how can I live without Frede?"

At five her breathing changed again—and again for the worse. The night nurse was a Miss Patterson. I did not like her—she seemed a hard, unsympathetic woman; but I must say she was skilful and attentive. The day nurse was a Miss Ince—a girl from Barbados—a very tall woman with snow-white hair. Yet I do not think she was much past girlhood. Her personality was very charming and individual.

At six Frede wakened out of the morphine sleep, muttering in delirium. From then until seven we thought her dying. I stood by the bed and watched while the nurse strove to rally her, feeling as if I were in some hideous nightmare—or in some narrow cell of torment from which my agonized soul looked out on what was passing around me.

At seven Frede rallied. She became conscious and her pulse improved. But I knew there was no longer any hope. It was only a question of time. I dragged myself back to the apartment, forced myself to swallow a few mouthfuls of food and returned to the Infirmary. Frede was lying calmly on her pillows. I bent over her and asked her how

---

176   Noisy and laboured.

she was. "I feel fine," was her answer. I would rather have heard the complaints of the day before. *That* would have meant nature was still fighting. *This* meant that she had given up the struggle.

The day dragged away. Frede took little notice of anyone. She muttered to herself incessantly; but when I spoke to her she always answered clearly and rationally. At dusk, as I sat beside her bed she made the only reference to her condition that she made that day. "My breath is getting very short," she said. The fact did not seem to alarm her. I went out while the nurses prepared her for the night. Then I went back and walked softly up and down the room, clenching my hands and praying wildly and despairingly. Then poor Frede came back once more—*for the last time*—from the Valley of the Shadow. And she make a little joke—the last of all her gay and merry jests. Oh, Frede!

"I would like to see Stell with the influenza," she said. "The specific gravity would go up to 90."[177]

"Specific gravity"—Frede and I had made a jest of it for many a day. Poor Stell was always writing that a certain "specific gravity" had gone up so many degrees, in every upheaval of her nerves. Frede and I had tossed the phrase back and forth like a ball in our meetings. And now!

I made myself laugh. "It certainly would," I said. The tears were pouring down my face under that stifling mask. Oh, my friend—*my friend!*

Miss Hill and the nurse insisted that I should take a veronal pill and lie down in the adjoining room. I did not want to. But, as they truly said, I owed a duty to my children and I could do nothing for Frede, who had sunk back into her muttering semi-stupor. I realized this and allowed myself to be led away. Miss Patterson said she would wake me at the slightest change.

I took the tablet almost greedily—it would mean a few hours blessed oblivion and relief from pain.

At five o'clock I was called. I sprang up and hurried in. The end was coming. I bent over Frede and asked her how she felt. "Fine," was her response, firm and clear. But the brave heart was almost worn out—it was failing—failing. She lay, muttering and unnoticing, but to the last my voice had power to bring her back for a moment.

"Frede," I said, "I am going to write to your mother today. Have you any word to send her?"

---

177   Specific gravity is the ratio between the density of a given substance and a "reference" substance, usually water. The joke presumably was that Stella did not fully understand the meaning of the term but used it to describe her poor health, real or imagined (LMM and Frede had long felt she tended to hypochondria).

"Yes. Tell her I want to know exactly how her hand is," she said.

This was a commonplace message. It came from the conscious mind. The next was different. It came up from the subconscious deeps.

"I think I'll write to Cam, too," I said, as soon as I could control my voice. "Is there anything you would like me to tell him?"

"No, only that I wish for him the courage of the strong," she replied.

I walked up and down the room a few times. There was yet something I must say to her—but I must put it in such a way that it would not alarm or shock her with any sudden realization that she was dying. Such a realization could serve no good purpose now—and it might worry her. Yet I *must* remind her of a certain promise in words whose significance she might not grasp just then but would when—and *if*— the freed, conscious and intelligent spirit was released from the clogs of the failing body.

Years ago Frede and I were discussing, as we often did, the mystery of the hereafter—

"Whether 'twere ampler day divinelier lit

Or starless night without."[178]

And we made a compact. When in the course of years, few or many, one of us died that one was to come back and appear to the survivor *if* it were possible to cross the gulf. I *must* remind her of this.

Again I bent over her. "Frede," I said earnestly, "you won't forget your promise to come and see me, will you?" "No," she said. "You'll be sure to come, won't you?" I insisted. "Certainly," she said, clearly and loudly. It was her last word.

But oh Frede, you have not come yet. The dead *cannot* return or you *would* have come. I cannot—I *cannot* bear it.

I sat down beside her. I was sick to my soul with agony. Oh, is there not after all something in that old superstition that the Immortals who control our destinies are jealous beings—jealous of a too-great love or a too perfect friendship which makes us too much like them?

Poor Frede seemed unconscious of all that went on. Yet once she put out her poor thin hand, her hand that had been so beautiful and shapely—one of her best points—and laid it on my arm as if appealing to me to help her—to me, who was so helpless. I could do nothing for her—nothing—I, who would have done anything. I took her hand and held it until she drew it away again in a sudden restlessness.

Her breath grew shorter and shorter. At seven it ceased. She died as peacefully and gently as a tired child might fall asleep. *She died*. And I

---

178   From English poet William Watson's (1858–1935) "The Great Misgiving," a meditation on the mystery of death.

live to write it! Frede is *dead.* "After life's fitful fever she sleeps well."[179]
But *I* wake and must face the dreary years without her. I *must* live
as long as I can for my children's sake. I
must live—without that blithe comradeship, that intellectual companionship,
that faithful, earnest friendship—live,
knowing that Frede will never come
again under my roof—that never again
will come to me a letter addressed in her
old familiar hand—that I will never hear
her laugh—never save up a joke to tell
her—never walk with her again under
the Park Corner birches or over the old
bridge in the summer twilight! How *can* I

Frede under the Park Corner birches.

go on living when half my life has been wrenched away, leaving me torn
and bleeding in heart and soul and mind. I had *one* friend—one only—
in whom I could absolutely trust—before whom, I could in Emerson's
splendid definition "think aloud"—and she has been taken from me.
Truly, as has been said, in such an instance as this "it is the survivor
who dies." Yes, Frede, you did not suffer the pangs of death. It was
I—I—as *you* would have suffered had it been I who went away!

She died just as the eastern sky was crimson with sunrise. She "went
out as the dawn came in"—like old *Captain Jim* in my *House of
Dreams.*[180] When I realized that she was dead I stood up—I felt Miss
Hill's arms around me—I heard her whispering at my ear, "Look at the
sunrise—look at the sunrise." It was one of those absurd things people say, in a desperate effort, I suppose, to be kind and inspirational. I
could have shrieked with derision at it. The sunrise had no message
for me. I went out of the room with an unbearable agony tearing at me.
Tears had ceased to flow and I had not that relief. If I had been alone
my anguish would have found vent—and so relief—in screams. But I
must not scream out of consideration for the others there. I crushed
back the impulse to shriek—I went into another room and sat down on
the bed. Suddenly I found myself laughing. In a moment my hysterical
peals of laughter were ringing through the hall.

---

179   From *Macbeth* 3.2, lines 19–23. Macbeth says of the deceased king, "Duncan is in his
grave; / After life's fitful fever he sleeps well."

180   In LMM's 1917 novel, *Anne's House of Dreams,* a beloved family friend dies in a chapter
entitled "Captain Jim Crosses the Bar." (The title of the chapter is taken from Tennyson's "Crossing the Bar," a poem that likens death to a journey out to sea).

I have never before in my life had hysterics—and I have always felt a little contempt for women who have had them. Well, I ask their pardon.

I laughed—and shook until the bed shook under me. Miss Hill put her hands about me and held me tightly. The nurse, seeing that I was trying to check my horrible laughter said, "Don't try to keep it back, Mrs. Macdonald. It will injure you if you do." So I laughed on.

Well, Frede and I have always laughed. It has been the key note of our life together. So there was an ironic fitness in the fact that I mourned her with laughter.

The nurse finally brought me a drink of some stimulant. I drank it and regained my self control. The next moment I fell asleep on the bed exhausted.

Miss Hill had presently to awaken me to ask me what dress they should put on Frede. We decided on her pretty "Khaki-kool."[181] And my thoughts went back to the time Frede bought it. It was in May 1917, when I was with her at Macdonald just after her marriage. Her bridal had been too hurried to include a trousseau and it was necessary for her to get a new dress for the social functions which were to come off in our joint honor. We went into Montreal for the day and scoured the stores for a suitable dress. For a long time we could find nothing; but at last a clerk brought out a sample dress of the new fabric "Khaki-Kool" and we were both delighted with it. Frede tried it on. It became her from every standpoint. "You will make no mistake in taking it, Frede," I said. "It will be suitable for anything, except a dance or a formal dinner."

Suitable for anything—ay, even for a shroud! Dear God, it is well that the future is hidden from our eyes.

I took off the mask and overall and went back to the apartment. The hideous suspense was over; the still more hideous certainty had to be faced.

All that day I walked the floor of the beautiful living room—all the next interminable day I walked it. I could not sit down. Miss Hill and Miss Philp were consideration itself. They did not torment me with platitudes of consolation—they did not urge me to "rest." They knew no rest was possible for such pain as mine.

---

181   Khaki-Kool was a popular novelty fabric developed during the war, at a time when cotton and wool textiles were in short supply as a result of military needs. The fabric was woven from lower-quality "slubbed" (uneven) silk yarn.

I walked—and walked. Tears came freely at last but brought no relief. I "thought forward"—I lived out the allotted span of human existence in a few hours—*without Frede*. All the pain that should have been spread over many years—all the loneliness—all the longing—was concentrated in those hours. And I saw my whole past friendship with Frede in a series of vivid pictures, which

Lecturers in HouseHold Science. Standing Miss Hill, Miss Campbell, MIss Zollman Sitting Miss Fisher, Miss Philp, Mrs. Rutter.

burned in upon my consciousness and with them the unbearable torture of realizing that I would never see them in life again—Frede sitting in my old room at Cavendish, sleeking[182] her beautiful black hair before my mirror—Frede squatted on the floor of her room at Wedlocks discussing the universe—Frede standing laughing at the well at Park Corner—Frede setting bread in the old porch—Frede hunting for snacks in the pantry—Frede with "Sonny Punch" in her arms—Frede at my Christmas table, flushed and handsome, flirting with Fraser[183]—Frede coming to meet me

Frede with quote Sonny Punch

in Montreal station in that old homespun suit of hers—Frede sitting by my kitchen fire with Daff in her lap—over and over and over again I saw her—and knew that I should never so see her again.

At dusk Miss Ince came over and told me that the casket had been closed—she had thought it better not to send for me. I was shocked by this—I found that I had unconsciously been looking forward to seeing Frede *once more*. For a moment I felt that I could not bear *not* to see her—I *must* see her. But it was no longer possible. With a shiver of agony I resigned myself to it. After all, perhaps, as Miss Ince said, it was

---

182 Making hair smooth, usually by applying moisture or pressure.

183 A local Presbyterian minister, James Fraser (b. 1867); he is mentioned again a few pages below (see also note 188 as well as LMM's entries for August 8, 1918, and April 12, 1921).

best. I think perhaps they were all afraid I would break down again if they had sent for me. They need not have so feared; but I don't think I would want to remember Frede's dead face—cold, unresponsive, pallid—"that sad shrouded brow"[184]—no, it was better not. And yet how I hungered—and hunger—for that denied last look! In life Frede and I never said good-bye to each other. We had made a compact to that effect—we both hated saying "good-bye"—and we agreed years ago that we would never say it—we would always part with a laugh and a gay wave of the hand. On the November afternoon when I last left Park Corner Frede sprang on the back of the buggy and came down with us to the road. She wore her green "Household Science" uniform. As she dropped off I said "Well, Freddie, when shall I see you again?" "Oh, I don't know," she said—and she ran back up the old lane. There was no good-bye—and there was to be none now. Frede had gone on and I was left. Her work was done—mine, it seemed, was not.

One of the windows of the living room looked across the campus to the college rink. That Saturday evening it was aglow with electric lights and gay with whirling figures. I thought it a little strange. When death was on the campus—and the death of a member of the faculty at that—I thought it would have been more appropriate if the customary sports were omitted until after the funeral. As I looked at the gay skaters I asked that old, stupid, selfish question. "*How* can they be enjoying themselves there while Frede is lying *dead* in that dark room yonder?" The old, old question—how can there be light if *our* sun is blotted from the heaven? "Oh, never morning wore to evening but some heart did break,"[185] but the rest of the world is none the less gay for that.

I walked—and fought for some little transient respite from torture in foolish childish visions and pretendings. Fred wasn't dead—the door would open presently and she would pop in with her gay laugh—it was all some dreadful dream—some silly mistake—how nice it would be to waken!—how we would laugh over the blunder and my tragic suffering over it! To *waken*—yes, that was it—waken up in the Braintree bungalow again and know that Frede was alive and I was going to see her at Macdonald in a day or two and talk all our family and personal problems over with her. Oh, to waken!

---

184   A slight misquotation from Byron's 1813 poem *The Giaour*. The lines in the poem describe a man looking at the day-old corpse of a woman as a metaphor of the mysteries of time: "He who hath bent him o'er the dead / Ere the first day of death is fled, / The first dark day of nothingness, / The last of danger and distress / (Before Decay's effacing fingers / Have swept the lines where beauty lingers,) ... but for that sad shrouded eye, / That fires not, wins not, weeps not, now ...."

185   The title of an 1894 painting ("Never Morning Wore to Evening but Some Heart Did Break") by British artist Walter Langley.

I dreaded going to bed that night but when I did I slept at once and unbrokenly till morning. Then I got up and lived through another day of horror. My pain seemed *physical* as well as emotional. It wrung my body with actual pangs. People came and went and were sympathetic. They were shadows—shadows! When one of the Macdonald professors heard of Frede's death he exclaimed, "Oh heaven, what a loss to the country!" But I thought then only of *my* loss.

Monday brought a different form of martyrdom. Frede's body was to be taken to the Crematory in Montreal for cremation.

Frede and I had often, years ago, talked, as we talked of every other subject under heaven, of the best way of disposing of "worn-out fetters that the soul had broken and thrown away."[186] We were both agreed that the proper and sanitary way was by cremation and we both declared that when we died we wanted to be cremated. With me this was merely an academic opinion. But Frede seemed to feel very deeply on the subject. She had a horror, she said, of being buried alive; and she had another horror of the slow process of decay in the grave. She often adjured me to see that she was cremated if she died before I did. I promised lightly enough—I had little fear then that Frede would go before me. When Frede was dead Miss Hill told me that when Frede first knew she had flu she asked for pen and paper and wrote out instructions for her cremation if she did not recover. Miss Hill said she was a little delirious at the time and appeared to think she might not have meant it. But I, remembering our old compact, knew that she did when I looked at the few faintly scrawled words "If I die I hereby direct that my body be cremated. Frederica MacFarlane"—the last words she ever wrote; and though I did not know how Aunt Annie and Cam would feel about it I determined to carry out Frede's last wish and ordered the arrangements made for it. I am satisfied that I did it. But for my own part, although I still believe and always will believe, that cremation is the right way to dispose of the dead, I shall never ask that it be done in my own case. *It is too hard for the living*. It is far harder than giving our dead to the earth. *Then* one seems to possess them still in a measure. But in cremation they seem absolutely gone—*nothing* is left—the sense of utter desolation is dreadful.

On Monday morning there was a brief funeral service in the reception room of the Girls' Building. Mr. Lancaster, the minister of the St. Anne Anglican church conducted it. He had been a personal friend of Frede's and she had attended his church. Then we drove to the station

---

186   From Longfellow's 1893 poem "Slavery" about the death of a slave: "For Death had illumined the Land of Sleep, / And his lifeless body lay / A worn-out fetter, that the soul / Had broken and thrown away!"

[Sleighing in Mount-Royal Park Montreal.]

and waited for some time for the train. The casket was before us, covered with flowers—my sheaf of red roses among them. On the evening before Frede died a friend had sent her a beautiful pot of freesias with a note referring to some mutual joke regarding "favorite" flowers. It suddenly occurred to me that, with all our interchange of opinions, I had never heard Frede say what her favorite flower was. I asked her then; and she answered, in the strange, clear, decisive fashion she employed in those last, semi-conscious hours, "A red rose!" It was a good choice. I might have known it. The red rose was just what Frede, the vivid and dramatic and intense, would like best. So I ordered the red roses for her casket—the last thing I could do for her. Oh, Frede!

We went into Montreal—we drove up the mountain—up—up—up. As we passed the gateway of the crematory grounds the bell in the belfry just beside it began to toll. I felt as if each toll smote on my brain like a physical blow. Was that melancholy sound for Frede, the laughing and the brilliant? It had nothing in common with *her*.

Presently I found myself standing between Miss Hill and Miss Philp in the little hall of the crematory, with the palms and blossoms on either side. The casket was before us and Mr. Lancaster was reading the burial service—"ashes to ashes—dust to dust"—do human love and companionship end so? Was all that had been Frede pent up in that black box before me? Or was her spirit by my side, pitying my anguish—suffering in her inability to reach and comfort me? Wild tormenting thoughts rushed through my mind—then concentrated in one weird obsession. Frede was lying in that box—*dead*—and if I bent over her and *told her a joke she would not laugh*. This realization beat in upon me and tortured me. Over and over and over the thought repeated itself—"she wouldn't laugh."—yes, she must indeed be dead if she wouldn't laugh! This sounds ridiculous I suppose. It was the keenest anguish I had ever experienced in my whole life.

The service was ended—the ashes were sprinkled on the casket. Suddenly the grim black doors in front opened—the casket was pushed through them—they closed. What an unbearable moment! All the suffering of the past five days was repeated and concentrated in it. To see

Margaret MacFarlane

those doors close *between us* was far harder than hearing the clods fall on the coffin in the grave. It symbolized so fearfully the truth that the doors had closed between us for all time. I was here—Frede was there—between us the black blank unopening door of death.

I went back to St. Anne's. I made arrangements for sending Frede's ashes to Park Corner for interment in the old plot at the Geddie Memorial Church, beside George and his little son.[187] Three who sat at that table of thirteen are gone.[188] Is the tale fulfilled?

Tuesday I faced a task I knew must be done, though I shrank from it with cringing. I did not see how I could do it—but done it had to be. Accompanied by Margaret MacFarlane—Frede's sister-in-law, who had arrived on Sunday evening—a nice girl—I went over to Frede's room in the Men's Building. It was not the pretty gray-and-old-rose room she had occupied in the Teacher's Residence when I was with her at the time of her marriage. Owing to the coal famine the teachers had had to give up the residence and move over to the Men's Building. The room had been disinfected and aired but otherwise was just as Frede had left

187   Located on the north shore overlooking New London Bay, Geddie Memorial Church was built in 1836–37 as a meeting-house style church. It remains a local landmark.

188   See LMM's entry of July 30, 1918.

it. I stifled a moan of agony as I looked around. The room was so full of her—her favorite pictures on the walls,—mine, Aunt Annie's, Margaret Stirling's, and one I had given her of the old home at Park Corner, enlarged and framed. Her pen and her books lay on her desk—her little toilet articles on her bureau, everything stabbed me.

What was the thing that hurt me most? Another ridiculous thing. On a table behind a screen were the remnants of some little supper poor Frede had cooked up for herself some evening when she had come in late from a country trip, hungry and tired—likely that very last evening when she had returned from her fatal trip to Waterloo. She hadn't eaten it all—in a small dish was a pitiful little scrap of cold bacon—cold bacon—yes, that *did* hurt the most. Frede and I had had so many of those little chummy, delicious bed-time snacks together.

I had felt very helpless over the problem of just what to do with Frede's belongings. Therefore it was a great relief to find, in the drawer of her writing table, a letter addressed to me and her mother and Cam. She had written it in October when the first flu panic had fallen on Macdonald. It began, "Dear Maud or mother or husband." Was it only because Cam was overseas and because she knew I would be the likeliest one to find the letter if she died? Not altogether I think. My name came first to her instinctively—before even that of the mother she loved but who had cruelly misunderstood her in her earlier years and before the boyish husband who had caught her fancy in the glamor of his uniform and his overseas experience, coming into her life at a psychological moment of loneliness. No, *I* came first—the old friend to whom she had always turned in her hours of need—to whom she turned at the last when the shadow of what might be fell over her.

The letter made our task simpler—nothing could make it easy. We spent the whole day going through her possessions and assorting them according to her wishes. The wedding presents from Cam's friends to his people—her books and his letters and gifts to him—the rest to her own people. I worked and cried until I was almost blind—everything rent my heart—the pretty things she had been given or had bought for her expected home—the hats and dresses I had seen her in so often—the cards I had sent her since my marriage, full of little intimate jesting messages only we two could understand—little clippings, little snaps I had sent her and which she had kept like precious treasures. Oh Frede, I wonder if anyone will ever go over *my* possessions with the agony that was my portion when I went over yours. I hope not—I believe not—for I will leave none behind me to whom I will mean what you meant to me—no, not even if my husband outlives me. For men do not feel these things as women do.

On Wednesday we finished our task and packed everything into boxes and trunks, most of them to go to poor Aunt Annie. Frede had directed in her letter that I was to have "first choice" of her little treasures but I took very little. I needed nothing—to use anything of Frede's would always wring my soul.

When Frede married I gave her a beautiful silver tea and coffee service. She had taken great pleasure in it—I am glad to think of that now—and always used it proudly at her afternoon teas. I took this back and have packed it away. Some day Chester, if he lives, may marry and then I shall give, or cause to be given to him his "Aunt Frede's set." I believe that is what would please her most. She loved Chester so—her old "Captain" of his baby months. I know there is no living human being she would rather have get it.

I also brought home her "Good Fairy."[189] That morning in May when I arrived at the Teacher's Residence Frede took me up to her room and delightedly showed me her "first wedding present"—a pretty little bronze statuette called "The Good Fairy" which had been given her by two of the staff. Being her first wedding gift it seemed to have a special significance. She always kept it on her bureau. I shall put it somewhere where I shall see it often and perhaps in days to come it will give me pleasure and not pain.

Among Frede's little bits of jewelry were a pendant of peridots and pearls and a pair of drop earrings to match. They were given her by an ardent lover of hers in the west—an Ed Willetts. She liked him very much—she was very near marrying him. But somehow she found she couldn't—and didn't. I brought the pendant and earrings home with me and packed them away. I don't know yet what disposal I shall finally make of them. Perhaps one of the little girls at Park Corner shall have them some day. Or perhaps some misty little unborn bride of Stuart's may wear them. She will not be haunted as I would be by visions of Frede as I saw her at my Christmas dinner table two years ago, laughing and jesting with Fraser,[190] her cheeks flushed, her eyes black and brilliant, the pendant glistening on her breast, the earrings caressing her cheeks.

Miss Hill and Miss Stuart had together given her a little set of afternoon tea cups and saucers of old-fashioned design. Miss Hill said she thought Frede would like me to have that so I brought it, too. The

---

189   The statue was manufactured by Jessie McCutcheon Raleigh Nelson [1916]. It was sculpted by (and rarely credited to) Josephine Kern (Mrs. James Mapes Dodge). See http://lmmontgomeryliterarysociety.weebly.com.

190   Mr. Fraser (b. 1867) was the minister at Uxbridge. He was a widower with two young children who had been interested in Frede.

rest of her gifts went to Park Corner.

When I returned to the apartment Wednesday night I found that my martyrdom was over. The fierce flame of torture had at last burned itself out—and gray ashes were over all my world. I was calm and despairing.

I left on the 11.20 train. It bore me away into darkness. There was no Frede behind—no Frede anywhere in the world—nothing but a little handful of ashes. *Where was she?* That wit, that strength, that vivid, brilliant personality—*these* could not be gray ashes—these must be somewhere in existence still. But nowhere where I can reach them—see them—feel them. And therefore, as far as my world is concerned, lost to me.

I reached Toronto in the morning and spent the day doing some necessary shopping. I came home Friday—have been home a week—a gloomy, bitter week. I can do nothing in the day—at night I cry myself to sleep. This house seems so full of Frede—everything is connected with her—everything tortures me. I think of her constantly. I realize, as never before, how intimately the strands of our lives were woven together. Does Stuart say some quaint, funny thing I find myself thinking "How Frede will laugh when she hears this," *before* the new consciousness that she is gone can prevent it. I find a passage in my reading that arrests me—"I must send this to Frede"—"how Frede will enjoy this." Some of the things that have rent me with the keenest pangs are absurd enough, too—for life always mixes up tragedy and grotesqueness. Today when I was hanging up my beef hams to dry I broke down and cried because Frede could never come to taste them. "Maud," she used to say, "I love you but even if I hated you I would come to see you for the sake of getting some of your beef ham."

It seems to me now that Frede and I must have been intimate and congenial friends all our lives. It seems to me quite unbelievable that I was 28, with a lifetime of bitter experiences behind me when Frede and I found each other. Yet such was the fact.

In my journal of the winter I spent at Park Corner in 1892 Frede's name is not even mentioned. This is not perhaps to be wondered at. I was then seventeen—practically a young woman with my head full of the beaux and parties and amusements of budding bellehood. Frede was a child of eight. Naturally there could be little in common between us. The strange part is that I have so little recollection of Frede during that winter. This is odd, because she was always around and one would think that vivid, magnetic personality of hers must have been manifest even in childhood to a sufficient extent to impress itself on my memory. It did not, however. I scarcely remember Frede at all, though I do remember that I used to make her frightfully mad by teasing her about "Mel Donald," a little freckled urchin of her own age who went to school and whom Frede hated. She always got in a baby rage when I teased her about him and I am afraid I was mean enough to delight in doing it rather often. I should think she must have hated me. In fact, I believe she did; but also she accorded me a reluctant admiration. "In spite of my hatred I thought you very handsome," she once told me laughing, and averred it was one of the chief delights of her small existence that winter to get into my bedroom when I was dressing to go out or entertain company, and sit curled up on the bed to watch me while I combed and curled and frilled and plumed myself. I have no recollection of this. I was too full of the egotism of early youth to think about her and no prescience came to me of what this small, black-haired, sallow-faced mite was to mean to me in the future.

I might remark that this same "Mel" Donald, who was a second cousin of our own, later on developed into a quite smart and nice-looking young man and an excellent friend of Frede's. They were very intimate and congenial, though there was never any "lovering" between them. Frede outlived her hatred both of Mel and me!

Years passed. Frede grew up; I grew older and sadder and—let us hope—a little wiser. I must of course have seen Frede whenever I was at Park Corner. The first mention of her in my diary is in the winter of 1893, when I speak of her popping out of Park Corner school to greet me one day, when I called there on my way over to Aunt Annie's. The next mention is not till December 1898, when I speak of having been at Park Corner and finding it changed. "Cade and Frede are away. Only Stella is left." There is a note in this as if I missed Frede, which must have meant that we had been more companionable but if so I have no memory of it. At this time Frede was at P.W.C.[191] In 1899 I mention a

Frede in 1902.

summer visit to Park Corner, where I had a pleasant time "as Frede and Stell were both home." But it was not until August 1902 that Frede and I "found" each other. Our friendship seemed to open into full bloom in a single night. Before that we were mere acquaintances; after that we were to each other what we were to be for over seventeen, beautiful, unmarred years of comradeship and understanding.

I recall the night distinctly. It was a hot night. For some forgotten reason we all three occupied Stella's room. Stell herself slept on the floor. Frede and I were in the bed. We began to talk confidentially each finding that we could confide in the other. Stell was furious because our chatter kept her from sleeping, so we buried our heads under the blankets that sweltering night and whispered to each other all our troubles—I, the woman of 28, Frede the girl of 19. We discovered that our souls were the same age! She told me her love troubles—I told her mine. In those years love

191   Prince of Wales College, which LMM had also attended, 1893–94). Prince of Wales College merged with St Dunstan's University in 1969 to form the University of Prince Edward Island.

troubles seemed to us to be the only things worth worrying about. We both had had bitter and heart-rending experiences. We talked, until dawn. Many times I have regretted the fact that nearness and darkness have betrayed me into confidences that were foolish and unwise. But neither of us ever regretted the mutual revelations of that night—never did we wish a word unsaid. From that hour we were—as Aunt Annie writes me that Life Howatt said when he heard of her death—"part of one another." Oh, Frede, Frede!

Frede taught in various schools and in 1905 she came to Stanley. She was comparatively near me then and we met quite often. It was a boon to me beyond price in those hard, lonely years. I could not have endured them without Frede's sympathy and encouragement and jolly companionship. When I made a hit with *Green Gables* and saw a little money assured my first determination was to help Frede. She was, I knew, tired and discouraged, seeing nothing before her but endless, monotonous years of teaching country schools for a mere pittance. I insisted that she should go to Macdonald or McGill and I would pay her way—I told her I wanted to "help her little ship to come in." After much urging

she assented. She chose Macdonald and Household Science.[192] She had a busy, happy two years there and led her class in graduation. She spent a year in Red Deer

School of Household Science, Class 1912.

College, Alta. and then went back to Macdonald as Demonstrator to the Home-Makers' Clubs of Quebec.[193] She did a wonderful work there

192　Frede had earned a degree in Household Science from Macdonald College in 1912. The Alberta Ladies' College of Red Deer opened the following year, in 1913. Along with Macdonald College, it was built as part of a country-wide initiative to create educational opportunities for young rural women. However the College was overwhelmed by debt, and in 1916 sold the building to the provincial government for use as a psychiatric hospital for soldiers returning from the war.

193　Frede had been Superintendent of Quebec Women's Institutes from 1913 until her death in 1919. Macdonald College still offers a Frederica Campbell MacFarlane Prize of $100 to stu-

and won recognition as one of the cleverest women in Canada. She was specially fitted for such a work, for not only had she the brains, training and personality for it, but she had the practical upbringing on the farm which enabled her to have a complete understanding of all the problems of farm life—an understanding no city-bred woman could ever attain. She had hosts of warm devoted personal friends—and a few virulent enemies, for a certain class of people hated her truth and sincerity and her clear-eyed and uncompromising penetration of their shams and hypocrisy.

[Frede and two others]

Frede, like myself, had a somewhat lonely and misunderstood childhood. She was "different" from the rest of her family. She was, as she expressed it, "the cat who walked by herself."[194] Her sisters were a good deal older than she and George was no kind of a companion. She has often told me that her mother "never loved her," until the older girls left home and Aunt Annie was forced to turn to Frede for companionship in her loneliness. Frede,

[Frede and two others]

dents from rural regions of Quebec. The Women's Institutes of Quebec have raised money for this fund annually since 1920.

194   From Rudyard Kipling's *Just So Stories for Little Children* (1902). The stories are a collection of fables to explain different phenomena. In this tale—a favourite of LMM's—the cat cannot successfully be domesticated by man, and insists on maintaining some independence.

not being a mother herself, was mistaken in this. Aunt Annie *did* love her; but it was only the love of maternal instinct. It is certain she never understood her. Frede was an odd, lonely, homely little thing. Homely? Yes, especially in childhood. Frede was always the plainest of the three girls. Her enemies called her ugly but she was never *that*. There was always too much spirit and character in her face for that. She had beautiful thick glossy black hair, greenish-gray eyes that, like mine, had the Montgomery trick of seeming black at night, owing to the dilation of

A Macdonald group.

Groups at Macdonald College

the pupils, and a fine figure. But her features were irregular and her complexion—her worst point—sallow and freckled. Yet I have seen Frede look positively handsome. As in my own case her appearance depended vastly on the way her hair was arranged. In evening dress, with flushed cheeks and brilliant, mocking eyes, Frede had a certain *beaute du diable*[195] that was

195 "Devil's beauty," a beauty associated with youth, and often associated with a mischevious personality.

Macdonald College

SCHOOL OF HOUSEHOLD SCIENCE

This is to certify that

Frederica Campbell

has completed the Professional Housekeeping course in Household Science having made the record shown.

F. A. Fisher
Head of School.

F. C. Harrison D.Sc.
Principal.

*Macdonald College, Que.,
Canada.*

13th June 1912.

CANDIDATE'S EXAMINATION RECORD

Class *Housekeepers*
Max. Mark ... *1750*
Mark Gained ... *1404*
Rank in Class of *5* ... *1st*
Percentage ... *80%*

SUBJECTS	MAX.	MARKS GAINED
Bacteriology	100	75
Chemistry	150	93.5
Cookery	300	240
Electives :		
Dairy		
Horticulture		
Poultry		
~~English~~ *Biology*	100	75
Home Nursing		
Household Accounts		
~~Household~~ *Institution* Administration	100	78.5
House Furnishings	150	109
House Practice		
Laundry (*Institution*)	100	82
Millinery		
Needlework and Dressmaking	300	260
Physics	100	92
Physiology		
Physical Culture		*Good*
Practical Housekeeping	100	85
Punctuality and Conduct		
Dietetics	100	83
Demonstrating	100	80
Experimental Cooking	100	90

fascinating. I have seen her look exactly as she does in this picture of her, holding a flower, taken at the time of her marriage. But ordinarily the one below, snapped in a Macdonald greenhouse with a friend, is

"The cat who walked by herself."

truer of her. I think it is the truest picture of Frede she ever had taken.

In spite of her plainness, Frede found admirers and lovers wherever she went—her wit, vivacity and magnetic personality assured that.

Frede was clever from childhood. She passed for First Class License at Prince of Wales when only fourteen. If she could have gone on there or soon after to McGill or Dalhousie she would have had a brilliant college career. The thing should have been done. But there never was any ready money; and neither Uncle John nor Aunt Annie seemed to have any ambition for their family beyond giving them enough education to enable them

[Frede and Jen Fraser in greenhouse]

to "earn their own living" in a very humble way; George squandered enough on horses, new buggies and carouses every year to have paid for Frede's college course. It is a maddening thing to think that a girl with Frede's brains and in a home where the inmates ought to have been comparatively wealthy had no chance. She could not save enough to send herself to college out of the wretched salaries paid to teachers then—$180 or $230 a year.

She taught near home at first in Sea View and Irishtown.[196] She was always a marked success as a teacher—later on Dr. Anderson[197] said she was the best teacher in P.E. Island. She had in a marvellous degree the power of drawing out and inspiring her scholars. They invariably worshipped her.

Frede and Dan

When she was nineteen she had her unhappy love affair—the real tragedy of her life. She met and passionately loved my cousin, Will Sutherland,[198] then a young doctor in his first year of practice. It would have been an ideal marriage. They were suited to each other perfectly. As the wife of the successful man Will has become Frede would have been in her element. She would have made him an ideal wife. But it all came to nothing. I don't know that Will cared for Frede. Sometimes I think he did! But he was already engaged to a girl he had met during his medical course. She was a Catholic and a trained nurse. He married her a year or two later, much to his mother's grief.[199] I have met her. She seemed a rather likeable common girl—not to be mentioned in the same breath with Frede. But perhaps Will really loved her and is happy with her. Frede and I never knew—never will know. Frede eventually outgrew her unhappy love for Will. But it marked her for life. She was never quite the same again. Her cousin, Jim Campbell, went with her for several years. Frede was very fond of Jim. She never loved him but she might have married him if he had not been her first cousin and uneducated. When she was out west Ed Willetts was wild about her and never gave up hope of winning her until she was married. When she went back to Macdonald she had another quite serious affair with Dr. Walker,[200] a very clever and interesting man but, as far as I have been able to discover, a very untrustworthy one. He, too, was engaged to another girl of whom he

---

196   Sea View and Irishtown are in the central portion of Prince Edward Island, in Queen's county, north-east of Kensington.

197   Alexander Anderson (1836–1925) was been Principal of Prince of Wales College from 1868 until 1901, when he became Superintendant of Education for Prince Edward Island.

198   A Montgomery cousin who lived in the Park Corner area.

199   In this era, there was still a cultural gap between Protestants and Catholics.

200   John J. Walker had been Physician for the Men's Building at Macdonald College from 1908 to 1914. (There was also a female doctor for women students.)

was tired. Frede, I think, thought he would have married her if it had not been for that. But I doubt it. They eventually quarrelled; later he broke his engagement and married a third girl. It was something of a blow to Frede at the time but later on she realized that she had had a fortunate escape. It had not gone nearly so deeply with her as in the case of Will. She realized that her infatuation for Walker was an unwholesome one and could never have resulted in happiness. She always saw quite clearly with her brain what manner of man he was, in spite of the fascination he exercised over her for a time.

Frede and Miss Ferguson.

Well, it is all over. It has been my privilege to possess for seventeen years a rare and perfect friendship—something that

is very rare in this world, especially between women. Perhaps some day I may be thankful that I had it even at the cost of losing it. Just now the agony seems too great a price to pay. When I went through Frede's things I found in her desk some little pen and ink sketches she had made. They were of no value to anyone

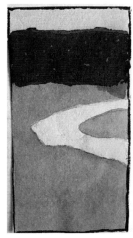

but me so I brought them home with me. I am going to put them here in my journal to keep them safely. To me they are full of Frede.

It has been dreadful to write all this out.

On every page I
cry my heart out.
been a strange
as if it brought
to write thus of
the grave were

have had to stop and
And yet there has
sad comfort in it—
me nearer to Frede
her—as if death and
cheated for a little

while. Oh St. Paul, you never lost anyone vitally dear to you or you would not have shouted so magnificently "Oh death where is thy sting? Oh grave where is thy victory?"[201] The sting is that we lose our comrades out of this life—the victory that we can never see them again on this side of the grave.

Well, I must make an end now and face life without her. I am forty-four. I shall make no new friends—even if there were other Fredes in the world. I have lived one life in those seemingly far-off years before the war. Now there is another to be lived, in a totally new world where I

---

201 1 Corinthians 15:55.

think I shall never feel quite at home. I shall always feel as if I belonged "back there"—back there with Frede and laughter and years of peace.

Saturday, Feb. 8, 1919
Leaskdale, Ont.

Had a dull headache all day. Felt a little better in the evening so compelled myself to write long letters to Aunt Annie and Stella, giving them the details of Frede's going. I have walked the floor since and cried until I am spent. I want to go to bed—and sleep—and forget. But the waking is so bitter.

Sunday, Feb. 9, 1919
Leaskdale, Ont.

I had such a ghastly dream about Frede last night—the first time I have dreamed of her. I was at Macdonald College in a large upper room. Several people were in it—Miss Philp, Miss Zollman, Miss Hill and several strangers. Frede was lying on a couch, alive, but seemingly very ill. I went over to Miss Philp in a far corner and said to her in a whisper "What does this mean? Didn't Frede die?" Miss Philp, with a look of horror on her face pointed to Frede. *"That,"* she said, "has been here ever since you went away. Now you know as much about it as I do." I went back to Frede. I felt none of the horror which seemed to entrance the others. There had been some awful mistake—but Frede was still alive and must be cared for. I gave her a drink of milk and then endeavored to tuck the bedclothes warmly around her. Suddenly I found that I held, not a quilt but a coffin lid and that I was pressing it down on her while she struggled feebly beneath it. I woke in horror and have been haunted by it all day.

Friday, Feb. 14, 1919

Have been very lonely and heartsick all the week. So many letters come which wring my soul. Some of them are from my friends sympathizing—mostly with the old stock platitudes. Some from friends of Frede, ranging from the Atlantic to the Pacific, begging me to write them and tell them about her death. Each and all say the same—they never knew a friend like her and never will again. I must write them—but oh, it is hard!

Saturday, Feb. 15, 1919
The Manse, Leaskdale, Ont.

It would be easier for me if I were living in some place where nobody had ever heard of Frede. She was so well-known here and everywhere I go people ask me about her death. Some betray such a heartless curiosity regarding details and ask tactless questions that are like a stab to me. Today I was up to see the old Oxtoby girls and Lizzie raved about Frede's being cremated—"it was so barbarous."[202] I told her curtly that it was Frede's own wish and dying request. I felt I was foolish to let the strictures of an ignorant and narrow-minded old maid hurt me—but everything hurts me now.

Monday, Feb. 24, 1919
The Manse, Leaskdale, Ont.

Tonight we were out to tea at a near neighbor's, so took the children. When we came out Stuart looked up at the begemmed sky and exclaimed, "Oh, see the beautiful stars!"

---

202   LMM and Ewan had first boarded with the Oxtoby sisters, Lizzie and Mary, when they moved to Leaskdale. In her long retrospective entry of September 24, 1911, LMM described the "two old maids, Mary and Lizzie Oxtoby, who would have delighted Dickens. No pen but his could do them justice. And oh, they are queer—at least it was only their queerness I saw that first night. And I have never liked Lizzie who is a narrow-minded gossip ..."

I think Stuart has inherited my love for natural beauty. I doubt if Chester has—at least, so far he has given little indication of it. I think he "takes after" his father in this respect. The beauty of the world of nature means nothing to Ewan. He seems to be as totally unaware of it as a blind man. I remember that Chester once, when he was about four, exclaimed as we were driving along a very pretty wooded road, "Oh, see the dear little tiny darling road." But never since have I heard him make any reference to pleasure in natural scenery. I hope it will develop later. One who has it not misses so much out of life. I am anxious for both of them to possess it for I consider it one of the greatest of happiness-yielding gifts.

The two boys are amazingly unlike each other. Chester is of a very reserved nature. He is much harder to understand than Stuart, who is frank and open. He gives an impression—and always has—of unyielding *sturdiness*. Stuart gives the impression of beauty and charm. Physically he is a very lovely child, so clear and rosy his skin, so brilliant his large blue eyes. He worships me with a strange intensity. This isn't vanity—or maternal idiocy—or anything but a simple statement of fact. Chester is very fond of me with the average boy's love for his mother. But he is quite as fond of his father. Stuart, on the other hand, seems to care nothing for anyone but me. "My *dear* mother," he exclaims passionately, throwing his arms around me, "*do* you like me?" He is never happy away from me—he cannot bear that a cloud should come between us for a moment. He is rather jealous and does not like even Chester to kiss and hug me. He will push him away, exclaiming, "*You* have a father. This is *my* mother." Why he should not feel that he has a father too, I cannot understand for Ewan has always made quite as much of him as of Chester. But "*my* mother" seems to be the only person in the world for whom, as yet, Master Stuart has any real love. He centres all his affection on me—alas, I fear he has inherited from me something besides my love of beauty—my passionate intensity of feeling and my tendency to concentrate it all on a few objects or persons unspeakably dear to me.

Friday, Feb. 28, 1919
The Manse, Leaskdale, Ont.

I had a wild, distracted, incoherent letter from Ella today. I really fear that woman is going out of her mind. She has always been in the habit of pouring out her woes to me in letters and I have always sympathized with her and tried to give her as good and sensible advice as was in my power, for I have been keenly alive to the bitter things in her lot, as well as the weakness of character, or rather of mentality in her that rendered her incapable of grappling with them. But she is really going too far. I am ready to assist her in real difficulties but I cannot have her dumping a lot of purely imaginary troubles on me like this. I have written in answer rather sharply, simply because I think she needs a bit of a tonic and will pull herself together the better for it. I do not think I have been harsh or impatient but I have told her a few plain truths that may act as a bracer. Her letter spoiled my day and made me unhappy. Frede and I used to share the "problem of Ella" as we shared "the problem of Stell" and now I have no such assistance.

Ella entreated me to "burn" her letter. I did not and shall not do it. I shall keep it to justify my own, should the necessity ever arise. Some bitter experiences in the past have taught me the wisdom of this.

Saturday, March 1, 1919
Leaskdale, Ont.

Today was a raw, surly day with wind and showers—quite lion-like. But we have had a wonderful winter. It has been more like one long spring. There has been no snow and hardly any cold weather. Cars and buggies have run all winter. It is well that it has been mild for we could not get any coal at all and have had to burn wood. It is not suited to a coal furnace and we have been almost smoked out. Nevertheless we are thankful to have any fuel at all.

Tonight I was casting up my financial accounts for the year. I find that I am worth about fifty thousand dollars now, and have earned by my pen since that first wonderful three dollars of 1896 about seventy-five thousand dollars. How the thought of possessing such a sum would have made my eyes stick out twenty-four years ago! It is not a bad showing, considering my initial equipment—my pen and the scanty education I managed to get. If I could only have had a couple of thousand of it twenty-five years ago when I wanted so much to take an Arts Course! But it does not matter much now. I daresay I would not have done any better, if as well, if I had got the B.A. degree I hungered for. "There's a divinity that shapes our ends"[203]—yea, verily. We are only clay in the hands of a mysterious Potter, who will not give us even the sorry comfort of knowing at the time the reason of our anguish.

Monday, March 3, 1919
The Manse, Leaskdale, Ont.

Wrote during the forenoon and then drove to Uxbridge over very bad

---

203   From *Hamlet* 5.2 lines 8–12: "There's a divinity that shapes our ends, / Rough-hew them how we will."

roads and read a paper on Astronomy to the Hypatia Club.[204] Had tea with Mrs. Sharpe[205] and came home in the evening. After nine I read till bed-time—my only time for reading. My book was a novel called "The Blue Germ"[206] and a very fascinating yarn it was, though its ending was weak. I fancy the man who would suddenly make human beings immortal would rather make a mess of things, especially in a world where every custom and law is based on the fact of mortality. After all, wouldn't immortality be rather boring in the long run—say, a few million of years. Even a soul, I think, must get tired and want a rest from "the fever called living,"[207] just the same as the body.

Thursday, Mar. 6, 1919
Leaskdale, Ont.

Ewan and I drove to Vallentyne parsonage this afternoon and had tea with the Methodist minister and wife on that circuit. He is an insufferable Cockney plus English Methodist,[208] but his wife is a nice little person though her face is exactly like a rabbit's. I gave a programme of readings from my books before their Guild—a new departure for me.

There is always something to hurt me now. When the secretary called the roll one name on it was "Fred Campbell." It brought back to me all I had temporarily forgotten. Oh, Frede!

Friday, March 7, 1919
Leaskdale, Ont.

Have been haunted all day by thoughts of Frede. Some days are more like this than others. This house is so full of her. I can't even make a cake without a stab of agony for my recipe book is full of the Macdonald College recipes she gave me. And in every room I see her in some

---

204 Hypatia (c.350–415 CE) was a female philosopher and mathematician who became head of the Platonist school in Alexandria. The concept of a Hypatia Club, a self-improvement organization for women, dates to 1886. The Hypatia Book Club in Uxbridge continues to this day.

205 Mabel Crosby Sharpe was the widow of Colonel Sam Sharpe, who had returned from the war in 1918 suffering from "shell shock." As LMM records in her entry of May 29, 1918, he committed suicide on May 25 (see note 52, page 21).

206 *The Blue Germ* is a 1918 novel by British psychiatrist and author Maurice Nicoll (1884–1953), in which a germ is developed that eradicates both human disease and human desire.

207 From the poem "For Annie" by Edgar Allen Poe (1809–1849): "Thank Heaven! the crisis—/ The danger is past, / And the lingering illness / Is over at last— / And the fever called 'Living' / Is conquered at last."

208 A "Cockney" is a native of East London, UK. At the time the term was often somewhat pejorative; in LMM's usage here it might well be suggestive of a low-bred, working-class background. It is also worth noting that there was some tension between Methodists and Presbyterians.

favorite position—she haunts my dining room table, sitting opposite the mirror and looking into it according to the habit about which Ewan used to tease her. She had the habit, though it was not born of vanity.

Tuesday, Mar. 11, 1919

Another day of bitter loneliness for Frede. Oh, it is so unbearable to think she is nowhere in the world—not even in the old Geddie Memorial graveyard at Spring Brook. There is nothing *there* but a little handful of gray ashes.

Yet am I not wholly desolate. Tonight, Chester, when I was undressing him, suddenly looked gravely up in my face and said "I don't know how I could live without you, mother." It is rare that he shows his affection like that. It comforted me. Life can't be *un*livable as long as one is necessary to somebody's happiness.

I began work on my tenth novel today. It is to be another "Anne" story—and I fervently hope the last—dealing with her sons and daughters during the years of war.[209] That will end *Anne*—and properly. For she belongs to the green, untroubled pastures and still waters of the world before the war.

Wednesday, March 12, 1919
The Manse, Leaskdale

We were out to tea tonight. I found it dreadfully hard to keep up my end of "small talk" and appear bright and interested. I was dull, depressed, and lifeless—as if the "youth of the soul" were gone, as well as the youth of the body. These pastoral visitations are rather dreadful to me just now.

Had a paper from Miss Philp today containing a sketch of Frede. Could I ever have pictured myself reading Frede's "obituary?" How she hated that word—"that fat and unctuous and objectionable word." I remember once, many years ago, telling Frede that I did not believe that I would live to be old. "I have a feeling," I said, "that early middle life will see the end for me. I cannot see myself *old*."

"*I* can," said Frede with a shudder. "I can see myself a wrinkled, shrivelled old woman." But her vision of herself was never to be. She went away in her prime of womanhood. Yet she had *lived* more in her thirty five years than most women do in ninety.

---

209   This novel would be *Rilla of Ingleside*, published by McClelland & Stewart in 1921. The novel is dedicated to the memory of Frederica Campbell MacFarlane.

Shall I live to be old? I have, as aforesaid, never felt that I would. Yet Frede was wrong in her "feeling"—I may be wrong in mine. It doesn't matter, if I can only live long enough to see my boys educated, well-started in life and—if the fates are kind—happy in homes of their own.

Saturday, Mar. 15, 1919
Leaskdale, Ont.

A chilly day—and a dreary one. I had a letter from Ella today—abjectly apologizing for her wild letter of a few weeks ago and evidently very frightened that she has "lost my friendship" because of it. I will reassure her on that point but I think the little alarm has proved salutary. My plain speaking has braced her up temporarily at least—but I fear only temporarily.

Stuart has just pulled my arm. "Oh, mother, look at Daffy licking the *underclothes of his bunky.*"

Daff has been sitting on the floor performing that engaging feat for which his spine is as yet quite limber enough—licking smooth his cream-colored stomach.

Saturday, Mar. 22, 1919
The Manse, Leaskdale

I have been dull and nervous continually. And the event of yesterday will not help me. Our little black mare "Queen" got kicked last night, had her leg broken and had to be shot. We have had her ever since we came here and she seemed like one of the family. She was such a dear little thing, with every good nag quality—speedy, gentle, trusty. Last evening was heart-rending. I cried all the evening. Chester, too, feels very badly. "Mother," he says pitifully, "my heart makes me sick when I think of Queen."

I have never had much

Chester and Queen

to do with horses, although I was brought up on a farm. Grandfather was a man who never let anyone have a horse to drive anywhere if

[Queen]

he could possibly help it. After his death Uncle John[210] coolly took possession of grandmother's two horses, worked and used them, but was so disagreeable about letting me have one to drive that after two experiences of it I never again in all the years I lived there asked him for one. I walked or stayed home. "Doctor," Alec Macneill's horse, and "Miss Flo," Lou Dystant's pretty mare were two nags I was very fond of. I never cared for any other horse until we got Queen. She has been a great pet and this cruel ending has hurt me horribly. What is the use of loving anything? It only means more suffering.

Sunday, Mar. 23, 1919
Leaskdale, Ont.

Alone this afternoon I read all Frede's old letters. I felt impelled to do so. Lately I have been so tortured by the thought that I can never again look forward to getting a letter from Frede. So I got out all her old letters. The reading of them was not painful—on the contrary, it was a comfort and a strange, bitter pleasure. While I read them Frede was *alive*, she existed—she was somewhere in the world. The vivid personality behind those letters *could not* have been blotted out.

Frede and I never corresponded very regularly before she went to Sturgeon. We had never corresponded at all until the fall she went to the Magdalens and the winter blockade soon ended that. During the three years she taught in Stanley I saw her so often that letters were seldom necessary. But after she left there our correspondence was regular. The first letter I have of Frede's was written from "Grindstone Island" in the Magdalens. The last is the little note received from her when I was in Braintree.

Many things in the letters hurt me, of course—especially the little instances of her solicitude for me scattered through them. Writing me

---

210   This is a reference to John Franklin Macneill (1851–1936), a son of LMM's maternal grandparents (Alexander Marquis Macneill and Lucy Woolner Macneill). By all accounts Uncle John was a domineering man.

before Stuart was born she said, in urging me to take things easier and spare myself a little, "I know of no woman who works so hard as you do and takes so little recreation. Missionary meetings and Guilds and visits in Zephyr are *not* recreations!"

Again, in the same strain she wrote, "Maud, I want you to remember that you are Ewan's wife and Chester's mother and my dearly beloved friend and we cannot do without you. I have lived in a great many houses and I have never known a woman who considered her husband's work as you do."

I think what hurt me so keenly in these was the fact that there was no one left on earth to understand or note these things.

In one letter from Sturgeon, written one winter when I was not feeling well she said, "I tremble to think of what the world would be to me without you."

Oh, Frede, you never had to learn it. It is I who must find that out.

Ella writes me that she has called her baby "Frederica MacFarlane." I am glad of this and will remit many things to Ella because of it. I like to think that in days to come there will be another Frede Campbell at old Park Corner. Little Maud is not much older and the two will be companions for each other as Frede and I were before, I hope. Frede has no other namesake. She hated her name—"Frederica Elmanstine." She was called after the German wife of an uncle who had married in a western state. Yet, somehow, the odd striking name suited her odd striking personality. Frede couldn't have been a Lilian or a Jennie or a Mary.

Speaking of namesakes I have six—Christine Maud Agnew, Anita Maud Webb, Maud Dingwell, Maud Beaton, Maud Campbell, and a small Maud Quigley here in Leaskdale. I had a small French namesake also—"Tennis" Doiron down home called one of his numerous progeny after me but the poor little thing died last winter from an epidemic of diptheretic sore throat.[211]

I wish that Frede had left a child—that her life went on in something. Perhaps Cam would have let me have it. Upstairs I have a trunkful of pretty baby clothes. When I looked them over last spring I thought, "Some day Frede may have a baby and I will send her these." But they will never be worn by a little child of Fred's. When we were together at Macdonald after her marriage she said once, speaking of my two boys, "I hope I'll be as lucky as you." But last fall at Park Corner she spoke in a different strain. She said if it were not for Cam's sake she would not care if she never had a child. "It was too much risk—they might

---

211   A bacterial infection often marked by a severely swollen neck.

turn out changelings as George had done etc. etc." I think she felt that she had not the strength, physical or emotional, for motherhood. Her intense life had exhausted both.

Monday, March 24, 1919
The Manse, Leaskdale

"Mother," said Chester solemnly to me today as we drove home from Uxbridge, "who were the father and mother of the first crow?"

I couldn't tell him exactly.

One crow doesn't make a spring; but evidently spring is near. The roads were dreadful and I am tired out. Besides, the "war" news was rather depressing. The Peace conference doesn't seem to get anywhere and Hungary has gone Bolshevik.[212] Where will this Bolshevik madness break out next? The whole world seems infected with it—the sick feverish world with its desperate nightmares and delirium.

Thursday, March 27, 1919

Yesterday I had to go to Lindsay to a "Presbyterial" meeting. Worse still, I had to take a fat stupid old dame of the parish with me. We came back to Uxbridge late in the evening and had a dreadful drive home through the pitch dark night over the worst roads that this part of the country has known for years. Had it not been for Ewan's flashlight I don't think we would ever have got home. It was half past nine when we reached here. Do you think I could then go to my welcome bed? Verily, no, I had to dress up and go to a wedding reception. Ewan said he was too tired to go and I knew the people in question would be offended if one of us didn't go, so I was the victim. I went up with the Cooks and had to sit there until three o'clock in the morning; before old J.C., who is seventy, could tear himself away from the scene of revelry. I talked to scores of the women who were sitting around the room in rows, until I felt like a machine that just talked on without any volition. My head ached, my back ached, my mind and soul ached. I talked hens and eggs and markets and high prices and roads and all the other entrancing subjects for "conversation" which prevail hereabouts—at least, when "the

---

212   The Austro-Hungarian Empire had fought against Allied Powers during World War I. Following armistice on November 11, 1918, Austria-Hungary collapsed as a political entity. The Kingdom of Hungary, as it had been since the Middle Ages, became a Republic. Over the next few years, Hungary saw considerable political turmoil. The Hungarian Democratic Republic, declared in 1918, was short-lived. In March 1919, another revolution created the communist Hungarian Soviet Republic (part of the larger "Bolshevik" or socialist revolution).

minister's wife" is present. I have a suspicion that when she isn't they talk racy and malicious and interesting gossip and enjoy themselves much better. But alas, ministers' wives dare not meddle with gossip else would their tenure in the land be short and troubled.

Friday, Mar. 28, 1919
Leaskdale, Ont.

Tonight there was a concert in the "Little Methodist Church" up north. The promoters thereof had asked me to recite and I had to promise because I have to depend on several of the Methodist youth for music in my Guild Socials—I am President of the Social Guild not only in Leaskdale but also in Zephyr this year! So tonight, after a hard day's work, and in place of a precious hour of reading and an early bed I had to dress up and prance up to "the north church." Ewan had a cold so didn't feel like going out, so I had to walk up in the teeth of a biting north-wester for a mile. The concert was a crude affair ending up with a box social. The young fry enjoyed it all enormously. I sat jammed up in the corner of a pew, where the draught from a window gave me shoulder-ache and tried, more or less successfully, to abstract myself from my surroundings and wander in that old ideal world of fancy and imagination which has always existed for me side by side with the actual business of life. My body sat there, crowded, warm, uncomfortable; my soul was faraway, enjoying brilliant adventures, starry dreams, ideal friends and companions.

Saturday, Mar. 29, 1919
Leaskdale, Ont.

Tonight I enjoyed the treat of a "good read." I read "The Twentieth Plane," the book which has made such a sensation in Toronto.[213] I was much disappointed in it. It was absolute poppycock—utterly unconvincing. And I was so ready to be convinced for since Frede died I would give anything if I could only be convinced that she still exists and that there might be a faint hope of getting some communication from her, even by the medium of the ouija-board.[214] But my intellect absolutely

---

213   *The Twentieth Plane: A Psychic Revelation* (1919) by Albert Durrant Watson argued that there are souls living on an astral plane who are willing to communicate with the living.

214   A Ouija board consists of a flat board printed with letters and numbers; users place their fingers on a pointer that moves about the board, pointing to different letters or numbers. The Ouija board had been a parlor game since the late nineteenth century. During World War I, however, it became popular as a means of communicating with spirits of the dead. LMM records Ouija "séances" several times below. (Nowadays the "ideomotor effect" is used to explain this

refused any credence to the so-called "revelations" of "The Twentieth Plane." As a stunt of the "subjective mind" or whatever strange occult power is responsible, it *is* rather remarkable. But as a proof that communication is possible with the spirits of the dead it is nil. There was a certain enjoyment in the book, though, because it is really exquisitely funny—all the funnier because it is so deadly serious. The "pink twilight" and the "orange sun" of the Twentieth Plane don't appeal to me, and the "bill of fare" which the departed eat is farcical—"synthetic beef tea" and "juice of a rice product!!" Ye gods, if one must eat in the world of spirits I would prefer something more appetizing. How Frede would have howled over that! What fun we could have had if we had read this book together!

In the whole book there was only *one* thing that seemed to me rather inexplicable on any hypothesis other than that of a communication from another world. But I have a long long way to go before I can believe that the spirits of the dead can spell out messages on the Ouija board or that they live in an eternal pink twilight on synthetic beef tea.

But I will say that Dr. Watson is choice in the spook company he keeps. There isn't a single non-famous spirit on his calling list, except his mother. Shakespeare and Plato and Wordsworth and Lincoln etc. etc. etc. jostle each other for a chance to expound through the Ouija board—and all use precisely the same literary style and a very awful one at that. There don't seem to be any grocers or butchers or carpenters on the Twentieth Plane—though one would think that a few butchers at least would be needed to convert the synthetic cows into the synthetic beef out of which the synthetic beef tea is made!

The denizens of the Twentieth Plane never by any chance "go to bed." They invariably "retire to the silken couches of rest."

I think I will retire to my silken couch of rest!

Tuesday, Apr. 1, 1919
The Manse, Leaskdale, Ont.

Yesterday and today have been bitterly cold with high, tempestuous winds. Ewan was away last night, so I took both the boys to bed with me, fearing that the little creatures would be cold in their own bed. We snuggled cosily down; myself in the middle, Chester on the right, Stuart on the left, and listened to the wind howling outside. I love to have them sleep with me—I hate to think of the day when they will be

---

phenomenon: here, unconscious movements of the people controlling the pointer appears to spell out words.)

too big. They are such delicious little souls in bed—so plump and warm and soft and cuddlesome, with their whispered confidences and their sleepy kisses.

Sunday, April 13, 1919
Leaskdale, Ont.

Last Monday I went into Toronto and stayed a week. I had much shopping and business to attend to, and I also wanted a little change for a tonic—something to stimulate me a little. I had "sagged" all the previous week—was depressed and nervous—thought constantly of Frede and cried about her all the time I was alone. This cannot continue if I am to have strength and energy for my work and duties. So I went to town and feel much better for it.

I stayed with Laura[215] and we had pleasant evenings. There is no one like one's own. I invested in a good Victrola while in.[216] I have never had any musical instrument in my home since I was married. When I left Cavendish I gave my old organ to the Sunday School there. I intended to get a piano but there was so much else to get that the first years of our marriage slipped away and I did not get one. Then the war came and while it lasted I did not think I ought to spend any money for unnecessaries. Now that it is over I felt I must have something. But for some time I have grown out of concert with the piano idea. I have no daughters; none of us has any musical gift. Rarely does anyone come to the house who could play well enough on one to give us real pleasure. On the other hand, the Victrola records bring the best music of the world into your home; I think it will be a splendid thing for the children; and as a means of entertaining visitors it is far ahead of a piano nobody could play. So a Victrola I did buy me. The agent was of the usual slick type and was very anxious that I should be made aware of all the good points of the machine. Pulling out a little contraption at the side he said confidentially, "You see, if you want a little *dance music* some Sunday evening and *don't want it to be heard on the street* just pull this out—so."

I had a vision of myself sitting in the Leaskdale manse parlor some Sunday evening, when Ewan was away preaching to the Zephyrites, listening to "dance music" with the soft pedal on!!!

---

215   That is, Laura McIntyre Aylesworth, a cousin from Prince Edward Island, who now lived in Toronto.

216   The Victor Talking Machine Company had introduced a turntable with the amplifying horn tucked away inside a wooden cabinet to resemble a piece of furniture, trademarked as the Victrola.

Just to see if it would be possible to make an agent shrivel I said smilingly, "I am a minister's wife so I don't expect to have *much* occasion for dance music on Sunday evenings."

I shall never be absolutely certain whether he blushed a little or not. But the odds are against it.

I spent Tuesday evening with Marshall Saunders[217] and we talked shop and Page. He was her first publisher also and cheated her without pity and without remorse. The man must simply have an obsession of dishonesty. Most certainly he could make more money by being honest. Wednesday evening I went up to see the MacMurchys and spent quite a pleasant evening talking with Marjorie who was in one of her agreeable moods.[218]

Thursday I attended a luncheon given by Mr. McClelland at the National Club. Several nice and interesting people were present but conversation was annihilated by Mac's announcement that the new Copyright Bill[219]—which has passed the Commons and is in Committee in the Senate and which we have all been considering a most excellent thing—will, if passed in its present form, simply ruin Canadian authors for a time at least, because they will not be able to secure copyright in the U.S. Horrified, we all began questioning and exclaiming and kept it up the entire luncheon. Life is certainly one darned worriment after another.

On Friday evening Laura, Ralph and I had a very interesting seance with the Ouija board. A wave of Ouijaism has flooded Toronto as a result of the publication of *The Twentieth Plane*. Honest dealers in Ouija boards have made small fortunes.

A rather strange thing happened. When we asked if any spirits were present the answer was—as usual—"Yes." "Frede" was present and wanted to speak to "Maud." This is the ordinary thing at seances like this. I was minded not to go on. I did not believe that Frede was there—and yet—I did hunger so for some communication from her. Why not try? So I crushed down a certain distaste and asked Ouija to give me the message.

---

217   Margaret Marshall Saunders (1861–1947), a Canadian author and early advocate for animal rights. Her novel *Beautiful Joe* (1893), written from a dog's point of view, has been likened by some to Anna Sewell's *Black Beauty* (1877), selling over seven million copies .

218   Marjory MacMurchy (1870–1938), whose first name LMM spells as "Marjorie," was one of Canada's most prominent early female journalists.

219   The Berne Convention for the Protection of Literary and Artistic Works had been introduced in 1886 to establish international standards for copyright protection. Canada had joined the Berne Convention in 1886 as a British colony, but the United States had not. It had long been a matter of concern that authors whose works were first published in Canada had virtually no protection under US copyright laws. To address this concern, Canada and the US signed a bilateral agreement that took effect in 1924.

Ouija thereupon began spelling out rapidly. In passing, I may remark on the curious fact that whenever *I* am present at a Ouija seance the Power that moves the pointer always spells *phonetically*. As I have not heard of this occurring when I am not present I must conclude that the reason is in me. But why? I have always detested the idea of phonetic spelling and have virulently opposed the idea all my life.

To resume:—Ouija spelled out,

"Has she cashed the second check?"

I was rather staggered. Certainly it was not the sort of message I had expected from Frede—or whatever power or personality was imitating Frede. Who was "she?" And I had no idea what "the second check" referred to. I asked of Ouija, *"Who is she?"* "Miss B.A. Hill" was the reply. Now, Miss Hill's initials are A.E. I did not know this at the time but I knew one of her initials was "A." Neither Laura nor Ralph knew of the existence of Miss Hill, so this answer *must* have come either from my subjective mind or from some outside intelligence. I said to Laura, "When I see Miss Hill I will ask her what it means." Instantly Ouija began to spell and spelled, "Trust a clear appearance, dear Maud." I then asked, "Shall I write Miss Hill or wait till I see her?"

Answer. "Better visit her. Her talk will convince you that I am right. Trust your uncle F.C."

Laura and Ralph laughed at the "uncle," thinking it nonsense. They did not know that in our family circle we have always called Fred—and she called herself—"Uncle Fred," as a little joke on her masculine nickname. But she *never* called herself, or was called, "Uncle *F.C.*"

I then asked if when I saw Miss Hill, I should ask about that "second check" or wait until she introduced the subject herself.

Answer. "Just let her talk."

I asked. "Where shall I see her?"

Answer. "Tomorrow at Uxbridge. She is on her way now."

Up to this time I had been feeling rather weirdly credulous. But now I knew this was not the truth. I knew perfectly well that Miss Hill would not be in Uxbridge the next day. However, I asked,

"Where shall I see her in Uxbridge?"

Answer. "Willis' drug store. Good-night dear Maud."

That ended Frede's communication. I did not—could not—believe it came from her. Yet it gave me a queer comfort—as if I really had been talking to her. I *knew* Miss Hill would not be in Willis' drug store. Yet when I reached Uxbridge Friday evening I induced Ewan to drive up to Willis' through the vile mud, alleging that I wanted to get some notepaper.

I did *not* find Miss Hill there!

Now *whence* did that message come? Why was part of it a lie? And is there any meaning or truth in that "second check?" Shall I ever know?

We had some other funny communications. The Aylesworth Ouija has, it seems, a great spite at Laura and always says something sarcastic to her. As soon as we stopped asking questions it started in of its own accord.

"Now Laura will dance. Tee-hee!"

Really, one could almost hear the sardonic chuckle. Laura said teasingly, "But, Ouija, I have no music. I can't dance without music." "Oh, Maud will whistle," retorted Ouija.

Again we all asked Ouija to tell us our worst faults. Ouija promptly told Ralph and Laura theirs but all I could elicit was the mysterious remark.

"Ewan knows."

Ralph's father, Dr. Aylesworth, believes that the power behind Ouija is a demonism. He may be right. But evidently some demons have a sense of humor!

Monday, Apr. 16, 1919
The Manse, Leaskdale

We have had five dark, dull, wet, cold, *wicked* days. Again I have been depressed and heartsick. Last night I cried half the night about Fredc and when I fell asleep I had a horrible dream of seeing her drowning and trying vainly to rescue her. The gloom of it has been over me all day.

Today I had a letter from Stell. She was married on April 11 to Lowry Keller who is just home from France. I have been expecting it. She told me about him last fall and a week ago I had a letter from her saying he wanted her to marry him at once. She has been engaged for nearly fifteen years to Irving Howatt.[220] Twice she has been all ready to be

---

220   Irving Howatt had been a neighbour from the Park Corner area. In a longer retrospective entry of January 5, 1917, LMM recalls an interest in Irving Howatt around 1892: "I had a romantic passion for Irving Howatt, who was not in the least interested in me. It went a little deeper than any of my previous ones. I did a great deal of day-dreaming that winter, with Irv as central figure; but I was not in the least unhappy because he was not in love with me ... Irv Howatt was at Dalhousie the winter I was on the *Echo* staff. He began calling to see me and 'seeing me home' from Fort Massey. He was very 'soft'—yes, 'soft' is exactly the word, horrible as it is. If I had wished I could have had him at my feet—have been engaged to him in short order. I did not wish it; he bored me to tears; I loathed his attentions; I could not imagine what in the world had ever attracted me to him ten years before. I snubbed him so pointedly that he took the hint and came near me no more."

married and he put her off on the plea of not yet being able to afford it. He certainly was badly pinched in the real estate slump that followed the outbreak of the war. But I think he was long ago tired of Stell. Her complaints and hysterics would wear out any man. But he behaved like a cad—as poor Frede said on her death bed. It is just as well she has dropped him.

And so "the problem of Stella" is solved. I am thankful. I don't think I could have borne it alone. Her husband will now be responsible for her vagaries and aberrations—*he* will have to endure her complaints, her aches, her agonies, her threats of suicide, her spasms of temper. He is madly in love with her at present. Let us hope it will last. Anyhow, Stella Campbell is now Stella Keller. Escape from old maidenhood, a home, support, companionship may work a change for the better in her neurasthenic outlook. But one thing is certain—she will always find plenty in life to grumble about. And heaven help L.K. if he ever tries to counter her.

Wednesday, April 23, 1919
Leaskdale, Ont.

Last Friday Cameron MacFarlane[221] came for the Easter week-end and stayed until yesterday.

I think I understand now why Frede was taken away. It does not lessen my grief but it has lessened my rebellion. She would never—could never—have been permanently happy with Cameron MacFarlane.

When she married him I feared much more than I hoped. I thought— and think—that I understood how it came about. Cam was home from the front and felt lonely and out of place. The girl he had been engaged to had been very disagreeable about his enlisting in the first place and eventually had broken off her engagement on the score of it. He met Frede frequently; they had

Cameron

---

221   Frede's now-widowed husband; see note 137, page 74–75.

always been friendly; he found her sympathetic and jolly and imagined himself in love with her.

Frede was also lonely and disillusioned. She had begun, as she had confessed to me the preceding Xmas, to experience the bitterness in the lot of a woman whose youth is almost gone—the social neglect, the heart's loneliness, amid the crowd of younger girls. She was caught in some measure, too, by Cam's uniform and the romance of a "war marriage." All these things combined to hurry her into it. Then the excitement and pleasure of being a bride hypnotized her into thinking she was happy.

Before I met Cam some things I had heard others had said of him, some unconscious betrayals by Frede herself made me suspect that there was not much in Cam from an intellectual point of view. When I met Cam that night in Montreal for a brief time—well, I certainly did not dislike him but quite as certainly he did not attract me in any way. Since then we exchanged occasional letters and his letters had as little effect on me as his personality. They never made me feel in the slightest degree acquainted with him. I regretted this. I felt it would be a tragedy if I could not like and feel at home with Frede's husband—if I continued to have that baffling feeling of strangerhood.

Well, Cam has been my guest for five days. He is a puzzling personality. I cannot decide whether he is painfully deep or painfully shallow—but I think the latter. He was in excellent spirits. Once or twice he referred to Frede very flippantly. One time we had been talking of Aunt Annie's sore finger and I told him of the tendency all that family had to blood-poisoning and added, "I remember that Frede had a troublesome wart on her finger two years ago and she burned it off with nitric acid[222] and that gave her blood-poisoning." Cam laughed and said—and in Lily's presence at that—"Served her right for being so vain as to try to burn it off."

I felt as if I had been struck in the face.

There were two or three more such incidents. But I would have found some excuses for Cam in his youth—he really belongs to another generation—if it had not been for his behavior on Monday evening.

The two old Miss Oxtobys were in their own way very fond of Frede, who always went to see them when she came here and was always nice to them. Naturally they wanted to meet her husband. So old Miss Mary toddled down here Monday afternoon. Cam was away with Ewan for a motor drive so Miss Mary asked me to bring him up in the evening.

---

222   Nitric Acid was commonly used for removing warts, corns, moles, and callouses.

When Cam came home I told him. I did not expect he would want to go for enduring boredom is *not* one of his strong points; so I was agreeably surprised when he said heartily "Sure I'll go," and I forgave him many things I had resented.

We went up; we stayed about half an hour; and I never felt so bitterly ashamed and humiliated in my life.

Cam behaved during the whole call, like an absolute *buffoon*—I can call it by no milder term. If he had been a stranger to me I would have said, "That man can't be in his right mind." Every question those poor old souls asked, or every remark they made, he insulted them by a flippant or irrelevant reply. He said things that were in the vilest bad taste. For example—I had been speaking to Miss Mary of Lily Shier, who had been ill, and I remarked to Cam, "She was a maid of mine. I have married off two of my maids from the manse."

"Good!" said Cam. "I wonder what kind of luck you would have if you tried your hand on me." This from a man whose bride had died three months ago!

I tried to get him away but could not. He was enjoying himself too much for that. When I hinted that it was late he laughed loudly and said, "Oh, yes, I suppose these *young ladies* want to go to bed. That's the advantage of being single—you can go to bed when you please."

The "young ladies," who are well over sixty, must have liked this.

Finally I did get him up—then he suddenly pranced around to the corner where Lizzie O. was sitting, got behind her, and bent over her. I swear I thought he was going to kiss her and I believe she thought so too for she jerked to one side like a flash. Cam, however, only whispered something to her—what it was I'm sure she doesn't know yet for she was too much upset by his caper to take it in. Then he said, with another guffaw,

"But then you know I'm just as happy as if I were sane."

I got him out then.

"Say, didn't I shock them!" he chuckled, as we went down the walk.

I was literally cold with rage. I wanted to say with biting sarcasm,

"Oh yes, you shocked them—and me—if that is anything to be proud of. You have repeatedly insulted two old women who were friends of your wife, you have disgraced Frede's memory, you have shamed and humiliated me before the members of my husband's church and you have made an unforgettable ass of yourself. Chuckle—do! It's well worth it."

But I was not going to quarrel with Frede's husband. I said nothing. I walked down the road beside him tense and silent. But I made a resolution that I would never ask him to my house again; and I knew that death had been a friend to Frede—had undone the mistake of her marriage to this crude, conceited, ill-bred boy who was not and never could be "of the race of Joseph." Frede, my darling, I would rather you were dead than unhappy even though it means my lifelong loneliness.

Cam left yesterday. I feel that I do not want to see him again. Somehow I resent his having any share in Frede when he was so unworthy of her.

When Cam wrote me after Frede's death he said that in one of her recent letters to him she had said she "wished she were dead." Why, he did not know—she was to tell him when she saw him. On the day before her death she said to me, "Maud, I should never have married Cam when he urged me to." I thought then that it was mere delirium—but now, I do not know. I think she had realized her mistake and had begun to dread the life before her. But she has gone—my brave, gay, gallant girl—and her going sits very lightly on her bridegroom.

Sunday, May 4, 1919
The Manse, Leaskdale

Today was cold and rainy, as the spring has been almost constantly so far. I dread these Sundays when I am alone. I get so bitterly lonely, now that Frede is not" next door" at Macdonald. This afternoon I cried bitterly. Oh, Frede, Frede!

Friday, May 9, 1919

A typical day. Worked hard all day, carrying the books out of the library preparatory to cleaning it. Then in the evening when I was horribly tired and should have gone to bed I had to motor to Zephyr instead and give a programme for the Social Guild. Didn't get home until nearly one and am now too tired to sleep.

It didn't rain today for a wonder. It *has* rained almost every day this spring and been bitterly cold also. It is so difficult to get housecleaning done. We have been struggling with it for three weeks and are only at the library now. I seem to have so little strength mental or physical to grapple with it this spring. I waken in the morning tireder than when I went to bed. I seem to have only one real wish—to lie down somewhere and sleep for a month. Perhaps I would "catch up" then.

Chester began to go to school last Monday. In a way I hated it—it seemed that I was giving him up to the world—as if he were no longer mine. He goes to the school along the side-road. It is too far away for

A Road to School

C's school

Off to School

him to come home to dinner, which I much regret. It is also a very small school which is another drawback—and the teacher is a sleepy mortal named Miss Brent[223]—which is a third. He seems to like it very well, so far as we can find out—for Chester, like his father, never tells anybody anything of his own accord!

Sunday, May 11, 1919
Leaskdale, Ont.

Another rainy, gloomy, dull Sunday. I did not feel well enough to go out today and yet it was a bad thing to be here alone all day. I felt nervous and depressed. Last night, too, I heard a horrible thing.

Miss Fergusson,[224] the nurse I had when Chester was born, was married soon after to a Mr. Jenkins of Montreal. Last winter she died of flu,[225] leaving three little children. This has haunted me all day. What fun she and Frede had here together that happy summer! And now they are both dead!

Miss Ferguson

Wednesday, May 21, 1919
The Manse, Leaskdale

This afternoon Lily and I were busy housecleaning when Chester suddenly arrived home from school. I almost fainted at sight of him. I thought his eye was out. He was a dreadful sight. Blood was running

---

223 Irene Brent taught at the Leaskdale school for two years, followed by Elva MacKay.

224 Isabella W. Fergusson had been trained as a nurse at the Toronto General Hospital. She had attended the birth of LMM's first son, Chester, in 1912.

225 That is, the influenza pandemic of 1918. For more information, see note 132, page 68.

down over his face from two cuts above the eye. The flesh was black and swollen; the eye was closed and—most terrifying thing of all—blood was oozing out between the lids. What had happened to the child's eye inside?

The boys had been playing down at the brook at noon recess and Chester had been struck, accidentally by a stick, or rather an old, dried, many-pointed root flung by a chum. I got the poor frightened child to bed and sponged off the blood. But those drops continued to ooze out between the lids and after supper we sent for the doctor.

Dr. Shier arrived at dusk with one of his characteristically reassuring remarks!

"I hope the eyeball isn't cut."

He said it with such dark significance that I, upset and nervous enough already, felt as if he must think the eyeball *was* injured. He examined Chester and said he must give him a little chloroform in order to be able to open the eye.[226] Chester has never had any chloroform and I could not know how it might affect him. Reason told me that he would probably be all right; but that did not prevent me from going to pieces nervously. I made Ewan go up with Shier for the examination. Once I could have gone—but since the flu I have *no* nerve. I *could* not go. Instead, I shut myself up in the parlor and sat right down on the middle of the rug with clenched teeth and hands to wait.

"Oh, if Frede were only with me!" I moaned.

Then I thought, "Perhaps she is. If human personality survives death I *know* that Frede would come to me in any crisis. But I want to *know* it."

Daff had come in and was sitting gravely over by the door. I recalled reading that animals are aware of presences which human beings cannot sense. Perhaps it was also true that those presences could influence animals. If Frede were with me could she make Daff do something which would prove her presence to me? I thought for a moment. I would ask for some unlikely thing—something that Daffy would never think of doing normally.

Daffy

"Frede," I whispered pleadingly, "if you are here *make Daff come over to me and kiss me.*"

Daff *never* offers any caresses or seeks

---

226   Chloroform was used as an anaesthetic in the late nineteenth and early twentieth centuries, although there were questions about its safety.

or enjoys petting. Yet it is the actual truth that hardly had I spoken when Daff walked gravely across the floor to me, lifted his forepaws and placed them on my shoulders, and touched my cheek with his mouth. Moreover, he did it twice.

Written out thus, the thing looks ridiculous. Why do such experiences always seem ridiculous when written or told? Perhaps because they should *not* be written or told—only lived. There was nothing that seemed ridiculous at the time. Instead, I felt sure that Frede *was* there with me and had made our old furry comrade the medium of her message. The conviction brought comfort and strength and calmness.

Presently Dr. Shier came down and said Chester had come out of the ether and he had found that the skin of the eyeball was cut but did not think there was any further damage. He could not be sure for a few days, however. So there is no sleep for me tonight I fear.

Friday, May 23, 1919
The Manse, Leaskdale

After two days of intense worry we are assured that Chester's eye is not seriously hurt and that the skin of the ball will heal up without scar or disfigurement. We finished housecleaning today and I am very thankful. We have been at it a month. It was doubly hard this year because of cold and wet, and delays and confusions caused by paper-hanging.

Next week will be a hard one, for the Forward Movement[227] meetings will be on and I shall have a houseful of guests all the time. Lily and I will have to spend our days cooking and dishwashing; but once it is over I hope I shall have a quiet summer of rest. I need rest so badly after the grief and worry of last winter and the hard physical grind of the spring. I really feel tired all the time. And these last few days of worry over Chester and broken rest while waiting on him at night have about used up all the little strength I had left.

I had a letter today from a Miss Gilchrist of England who turns out to be the "Quincunx" who wrote of wallpapers in the *Westminster Gazette* last year.[228] After all, her sentence, "wallpapers which went in and out according as you looked at them with the right kind of eyes," did not mean what I thought it meant. She meant merely that the pattern changed from convex to concave as you looked at it from one angle or another—a very different thing from my "seeing wallpapers." Well, I'm

---

227   The Forward Movement was a revival program involving evangelism, missionary work, and social concern, and would be formally accepted by the General Assembly of Canada in June 1919.

228   See LMM's entry of September 5, 1918.

a wee bit disappointed. I thought I had at last discovered a "kindred spirit" who would not think I was crazy, mendacious, or possessed of the devil when I talked of being able to see wallpapers in miniature.

Saturday, May 24, 1919
The Manse, Leaskdale, Ont.

"Queen's weather" for the 24th. Today was delightful—so bright and warm. Lily took a holiday and went to town but my holiday consisted in working hard from blushing morn to dewy eve—and after—finishing up the little left-overs of housecleaning before the F.M. meetings began. I managed to do it and then got supper for Dr. Drummond of Hamilton,[229] who came tonight and is to preach tomorrow. He is a very nice and intellectual person but I am too tired to enjoy his company. I envy the fairy tale princess her hundred year nap. How glad I shall be when this coming week is over and I can have a little leisure and rest.

September 1, 1919
The Manse, Leaskdale, Ont.

"A summer of leisure and rest!" That was what I hoped for and looked forward to when I wrote on May 24th. It has a very ironic sound now in view of the hideous summer I have passed through—the most dreadful summer I ever lived in my life—the horrible climax to a horrible year of illness and grief and worry. 1919 has been a hellish year. I am so hopelessly tired—too tired ever to get rested again. I've got too far behind with rest—I can never catch up. At least that is how I feel just now.

Well, to tell the tale. On the Sunday after my last entry all went well. We motored to Zephyr with Dr. Drummond and after the service took him to Uxbridge. Ewan seemed perfectly well and in excellent spirits. On the preceding Friday he mentioned that his "headache and weakness was coming back." He was referring to the winter he spent in Glasgow, when he had suffered continually from headache, and insomnia. At the time I knew of the headaches and insomnia but I did not know of the "weakness." When he came home in the spring he seemed perfectly well and assured me that his trouble was merely the result of not "being acclimated." I thought this a peculiar thing but as he was quite well again I ceased to worry, having no realization of what his malady really was.

---

229   The Reverend Dr. Daniel Robert Drummond (1868–1931) was a moderate on the topic of Church union, arguing in favour of a federation rather than a union.

When he spoke that Friday of his headaches returning I felt anxious but it seemed to pass away very quickly and all Sunday and Monday he seemed perfectly well. Monday morning he took Dr. Drummond away and brought back Mr. Rae of Unionville[230] and Mrs. Dodds of Sonya who were to be the speakers that night. In the evening Mr. Rae spoke here while Ewan took Mrs. Dodds to Zephyr. They returned at 10.30. I made tea for them and we sat up until nearly one talking. I never saw Ewan seem better. He was as jolly as any of us. That night, as Mr. Rae had the spare room I took Mrs. Dodds in with me and Ewan slept with Chester—or rather, went to bed with him for, as he told us at the breakfast table, he had not been able to sleep at all. This in Ewan was surprising for he generally sleeps like a log. What was still more unusual and which should have alarmed me if I had realized the full significance of it, he had risen in the night, dressed, and gone for a long walk up the north road. I felt vaguely uneasy over this extraordinary proceeding but Ewan seemed as well as usual all day and quite cheerful and jolly. He went with Mr. Rae to Zephyr at night and slept well afterwards. Nevertheless, he seemed dull at breakfast and spoke of a headache.

[Ewan, Chester, Stuart, Mr. and Mrs. Dodds]

From that out the rest of the week seemed like a dreadful nightmare to me. We had company right along and I had to conceal my anxiety and plan and manage and laugh and talk as if nothing were the matter. Wednesday forenoon we motored to Uxbridge. Ewan went to the manse while I did some shopping. It was warm and I was very tired. When I went down to the manse I found Ewan complaining of headache again. Somehow, there was something about him that worried me—I could not tell what it was. We brought Revs. Smith and Lawrence, the speakers of the evening, home with us, also old Mrs. Collins,

230 Below LMM mentions local ministers and other speakers involved in the Forward Movement. Rev. J.W. Rae, for example, was minister at Newcastle, 8 km (5 miles) south-east of Leaskdale.

who is "Mrs. Nickleby"[231] in the flesh. She is hard to endure at any time but when one is tired and possessed by worry she is intolerable. She talked incessantly and inconsequently, detailing to me all the items of her recently deceased husband's illness and death, even to the kind of underclothes she put on him to "lay him out." I talked to her with one corner of my mind and wrestled with my dread in the other corners. Ewan was very dull at supper time. He took Mr. Smith to Zephyr and when they came back he sat dejectedly in his chair, looking dully before him, taking no part in the conversation at all. By this time I was feeling terribly alarmed and anxious although as yet no realization of the nature of his malady had dawned on me. Ewan did not sleep that night but got up and went out walking again. Smith and Lawrence departed and Mr. Lord, his son Lieut. Lord, and Mr. Mutch came. Ewan sat among us in silence and gloom. He got someone else to motor Mr. Mutch to Zephyr and remained at home lying in the hammock. He would not or could not talk and my pleadings to go and consult a doctor were in vain—no doctor could do him any good, he declared moodily. He alternated between fits of dull apathy and spells of restless walking.

Friday night Mr. Brydon was our guest. When Ewan took him to Uxbridge in the morning I insisted on his going to Dr. Shier. Dr. Shier told him he had a "nervous breakdown" and must go away for a change. Ewan said he would not do this. Dr. McKay[232] came that night. I made Ewan take a veronal tablet. This made him sleep but he was no better next day. In the evening we motored Dr. McKay to Wick where he was to speak. On the way back the night was beautiful and moonlight. I was too tired and worried to talk and sat silent in my corner. As we neared home Dr. McKay said, "What a pleasant, restful drive this has been!" I smiled bitterly. It had been for me an hour of the most horrible unrest and worry. Dr. McKay and others supposed Ewan's trouble to be physical—a little breakdown which a short rest would put right. I could not believe it. Ewan had been perfectly well right up to that week and he certainly had not been working hard all winter. Ewan is not the type of man who overworks—he "takes things easy" in all respects.

But I was determined to find out what was wrong. I pleaded with Ewan until he at last confessed the truth. He said he was possessed by a horrible dread that he was *eternally lost*—that there was no hope

---

231   A reference to Dickens' *The Life and Adventures of Nicholas Nickleby* (1839). Mrs Catherine Nickleby brings much comic relief to the novel for her stupidity and poor grasp of reality.
232   The Reverend Dr R.P. MacKay, D.D. (1847–1929), later a leader in the Church Union Movement.

for him in the next life. This dread haunted him night and day and he could not banish it.

Never shall I forget my despair when I discovered this. I had always known it as one of the symptoms—*the* symptom—of religious melancholia.[233] Unutterable horror seemed literally to engulf me. Was my husband going out of his mind? He had every symptom given in the encyclopedia on that type of insanity. It was one of the things I had always had the most deeply rooted horror of. Every trouble I had had in my life seemed as nothing beside this. I do not know how I lived through the days that followed.

I made other discoveries. This was not Ewan's first attack. When he had gone to P.W. College[234] at about eighteen he had had a slight attack. Six or seven years later at Dalhousie college he had suffered from it for two years—though in a much milder form than this. Then that winter in Glasgow he had had a very bad recurrence—and now this, the worst of all.

I was horror-stricken. I had married, all unknowingly, a man who was subject to recurrent constitutional melancholia, and I had brought children into the world who might inherit the taint. It was a hideous thought. There *was* a ray of light, though, in the fact that he had recovered from the former attacks—he might recover from this one, too.

Dr. McKay went away the next morning and I was thankful. The nightmare of guests was over and I could wrestle with my terrible problems. I did not know *what* to do. Never was I in such a terrible position. That day was fearfully hot. I tried to put in a little bit of garden for Ewan declared he could not work and would not try. That night I felt sick with despair. Ewan lay in the hammock, his eyes staring before him, his mind possessed by that horrible, unnatural idea. I sat by myself in the dusk in the corner of the veranda and cried bitterly for Frede. If she were only alive! She was the only human being to whom I could have gone with my trouble and my fear. I was determined no one else should know of it if it were possible. For Ewan's own sake and the childrens' the impression must not get abroad that his mind was unbalanced. It would ruin his prospects. I talked to the people of his headaches and insomnia but I fenced the world from him as much as I could lest the other deadly thing should be suspected.

---

233   Nowadays Ewan Macdonald's "malady" would likely be described as a major affective mood disturbance, resulting in depression, loss of normal involvement, and a sense of guilt. "Religious melancholia" is a mental illness characterized by extreme guilt about religious matters or over-concern about one's individual guilt. In the Presbyterian faith, it manifests itself as an obsession with predestination—that is, with not being one of God's "elect" souls destined for heaven.

234   Prince of Wales College.

Ewan slept one night out of three naturally. The other two he did not sleep unless he took veronal. I induced him by tearful pleading to give up going out for walks before daybreak. I knew if he were thus seen wandering around people would begin to wonder and suspect. As for me, I hardly slept at all. A plague of heat and mosquitoes was also upon us. Some days Ewan would seem a little better and be able to interest himself a little in reading. But for the most part he sat or lay in gloomy silence. He was so utterly unlike himself that he seemed to me like a stranger. He never took the slightest notice of the children and seemed to have absolutely no interest in them or anything. I suppose in a way this was reasonable enough. Granted that you believed completely—and *felt*—that you were doomed to hell fire for all eternity—that hideous old mediaeval superstition which Ewan normally believed in no more than I did—you wouldn't feel much interest in anything else.

Hour after hour in the long nights I would get up—I was sleeping with Stuart in the spare room—and tiptoe down the long hall to the door of our room, listening with suppressed breath to find if Ewan were asleep. If he was I went back and dozed a little myself. If not then I slept not. Oh, what nights of horror those were when my dread was too great even to find relief in tears. And at dawn the birds would sing madly and joyfully outside and I would ask myself in dreary incredulity if it could be the same world it had been two weeks before this awful thing swooped down—when we had been so busy and eager and—by comparison at least—so happy. Was it not some hideous dream? Oh, if I could only waken!

Some days or nights stand out in my memory of this time unique in horror. One was, the first Sunday night after the Forward Movement meetings, when Mr. Fraser of Fenelon Falls supplied for us. Ewan seemed a little better in the forenoon but would not go to Zephyr with Mr. Fraser. He got Alex Leask to take him. After dinner one of the most dreadful thunderstorms I have ever seen came up. I was almost terrified by it. Ewan took no notice of it or me but walked the floor wrapped in his own morbid thoughts. The rain came down in a sort of cloud-burst—a perfect river rushed down the hill and swept our garden out of existence in a twinkling—the garden I had worked so hard to get in, doing all the digging and preparing myself. I was so tired—so worn out—this seemed the last straw. I burst into tears and sobs. Ewan looked at me unsympathetically and said if that was all the matter I had very little to cry about.

The very hardest part of my trial was this same lack of sympathy on Ewan's part. My sufferings mattered nothing to him. His attitude was

"You do not believe that I am to be damned or that you are so I do not see why you should worry." I was absolutely alone in my despair. I was never in all my life so wretchedly unhappy as I was in those awful days when I went about trying to work and plan and smile with that fear that was not to be mentioned hanging over me.

Ewan went to bed that night at nine. I sat on the veranda until 10.30 and talked to old Mr. Fraser. It was a beautiful silvery moonlit night— such a contrast to my inner misery.

At the end of a fortnight Ewan was no better and I decided that something must be done. I could not get him to go to Toronto and consult a specialist. "I don't want a doctor—I want a minister" was the absurd reply he would always make when I urged it. I thought it over and decided that he must go away for a change. I could not go with him. The children must be looked after and besides Stella was coming in a few days on her way to the Island so I could not leave. But if he went to Flora's he would be looked after and I could write her to get the opinion of a nerve specialist. Ewan was unwilling to go—it involved an effort which he declared he was too weak to make. The delusion of weakness possessed his mind equally with the other—or rather, as the specialist later told me—was the result of it. The subconscious mind produced the belief in weakness to secure him against any effort that would necessitate his dragging his attention from the hideous subject he was worrying over. But I was resolute. I made all the arrangements and literally forced him to go.

The evening before he went we motored down to Uxbridge for some household supplies. Ewan seemed a shade better when we got there and after our errands were done he suggested some ice cream. We went into an ice cream parlor. It was crowded with gay laughing people. We sat down at a table. Ewan stared fixedly before him all the time we were there. I could not swallow the ice cream. It choked me. I got up, got him out and we started for home. It was a hideous drive through that

Uxbridge

beautiful blossomy spring twilight. Ewan would not talk and I could not. I crouched in the car with only one wish in my mind—if I could only spring out of the car and run away across the fields—run till I dropped—anywhere—anywhere—if I could only escape the fate that seemed to be drawing nearer—nearer all the time like a menacing shadow. When we got home I flew upstairs, shut myself in my room and broke into crying that was almost hysterical. "I *can't* bear it—I *can't*" I moaned, over and over again. Presently Ewan came up. He seemed to feel for me a little. "Oh Ewan, come back to me—come back to me," I sobbed. "I will—yes, I will," he answered agitatedly. "Don't cry, dear—I'll come back." But ten minutes later he was again sunk in gloomy reverie, lost to all realization for any external matter.

The next morning we went to Toronto. From the time we left Ewan never spoke unless I spoke to him. It was a hard journey. In the Union Station Waiting room we found Stella, just arrived from Los Angeles.[235] I may say that I paid her way from California to P.E.I. and back, in order to give Aunt Annie a little comfort and cheer. But there is nobody to give me any of that, now that Frede is gone.

I had not seen Stell for nearly six years. Before Ewan's illness I had been looking forward with pleasure to her visit. Now I wished her a thousand miles away. She had, I knew, never liked Ewan. She *must not* suspect what the real trouble was. I poured a tale into her ears of Ewan's headaches and insomnia—all perfectly true—but said nothing of his mental state except that he was in low spirits over his breakdown.

Stell and I left for home on the afternoon train. Ewan was to leave for Boston on the night train. He seemed a little brighter when he bade us good-bye but I never had a heavier heart than when he got off the train. I clung to the hope that the change might arrest the progress of his malady and turn him back to normality. But the hope was a very faint one and I was sick at soul.

Nevertheless, the ensuing ten days were easier in many ways than the preceding fortnight had been. I was not constantly tortured by the sight of Ewan sitting in gloomy, unheeding reverie. I did not have him on my mind like an incubus all the time. And at night in spite of my anxiety I slept well—something I sadly needed to do—and did not spend the night lying miserably listening for tip-toeing from room to room like an uneasy ghost. Then Stella helped considerably, for between her frequent spasms of growling over the heat and mosquitoes—which were certainly pretty bad—and her aches and pains—which

---

235   Stella had moved to Los Angeles, California, with her new husband Lowry Keller.

were non-existent except in her own hypochondriac imagination—she could be and was as jolly and full of fun as of yore. Then, too, it was a pleasure, spiced with sadness, to be again with someone with whom I could talk over old times, old friends, old foes.

As for Stella's prospects in life I have some painful doubts. Her husband seems to be a good fellow; but she does not love him and it is easy to see that she is far from contented with affairs as they are. Given her temper, tyranny, selfishness, and delusions of illness I foresee rocks ahead for their matrimonialship.

We sat up most of the first night thrashing out various family problems and talking over all that had happened in the six years since we parted last. I had a fair sleep afterwards with poor little Stuart cuddled close to me. The next day I was busy all day preparing for the social Guild which was held here at the manse. The guests sat on the moonlight lawn and I moved the victrola to the front door and gave a victrola programme. I had to dress and smile and chat as if I had the lightest heart in the world. Had Ewan's malady been some physical illness I could have shown my anxiety. But as it was I must hide it. When I had put a record on I would slip out to the darkened kitchen and walk the floor until it was time to go back, praying desperately. Where was Ewan and how was he? He should be in Braintree. How had he stood the journey? What would the news be in his first letter? These questions tortured me. But I smiled gallantly—have I not had good training in so smiling most of my life?—while the fox gnawed.

The worst hours of that week were when I went down to the office to get the mail. It was worse than the days when I waited for the war news. I don't know which I dreaded most—to get a letter from Ewan or not to get it. I had hoped that on Saturday I might get a card written from Montreal but none came and this made me feel that he must have been very miserable when he arrived there. After I went to bed, having smiled all the evening lest Stell should suspect—I *would* not have *her* think that my husband was going insane—I had a breakdown and a bitter cry. The next day—Sunday—was very hard. It was so terribly and unseasonably hot. I was unhappy—dispirited in mind and not too well in body. On Monday a note came from Ewan. It was not very satisfactory and did little to disperse my worry and dread. It said briefly that he had arrived in Braintree the night before "much exhausted" but felt a little better that morning. I afterwards discovered that he had reached Flora's almost in a state of collapse, after a dreadful journey of mental suffering—which, no matter how irrational the cause, must have been terrible. It must be more awful than we can realize to be haunted by the dread that you are doomed to an eternity of torment. In his normal state of mind Ewan does not believe any more than I do in that blasphemous old idea of a "hell of fire and brimstone." But he was not normal and all the gloomy teachings he had listened to in his childhood from ministers of the old school had taken complete possession of his thoughts. I have heard him mention more than once the impression made on him long ago by a sermon one of those ministers preached on "hell." I believe that sermon is responsible for his delusion—as such sermons have been responsible for many tortured hearts and souls.[236]

I had no letter again until Wednesday when another brief dull note came. He said merely that he had been to see a specialist and nothing else. I spent the rest of the day in agony of mind and in a miserable physical condition with a burning, tingling sensation all over my body—the protest, I suppose, of tortured nerves.

The next day Ewan's note said he felt a little better and had slept well the preceding night. This helped me through the day. Again on Saturday another note came saying that he felt "a little better." How I grew to hate that phrase! He was always "a little better"—but never really any better. He said he would have to stay five weeks at least.

On the following Monday—June 23rd—I went to Toronto with Stella. She left on the night train to Montreal and I saw her off with a sense of relief. Then I went to the Carls-Rite[237] and spent a poor night, half sleepless and tormented by bad dreams of Ewan. One of them was very awful—he was looking at me through a barred window and weeping—the horror of it wakened me and I slept no more.

I came out on the 8 o'clock train and came up with the mailman. I found two letters from Ewan. I opened the one which had come the day before and it held good news. Ewan wrote that he felt better than any day yet. Cheered and encouraged I opened the other. He said he was very miserable—the specialist was doing him no good—he was going to try an osteopath—the whole brief, disconnected epistle reflected the gloom and turmoil of his distracted mind. I threw myself on the bed and cried bitterly. But I could not indulge in the relief of tears long. There was work to do. I changed my dress and went downstairs to get a bite of dinner.

Just as I reached the foot of the stairs the telephone bell rang. I went to take the message. My heart stood still with a horrible fore-knowledge when I heard that there was a telegram for me. It was from Flora and said, "Ewan is no better. Can you come at once?"

---

236 Most likely Ewan's mood disturbance was the result of genetic factors rather than a specific event.

237 The Carls-Rite, built as the Grand Union Hotel on Front Street, is no longer standing.

I hung up the receiver. Now that the blow had fallen I was calm and collected. I thought quickly and clearly. I *must* go. I must leave those two poor little boys in Lily's charge and go. She was a good girl as girls go—but to leave my children alone with her! Still, there was nothing else to do. Flora would not have sent for me unless the need was urgent. My own belief was that Ewan had finally gone completely insane. But I did not think about *this* then—it must be considered later. The first question was—how soon can I get to Boston? If I went on the evening train from Uxbridge I would catch the second train to Montreal. But I knew that that train very often missed connection with the Boston train leaving Montreal in the morning. Then I would have to wait in Montreal all day and could not get to Braintree until Thursday morning. But if I could catch the two o'clock train from Uxbridge I could connect with the first Montreal train and get to Boston by Wednesday night. It was a quarter past one. Could I catch that train? I could and did.

I had no money. I 'phoned the Dominion Bank Manager to have a hundred ready for me. I asked Mr. Warner to motor me to Uxbridge. I flew upstairs. In fifteen minutes I was ready, and Lily had tossed a few necessities into my grip. We left at twenty-five to two and reached Uxbridge in twenty minutes. I did not think much as we tore down the Seventh at a breakneck pace in that old Ford. My mind was concentrated on catching that train—later on thought would come. I caught the train. All the way to Toronto I was calm and did not suffer much. Feeling seemed numbed or held in leash by the need for prompt action. We got in at four. I had to wait until 7.20. I sat in the crowded station and wondered if anyone else in the passing throngs faced just what I did. I had eaten nothing since my 7 o'clock breakfast. I went into the lunch room and got a sandwich and a cup of tea. But I could not swallow one morsel of the sandwich. It stuck in my throat. I gulped down some of the tea. It was a rank black brew and scalding hot but it gave me a little needed stimulation. At last, after what seemed years of interminable waiting I found myself gliding out of the dingy old Union Station on the Montreal train just 24 hours after I had seen Stella off on it.

Then my composure failed me for a time and I broke down and cried bitterly. This relieved me somewhat and when I regained self-control I got the porter to make up my berth. It was an upper one—I could get nothing else on such short notice and indeed was lucky to get that. It was the second time in my life that I had to sleep in an upper berth. The first time was twenty-nine years ago when I went out west with Grandfather Montgomery. I spent my first night on a train in an upper berth—and slept as little that night as this. I dozed brokenly for a couple of hours and then lay there till daylight. When morning came I found the train was an hour late and I was racked with anxiety lest I miss the Boston train after all. But I did not—fortunately, for I *could not* have endured waiting all day in Montreal. I had however only fifteen minutes to get my ticket and have my grip checked—no time to get even a cup of tea. It mattered little—I was not hungry; but when the Boston train pulled out I realized that I was weak from lack of food. I had eaten nothing since my breakfast at the Carls-Rite the preceding morning.

That day was beyond any comparison the longest and most horrible I have ever spent in my life. The train seemed to crawl. I tried to think—to plan—but it was impossible. My mind refused to work. If Ewan had gone out of his mind completely *what was I to do*? I had *no one* in the world to go to for help—neither father nor mother nor sister nor brother. If this horrible thing had happened—and I fully believed it had—the only thing to be done was to put Ewan in some good sanitarium and go back to the children. Our home would have to be broken up and we must go—where? I asked myself a hundred questions—I could not answer them. A hundred sickening possibilities haunted my distracted thoughts. I could not read. I bought a magazine and forced myself to look at it but the lines made no sense. At twelve I went to lunch and forced a few mouthfuls down. Somehow it seemed to me that my distracted state of mind must be reflected in my personal appearance and I shrank from the sight of the other passengers in the car, even though I knew the feeling to be absurd.

At one station, I remember, a bride and groom got on—just newly married, as was evident from the rice on their hats. They sat before me. She was very young and very pretty. They were both insultingly happy. My thoughts went back to my own wedding day nearly eight years ago, and the thing that flashed first into memory was something that had happened as we drove to the station. Not long after we left Park Corner a *hearse* came out from a sideroad and drove on ahead of us, on its way back to Kensington from some funeral. That ill-omened thing headed our procession all the way to the station. We never got quite close enough to pass it. I was not superstitious and we all laughed at the "bad omen." It came back to me now and haunted my mind like a black raven. As for the gay little bride and groom I owed them no ill will nor felt any but I hated the sight of them—they seemed so to emphasize the bitter contrast between my feelings and theirs.

Well, even to those who were stretched on the rack or bound to the stake came an end of torture. At eight I reached the North Station at

Boston, caught a street car and got across to the South Station, to find that the Braintree train had just left and I must wait until 9.15 for the next one. I sat down in the waiting room, passed and repassed by throngs, not one of whom I knew. I was sick, tired, racked with anxiety. But that hour passed, too. At ten I got to Braintree, found a cab, and drove to the little bungalow on the hill. I steeled myself for the worst—in a few minutes I would know all. As we drove

The bungalow on the hill.

up to the door a light flashed up in the porch where they had been sitting in the twilight and I saw Ewan coming down the steps with a smile!

The reaction from the horrible dread from which I had suffered ever since getting that telegram left me so weak and trembling that I could hardly stand. I clung to him, asking tremulously, "Ewan, how are you?"

"I have felt better today than I have for four weeks," he replied.

For the time being I was almost light-hearted. The relief at finding him sane and better was so indescribable that I will not try to describe it. I got in, greeted Flora and Christy Viles—who was there—got washed and dusted and sat down to supper. I was hungry now and ate heartily. We were all quite gay and Ewan seemed indeed more like himself than he had been since the attack came on. Afterwards, as I helped Flora wash up the dishes she told me what a terrible time they had had on Monday and most of Tuesday. Ewan had walked the floor ceaselessly, wild with unrest, declaring that there was no hope for him—that he would never be better, and so on until poor Flora was nearly distracted. Tuesday morning he had asked her to send for me—"she may as well know the worst" he said. So Flora had sent the telegram. Then, Tuesday night, Ewan had taken a turn for the better. For the first time since he had arrived in Braintree he had slept naturally and all day had felt well. Christy said she believed his malady had passed the crisis—and indeed, in spite of all that came afterwards I believe she was right. Certainly, he was never anything like so bad again.

After we went to bed he told me of his attack. He said he had had *a vision* of himself and the children in *hell*. Well, I knew that *that* had been absolute insanity while it lasted. The question was—would it return—and last longer?—or was that the crisis and had he turned back finally to comparative sanity? After he had talked out his troubles and I had soothed him as best I could he slept four hours and I slept not at all. In the first place I was too tired and nervous. In the second, I was frightened to go to sleep lest a movement of mine in sleep should waken him—and it was so terribly important that he should sleep. But his sleep was certainly anything but sound or restful for his body was full of nervous jerks and twitches and he sighed, moaned and moved continually.

The next day he seemed fairly well until dinner time. Then we went in to Boston, as he had an appointment with Dr. Garrick, the nerve specialist whom he had consulted.[238]

We walked down to East Braintree station through the little wood

path down the hill which I trotted over so often last winter. On the way silence descended suddenly on Ewan. At the station he walked the platform restlessly. All the way in he was in the old black reverie. In vain I urged him to pull himself together—in vain I pled and reasoned. The

The little wood path

nature of his malady was such that he could not make an effort—will was paralyzed. The noise and crowds of the South Station made him worse. The roar of the subway as we thundered through it tortured him. When we finally reached Commonwealth Ave. Ewan was worse than I had ever seen him. I felt almost distracted with anxiety and terror. *What* was it I was fighting? If I only knew my foe!!

We were half an hour ahead of time, so we sat down on one of

East Braintree Station.

238   Nathan Garrick was a professor in neurology at Boston University Medical School and would become the Head of the Health Service there.

the seats of the boulevard. Ewan's head fell on his breast. He was in the deepest gloom—nothing I could say or do roused him in the least. I said some bitter things—hoping to make him angry—I believed it would do him good if he could just become really angry. But it had no effect—never had any effect. All through his illness he was never in the least angry or vexed, no matter what provocation he had. This was abnormal for although Ewan is in the main a good-natured man he can be angry enough on occasion.

On either side of us rolled past an endless stream of fine cars filled with fashionably dressed people. Not *all* in that procession could have been happy or carefree—no doubt many of them carried anxieties and problems as bitter as mine. But they all *looked* happy and prosperous and I felt as if I were alone in my world of misery—hopeless and heartless. Life could not be faced.

On a seat not far away a man was sitting. He, too, seemed to be down and out. He was shabbily dressed and he sat, leaning forward moodily, never glancing up, the picture of dejection. I think he was some poor derelict, out of work and utterly discouraged. Anyway, I felt that the three of us all looked and felt alike.

It is a curious fact that when I am badly upset in mind, worried and nervous, I always feel *dirty and dishevelled*—as if I were physically unclean and untidy. I was not—I was neatly and carefully and quietly dressed, but I felt like the veriest drab and shrank from the eyes of every passerby as if he must notice and wonder over my unkemptness.

At last the hour of our appointment came and we went in. I liked Dr. Garrick immensely. He impressed me as being a strong, kind, competent man. After he had seen Ewan he took me away for a short talk. I knew Ewan had not told him about his conviction of having "committed the unpardonable sin" and so forth—so I told him the whole facts of the case. He said frankly that the case puzzled him. The idea about his future fate which haunted Ewan was one of the hall-marks of insanity but he was inclined to think that Ewan's malady was simple melancholia.

"On the other hand," he said, "we must face the possibility that it is manic depressive insanity."[239] He told me not to argue with Ewan on the subject of his "phobia" and *not to let him out of my sight*. My heart sank like lead at this hint—it seemed to voice a fear I had not dared to face though I knew it had been lurking in my mind from the very first. He went on to say that possibly the malady had a physical cause

---

239 "Manic depressive insanity" would now probably be labelled as bipolar disorder or major depressive disorder.

which might be found in the condition of the kidneys which were not functioning properly, as analysis showed. More than half the poisonous elements were being retained in the system. Whether this were a cause or an effect, Ewan must drink all the water he possibly could. He also gave me some chloral tablets[240] to produce sleep.

Then we left. I felt very wretched. Ewan did not even ask me what Dr. Garrick said. He was in terrible mental distress all the way home. It was like a nightmare to me but we got to Flora's at last. Ewan continued miserable all the evening. I broke down and cried hopelessly, to Flora's dismay. After I had sobbed myself calm I rose up, grimly determined to renew the fight, made Ewan take a drink and a dose of chloral and went to bed myself.

It was the next day that I began to write notes for my journal, partly by way of easing my mind by the old resource of "writing it out." These entries I will copy here. They reflect with tolerable accuracy my summer that I had hoped would be "quiet and restful!"

++*Friday, June 27, 1919*
East Braintree, Mass.
30 Dobson Road

Last night I took a veronal tablet. I have kept veronal by me for the last fifteen years. Dr. Jenkins prescribed it for me once. Realizing fully the danger of forming a drug habit I have never allowed myself to take it, save in cases of great emergency, and I considered this one, since I am almost exhausted from my recent loss of sleep. So I took my tablet and went to sleep in the "den," on the lounge by the long low window. It was no use to think of going in with Ewan. I would not sleep myself and I would very likely disturb him. I had one night of blissful oblivion, at least, though I woke early this morning. Ewan slept three hours after the first chloral tablet last night and three hours more after a second. He seemed bad all the morning until ten. Since then he has seemed better. Once he called me "Pussy"—the old nickname he has never used since the beginning of his trouble. Also, this afternoon he read three hours unbrokenly and seemed really interested. This, too, is a new and good sign. I make him drink water mercilessly, compelling him to swallow a brimming goblet every hour. Ewan himself would never take anything. His argument is that his trouble is that he is "outcast from God" and drugs will not help that. So I have to make him take his medicines etc. I carry the glasses to him and stand over him

---

240   Chloral hydrate, to induce sleep.

until he drinks it. It is no light ordeal either for the water here is miserable stuff. Flora does not have ice and the water is tepid; also, being filtered, it is flat and insipid. I loathe it and long for a drink of the cold sparkling water from my good old Leaskdale pump.

++*Saturday, June 28, 1919*
30 Dobson Road
East Braintree, Mass.

Today was cool—such a beautiful change from the "hot wave" in which we have been sweltering. I had to take veronal again last night. But I feel encouraged about Ewan. Last night he slept five hours without any drug. All the afternoon he has been reading. Once he made a small joke—again he read me something out of the paper—he asked for and read a letter that I had received—he spoke about Chester and wrote a note to him—all small things in themselves but tremendously significant when compared to the utter absence of all such indications this past month.

This evening it was necessary that I should go somewhere to buy a few necessities to supplement the scanty contents of my hurriedly packed grip. So I motored to Quincy with the Reids.[241] In spite of the improvement in Ewan I hated to leave him. All the time I was away I was worried and so nervous I could hardly sit quietly in the car and compel myself to talk composedly to the Reids. When we reached Quincy we separated and I made my purchases alone. Then I went and sat down on the low stone wall surrounding a church green and began to read a magazine which I had bought. Presently a policeman came up and ordered me off none too politely. The church people, he said bluntly, had told him not to allow people to sit on the wall.

I don't think I hurt the wall much by sitting on it—there was no visible dent in the granite when I got up. For of course I did get up. One doesn't dispute with a policeman. But this trifling incident had an exaggerated effect on me, owing to my worn-out condition. At another time it would have either angered or amused me. Now it hurt me—hurt me bitterly. As I walked away the tears came to my eyes. Foolish as they were I could not check them. I was surrounded by a gay Saturday night mob of strangers. I was dreadfully tired—so tired that I could hardly stand—and to be ordered off that wretched wall was really the last straw. I shall detest Congregational churches forever.

---

241   Quincy is located 8 km (5 miles) south of Boston. The Reids (and the Dobsons, mentioned in the next entry) were neighbours of Amos and Flora.

I walked wearily up and down for half an hour—and it seemed half a year—before the Reids came. When we got home I found Ewan standing on the corner talking to a group of men—something he had not done for a long time—never since he came to Braintree. He came to meet me with a smile. I had been dreading to come back and find him plunged in gloom again—I felt that I could not endure it if he were. But it was so blessedly different from what I had feared. Later on Flora told me that while I was away he had been chatting to her quite brightly of old friends and old times and seemed quite like himself. Oh, if this only lasts! I feel better now than I have for a long while and I am hungry for the first time for a week.

++Sunday, June 29, 1919
30 Dobson Road,
East Braintree, Mass.

Fine and cool. Ewan slept fairly well but took chloral once through the night. I continue to sleep in the den. I like to lie there, even if I cannot sleep and watch the beautiful branches of the big oak at the back door waving against the sky and the lights gemming the dark hill across the valley. Ewan seemed *much* better all day. He read, talked, and actually laughed a little. Once he said to me, "It is blessed to be able to think rationally again," and later on, "I feel as if I were in a convalescent hospital." I take this to mean that those horrible ideas have loosened their clutch on him. We took a walk in the afternoon and evening—dull affairs, for Ewan does not talk much yet. I found the day long. I could not read for my mind is not yet sufficiently at rest. I keep fearing Ewan's improvement will not last.

The Dobsons called in the evening. Their daughter, Mrs. Marston, has the most awful voice I ever heard in a human being—high-pitched, shrill, raucous. It caused me actual physical pain in the raw state of my nerves. My relief was enormous when I saw her finally walk out.

Another hopeful sign in Ewan—he *criticized Amos* to me today—rather deprecatingly, it is true, as if he were doing something very reprehensible. Still, he *did* criticize him. Amos deserves it. He is an intolerable bore. When I am well and easy I don't mind him but just now he grates on the raw. He is one of those people who are always trying to start an argument just for the sake of argument and he is everlastingly trotting out some ancient "heresy" which he plainly thinks must prove very shocking to anyone so orthodox as he evidently supposes a Presbyterian minister and wife must be. If poor Amos only knew how out-of-date his questionings are to me—the hoary old problems of Cain's wife and the seven-day creation and all that. I used to humor him in the winter and argue away as solemnly as if I thought all his queries brand-new and startling, but I haven't the patience for that now and I feel like shrieking or throwing something at his head when he begins. This afternoon he started up on "the unpardonable sin"—of all subjects in the world, the very last one I want referred to in Ewan's hearing just now. Why, it might tear open afresh something that was just beginning to skin over. I choked Amos off so quick that he has been in a dazed condition ever since, not knowing just what happened to him or why.

++*Monday, June 30, 1919*
East Braintree, Mass.

I slept fairly well—Ewan also, though he seemed to jump and start a good deal, as I heard in my frequent toe-trips to listen at his door. Nevertheless, he does sleep and without any "dope." He seemed real well all day but complained of headache in the evening. He seemed cheerful, however—really more cheerful than I. I feel awfully dull and flat.

I had a letter from Lily today—a very ill-spelled and ungrammatical epistle but the most eagerly welcomed one I ever got in my life—for it told about my dear little boys—that they were well etc. It is so dreadful to be separated from them like this.

Tonight I felt a little better and easier than I have for a long time. For the first time I dare to hope that the worst is over and that Ewan will continue to improve. Yet I will go softly and in dread for many days yet.

++*Tuesday, July 1, 1919*
E. Braintree, Mass.

Last night I went in with Ewan because when I sleep in the den, the getting up and prowling about of Amos at four always wakens me and I cannot get to sleep again. He has to leave at six and he is so slow that it apparently takes him two solid hours to dress and eat his breakfast. Flora, too, is given to night prowling owing to her chronic indigestion. So I went with Ewan hoping for a good-night's rest but I was out of the frying pan into the fire. Ewan slept, though very nervously, but I could not sleep at all. I was afraid to move a muscle, so great was my dread of waking him, and I grew numb and cramped. Sleep was impossible. I heard millions of sounds—trains incoming and outgoing with grunts and puffs and shrieks, motor cars chugging and honking, and each and every sound got on my nerves because of my dread that it would wake Ewan. Plainly, there is nothing for me but the den.

Today was terribly hot. I had a letter from Stell, written on her way home. She saw Cam in Montreal and he had said, in referring to Frede, "Well, we had a ripping good time while it lasted." And again, that he "wasn't going to carry any excess baggage"—meaning a second wife!— "for awhile."

I sometimes wonder if Cam is quite normal. He really doesn't seem like any sane person I have ever known.

This afternoon I went to Boston where I found the heat terrific. I had a good talk with Dr. Garrick. He was delighted to hear that Ewan's abnormal ideas had disappeared so quickly. The trouble was only simple melancholia he said, and Ewan was probably over the worst. I went away with a heart wonderfully light compared with my previous visit. To be told your husband has religious melancholia *is* good news when you have been dreading to hear that he has manic depressive insanity! Everything is measured by contrast in this world. I almost enjoyed my hour of shopping in spite of the dreadful heat and mugginess. Under all, of course, was the undercurrent of dread lest I should find Ewan worse again when I got home. But he was all right.

Tonight I have felt a peace that almost amounts to exhaustion. For the first time since May 28 I feel off the rack. There seems no longer any reason to fear that Ewan will become violently insane. I feel as if I had been lifted out of hell. Tonight I lay on the couch out in the porch, utterly relaxed in body and mind, limp, inert, resting absolutely. I cannot describe the wonderful release from intolerable torture and fear.

++*Wednesday, July 2, 1919*
E. Braintree, Mass.

Last night I could not sleep till late in spite of my reaction—or perhaps because of it. But I did not mind. I lay on my couch in the little den and watched the earth-stars and sky stars and was happy. My mind was strangely active. Rebounding from its long repression thought was brilliant and sparkling and varied. I felt *re-born*. All today I have felt utterly tired but peaceful.

++*Thursday, July 3, 1919*
E. Braintree, Mass.

I slept miserably last night owing to heat, a sore throat, and prowlers. Ewan slept fairly well but complained of nightmares. The heat today was such as I have never experienced. The thermometer was 101 and with it humidity and general mugginess. Flora, too, was not well all day—very nervous and inclined to crying spells. She is really a chronic neurasthenic,[242] poor soul. Between the two of them I felt as if I were going to fly to pieces myself. We have been three rather uncanny people.

++*Monday, July 7, 1919*
East Braintree, Mass.

Friday was a day of breathless heat—we sat and sweltered. Saturday was worse. At noon Mr. Viles came to motor us over to Newton for the weekend.[243] It was a beautiful drive and not unpleasant in spite of the heat, as the motion kept our faces dry and we could endure it better.

The Viles live in a very old house—200 years old. It was dusty, musty and "old"-smelling. Christy is an untidy housekeeper. But she can at least get up a regular old "Montgomery" meal, and there is nothing the matter with her cooking.

We went to bed in a large old room upstairs and in spite of the heat and mustiness I hoped for a decent sleep, for I had slept very poorly the two preceding nights. It was not to be. The house was built at one of the busiest motor corners in Newton. Until two o'clock an unbroken stream of cars tore by and as the corner is a dangerous one every car honked or shrieked or yodelled according to its horn. I might as well have tried to sleep in Pandemonium. The strange part is that Ewan slept and all the racket never woke him, although he sighed, moaned and turned from side to side continually. Worn out from loss of sleep I began to suffer from an annoying form of nervousness—a sort of "burning unrest" in which the unrest is of the nerves and the burning sensation physical—especially in my feet. I have seldom passed a more unpleasant night. But a thunderstorm at dawn cooled the air and yesterday was much pleasanter. But I was miserable all day with suppressed nervous unrest and was glad when we got back to Braintree. Then I found a letter from Stell that got under my skin. She said "her mother thought she or Clara should have Frede's peridot necklace." There is gratitude for you! After all I've done for that family and the hundreds and hundreds of dollars I've given them—after paying Stell's expenses for her trip home. I was sick with disgust. The minute I go home I'll pack that necklace up and send it to Aunt Annie. If I choose

---

242 "Neurasthenia" was a term used to describe a basket of symptoms such as fatigue, anxiety, depression.

243 Newton is about 8 km (5 miles) east of Boston.

to keep it, they could do nothing. That letter of Frede's to me, since it was written and signed by herself, was a legal will in the province of Quebec and has been probated as such. In it she left me "first choice" of all her things. Yet I took little. She owed me $140 dollars which I had lent her to pay some bills and in her "will" she directed her mother to pay this out of her life insurance. But I told Aunt Annie I would not take it and let her have all the Insurance. And this is how she behaves. Of course Stell put her up to it—Stell's greed and selfishness is abnormal—but the whole thing sickened me. I broke down and had a good cry—after which I felt much better. What a relief tears are!

Today was cool and pleasant—such a blessed change. It is dear little Chester-boy's birthday. He is seven years old today. It is the first birthday we have been separated. I had a letter from Lily today. Both boys are well. But at times I shiver over the thought of them—two little creatures only 7 and 3 1/2 away up there, a thousand miles away from me, absolutely alone, save for a servant girl and some kind neighbors. Why, they might take ill and die before I could get to them—they might be killed by a car—but it doesn't do to entertain or encourage thoughts like these. I resolutely put them away. But when I am tired or nervous they creep in. I can't hear the 'phone ring without a dreadful feeling—born of the time when I got the wire of Frede's illness last winter; and if it turns out to be someone asking for me I turn sick lest it be a wire from Leaskdale with bad news.

Ewan's head continues to bother him considerably and that worries me. But thank God, there is no return of his delusions.

++Thursday, July 10, 1919
East Braintree, Mass.

The preceding days have been cool and livable. Ewan has kept better and sleeps pretty well—better than I do, indeed. Last night I slept very little but lay and watched the full moon as great dark clouds sailed over her. The effects were very fine. I thought of many things as I watched them—events of long-past years, friends gone over, buried hopes and fears and loves and hatreds. After all, life has been in the main a hard thing for me. What happiness I have had has been far out balanced by suffering. Yet I have always found life interesting and I have never wished to stop living, save in temporary moments of torture. There is always the lure of something further on—something in hiding just around the next bend—to lend spice to it. It may be only a trick—it has always seemed to be a trick hitherto—but it serves.

Flora and I went into Boston this afternoon to see the much advertised movie "The Fall of Babylon."[244] Like the curate's hackneyed egg[245] it was very good in spots. The siege of Babylon was wonderful. But the heroine, the so-called "mountain maid," was nothing but a very sophisticated chorus girl and there was never for a moment an illusion of anything else.

We came home very tired and found E. reading and in pretty good spirits but with a handkerchief tied around his head. I always hate to see that flag of distress appear.

++*Tuesday, July 15, 1919*
East Braintree, Mass.

I feel distressed and anxious tonight. These past three days have not been unpleasant—not too hot, and Ewan kept pretty well. We were full of plans for leaving for home next Monday and I have been looking forward to it hungrily. I want to be home so much, with my children. All this forenoon Ewan was very well. Friends came to lunch and after lunch took us for a motor drive. When we returned our guests left and I was helping Flora wash the dishes when I suddenly noticed that Ewan was walking the floor again as he has not done since I came. In response to my anxious questions he declared he was all right, only a little restless. But I feel disturbed. He has been quiet since but I "sense" that he is not feeling so well. I played "Halma"[246] with him as usual this evening but felt he was not so interested in it as usual. The game bores me but Ewan likes it and as it is not well for him to read too much and as there is so little to amuse or interest him in this quiet place—really the quietest I ever was in—I play it a great deal with him.

++*Wednesday, July 16, 1919*
E. Braintree, Mass.

I slept poorly and woke early. At six Ewan came out dressed—a bad sign, for lately he has been sleeping till nine or ten. He admitted he had not slept well but protested he was all right. This could not deceive

---

244   Also known as *Intolerance*, this epic three-and-a-half-hour-long silent film interweaves four separate historical narratives, including the fall of the Babylonian Empire to Persia in 539 BCE. It is considered a masterpiece of silent film.

245   Expression suggesting something that is mostly bad, but described euphemistically by a few redeeming good qualities.

246   A strategy board game invented in the late nineteenth century, similar to the more modern game of Chinese checkers.

me. He has been dull all day and complains of his head. I feel sick from dread. How can I bear it if he has another attack? It has rained all day and been very depressing.

++*Thursday, July 17, 1919*
E. Braintree, Mass.

I know just how a wretched little mouse feels when it has crept a little bit away from the clutches of the cat and is pounced on again.

Both Ewan and I slept poorly. He got up very early, dressed, and came out, determined to go out walking. I pleaded with him until he consented not to go. I dared not let him go out alone after what Dr. Garrick had said. All the forenoon he was dull and I was heartsick from worry. After dinner we had to go into Boston to consult an oculist about Ewan's eyes as Dr. Garrick had ordered. It was another terrible trip. Ewan seemed to be and declared he was as bad as he had ever been. Owing to the car strike we had to walk from the station to Commonwealth Avenue and the clatter and traffic of the streets seemed to upset Ewan completely. At one time I thought he would simply collapse on the street. I did not know what to do. I took him into a drugstore and got a dose of aromatic ammonia[247] for him. It did not do him any good. His "weakness" was not real, but merely a delusion, so not to be acted on by drugs. At last he yielded to my pleading and consented to make another effort. He admitted that his terrible ideas regarding his destiny had returned. This seemed to me the worst of all. There is something about it that paralyses me. It seems so unnatural—so morbid—so alien to the world of reason and sanity. I feel so powerless before it—as if I were menaced by a foe whose face I could not see—by something creeping upon me in the dark—formlessly, shapelessly horrible.

We got the visit to the oculist over. Somehow I got Ewan down to the station again and on the train. We got to Braintree—we walked home. I had kept up until this. Now my strength gave way. I went to Ewan's room, flung myself on the bed and cried despairingly. My agony at last seemed to pierce even Ewan's apathy and he roused himself a little and vowed he would fight against the gloomy suggestions of his malady. But I have given up hope entirely.

We were to have started for home next Monday. How eagerly I had looked forward to it! Now it is out of the question to think of going. Oh, my poor little boys!

---

247 Used to prevent fainting by inducing deep breathing.

++*Friday, July 18, 1919*
East Braintree, Mass.

Last night I gave Ewan chloral twice before twelve and it had no effect on him. Then I gave him veronal and he slept. I took veronal myself but it had little effect. I only dozed fitfully. This morning I felt as if I *could not* get up. But I had to. As the day wore on I felt a little calmer. Ewan seems better again. He is quiet but not moody. It is possible that this attack will not last as long as the others but I am afraid to hope.

We spent most of the afternoon sitting down under the oak trees of the woods on the hill and talking. Ewan seldom tries to "talk out" his dreads. It would be better for him to do so and I always encourage him when he takes a notion to. Yet it is very dreadful to hear the things that possess him. They are so appallingly irrational and absurd.

The Woods on the Hill

I had a letter from home today. Chester had a bilious spell.[248] He was better but the news has added to my anxiety. Mr. Dobson motored me to Quincy tonight to get more chloral for Ewan. I had hoped he would not have to use it again.

++*Saturday, July 19, 1919*
E. Braintree, Mass.

Very close and muggy again. The "mugginess" is really dreadful. I had a bad night again. Ewan took veronal and seemed calm all day. We spent the afternoon under the trees. In the evening I had to go to East Weymouth on an errand. I had never been there before. I got on the wrong car and was carried miles out of my road but eventually got to my destination and home again. I shrank from the eyes of the people in the car or on the street. It seemed to me they must all know how miserable I felt. I *knew* they couldn't but there are times when reason has no effect on feeling and this was one of them. And then there was the dread of what I might find when I got back. But Ewan said he felt

---

248   A term now rarely used that indicates either an upset stomach, or an upset stomach accompanied by a heachache.

restful and Flora said he had been chatting quite naturally.

Oh, if I could only get *one* good night's sleep! I won't take veronal more than once a week and I don't sleep unless I do but lie awake and think of a thousand hideous things that may happen. They can't *all* happen but they all torture me.

++Sunday, July 20, 1919
E. Braintree, Mass.

Muggy—muggy! I had my bad night. Ewan seemed better most of the day— even laughed and joked a little. I felt encouraged. Mrs. Dobson asked us all over to tea—they live just across the street—and Ewan seemed quite willing to go. But just as we got there I saw at once that he was in the throes of another bad attack. He sat

Dobson House

through the meal in absolute silence. I tried to eat—but every mouthful choked me. I tried to talk—I don't know what I said. I was in an agony of dread—and of humiliation as well, for I felt sure the Dobsons would realize that Ewan was "melancholy"—as we used to say long ago in a whispered tone as of something both shameful and terrible.

Ewan got up erelong and said he must go home. I asked to be excused and followed him. I was thankful to get away—and besides I dared not leave him alone. I came home and had a bitter crying spell. I had a sensation of unbearable, internal agony—a terrible sensation, almost physical, in the region of the solar plexus. The feeling is so dreadful that I cannot describe it.

++Monday, July 21, 1919
East Braintree, Mass.

I cannot realize that it *is* July 21st—that the summer is almost over. Time seemed to me to stop on May 28.

This is the night we were to have left for home. I have no idea now when we can go.

Last night I walked the floor until midnight and then took chloral.

I woke at 3 and slept no more. Ewan had to take veronal. Flora went away this morning to a picnic. I was glad for I saw she was upon the verge of one of her nervous spells and I felt that I simply couldn't endure the two of them in that condition. I housecleaned Ewan's room. At first I had to force myself to work but eventually I grew calmer and able to think of what I was doing. Ewan seemed really better. He read part of the day. We played Halma the rest of the time. He was very nervous at supper and later on some of the remarks he let fall got on my nerves. I was threatened with an hysterical outburst but managed to tide over by shutting myself in the spare room and walking the floor.

++*Tuesday, July 22, 1919*
East Braintree, Mass.

Wet and muggy. Ewan and I went in to Boston as he had to see his oculist again. I was half sick with dread lest I should have another such experience as I had last time and the strain was dreadful. But he did not and kept at least as well as when we left home. Nevertheless, I was expecting every moment that he would "slump," and I went like a cringing dog expecting a second lash.

We went first to see Dr. Coriat who is the author of several books on nervous disorders.[249] His personality did not appeal to me. I did not like him at all. But he said Ewan would be quite well by the fall.

This gave me a little courage to go on with. We then went to see Dr. Garrick, who also spoke hopefully and I felt much better psychically when we came away. But physically the trip home was almost the last word. It was "rush hour." The subways and station were simply packed solid with sweating crowds. I felt as if I would smother in the heat and odor. The possible effect on Ewan worried me too. But he did not seem to mind it half as much as I did. I am almost worn out and feel as if the only thing that would do me any good would be to get away out in some lonely waste place and shriek at the top of my voice for half an hour.

++*Wednesday, July 23, 1919*
East Braintree, Mass.

I had to take veronal last night. It may be a dangerous drug but without it this summer I could not have carried on. My best news is that Ewan

---

249   Isidore Henry Coriat (1875–1943), psychiatrist and neurologist, published several books on mental disorders including *Abnormal Psychology* (1910) and co-authored *Religion and Medicine: The Moral Control of Nervous Disorder* (1908).

had a good sleep all night without any drug and seemed real well again all day. As for the weather, it has poured rain and been of a mugginess to cut with a knife. Ewan's glasses came in the mail and were broken. This meant that I must hie me into Boston and get the lens replaced. The oculist, by the way, found a bad astigmatism in both eyes and says that Ewan has only had half sight all his life.

Off I went, caught a train, got in, got the glasses, and *got* home again. I am woefully tired but my mind is easier and I do not mind mere physical tiredness. Played halma all the evening. How I detest it!

++Friday, July 25, 1919
E. Braintree, Mass.

Today was cooler—high time. I think I couldn't have borne another day of that darned mugginess. Ewan has been fine lately. Has slept well at night and has had no trouble with his head.

++Saturday, July 26, 1919
30 Dobson Road, E.B., Mass.

Last night, after I lay down on my couch by the den window I had a cry over the thought of Frede. The pain of her loss is coming back to me as the later pain subsides. I slept only from twelve to three.

Ewan seems well. We went into Boston and saw Mary Pickford in "Daddy Long-Legs."[250] It was very good and Ewan laughed heartily over it. He has not laughed like that since May. It is a good sign. I feel sure he is really recovering but he is far from normal yet.

++Sunday, July 27, 1919

We all slept well last night. What a blessing good, sound, normal sleep is! I have always been a good sleeper, save for an odd night when worry or excitement kept me awake, until this summer. Ewan was better to-day than any day yet. I found the day long and tedious. I am so home-sick—and *boy*-sick!

++Monday, July 28, 1919
E. Braintree, Mass.

A horrible day—hot and humid again. I felt very nervous all day. I slept

---

250   Canadian-American silent film actress Mary Pickford (1892–1979; her real name was Gladys Louise Smith) starred in this comedy-drama about an orphan who grows up to success.

badly and had a headache. Had a letter from Stella—all growls over trifles. Ewan, too, seemed quiet today and I fear another "slump."

++*Wednesday, July 30, 1919*

Ewan is *not* well. He denies that he feels worse but he cannot blind me. He is not sleeping well again—has to take chloral. But neither headache nor abnormal thoughts have returned yet.

++*Saturday, Aug. 2, 1919*

Ewan kept about the same until last night when we were both sleepless. I was in with him and he confessed that his "phobia" had returned. I could hardly suppress a sob of despair when he admitted this. We had a miserable night and not even veronal could give us rest. He got up early and went out for a walk. I had to let him go alone—I was too exhausted to go, too. He seemed better when he came back. We "talked out" all his trouble again, though I felt as if I couldn't bear to thrash it all over again—and never get anywhere. Yet I feel it does him good to talk it out. I had to go into Boston to see about getting our tickets etc. for we had planned to leave for home Monday. I don't feel that we are going to get away and I don't see how I can endure another disappointment. I went to the South Station and across to the North Station in a daze of pain, got the tickets, and came home. Ewan was away, having gone to East Weymouth to see Mr. Hyde, an Anglican clergyman. I was so tired I couldn't control my nervousness and I walked the floor for two hours. Then Ewan came home and told me he felt much better. I couldn't believe it at first but as the evening wore away he *did* seem so well that I heartened up a bit again.

++*Sunday, Aug. 3, 1919*

This was a beautiful day, fine and cool. Ewan keeps saying he is better and of course he is to a certain extent but he is far from being as well as he was three weeks ago. He is dull and does not sleep without drugs. This evening Flora and I went over to the McCombs (our next door neighbors) for a few minutes. I wanted to say good-bye for we still plan to go tomorrow though I am in constant terror that Ewan at the last will not be able to go or will think he is not. The McCombs are nice enough people but their cat is nicer. He is an amazing creature. Weighs 26 lbs. and looks like the King of Catland. He sits on their veranda in the evenings and my hands burn to stroke him. But he is not over friendly to strangers.

Tiger

While we were there Ewan came in. In company I realize how far from well he yet is. There is not a scintilla of his old jollity in him. He sits in silence, hearing little and saying nothing. I got him away as soon as I could for I could not bear it.

This may be our last night here. I dread the journey home terribly. But Ewan is anxious to be home and I think if he can get there it will be better for him. He seems to be craving to get back to his work. There will be more there to take up his attention and keep him from brooding. And oh, I will be so thankful to get home!

On Monday evening, Aug. 4 we left Braintree. Ewan had been dull that morning but was better in the afternoon and seemed fairly well when we left. Flora went to the North Station with us. I parted from her with real regret. Flora is a stupid, uncultured, uninteresting woman but she has a heart of gold and she was kindness itself to us this summer.

Our train left at 7.15. I had taken a drawing room so we were by ourselves. There *are* times when a little money makes life easier. *What* would we have done this summer if we had nothing but Ewan's salary to depend on? If I had had financial worries on top of everything else it would have been the last straw.

We both had a good night, thanks to Veronal and reached Montreal in the morning. We had to wait there until Thursday morning as we wanted to come home by boat. Ewan was much better that day and the next. We went to several movies and enjoyed them. Thursday was very hot. We left in the morning on the train for Prescott where we took the boat. That afternoon we sailed through the Thousand Islands.[251] I was disappointed in the scenery. It was beautiful but it was not the fairyland I had cherished all my life in my imagination. When I was about nine years old a little booklet fell into my hands advertising a certain line

---

251   In the early twentieth century, the Thousand Islands was a popular resort, particularly among wealthy Americans. The region consists of an archipelago of 1,864 islands between the Canada-US border, along the Saint Lawrence River between Ontario and New York. Prescott, Ontario, some 180 km (111 miles) northeast of Montreal on the St Lawrence River, is sometimes called the "gateway" to the Thousand Islands.

of tents. It was filled with colored pictures purporting to be of the Thousand Islands—all with beautiful tents in them of course. I used to pore over them with never-failing delight and ever since then the Thou-

"In the Thousand Islands. St. Lawrence River, Canada."

sand Islands have meant to me the sylvan dells and wondrous colors of those pictures. Alas, the reality was very unlike and I couldn't forgive it for my disillusion. We saw the Islands at a disadvantage, through a haze, their greenery seared to dull brown by the summer heat. Under more favorable circumstances they would no doubt be more beautiful—but—well, they were *not* my Thousand Islands of Enchantment.

There was a heavy thunderstorm in the afternoon and a gale blew all night, so we slept little. But the next morning was cool and clear and bracing. We were in an atmosphere such as I had not felt since I left Canada. Moreover, we got into Toronto in time to catch the train for home. Dr. Shier motored us up and we got here at noon. Chester and Stuart nearly ate us, Ewan seemed quite bright and cheerful, and oh, but it was good to be home. We both had a good, drugless sleep that night and once more I ventured to hope that the worst was over.

Sunday, Aug. 10, 1919
The Manse, Leaskdale

I was up all last night with Stuart who suffered from severe abdominal pain. I was afraid of appendicitis, for it seems he has been like this for a week and getting worse every night. So I sent for Dr. Shier who said it was cystitis.[252] I am thankful I got home when I did.

Stuart

252 Inflammation of the urinary tract and/or bladder, usually caused by a bacterial infection. LMM herself suffered considerably from this condition.

Lily would have been frantic. I did not go out today. Mr. Fraser,[253] the old minister who has been supplying for Ewan all summer, preached. He will continue to supply until the first of September by which time Ewan hopes to be able to take up his work.

I feel dreadfully tired and discouraged tonight. I suppose it is owing to loss of sleep.

Tuesday, Aug. 12, 1919
Leaskdale, Ont.

I have been exceedingly busy trying to get things straightened out. Hosts of people have been coming to see Ewan, of course. I am woefully sick of going over and over the same routine of information re "kidney poisoning" etc. Ewan seems real well mentally. But last night he woke at one in a cold clammy sweat, such as he has had two or three times before this summer. I do not like it.

Thursday, Aug. 14, 1919

I have had to resort to the spare room to sleep. If I stay in my own room I simply can't sleep for fear of waking Ewan. Last night I got a good sleep. So did Ewan but for two nights before he had to take chloral. I am so sick of the sight of that brown bottle with its little white tablets. Ewan has not been so well these two days past. He is dull again.

As for me, I have begun work on my new book. I hope the ending will be more auspicious than the beginning. But it is time I got to work for I've done nothing all summer.

Saturday, Aug. 16, 1919
The Manse, Leaskdale

Today Ewan had the handkerchief around his head again. How my heart sank! Yet this evening he was much better again. So it goes—up and down, forward and back. I am still the mouse in the claws of the cat.

Sunday, Aug. 24, 1919

Ewan has seemed pretty well all this week. He has slept without drugs and been quite cheerful. Lily has been away for a week of her vacation

---

253   James R. Fraser (b. 1867). See LMM's entries for August 8, 1918, and April 12, 1921.

so I have been very busy. Miss Chapman, sub-editor of *McLeans Magazine*,[254] spent Wednesday here, to get material for an article on me and my "career." I talked brightly and amusingly—and watched Ewan out of the corner of my eye, wondering how he felt. That is my existence now.

"Rainbow Valley" is out.[255] The cover design is very pretty. My ninth novel—and I don't feel a particle of interest in it!

Frede will never read it!

One of the stories she would have recognized. It was the one of Mary Vance chasing Rilla Blythe with a codfish. Chester and Amy Campbell were the originals of that and Frede was never tired of laughing over it with her Macdonald cronies. The only other bit of "real life" in it is the ghost the children saw on the dyke. Of course that is the old ghost that Well and Dave Nelson and I saw, which turned out to be grandmother with a tablecloth.[256]

This afternoon I was alone and bitterly lonely. I took a wild spasm of longing for Frede. It seemed to me that I *could not* go on living without her—and that it was no use to try.

Wednesday, Aug. 27, 1919
The Manse, Leaskdale, Ont.

Ewan motored to Toronto to the Exhibition today. I never feel easy when he is away alone. But I could not go with him this time.

Today I happened to pick up and open at random an old scrapbook containing reviews of my books. A clipping caught my eye, written in 1910. Some editor had written me, asking some questions about my views on "Canadian Literature" and in my reply I find the following paragraph—rather significant in view of what has come since.

"I do not think our literature is an expression of our national life as a whole. I think this is because we have only very recently—as time goes in the making of nations—had any real national life. Canada is only just finding herself. She has not yet fused her varying elements into a harmonious whole. Perhaps she will not do so until they are welded together by some great crisis of storm and stress. That is when a real national literature will be born. I do not believe that the great

---

254   Founded in 1905, *Macleans* is a long-running Canadian news magazine, published weekly (in January 2017 it became a monthly publication).

255   See LMM's entry for December 26, 1918.

256   Wellington Nelson and his brother David had lived for some years with LMM's family when she was a child, following the death of the boys' parents.

Canadian novel or poem will ever be written until we have had some kind of baptism by fire to purge away all our petty superficialities and lay bare the primal passions of humanity."[257]

When I wrote that I had no premonition of the Great War. But if I had known what was coming I could hardly have described it better. Many a prophet's reputation has been made out of less! It remains to be seen if the rest of my prediction will come as true. I believe it will, but it may take twenty—thirty—forty years before it is made manifest. The great Canadian literature will come from the generation born of this conflict not from the generation that fought through it.

Sunday, Aug. 31, 1919
The Manse, Leaskdale, Ont.

Ewan came home last Thursday night. He seemed tired and admitted that his head had troubled him a good deal while away. He was duller on Friday than he has been since coming back. Last night again he was very dull. I got dreadfully blue. At times I feel that I cannot bear any longer this alternation of faint hope and sickening despair. If Ewan does not soon recover he must resign and I must get a house somewhere where I can make a home for the children while he goes to a good sanitarium for treatment. I can think of no other solution. It is very disheartening. He seemed so much better when we came home and for a week afterwards.

So this has been my summer! Well, I've lived through it and kept up for my children's sake.

Later on

After writing the above I went into the library and found Ewan sitting in his arm chair gazing gloomily before him. I made him confess that he is again haunted by conviction of eternal damnation. I went upstairs to my room, shut the door and cried wretchedly. This is the one thing I cannot endure. I can help him fight headache and insomnia but this other thing seems so unnatural that it fills me with such horror and repulsion that I can't face it. I can't help it—it always turns me against Ewan for the time, as if he were possessed by or transformed into a demoniacal creature of evil—something I must get away from as I would rush from a snake. It is terrible—but it is the truth.

---

257 From a newspaper article entitled "Our National Literature" published in *The Globe* (and later *The Island Patriot*) on January 6, 1910.

Tuesday, Sept. 2, 1919
Leaskdale, Ont.

Ewan slept last night without drugs. I went to the spareroom, so slept well and feel better. Ewan went away today for a visit to Sutton.[258] I dreaded to see him go; and yet it was a relief. I am good-for-nothing when I see him sitting gloomily around, a prey to dejection and delusions. When I don't see him I can at least work, no matter how heavy my heart is.

Last winter I began to copy my whole journal into a set of volumes all the same size. My journal, beginning in the fall of 1890, has been written in various "blank books" of equally various shapes and sizes. I resolved to copy it as aforesaid. It will mean a great deal of work and will take a long time, for I can only spare fifteen minutes a day for it. But it will be a satisfaction when done. I shall be careful to copy it exactly as it is written but I mean to "illustrate" it as I go along with such photos of the scenes and people who figure in it as I possess. How I wish I could have had in childhood and girlhood, a "kodak"[259] such as almost everybody now has. But of course such things were unknown then.

I find that when I am copying those old journals I feel as if I had gone back into the past and were living over again the events and emotions of which I write. It is very delightful and a little sad.

Today I was copying my account of the "peanut party" we had in one of poor Prof. Harcourt's classes.[260] At the time I thought it good fun. But if I were to write an essay on "Things I Am Ashamed To Remember" that peanut party would be one of them. Harcourt was a nonentity and his classes were farces. The time we spent in them was absolutely wasted. But all this did not justify us in such a performance. I was not

---

258   Sutton, Ontario, on the south shore of Lake Simcoe.

259   A popular, inexpensive camera, which used photographic film. The Kodak Company had been founded by George Eastman in 1888 and from the early twentieth century developed new technology that made the use of cameras much more widely available.

260   LMM's entry of March 8, 1894, while she was studying at Prince of Wales College in Charlottetown, records this event: "In college and had a gay racket during chemistry hour. We had previously voted to get up a 'peanut party' and all of us subscribed two cents each. At School Management hour the First Class girls, who do not take it, sneaked off uptown and got four pounds of peanuts. After recess we all went over feeling pretty mutinous. We got the peanuts distributed, cracked, ate them and threw the shells at one another. The air was thick with flying shells and beans, while a big carrot and a red herring also passed and repassed. Harcourt was furious but powerless. He took down—or pretended to—a lot of names and I expect we'll hear something more of it yet: but they can't kill us and Dr. A., who dislikes Harcourt, never pays much attention to the latter's complaints. Harcourt is no good whatever as a teacher and is not respected in his classes at all."

one of the ring leaders—I merely followed. But I enjoyed it, so I am condemned. I was a little beast—we were all little beasts.

A few years ago a brother of Prof. Harcourt's, who is a missionary in India, was here for a visit. He was a fine-looking, very agreeable man, with a decided and charming personality—a great contrast to Prof. Harcourt who always gave me the impression of a sneak—and a weak sneak at that. But if he had been ten-times sneakier that peanut party would still remain something to be ashamed of.

Wednesday, Sept. 3, 1919
Leaskdale, Ont.

Worked hard all day, then went to Guild at night and read a paper I had written. There were only a few there and I felt that the time and trouble the paper had cost me was practically wasted.

While I was writing my "fifteen-minute stint" of old journals today I found a reference to "Sam Wyand's field." Instantly fancy took wing and I was back among scenes that have now vanished from the face of the earth.

"Sam Wyand's field"—a most unromantic name for one of the most beautiful little spots I have ever seen—a spot to which in my childhood I gave the love I afterwards gave to Lover's Lane. For years "Sam Wyand's field" spelled Arcady[261] for me—to this day it shines in memory like a land of lost delight.

I think I was about eleven years old when I first saw it. I had gone down to spend an afternoon with Pensie[262] and we went picking strawberries in the fields and "stumps" at the back of their farm. In a corner of John Laird's back field we found a little lane leading through a belt of woods—a lane that might have been part of the woods of fairyland—narrow, winding, mossy, with soft resinous young fir boughs pushing out across the path to brush our faces. Here and there, on either hand were little "bays" filled with green ferns. At the far end of the lane the firs suddenly gave place to maples, with great sheets of ferns growing over their roots. Far on either side of us they stretched. Then just before us was a smooth old "longer" fence and over it Sam Wyand's field—the back field of a farm that ran at right angles out to Cavendish

---

261   Probably a reference to Sir Philip Sidney's *Arcadia*, a long prose work first printed in 1690, set in the semi-mythological province of Arcadia in Greece. The term "arcady" suggests a pastoral location of almost legendary beauty.

262   Pensie MacNeill (1872–1906), daughter of Charles and May Macneill, was a cousin and childhood friend.

Road. We picked berries there all the afternoon. That is—I picked part of the time and the rest I squatted amid the grass and *soaked in* the beauty around me. On every side but one, and for two thirds of that, the field was completely surrounded by thick maple woods. It was shut away from the world. No house was visible from it. In one corner the maple growth was particularly beautiful—so tall and even and symmetrical that afterwards Lu[263] and I used to call it "the maple orchard" and the leaves that turned up whitely in the afternoon breezes were the "blossoms." Anything sweeter than the whistles of robins that always used to ring through that "orchard" in the early evenings I have never heard since, nor ever expect to hear again until in the circle of Eternity I come back again to "Sam Wyand's field."

The field was never cultivated for four or five years. The soil was poor and so it was left for pasture and the sheep that were always nibbling peacefully here and there in it never seemed to interfere with the growth of wild, feathery grasses, purple in early summer, creamy velvet in the autumn, that covered it, or with the strawberries either.

After I had discovered the field I was not long—for in those days I was a most intrepid little explorer of unknown woods and fields—in finding a way to it from home and thereafter for many years Lu and I used to go back every other day in strawberry time. We used to go up across Uncle John's big hill field, climb into "Jimmy Laird's" field, turning on the fence—at least I did—to luxuriate in the glorious view of Cavendish, the gulf and New London Harbor visible from it. Hist[264]—I see it now as vividly as ever—oh, my heart aches, my eyes burn for it! Then we went through Jimmy Laird's woods by another beautiful lane of spruces and beeches which we called "the Intercolonial"—having at that time a passion, born of I know not what, for naming all the lanes we knew after Canadian railways. Beyond this we crossed a "back pasture" of Jimmy Laird's and connected up with John Laird's field and the lane to Sam Wyand's. We would put our lunch away under a clump of ferns in the maple orchard and our jugs beside it. I invariably carried a big white jug from our kitchen plenishings. Then we took a cup apiece and went a-picking, emptying our cups in the jugs as we filled them. Nine cups filled my jug, I remember, and then I picked a tenth and carried it home, emptying it into the jug just before I got there, for the strawberries always "settled" with the carrying home and one wanted to have one's jug brave and full.

---

263   LMM's cousin, Lucy Simpson Macneill (1877–1974), the daughter of her Uncle John Franklin Macneill.

264   "Hist" is a now somewhat archaic exclamation to call for attention or for silence.

There was a certain "etiquette" about berry picking which we always strictly observed. The strawberries grew in scattered plots called "beds" and when you had located a bed and planted yourself down in it to pick it was not permissible for any one else to come and pick in that bed.

It was a haunt of foxes and rabbits and we picked so quietly, snuggled down among the grasses, that we often saw the wild creatures running across the field. I remember one morning we arrived there we found five foxes in the field. How they ran, the red fellows! One autumn day Lu and I were back there just for a walk when we saw a fox come out of the woods and lope towards us, carrying something in his mouth. We stood so still he did not notice us until he was half way across the field. Then we yelled at the tops of our voices. Mr. Fox got the scare of his life. He stopped short, dropped what he was carrying, and fled. We ran to the spot and found half the body of a plump little gray rabbit. Brer Fox[265] had eaten the head and shoulders and was perhaps carrying the rest home to Madam or the little foxes. If so they never got it. Lu and I indignantly buried the half corpse, for we loved rabbits and entirely disapproved of their slaughter by foxes.

One summer we were much worked up over the dead bodies of sheep we used to find over the field which had been killed by dogs.

It was seldom anyone else came to the field. It seemed to belong to us. We sat in the corner by the maple orchard when noon came and ate our lunches with the zest of youth. We went home when the shadows grew long carrying our jugs proudly. Never were such happy days. I would give five years of my present hurrying over-worked existence for just one of them. But they return not.

Finally the field was ploughed up and we could pick berries in it no more. Then we went to "Montana"—the stumps and clearings at the back of Charles Macneill's farm. This place had been so named by Pensie and we imitated her by calling several other spots after States of the Union. We called Sam Wyand's field "Illinois" but the latter name never succeeded in displacing the former. Then there was "Indiana." This was a clearing right in the heart of the woods where we went to pick raspberries. A lane which we called the "C.P.R."[266] led from Montana to it through a long growth of young maple. Half way down an enormous fallen tree trunk lay right across the path. It was quite a feat to scramble over it. It was the biggest log I ever saw, as high as our waists. It was very old and I don't know what kind of a tree it was though from my

---

265   "Brer Fox" was a popular character from a collection of African-American folk tales. The stories were compiled by Joel Chandler Harris as *Uncle Remus, His Songs and His Sayings: The Folk-Lore of the Old Plantation* in 1881

266   Presumably after the Canadian Pacific Railway.

memory of its bark I think it must have been a gigantic maple, though I have never seen a maple so big.

Many years before I left Cavendish all these dear old spots had been spoiled or eradicated by clearings and cuttings. One side of the old "Intercolonial" was completely cut away. The dear old "maple orchard" in Sam Wyand's field was cut down. "Indiana" is now an open cultivated field.

I have made myself wretchedly homesick by writing all this and visualizing the memories evoked. It has been so real to me that it has filled me with a bitter longing to be in those spots once more—to taste the inimitable flavor of the wild fruit, to lie amid the sun-warm grasses, to hear the robins whistling, to tiptoe through the lanes of greenery and fragrance in the summer mornings of those faraway years. When I wrench myself away from their idyllic memories to the bitter, carking reality of life at present I sicken at the contrast.

Thursday, Sept. 4, 1919
The Manse, Leaskdale, Ont.

A pleasant day, filled up for the most part by the preserving of two huge kettlefuls of plums. I like this sort of work, however. Only, it takes so much time—and the Government won't extend the day to thirty-six hours!

Tonight in copying my old diary I found a mention of Norman Campbell.[267] Poor Norman! His life ended in tragedy.

Norman Campbell, when I knew him at P.W.C. and later, was a nice jolly fellow whom I always liked. We were "good pals" and where Norman and I were at any time laughter made a third. After teaching school for a few years Norman went to Charlottetown and took up the study of law. He passed in due time and was admitted to the bar. Meanwhile he had become engaged to Miss Ross, the matron of the P.E. Island hospital. Most of his friends thought it an odd match for she was his senior by at least fifteen years—literally old enough to be his mother. But Norman seemed happy enough and their marriage was on the point of coming off when Norman suddenly broke down with "nervous prostration"—at least that was the name given out. The real truth was—though this did not leak out for several years and may not be known to his family to this day—that it was the oncoming of the

---

267   Norman Campbell was a second cousin on the Montgomery side, and also a friend from her time at Prince of Wales College.

terrible insanity which is consequent on syphilis.[268] Sometime poor Norman must have tampered with forbidden fruit—and paid a terrible price. He went home to his father's "for a rest"; but it was evident erelong that his mind was giving way. The last time I was at Mary's she told me of his condition and what a dreadful time they had with him. I forgot how long he lingered—a few years—and then died. So closed a life that promised fair—gay, merry, clever Norman. It hurts me when I think of it. There are such terrible tragedies in life—things we never dream of when we are young. I recall Norman as I knew him—Norman laughing with me in the hall at MacMillans—Norman terrifying the soul out of my body with his weird ghost stories one dark night when a gang of us were out driving in Donald E's old pung—Norman and I dancing together all night in the maple-roofed pavilion on the night of Mary's wedding—Norman whisking me out to see the sunrise after it and kissing me unblushingly because he had a glass or two of Scotch courage in him after the Highland fashion at weddings and so was quite ready to dare anything. It was the only time he ever kissed me for there had never been any sentiment between us. And, as always, a jest on his lip and a twinkle in his eye. Somehow I cannot connect *that* Norman with the Norman Mary described to me—the furtive, unshaven creature, slinking furtively about the house, snarling at his friends, refusing to eat at the table but tearing food found in odd corners—repulsive, idiotic-mind, heart, civilization gone. "The wages of sin is death."[269] The life and death of Norman Campbell was a terrible commentary on that merciless old text.

Friday, Sept. 5, 1919
The Manse, Leaskdale

I was busy all day and consequently tired at night. Ewan came home at twilight. I went out to the gate, vaguely hoping that I might see his old roguish dimpled smile of welcome. But as he opened the gate I saw the drooping head and dejected bearing I have seen so often this summer. He gave a smile indeed—a forced, lifeless smile—then went into the house and into the library. I sat down on the veranda sick at heart. He is no better than when he went away.

---

268   Syphilis is a sexually transmitted bacterial infection (now treated with antibiotics). A condition known as neurosyphilis occurs when the bacterium associated with syphilis infects the brain or spinal cord. This may take place in people who have untreated syphilis a decade or so after the first infection. Symptoms include mental instability.

269   Romans 6:23: "For the wages of sin is death; but the gift of God is eternal life through Jesus Christ our Lord."

Saturday, Sept. 6, 1919

Fine and very warm—unseasonably so. Ewan did not sleep much last night. Neither did I, as Chester was not well. I felt indescribably badly all day—tired, nervous, despondent.

Sunday, Sept. 7, 1919
Leaskdale, Ont.

We both slept pretty well last night. Today was warm and close. Ewan went to preach at Wick, while Mr. Macdonald of Wick preached here. I felt fairly well all day till about 4.30 when Ewan came home. His head was troubling him and he was very dull and abstracted. Evidently he had found the day difficult. My own discouragement and nervous tension returned in the gloom of his presence. Tonight I feel as if I were beating my hands against a stone wall. Oh, how hard I have tried lately to convince Ewan that his gloomy fears are irrational and foundationless—I have tried every way—argument, "suggestion," entreaty, scorn, sympathy. I might as well have saved my breath. Nothing has the slightest effect. Reason has no power over the delusions of an unsound mind.

Monday, Sept. 8, 1919

"Black Monday" indeed. This has been my hardest day since July 16. To begin with, last night after I went to bed I broke down and cried bitterly for hours. Finally, calmed by the tears, I slept till 6. Ewan took chloral and so slept also. Today was terribly hot—almost as hot as any we had all summer—and exceedingly oppressive besides. Ewan was very dull all the morning. He went for the mail, brought it home, gave me my letters and went upstairs without a word. I read my letter—another of Stell's wild outpouring of complaints and whines and growls. Those selfish letters of Stell's have been almost more than I could bear this summer. She makes mountains out of every molehill and shrieks to the universe for sympathy as if no creature but her had any worries or troubles.

After reading it I went upstairs. Ewan was lying on the bed staring at the ceiling. I tried to cheer him up but he became angry with me, all because I would not agree with him that he was everlastingly damned, and said some things that hurt me, even though I realized that it was not Ewan's self that was speaking. I stayed with him all the afternoon, playing Halma with him, reading to him and making him read aloud to me, as a means of keeping his thoughts from revolving on their point of self torture.

In the evening I had promised to go up and see Mary Quigley and her mother. There were reasons why I was anxious to keep my engagement and as they had no phone I could not ask them to excuse me and I knew they would be expecting me. So I went, but with a heavy heart, leaving Ewan lying in the hammock. It seemed a long evening. Ordinarily I do not find it hard to talk to Mary and Mrs. Quigley. Indeed, they are the only two women in the congregation whom I find really congenial and whose company I enjoy. They are witty and intelligent. But tonight it was difficult to force myself to smile and talk while my heart ached behind my mask and my mind wearied itself with unanswerable problems.

I walked home alone under the stars. Somehow, strength came to me out of the soft September darkness. I said to myself, "I will *not* give in. I will fight on. Dr. Coriat said Ewan would recover this autumn and I will believe him. I *will* be calm and brave and resolute." And I felt so.

Nevertheless, it taxed my fortitude when I got home and found Ewan more miserable than ever. I gave him a bromide. Now I must go to bed myself but I dread the night for I fear I cannot sleep unless I take veronal.

Tuesday, Sept. 9, 1919
Leaskdale, Ont.

Today was cool again and I was very thankful, for a hot oppressive day like yesterday seems to make Ewan worse. But he was not well at all today. Last night, he had to take chloral twice. He was very restless all the morning. I read to him and played Halma. After dinner we motored to Uxbridge and after shopping went out to Alex. Mustard's where we had promised to take tea.[270] I had a hard time on the road for Ewan was in terrible distress of mind and I dreaded getting to Mustards' for I was afraid he would make an exhibition of his feelings before them all. When we reached there I gave him a bromide which quieted his unrest a little and he lay on the sofa during the afternoon, saying only that his head ached. As long as he was quiet I could endure. So I sewed feverishly on a bit of embroidery, held myself together by sheer will power, and talked to the family as if all were well.

---

270   The Mustards were a prominent local family; Hugh Mustard (1879–1917) and his wife Harriet (1865–1939) were the parents of Alexander, who married Zella Cook. Other siblings were James and John Mustard.

Had I been free to feel any emotion I would have felt very sorry over that visit. When I came here eight years ago Hugh Mustard and his wife were among my first and best friends. They were fine, upright, *sincere* people. We have had many pleasant visits there. Two years ago Hugh Mustard died. Our church has never seemed the same to either of us since, nor has that home. A few years ago Alec, the oldest son, married Zella Cook, a Leaskdale girl much older than himself. Zella was a girl with whom I had always been on good terms outwardly but I never liked or trusted her. We were thrown much together as she was very active in church work but she is one of those people in whose presence I am always ill at ease—always instinctively on my guard. I was sorry when Alec married her for I knew that Hugh Mustard's place would never be the same to us again. The old atmosphere of confidence would be gone. This proved to be so but as long as Hugh was alive Zella had to remain in the background. With Hugh's death came a change; and

finally Mrs. Hugh has decided to move to Uxbridge and leaves very shortly. Our visit of today was the last we shall have with her on the Sixth. We shall have to visit Alec and Zella of course but it will be the performance of

Hugh Mustard's House

a duty and no longer a pleasure.

Ewan seemed a little better in the evening and talked to the boys. But I was relieved when we got away and got home.

He is in bed now and I am sitting down here, because I dread the thought of going to bed, writing in this old journal which has been my confidant so long. I have no other.

Stuart.

When I went upstairs upon coming home little Stuart was still awake and he called out anxiously, "Did you have your supper, dear mother?" He is such a thoughtful little chap, always anxious that those he loves should be provided for. So far, I see nothing of that in Chester; yet, although he is undemonstrative, occasionally something—generally a little suffering—opens up a glimpse of his nature. A few nights ago he suffered most of the night from what used to be called "growing pains" when I was a child. I used to have them badly. I was lying beside Chester cuddling him and trying to comfort him, for the pain was pretty severe. Suddenly he put his arms about me, "Oh," he said, "I love my dear mother. I love to feel her sweet hands on my face."

Poor little chap, he and Stuart have made life possible for me this summer.

Wednesday, Sept. 10, 1919
The Manse, Leaskdale

Ewan was dull all day but on the whole seemed better than yesterday. There was no outburst and he did not seem so restless. But he complained a good deal of his head.

This evening we were playing Halma in the library when old Lizzie Oxtoby came in. She is a person in whose presence I always feel unhappy and defensive at any time so her effect on me in my mood of tonight may be imagined. I felt as if I would fly into little pieces every moment of her stay. I talked desperately to cover Ewan's moody and noticeable silence and oh, how thankful I was when she went away!

Thursday, Sept. 11, 1919

Ewan was very dull all day. We had promised to go over to John Lockie's[271] on the fourth to tea and we left about five. When we got there Ewan excused himself and lay down on the sofa, saying his head was aching. I sat and sewed and talked to Mrs. Lockie. At supper Ewan was very gloomy. He could not or would not talk. Before the meal was done he excused himself and went back to the sofa. There he fell asleep and, in spite of the talk around him—for Mrs. Lockie had several other guests—he slept soundly on. I recognized this as something new, for never before this whole summer has he slept anywhere but in his room and the slightest sound would make him moan and turn; if he did not actually wake. When he woke he sat up and make a joke—the first I have heard him make for a long time. As we drove home he said he felt better. I feel hopeful once more.

---

271   John Harvey Lockie was the Secretary Treasurer of the United Farmers of Ontario.

Friday, Sept. 12, 1919
Leaskdale, Ont.

Ewan slept last night without chloral but was very dull all day. I relapsed into discouragement and was so terribly nervous all day that I couldn't work or fasten my mind on anything. After supper I shut myself in my room and indulged in the relief of tears. After that I braced up again and played Halma with Ewan until nine, when he went to bed. I don't know what to do.

Saturday, Sept. 13, 1919

I have again almost given up hope. Ewan was as bad today as I ever saw him. He had to take chloral twice last night. He did not get up until noon and then was very dull. When I went up to my room to dress for the Mission Band I found him lying on the bed, evidently given over once more to his delusions. I felt as if I could not endure it. Though I knew it was no use I implored him for the thousandth time to banish such false and blasphemous ideas. "You have assumed responsibilities," I said. "You have brought two children into the world"—

"Yes, and I wish from the bottom of my heart I never had," he exclaimed bitterly.

That was more than I could bear. I felt as if a knife pierced my heart. That Ewan, who has always been so fond and proud of his boys, should say *that*—and if it were *not Ewan* who said it—well, that was a deeper horror still! With a choking cry I flung myself on the couch. I cried blindly. It was my darkest hour. Ewan got up and went out saying, "Well, I must go to meet Smith I suppose. Your idea is that I must go on till I drop."

This did not hurt me. Ewan never says such things in his normal condition of mind. But I cannot get over what he said about the children. It seemed so hideous. It is just because those horrible delusions of his make him believe that they are eternally lost as well as himself and so he wishes they had never been born.

Well, they never would have been born if I had known that Ewan was subject to constitutional recurrent melancholia for I believe no one has a right to bring children into the world who may possibly inherit such a curse. But now I cannot and do not wish them unborn.

After he went I got up, bathed my face, set my teeth and went to the Mission Band where I cut and sewed Shaker flannel patches[272]

---

272   Originally produced by the Shaker religious sect in the eastern United States, Shaker

for a hospital quilt with the children for an hour. Then I came back, walking through the beauty of the warm golden afternoon like a lost spirit through a heaven in which it has no part. Ewan is not back from the station yet. He has gone to meet Captain Smith who is to preach for him tomorrow and will be here until Wednesday.[273] I dread it. Capt. Smith is an old P.E.I. acquaintance and I hate to have such see Ewan as he is now, lest they suspect his mental condition and scatter the news broadcast. I have kept the mental side of Ewan's trouble a secret from all but Dr. Garrick and I cannot bear the thought of anyone knowing it, especially the people I know down east. Stella, too, is coming next week. I feel like a caged creature. Turn where I will there is nothing but dungeon bars.

Sunday, Sept. 21, 1919
Leaskdale, Ont.

Is it only a week since my last entry? Yet what a difference. For what seems like a miracle has happened. Ewan is—or seems to be—*absolutely well.* It seems too good to be true. And I cannot help fearing that the recovery has been too sudden to last. Yet the onset was sudden. And he recovered just as suddenly from the attack he had that winter in Glasgow.

Last Saturday when he left to meet Captain Smith at the station he was very very miserable. Two hours later, when he returned, he was well. That is all there is to it.

When he returned with Captain Smith he seemed quietly cheerful and talked easily about old times—as he and Capt. S. knew each other well down home. After supper we all motored over to Jas. Mustard's and stayed for an hour. Ewan seemed his old self, laughing and joking. When we came home he started up the victrola, something he has not done since last spring. That night I slept in my own bed but lay awake most of the night, afraid to move as usual. But I noticed a change in Ewan's sleeping. For the first time he never sighed or moaned in his sleep, although he moved a good deal and woke twice. He kept well all

---

flannel was a mixed wool and cotton blend of superior quality with a light nap and soft finish.

273   Edwin Smith, born probably around 1970 in Prince Edward Island, had (like Ewan) studied at Pine Hill Theological College. Smith married in 1897and eventually fathered 7 children. He had been a minister in Prince Edward Island, before moving to Tillsonburg, Ontario. When war broke out Smith joined the Royal Navy Volunteer Reserve Force; records show he was a lieutenant in command of a Motor Launch (an originally Canadian-made small military vessels designed for harbour defense and chasing enemy submarines). As such Smith was one of many Canadians who served on motor launches during the war. There is no record of any military decoration.

day. Sunday night I slept on the box couch and slept well. When Ewan got up in the morning he said, "This has been the first night since last May that I have slept a *real* sleep and felt rested on waking." That day I felt a lightness of heart long unknown to me.

Captain Smith stayed until Wednesday and we enjoyed his visit very much. About twenty years ago Edwin Smith was the minister in Kensington and Long River. I never met him but as the Park Corner folks were in his congregation I heard of him frequently through them. I always felt a certain unusual interest in him because it was hinted abroad that he was a writer of articles and so I felt profes-

Captain Smith and Ewan.

sionally akin. He was then a young man, lately married, very handsome

Rev. Edwin Smith, M.A.

and clever. The first time I saw him was on the occasion of a meeting of Presbytery in Cavendish during the "church row."[274] Fan Wise[275] and I were standing in the hall porch looking at the ministers on the platform, Edwin Smith among them. "That man is too good looking to be a minister," whispered Fan. Later on he preached in the new church on the occasion of Ewan's induction there. He was then settled at Cardigan; after that he went out to Alberta and when the war broke out was settled in Tilsonburg, Ontario. He had always had a hobby for sailing and wherever possible he kept a yacht. He had studied navigation and qualified as a captain. When the war broke out he offered his services to the British admiralty and was accepted. For

274   The "Old" Cavendish Presbyterian Church was torn down in 1901; a heated debate had ensued about where it should be rebuilt.

275   Fannie Wise (later Fannie Wise Mutch) was an old friend from Cavendish.

four years he has been an officer in the British navy, commanding a flotilla of submarine chasers. He had adventures galore and did such good work generally that he was personally thanked and decorated by the king.

The war was ended and he had to doff his gold stripes and return to civilian life. His nerves are rather shaken and he is at present agent at Oshawa for the Imperial Life Insurance Co. I very much doubt if he ever goes back to the pulpit—which is rather a pity, since he is a very good preacher.

I had expected to see a good deal of change in him. He is by now fifty years old. But he looks about 35. There is not a thread of gray in his thick black hair, not a line on his lean, handsome, almost boyish face, not a trace of stoop or stodginess in his slender, upright figure.

He entertained us brilliantly with his tales of adventure. He is certainly a rather universal genius, for he can preach, talk and write wonderfully well, is a Fellow of the R.A.S. of London,[276] and is full of personal charm and magnetism. I rather think he lacks steadiness of purpose, with all his gifts, and so has been surpassed in his professional career by men who were far his inferiors in mental capacity.

On Wednesday Ewan and I motored him to Oshawa. The day was fine. Ewan was in excellent spirits, and we had a delightful time. We came home in the evening, Ewan was as cheerful and merry as of yore, teasing me, and calling me "Pussy" and "Monkey." He seemed perfectly well and said he was.

I hardly know myself. The burden I have carried all summer has suddenly slipped from my shoulders and I think I feel a little light-headed—as if I were flying rather than walking. I cannot describe my feelings. It is easier to write out pain than joy. I feel as if twenty years had been knocked off my tale of birthdays.

Stella came last night. We motored down to meet her and all the way home and all the evening Ewan teased and bantered her as of old. Then she and I talked until twelve, of the incidents of her summer at home and the many seemingly insoluble problems of Park Corner.

Ewan preached today and had no difficulty in doing so. Oh, if it only lasts! I would not re-live this past summer for anything that might be offered me.

I must be a pretty wiry creature. When I was a child I was supposed to be delicate. I don't think I really was. Because my mother died of consumption[277] I think people got the idea that I must necessarily have

---

276   Royal Astronomical Society of London.
277   Tuberculosis.

inherited delicacy of constitution and the fact that I was subject to rather severe colds spread and deepened the impression. I have not had an easy life and yet, since I left childhood behind me I have not had a serious illness. And now, after a summer of unceasing care, worry, and hard work an Insurance Co. finds me a "first class risk"—heart, lungs, kidneys, blood-pressure all normal. That isn't too bad.

I took out $20,000 on my life. That will provide for the boys' education if anything happens to me.

Monday, Sept. 22, 1919
Leaskdale, Ont.

I spent the morning doing up grape jelly. After dinner Ewan and Stella and I motored to Sonya to say goodbye to the Dodds who are leaving there—to my regret, for I like Mrs. Dodds and we have been quite chummy. Then we went to Uxbridge to meet George Millar, a P.E. Island pal of Ewan's who was coming out from Toronto for a brief visit. This evening we had a grand seance of fireworks on our lawn. I got them in the spring, intending to have them for Chester's birthday in July. But we were

Mrs. Dodds.

away then and since our return I have not felt much like fireworks until lately. So we had the fun tonight.

Sunday, Sept. 28, 1919
The Manse, Leaskdale, Ont.

We have had a most enjoyable week, motoring everywhere we could find an excuse to go. Capt. McGillvary came last night to speak on the Prohibition referendum.[278] He is a young chaplain who was overseas—very good fun and he and Stell and I have had much laughter together.

Stell goes tomorrow and I feel badly over it. We have had a very jolly week—a week that seemed like a bit of olden times. It is long since I have laughed so much and so often and so light-heartedly. I think it was because the mirthful side of my nature has been so completely repressed this summer. When it was again released it shot up like a spring and vibrated tremendously to the currents of life. In a little

---

278   Canada had passed a national prohibition of the manufacture and purchase of alcohol from 1918 to 1920 as a temporary measuring during wartime. Referenda were held to extend this measure as well as to ratify provincial prohibition law. (Most provinces voted to repeal the bans in the 1920s, except for Prince Edward Island, where alcohol remained illegal until 1948.)

Stella

while it will revert to its normal level and life will be sober enough again but for this week it has had full sway.

Anyhow, Stell and I have had a joyous week of mirth and good feasting together. When all is said and done, she is of the race that knows Joseph and the only person in the world, now that Frede is gone, who can enter with me into its heritage. She has been pretty well this time—fewer growls than I have ever known in her—and when Stell is in good humor there could not be a jollier companion. I hate to see her going so far away, where we can never meet save at intervals of years. But it seems to be my Kismet to go through life thus and I must e'en make the best of it.[279]

Monday, Sept. 29, 1919
Leaskdale, Ont.

This evening we motored Capt. M. to Uxbridge to speak at the mass meeting. On the way back we had a punctured tire and as a result didn't get home until nearly one. Cars are all right some times. At other times they are exasperating animals. When we got home Stell and I flew around and with many jokes got up a downeast lunch of cold corned tongue, sandwiches, hot tea and cake. We all sat around the table and ate and told jokes until nearly three. This morning we all motored into Toronto. Stella left on the Chicago train at 6. I bade her a dreary good-bye and Ewan and I started home again, getting here at 9, after a black and nerve-racking drive through thunderstorms and over muddy roads.

Thursday, Oct. 2, 1919
The Manse, Leaskdale

Ewan didn't sleep very well last night—sighed and moaned a good deal. This has made me feel anxious all day. I wrote two hours this morning and put up grape juice in the afternoon. In the evening we motored over to Zephyr to re-organize the Guild there—which of course slumped this summer when we were not able to shoulder it along. Midway in the big swamp, two miles from everywhere, a tire blew out,

---

279   Derived from the Turkish word for fate, "kismet" suggests a power that is believe to control events of the future.

and, as our jack, as usual, was not in working order we had a devil of a time getting the spare on. I'm all tired out.

Saturday, Oct. 4, 1919

Today I heard Ewan going through the hall shouting, "Last call for dinner in the dining car." It seemed good to hear the threadbare old joke again though in days past it often "got on my nerves" by reason of its vain repetition. I hadn't heard it since last spring and it meant Ewan was feeling O.K.

I was busy all day preparing for a visit to Toronto. I am going in Monday to spend a week with Mary Beal and am looking forward to it eagerly.[280] It will be *good* to be free of responsibility for a few days—no meals or meetings to plan etc. etc. etc. Ordinarily I like my household routine very well and enjoy carrying it out with the systematic planning that enables me, as Frede used to say, protestingly, "to do three women's work." But we all like a little playtime.

Tonight I was copying the entries in my old diary dealing with the "license exam." What an abominable system they did have at P.W. College in those days! We mulled for a fortnight over the college exams, studying hard and late o'nights. Then, when they were over, and we were all thoroughly tired and fagged we had to plunge right into another set of exams, on precisely the same work and rush through them at the rate of two and sometimes three a day. No wonder many always failed, even those who had made good marks in the college exams. It was barbarous. Not long after my time a saner custom came in and those who made a certain percentage in the college exams did not have to take the License exams. Possibly by this time the Powers-that-rule have had a further accession of common-sense and abolished the License exams altogether. If they haven't they should have.

Monday, Oct. 6, 1919
2 Nina Ave., Toronto

I came in this morning and Mr. McClelland met me at the train and took me to lunch at the National. I shopped the rest of the day and came up to Mary's in time for dinner. After dinner she and Norman and I went to a movie which was rather good. But it is only an occasional "movie" that I really care for.

---

280   Mary Beal came from an Uxbridge family and had been the Vice-President of the Hypatia Club in 1911–12.

Wednesday, Oct. 8, 1919
2 Nina Ave., Toronto

This is "the end of a perfect day." The weather was glorious. Mr. Mc-
Clelland, and Mr. and Mrs. Stewart and I motored out to Oakville today
on the Hamilton Highway and had dinner in the evening at the Mississauga Golf Club House.[281] Before dinner we went over part of the links
and I played my first round of golf. Made a fearful mess of it, of course,
but felt the fascination of the game. I have always thought that golf is
a game I'd love if I ever had a chance to learn and practise it. But then
I've never had a chance and never will have.

The scenery about the Mississauga Links is charming. I have seldom seen a more beautiful bit of landscape than the valley below the
club house.

Thursday, Oct. 9, 1919

Today Mary gave an afternoon tea for me. My soul loathes afternoon
teas. May the devil fly away with the individual who invented such a
form of entertainment. But for Mary's sake I went through the motions
gracefully—togged myself up in a French gown of shot pink and green
taffeta and honiton lace,[282] which I don't often get a chance to wear,
strung some "jools" on myself and pinned on the inevitable corsage
bouquet and receiving smile. I stood most of the afternoon shaking
hands and saying, "I'm glad you do" to women who told me they loved
my books etc. and whom I probably will never meet again and won't
recognize if I do. And this is in the year of grace 1919! How long does
it take a world to learn how to live?

But Mary was happy because her tea was a great success of its kind
and so wisdom is justified of her children.

We wound up by going to see "Mickey" tonight, a movie which is
attracting crowds and is hailed as a wonderful performance.[283] It really
bored me to tears. I could howl and tear my hair to see what should be
a simple, innocent, artless "backwoods" girl played by a sophisticated

---

281   In 1917 the first concrete road in Ontario, the Toronto–Hamilton Highway, was opened,
almost 64 km (40 miles) long, connecting the two cities. This road is today known as Lake Shore
Boulevard and Lakeshore Road. The Mississauga Golf Clubhouse (now the Mississauga Golf and
Country Club) was established in 1913.

282   A traditional hand-made lace from Honiton, Devon, in England.

283   The comedy-drama silent film *Mickey* (1918), starring Mabel Normand, was about an
orphan who has been brought up in a mining settlement, and is sent to New York to live with
her aunt.

movie star who rolls her eyes and indulges in the vulgar pantomime of a Broadway soubrette.[284] It really doesn't "go" at all.

Monday, Oct. 13, 1919
Leaskdale, Ont.

We have been having some fairy-like autumn days. Last Friday I wound up my shopping orgy, paid the bills—"some performance" nowadays, believe me!—and went to Mr. McClelland's for dinner at night. Met Mr. and Mrs. Hatheway, rather nice people. Saturday night I came home amid the Thanksgiving mob—no joke in Toronto's old station. Marshall Saunders, author of *Beautiful Joe*, came out with me for the week end.[285] A clever woman but a bit of a bore—talks too much and overloads her conversation with irrelevant detail. I was quite reconciled when she left this morning. Lily has gone for her second week of vacation and I shall be trebly busy for a time. Chester walked "around the block" with Douglas Madill this evening—a distance of five miles. Quite an exploit for a kiddy of seven. He was quite tickled and wrote in his diary about it. He has kept a little diary for a year now. Whether he will keep it up when I cease to be the moving power I know not but he is quite interested now. Dear boy, I hope he will never need a journal for what I have needed mine—the outlet of pain and bitter experiences which none shared with me and which I could tell to no other confidant.

Wednesday, Oct, 15, 1919
The Manse, Leaskdale, Ont.

Beautiful weather. Ewan motored to Toronto yesterday and didn't come back till tonight, so the lads and I were alone last night. I forgot to lock the doors but we slept none the less soundly and nobody ran off with us.

Copying my old diary tonight I came to a mention of Mamie Simpson.[286] Poor Mamie—the only one of those old Cavendish schoolmates

---

284   A soubrette is a stock comedy character, often vain, mischievous, coquettish and gossipy (such as a chambermaid or confidante of the main female character).

285   See note 218, page 136.

286   Mamie Simpson was mentioned by LMM in one of her earliest journal entries, November 26, 1889 (when LMM was age 15). In her longer retrospective entry of January 28, 1912, following her relocation to Ontario, LMM wrote of Charlie Simpson's family in Cavendish, "He and his wife and youngest daughter still live there. Mamie and Emma, the two older girls were my schoolmates. Both went to Boston several years ago. Emma married there. Mamie went under. She has trodden ever since the way that takes hold on hell."

of mine who took the road that leads down to death. Mamie and Emma Simpson were the two daughters of "Charlie" Simpson by his first wife. A man who is known all his life as "Charlie" is classed by that fact. Charlie S. was a notorious bigot in his religious opinions—he was of that sect which arrogates to itself the title of Christians and is known to those outside the pale as "Campbellites." In Charlie's opinion you were damned if you were not immersed—or if you played cards or danced. *His* girls were brought up to abhor such things; but it never worried him a particle that his girls were out on the roads, or "sitting up" with every Tom, Dick and Harry for all hours of the night.

Mamie was the older and was considered a very pretty girl. She was gay, merry, free from malice; everyone liked her. In the apt country phrase you "always heard her before you saw her"; she always had a new beau on the string—harmless, silly flirtation at first—then indiscretions—then hinted scandal. It never broke into open flame but in a few years poor Mamie's reputation was fly-blown. She went to Boston and erelong the inevitable followed there—open shame, rapid degradation. She has been the mistress of scores of men, she has been in the reformatory, in the brothel. Her name is never mentioned in her old home—she has never returned to Cavendish—never will. "'Tis an old tale and often told."[287] But in spite of that I think there are worse women in God's sight than poor, good-hearted, wrongly-trained, misled Mamie Simpson.

Thursday, Oct. 16, 1919
Leaskdale, Ont.

I had a letter from home today with two bits of news that rather saddened me. One was that Walter Simpson was dead, the other that Geo. R. Macneill had sold his farm and was going to move to Bonshaw.[288]

Walter Simpson was a brother of Arthur's but a very different type. He was clever, conceited, radical, with very liberal views on religion. He was a much hated man, for he was sarcastic and pugnacious and had not the slightest regard for anyone's feelings. But I never disliked him at any time for he was always very decent to me. When I was a

---

287   From Walter Scott's *Marmion: A Tale of Flodden Field* (1808), Canto II, XXVII: "'Tis an old tale, and oft told; / But, did my fate and wish agree, / Ne'er had been read, in story old; / Of maiden true betray'd for gold, / That loved, or was avenged, like me!"

288   Walter Simpson was a friend from Cavendish, who had been in the Literary Society with LMM; George Raglan Macneill similarly was a Cavendish friend and cousin, also a member of the Literary Society.

young girl he was one of the bright and shining lights of the Literary Society and I always enjoyed his verbal tilts with the other members. In those years his first wife was alive, a detestable narrow-minded, ignorant woman. After her death he married Ada Macneill[289] who civilized him to a great extent, aided no doubt by the mellowing process of years. Owing to my friendship with her and Myrtle I saw a good deal of Walter after that and rather enjoyed his company. But the reason I feel rather badly over his passing out is, I think, solely because he was one of the landmarks in the Cavendish of my youth. I would feel about the same, I verily believe, if it had been his brother Arthur whom I have always detested. He, too, was part of that old life, hatred and all, and every such passing seems to remove it further and further away.

Geo. R's Place

It is a real grief to me that Geo. R. has sold out. I hate to think of two old and dear friends like George and Eva going away from Cavendish for one thing; and for another, it has brought forcibly home to me how fast the name of Macneill is disappearing from Cavendish—of "our" Macneills, that is, for Albert and Alec and Russell are not really of our clan at all but only related to us by reason of their grandfather having married one of "our" Macneill's. They are of a different stock altogether, with far different traditions and atmosphere.

When I was a girl Cavendish was full of Macneills. A certain John Macneill[290] came out from Argyleshire, Scotland, to the Island, then mostly covered with forest and called Island of St. John, in the year 1772. On the way out he met on shipboard Margaret Simpson and

---

289   Ada Macneill was a schoolteacher who had given birth to Myrtle Macneill out of wedlock. From 1894 Ada lived with her aunt and uncle, David Macneill and his sister Margaret (distant relatives of LMM). In some respects this kinship relation was part of the prototype for *Anne of Green Gables*—David Macneill was notoriously shy, like Matthew Cuthbert, and Margaret shared qualities with Marilla Cuthbert. Ada married Walter Simpson in 1901, although Myrtle remained with David and Margaret. Myrtle would marry Ernest Webb in 1905. LMM and Myrtle remained good friends all their lives, but Myrtle herself was not the model for Anne.

290   John Macneill (1750–1815) and Margaret Simpson (1759–1859).

on arriving in Charlottetown they were married.[291] Their oldest son, my great grandfather, William Macneill, was the first male white child born in Charlottetown—a female child having been born before him.

In 1790 John Macneill settled in Cavendish where the Simpsons and Clarks also located. He had a family of nine sons and three daughters,—all clever, high-spirited and domineering—at least, so report goes. The only one of them who survived into my days of recollection was "old Uncle David" Macneill, who was the youngest of the family and so not so many years older than his oldest nephews. He was a very brainy old man and very pleasant and amiable in society, but, I understand, a tyrant and martinet—in his own home—as most of the old Macneills were, I believe.

John Macneill did not live out his days. One day he was suddenly seized with severe internal pain. All homely remedies being of no avail the resolute Macneill mounted on horseback and rode across the Island to Charlottetown by the old bridle trail, his wife sitting on a pillion[292] behind him. The Ch'town doctor's remedies availed nothing and he died soon after reaching there. Nowadays he would be promptly operated on for appendicitis and his life probably saved. But appendicitis was not discovered then and John Macneill died in ignorance even of the name of his malady. It was impossible to take his body home for burial through the woods by the bridle trail so he was buried in the old "Malpeque Road" burying ground at Ch'town and there his forgotten and unmarked grave cannot be even found today.

My great-grandfather, William Macneill, married Eliza Townsend, the daughter of an officer in the British navy, Captain John Townsend.[293] She came to P.E. Island with her grandfather, who was an officer in the British army and had been given a grant of P.E.I. land by George III.[294] This he called Park Corner, after the Townsend estate in England. Old William Macneill was a clever man. He went early into local politics, was for twenty years a member of the Provincial Legislature and "Speaker" of it for sixteen. He was Commissioner of Public Works for all the north side of Queen's County, and was also a magistrate for twenty years. He married all the people in the vicinity, wrote all the wills, and settled all disputes. He lived to be eighty-nine and was buried in Cavendish churchyard.

---

291   Here LMM has written in the margin, presumably at a later date: "Have discovered he met her *after* arriving on Island (1932)."

292   A sidesaddle allows the rider to sit aside rather than astride a horse; women in dresses often rode this way.

293   William Simpson Macneill (1781–1870) and Eliza Bliss Townsend (1788–1859).

294   George III (1738–1820) was King of Britain from 1760 until his death in 1820.

In my childhood there were ten families of Macneills living in Cavendish, eight of whom were "our" Macneills. Furthest west was John Macneill, an old bachelor who lived with his sister Jane. They have died since I left Cavendish and the farm has passed into the hands of a Simpson. Next to them lived William C. Macneill, Amanda's father. Then there were Mr. and Mrs. Macneill, their sons, Malcolm, Hamilton and Allan, and their daughters, Amanda and Tillie. Now all are gone except Mac and Ham, who are living there, two forlorn old bachelors whom nobody will marry. When they die another Macneill homestead will vanish from Cavendish.

Pierce Macneill lived next them.[295] He and his wife have no children, so at their death it is likely that farm will pass to another name also. David Macneill[296]—"young David"— who lived on the other side of the road, is dead and Ernest Webb owns that place now. Across the road from us Great-uncle James—"Uncle Jimmy"—lived. He has gone and now George has

Cavendish Churchyard

Wm. C. Macneill's

sold out to a Simpson. Grandfather is gone. Uncle John is still there but his son Ernest has no family. If he does not have any that farm will eventually pass away from the name, too. East of us, Charles, William and George Macneill lived.[297] Of these George was of our clan. He and his wife and all his big family have gone, except Arty.[298] He, too, is childless, so the name is doomed there. Of the

295　Pierce Macneill (1851–1936).

296　David Macneill (1836–1914).

297　Charles Macneill (1831–1908); William C. Macneill was the father of LMM's friend Amanda (see note 85, page 36); George Macneill (d. 1898).

298　Artemas Macneill, a brother of LMM's friend and cousin Alma.

"other" Macneills, Russell has two sons, Albert one, William, one and Alec none. These may keep the name alive but it will not be "our" name. The old stock is played out there, and 'tis a pity for 'twas a rare good old stock with all its faults. "Sic transit gloria mundi."[299] Into the dust they have gone, one and all, with their loves that burned and their hatreds that flamed and their woes that ached as hotly and fiercely and bitterly as ours of today.

Friday, Oct. 19, 1919
The Manse, Leaskdale

Twenty-four years ago I wrote in my diary, "I wish I could have lots of books." Looking at my library today one would suppose that I had attained my wish. In truth, I have. I have more books than I have convenient room for. But alas, I have not the time to read them, save by a hungry dip and bite now and then. So am I much the better off by reason of my granted wish? And will my children, who will have these hundred of books to revel in, get any more pleasure and nutriment out of them than I got out of the few well-chewed ones of my youth?

Saturday, Oct. 25, 1919
Leaskdale, Ont.

Today I realized that I have been feeling better these last few weeks than I have felt at any time since I had the flu a year ago. I have not felt tired or dragged or headachy. I have been full of vim and energy. I have slept well and wakened refreshed. The gods grant that it continue.

Last night I copied a lot of my old diary. It is like living over the past again and I always come back to the present with a little sense of unreality. Some of those old entries hurt me, too. For example here is one, apropos of a visit to Pensie's home: "What a dear old place it always is! Always the same and always certain of a good time." Alas, it is many years since it ceased to be "the same." Charles and "Mrs. Charles" are gone. Pensie has been dead for several years, her gay, ready, if not over-intelligent laughter, forever stilled. All the girls and boys have gone from the old place, save Russell, who was the one I never liked. His wife, Maggie Houston, is an odd, unamiable person, and to go there now is so little like what it used to be in the gay days of old that it is almost farcical.

Ches Clark figures quite frequently in the records of that particular time.[300] Ches and I were always excellent friends. We were never

---

299   "Thus passes the glory of the world" (Latin).

300   Chesley Clark was a Cavendish neighbour (see note 385, page 282). Lemuel McCleod, mentioned in the next paragraph, was from French River.

"beaux" though he occasionally drove me or walked home with me. We were simply "pals." In 1897 Ches went out to B.C.—and has never been home since. At first when he went out there he was coming home every "next year." But the years came and went and he returned not. And now he can never come back to the Cavendish he left—it is no longer in existence.

Ches was married a few years ago to some lady he met out there. They have no family and I have an idea that she is a good deal older than Ches. He always liked mature friends and sweethearts. I was four or five years older than he and so were all the girls he went with. I would like to meet Ches and have a talk over old times but it is not likely our paths will ever cross again. "Lem" too—I have just been copying the entry of his proposal. Well, as I predicted, Lem did not die for love. In no very long time he was going about with several other girls. I don't know why all his affairs with them came to nothing. Eventually he left Kensington and went into a store in Ch'town. There he met Maggie Sellars, a very pretty girl, and, I have heard, a very nice one. They became engaged and Lem went out west, set up in business for himself, and married his Maggie. Since then he has drifted out of my ken. He has no family and I have heard that he was not especially successful in business, but that last is mere rumor and may not be true.

Tuesday, Oct. 28, 1919
Leaskdale, Ont.

I have been reading Marshall Saunders' latest book "Golden Dicky" to Chester, a chapter every night when he goes to bed.[301] He has been keenly interested in it. Tonight I was reading a somewhat pathetic chapter detailing the adventures of a lost and starving dog. Suddenly I was interrupted by a bitter cry. Looking down I saw the child's face convulsed. "Oh, mother, I can't bear it," he sobbed.

"Why, lad," I said, "it's going to come out all right. Billy isn't going to die. She's going to find a good home and a kind mistress very soon." "Are you sure?" "Yes." "Well, just read me the part where it says so right off before you finish this chapter."

I never saw a child so keenly sensitive to accounts of suffering. He is even more so than I used to be—too keenly sensitive I fear.

Today in my old diary I came to a mention of Lula Gamble, my little girl-chum at the Bideford parsonage long ago.[302] It is years since her

---

301 *Golden Dicky: The Story of a Canary and his Friends* (Stokes, 1919). Marshall Saunders had written a series of animal stories, following her success with *Beautiful Joe* (1894).

302 Lula Gamble (1880–1963). In an entry of November 27, 1894, when she was teaching in

name has even occurred to me. She was twelve that winter and I was twenty but we were "just chums." I seem always to have had an aptitude for comradeship with girls much younger than myself—Frede, Nora, Lula. The gap between twelve and twenty is a very wide one—perhaps the widest possible. But Lula was mature for her age and so we bridged it easily. We slept together and plotted together to pull the wool over the eyes of the Reverend and cranky Estey, we talked and laughed together in the darkness. I remember Lula flinging her arms about me one night before we went to sleep and saying "Let me kiss your beloved face, teacher."

I don't know where she is or what has been her lot in life. I dimly remember hearing years ago that she was married. She was a clever little thing. I hope she has had as happy a life as she deserved.

Saturday, Nov. 8, 1919
The Manse, Leaskdale, Ont.

Chester has a knack of saying odd little things. He goes over to George Leask's every morning for our milk. It was very sharp this morning and when he returned he said, "Mother, when I got the milk and left Mr. Leask's I just kneeled down on the ground and asked God to make it warmer but when I got out of the gate it was just as cold as ever."

Last night he developed a sudden fondness for celery. When I said, "How is it you can eat it now when you have never liked it before?" he said gravely "I can eat celery now because God put the power into me."

I wonder if I made many queer speeches when I was a tot. If I did they were not recorded or remembered, save two, which I often heard told by way of a joke—something I did not at all relish. One day when I was very small an aunt asked me if I would go and bring home her turkeys from the shore field. I responded gravely, "I am afraid it would excite ridicule."

I remember saying this but I have no recollection of the other speech with which I am credited. There was company to tea—"quality folk"—Mr. and Mrs. Archibald, with another minister and wife who were visiting there. I came in late, very hot, breathless, and dishevelled. I had been down to the mill brook with "Katie," Uncle John's French servant girl, to water the cows. Grandma asked me why I was so late and I gasped out, "Katie and I went to water the cows and we had to chase *that bloody heifer* for nearly half an hour."

Consternation!

Bideford, LMM described Lula: "She is about 12 and is so far advanced that I hardly know where to place her."

Of course, I was merely repeating a phrase I had heard Katie use. The French "hired help" of those days were given to swearing. For that matter, I would not have known that "bloody" was a "cuss word." Nor, indeed, could I ever understand why it should be so considered until little over a year ago when I learned that it was, in that usage, not an adjective at all but a corruption of the old oath, "By our Lady"—"By'r-l-dy"—"bloody."

The other evening I heard Chester explaining "marriage" to Stuart. "A man and a woman go to a minister and he *preaches a sermon to them* and then they're married."

Wednesday, Nov. 12, 1919
The Manse, Leaskdale

I feel rather anxious tonight. At supper Ewan seemed rather dull and irritable and immediately after it went upstairs and lay down, saying he wanted "to rest." This seems so much like he was in August and September that it struck a chill to my heart.

Friday, Nov. 14, 1919

I feel half sick with despair. Thursday morning was cold and gray. Ewan and I motored to Glenarm, a distance of thirty miles, to visit Rev. Mr. Smith and family. I enjoyed the drive for Ewan seemed quite well and I thought my anxiety of the previous night groundless. But after dinner he complained of a headache and from that on I was worried. We had supper at Woodville with the Brydons and then motored home through a very black dour night. Ewan still complained of his head but seemed cheerful enough. Last night, however, he wakened at four and could not sleep again. He admitted that his "phobia" had returned. This was dreadful news to me.

It has been a terrible day—dark and cold and windy. I had to work at cleaning the dining room. Is the winter to be like the summer? I *cannot* face it here alone if it is—no, I cannot!

Saturday, Nov. 15, 1919
Leaskdale, Ont.

Another day and evening of something sadly akin to utter despair for me. Ewan had a poor night. I had to get out the chloral bottle again—I had so hoped I had put it away forever—but even it did not give him sleep. He had a poor day—headache and depression. I worked doggedly all day. The hardest thing I had to do was go over to the church in the afternoon to help with a practice for the S.S. Christmas concert. It is a job I dislike at any time and today it did not seem to me that I could face it. But I set my teeth, went over, selected and allotted recitations and dialogues and drills and kept my gnawing fear in the back of my mind. It got its revenge when I came home in the early autumn twilight. I shut myself in the dark parlor where no one could see me and the children could not find me and had a bad half hour. This evening after I had got the children to bed I sat here by the table, too despairing even to read. Oh God, I cannot face a winter like last summer!

Sunday, Nov. 16, 1919
The Manse, Leaskdale

There is no improvement in Ewan. He had a bad night and had to take chloral. Today he managed to get through his services by dint of reading an old sermon. The great trouble of course, in these attacks, is that he believes he is not "fit to preach," since he is a lost soul! He was very dull when he got back from Zephyr and walked the floor after supper. It is all just like last spring—only he is not quite so bad. But there is the dread that he may become so. Of course I don't sleep now either, so I feel miserable every way.

Monday, Nov. 17, 1919

Again a poor night for Ewan. He stayed in bed all the forenoon. In the afternoon we had to go to a funeral. Ewan managed to get through with it but I sat in misery lest he break down. He was very dull this evening. I have held myself rigidly in all day, keeping going by the exertion of will power, determined not to let myself slump or go to pieces.

Tuesday, Nov. 18, 1919

Another bad night. Ewan took chloral twice but it seemed to have no effect. I have begun giving him bromides again. Ewan was dull all day but in the evening said he felt "much easier."

Wednesday, Nov. 19, 1919
Leaskdale, Ont.

Last night Ewan had to take two doses of chloral but this time they worked and he got a good long sleep from them. I slept with Chester, who has a bad cold and sore throat, that I might keep him warm and covered. I slept little for outside a cold fierce gale was blowing and the shutters kept rattling and banging. Besides, my bitter thoughts haunted me. How long the night seemed! It was very cold all day. Ewan stayed in bed all the morning and seemed very dull all day. I am keeping up the bromide treatment and will give it a fair trial. I worked hard all day getting the kitchen cleaned.

A copy of the *Canadian Bookman* came today with a splendid review of *Rainbow Valley*.[303] It would have pleased me very much if it could have pierced through the fog of worry that surrounds me.

Thursday, Nov. 20, 1919

I slept with Chester again last night. Ewan took chloral twice and slept. He seemed much better all day. I began to hope although I was afraid to. But when we went out this evening to make a sick call he was so dull and abstracted that I was miserably sure people would notice it and discover that his mind was unbalanced. Coming after my little gleam of hope this was doubly hard. When we came out into the black, bleak, hard, cold November night I couldn't keep back the tears and cried silently all the way home. Ewan walked beside me in silence. It did not matter to him in the least that I was broken-hearted. This is one of the most dreadful phases of melancholia.

Friday, Nov. 21, 1919
The Manse, Leaskdale

Again I feel encouraged. Ewan slept well from 10 to 5.30 without any chloral and seemed more like himself all day. Mr. Forbes, a visiting missionary, came for over Sunday. I had expected he would bring his wife with him and I dreaded it under the circumstances but fortunately she did not come.

Saturday, Nov. 22, 1919

Again Ewan slept well and seemed much better all day. I went to S. S. practice again this afternoon and came home tired and dispirited from trying to get the children into line. Ewan and Mr. Forbes were away. It was dark and cloudy and cold. I found it very hard to compel myself to go to work. I wanted to go upstairs, fling myself on the bed and just give up. But I didn't—instead I went to work.

---

303   *The Canadian Bookman* was founded in 1919 by Canadian editor B.K. Sandwell (1876–1954). In 1921 it would become the official organ of the Canadian Authors' Association.

Had a letter from Nora Lefurgey—Mrs. Edmond Campbell—to-day.[304] She lives in B.C. and has three children. She wrote a gay, happy letter. Such letters are a little bitter to me now, in my own dread and unhappiness.

Stokes also wrote me that *Rainbow Valley* is to be translated into Danish and Swedish.

Monday, Nov. 24, 1919

Ewan has been sleeping well and seems fairly normal again. But I don't think I shall ever feel free from dread again. The attacks come so suddenly and relentlessly. But possibly it can always be controlled thus by the bromides. I must hope so anyhow, if I am to go on with life at all.

Tuesday, Nov. 25, 1919
Leaskdale, Ont.

A cold snowstorm. In the afternoon we went to Allan Gray's to tea.[305]

There are people who seem to take all the beauty, color, rhythm, sparkle and courage out of life and leave it ugly, gray, flat, dull and cowardly. The Grays are this kind of people. When I came away and drove home through the cold wintry night I felt depressed and cowed. We have to go back to the buggy now and so the drive home was slow and cold and dreary. I suppose I am feeling the reaction of my fortnight on the rack. Or else Mrs. Gray's "sweet supper" consisting of nothing but jam, pie and several kinds of poorly made cake has damped my spirits! No wonder they are dull and depressing when they live on such stuff.

Wednesday, Nov. 26, 1919
The Manse, Leaskdale

This morning Ewan, Chester and I drove to Uxbridge. It was bitter cold and it did seem very slow progress after skimming down in the car. But we've just got to resign ourselves to it and make the best of it. I shall not growl over this if other things keep bearable. Chester had to have his two lower front teeth taken out as the second ones were pushing through behind them. I try to keep sharp tabs on my children's teeth

---

304   Nora Lefurgey (1880–1977) was a friend from Cavendish. In an entry of September 23, 1928, LMM wrote, "Apart from Laura Pritchard and Frede Campbell, Nora Lefurgey (who in some respects is much the same type of girl) is the only friend I have ever had before whom I could, in Emerson's fine phrase, 'think aloud.'"

305   Allan Gray (1863–1943) was a farmer and leading member of the Presbyterian Church in Leaskdale.

in order to secure as regular a second set as possible. I have several of his first set filled in order to keep them in place so that the gum might not shrink and crowd the new ones. I have felt badly all my life from the ugly, crowded crooked appearance

Brock St. E., Uxbridge

of my teeth—at least of the lower ones—which might have been remedied if they had been attended to early enough. Of course, I inherited teeth with a tendency to be crooked from father but much might have been done to straighten them if they had been taken in time.

I have always envied people with nice white even teeth—something rather rarely seen. However, I have most of my own teeth yet and that is something to be thankful for. One's own teeth, even if they are ugly, are really better than a beautiful false set.

We got home in time for dinner and I spent the whole afternoon in writing a paper for Zephyr Guild tomorrow night and in arranging a "scrapbook" programme for our Leaskdale guild tonight. Then after supper I went to the Guild and "ran" it. Now I'm home, good and ready for bed.

Thursday, Nov. 27, 1919
Leaskdale, Ont.

I worked at Book 10 all the forenoon.[306] Then after dinner got ready and went to Zephyr and had tea at Frank Walkers—a performance almost as depressing as our visit to Gray's. To be sure, they are not quite as "gray" as the Grays but they are ignorant and trivial. Mrs. Walker told me she thought Ewan was "too fat" for real health and that his cough was "terrible" etc. He is no fatter than he has been for years and his cough is a temporary one owing to a bad cold he has contracted. But that sort of thing is depressing when one is rather down anyhow. I remember the first time I was ever there. It was in the winter before Chester was born. Mrs. Walker knew my condition, which was perhaps the reason why she entertained me with the cheerful accounts of three women she had known who had all died in childbirth. I did not

---

306   That is, *Rilla of Ingleside* (1921).

let it worry me. I knew there was a certain element of risk but I knew also that only a very small percentage of women die in childbirth. Besides, my sense of humor was in good working order then and it really amused me. But now when I am not feeling especially cheerful such a hostess rather gets on my nerves. I was quite willing to exchange her conversation for even the dark night and rough roads of the way to the church. Then, when we got there, there was no guild after all and I might have spent my precious two hours yesterday much more profitably. We came home over that long bleak hilly road. Ever since I came here those night drives home from Zephyr have been the bane of my existence. I get here chilled to the bone, tired and disgruntled. But a good hot drink and the consoling prospect of soon being cuddled down in a warm blankety bed with a blessed hot water bottle have raised my spirits somewhat.

Friday, Nov. 28, 1919
The Manse, Leaskdale

Worked at Book 10 all the morning. I feel rather discouraged over it. I can't seem to make it take shape and color as I wish. Had a dialogue practice here this evening, "licking a lot of young cubs into shape" for the S.S. concert. Now they are gone. I shut the door behind them with a bang of thankfulness and now that the day's grind is over, I'm going to have a blessed bit of a read.

Lately I came across in Byron his reference to the minor Scottish poet Hector Macneill, found in that vitriolic *English Bards and Scotch Reviewers*.[307] Hector Macneill was a collateral ancestor of my own, being a second cousin of the John Macneill who emigrated to P.E. Island. Most of his verse is negligible in quality but he wrote three lyrics that are equal to any in the Scottish or any other tongue. They are "I lo'ed ne'er a laddie but ane," "Saw ye my wee thing, saw ye my ain thing?" and the famous "Come under my plaidie," so often and wrongly attributed to Burns.[308]

Sunday, Nov. 30, 1919
Leaskdale, Ont.

I am forty-five years old today—not a particularly exhilarating fact. I don't look forty-five—strangers usually guess my age as 30. My hair is

---

307   *English Bards and Scotch Reviewers* (1809) is a satirical poem written by Lord Byron (1788–1824), a response to a negative review of Byron's first work of poetry. Poet, novelist, and well-travelled clerk, Hector Macneill (1746–1818) was born near Edinburgh, Scotland.

308   That is, Scottish poet Robert Burns (1759–96), a favourite of LMM.

still dark in general effect, my complexion is reasonably fresh and I have no wrinkles, owing I suppose to faithful cold-creaming and massage every night as well as to a series of facial muscle exercises I invented myself and practice regularly every day. And I don't *feel* forty-five—

at least, I don't feel as I once supposed a woman of forty-five must inevitably feel. But I *am* forty-five and life must be on the down-grade henceforth. One may as well look the fact in the face, distasteful as it is, and make the best of it. After all, most of the time I shall forget that I am forty five, or any age, and then it will not matter.

Last night we had one of the worst hurricanes that Ontario has had since 1896. The wind was terrific. It shrieked through our keyhole like the whistle of a steam engine. We are so well sheltered in this little dale that we seldom feel a wind but last night we got enough for a year in one capful. I sat here alone and tried to read but I was very lonely and so my book seemed savorless.

Making the best of it.

This afternoon was dull and cold and bitter. I copied down a goodish bit of my old journal. Lou Dystant's name figured in it conspicuously. Poor Lou! Of all the men who have loved me he was the slowest to recover. He did not marry until two years after I did. Then he married a nice girl and lives at Ellerslie and has a daughter. For years after I left Bideford he used to send me gifts at Christmas with a little note saying that he cared as much as ever and wanted to feel he could give me some small pleasure. A year or so before my marriage I met him at an Exhibition in Ch'town and as we walked about the grounds together he pulled up the lapel of his coat and showed me a little pin on which was my own face, reproduced from an old photo. I wonder what he has done with it since.

Friday, Dec. 5, 1919
Leaskdale, Ont.

Ugh! Those boys were here again for practice tonight. My nerves are frayed out. Ordinarily I like training small fry to do these things but these lads are certainly very raw material. One chap sat on the rocking chair and rocked fiercely all the time. One slumped down on his chair and it seemed impossible to get any energy into or out of him. I wanted to stick a darning needle into him to see if he could really feel or jump. One was pert and "Smart Alleckish." All were gigglers. There wasn't one nice or nice-mannered boy among them. I kept my patience admirably and put them through that dialogue until my head grew dizzy. Then I packed them off. It is 9.30 now and I am going to read Gibbon for awhile to take the taste of raw cub out of my soul.[309] I am on my third volume of him now. It is about twelve years since I read him through before. I read one volume, then I plunge into the most frivolous novel I can find by way of getting back to normal. He is so big and massive that he seems to suck one's individuality clean out of one—swallow one up like a huge, placid, slow-moving river. As I march with his stately procession of forgotten heroes and forgotten fools I get the uncomfortable feeling that I am as insignificant as a grain of dust amid so many centuries of "baffled millions who have gone before."[310] And I know I am—but it is an abominable feeling and one not to be tolerated, because it makes life impossible and silly.

Sunday, Dec. 7, 1919
The Manse, Leaskdale

Seven days of December gone, praise be. Not that I am in any hurry to get to the end of my forty-sixth year, thank you; but this winter is just something to be endured. This week has been very cold and gray and depressing. Our coal is poor so our house is not comfortable. Ewan, though fairly well, does not seem like his old self yet and I go in daily fear. I am lonely. I miss Frede hideously these gray days. Last night as I sat here alone I cried chokingly. If she were only somewhere in the world—if I might only hope to get a letter from her! But there is only blank and silence.

Cam is going to put on her tombstone the epitaph I selected.

"After life's fitful fever she sleeps well."[311]

It is the one I want on my own when I die. And I trust I shall sleep well—and dreamlessly. For I think it will take me a long while to get rested.

---

309   Edward Gibbon's six-volume History of the *Decline and Fall of the Roman Empire* (1776–88) recounts the history of Western civilization from the Roman Empire to the fall of Byzantium.

310   From Byron's "Epistle to Augusta": "Surely I once beheld a nobler aim. / But all is over. I am one the more / To baffled millions which have gone before."

311   From *Macbeth* 3.2, lines 19–23. See LMM's entry of February 7, 1919.

Monday, Dec. 8, 1919
The Manse, Leaskdale

Got home from a cold drive to Uxbridge to find a letter from Stell, all growls as usual and coolly demanding the loan of $2500 to start up a chicken ranch. That girl seems to be entirely without any sense of shame. She borrowed $1000 from me eight years ago, promising to pay 5% interest—and has never paid one cent. Yet now she asks for another loan, as if I were a bank on which she could draw at will. I am getting tired of lending money to her and her pals and never getting even interest on it. When I was poor and struggling nobody ever lent me a cent to help me along. I thought when Stell got married I would surely be free henceforth from her appeals and demands for money but I shall never be free from her. She has come to be a most disgusting compound of falsehood and effrontery and I'm out of all patience with her and her gang.

There, I've got that out of my system and feel better—and disposed to think I've stated it a bit too strongly. After all, old Stell is "one of us" and I suppose I must help her out. Perhaps she'll get on her feet and do better after this. But it is her callous taking-for-granted behavior that nettles me—as if I had no purpose in life than to earn money to help her out.

And I can never forget the way she behaved last summer about Frede's necklace.

Tuesday, Dec. 9, 1919
The Manse, Leaskdale

Ewan was not so well again today—said he felt nervous. In the evening I went up the hill and spent the evening with Mrs. Alex Leask who is ill. I talked small potatoes to her for two hours and hugged my fox of worry. As I walked home alone through the dense black night I shrank from what might be waiting for me when I got home. It is a hard thing to dread going to your own home. But Ewan seemed better again and I hope will not have a serious relapse. He sleeps well now and perhaps his recovery will be the more sure if it is not so sudden as last time.

Friday, Dec. 12, 1919

Tonight I had to go to Zephyr to give readings at a concert in aid of the Library there. One interesting feature of it—to me—was a little play which some of the scholars gave, taken out of my book "The Golden Road."[312]—the chapter containing "Great Aunt Eliza's visit." They did it very well and I really enjoyed it. The performance gave it a freshness which, for me, the printed page lacks.

But my evening was spoiled by the fact that Ewan's head bothered him a great deal and that he was staring at vacancy part of the time, immersed in gloomy reflections, instead of listening to the programme.

Saturday, Dec. 13, 1919

This was a dull gray lifeless day all through without a gleam of sunshine without or within—except a letter from Bertie which only made me feel so hungry for a talk with her that it made matters rather worse than better. I wrote in the forenoon and finished the skeleton of Book 10. After dinner I went to concert practice—a lifeless, dragging performance where everything seemed at loose ends and everybody seemed waiting for somebody else to go ahead and do things. After it was over I made a call on an old lady who may go into the kingdom before me but is a doleful inhabitant of this world. She sucked out what little "grit" I had left in me and I came home feeling like a squeezed orange.

The truth is, I'm starving for a little companionship. For eight weeks I've been mewed up here without one living soul near me who is any kin whatever to the race of Joseph. Ewan, in his present quiet, dull state of mind is rather worse than no company at all. So I'm utterly alone, and once in a while, when a dull, lifeless twilight is wrapping itself over a dull lifeless gray world I give up in a sort of despair and mutter, "I *can't* go on."

But my givings-up never last very long. When I get rested and cheered up by a bit of a dip into some interesting book—or even by a dose of confession in this, my diary—I rise up again and resolve to endure to the end. This little outburst here has quite refreshed me.

But oh, if I could only write to Frede or get a letter from her. That would keep life wholesome and normal. How I dread the thought of Christmas—the first Christmas on which I cannot hope to get even a greeting from Frede. Never again will she spend a Christmas with me. Christmas can never again mean anything to me but a day which must be made gay for the children's sake but which will only make me glad when it is over and done with.

---

312   Published by L.C. Page in 1913, this was the second in *The Story Girl* series.

Wednesday, Dec. 17, 1919
The Manse, Leaskdale

Life in weather as cold as these past three days have been is not life but mere existence. Monday and Tuesday were bad enough but today was still worse. This morning it was 16 below zero and we could not get the house warm. All day we have shivered and sighed. Mental work was out of the question. So I put on a sweater and *overboots*—for the kitchen floor was so cold that water froze on it at noon—and compounded my winter's supply of mincemeat. Now it is bedtime and I am glad. I shall go to bed with a hot water bottle and get warm.

Thursday, Dec. 18, 1919

I shut the manse door tonight behind those boys and said a fervent thanks-be. This was the last night of practice for them and I hope I'll never have such a gang to train again.

It was much milder today—we got the house warm—and life seemed a shade less gray.

I had a letter from Clara, giving some details of Stell's goings-on. Poor Stell—and yet when I think of some of the lies she has told Clara in order to cheat the latter out of her share in poor Frede's little leavings—I turn sick at soul.

Clara wrote that she had been to see "Anne of Green Gables" on the screen.[313] Page, by the way, sold the movie rights last summer. He would never sell them as long as we were in partnership because he would have had to share up with me. I knew he would do it as soon as he was free. He got $40,000 for the film rights. My share would have been $20,000—a nice sum to be cheated out of!!!

Mary Miles Minter is playing *Anne*. I've seen her in other plays. She is very dainty, very pretty and utterly unlike my gingery Anne. Clara wrote that she did not like the film at all and that everyone else was disappointed. The reason seems to be that their "favorite characters" are not included in the cast. Now, these characters do little in the books, but *talk* and unluckily talk can't be reproduced on the screen. Only the characters who *do* something can appear there. I do not expect to like the film myself—I never yet have liked any film I have seen that was reproduced from a book I had read. Nevertheless I am very curious to see it. Clara says Los Angeles turned out *en masse*—that she never had to stand so long in line in any city in her life to get a ticket.

---

313   The first film version of *Anne of Green Gables* was produced in 1919, a silent comedy-drama was directed by William Desmond Taylor, and starred Mary Miles Minter.

Friday, Dec. 19, 1919
The Manse, Leaskdale

Tonight was sharp as a needle. I yearned to subside into a rocking chair and have a good read "but wisest fate said no."[314] Instead, I had to go up and give a recitation at a concert and pie social at the north school. The whole evening was, as I expected, a sort of nightmare to me. Why then did I go?

Well, I am president of the Social Dep't of our Guild here. Six times a year I have to get up a programme. As there is not enough talent in the Guild to provide all this I have to get help from the Methodist young people up north occasionally. As a result, when *they* in turn ask me for assistance I must not refuse to "giff-gaff"—which I used to be told in childhood was a polite way of expressing the old Scotch proverb, "If you'll scratch my back I'll scratch yours."

I could not ask Ewan to drive me up. I knew the noise and heat of a concert and pie-social would be bad for him. On the other hand Lily and I could not drive ourselves up and look after the horse on such a bitter night. So we asked Herb Harrison the local storekeeper to go up with us.

We went. Lily and Herb talked gossip all the way up and back. I looked up at the stars and wondered if around those mighty distant suns revolved planets whose insensate inhabitants attended and enjoyed pie socials. We got up—we went in. The schoolhouse was packed with a crowd three times too large for it. The air became stifling. My head ached. My back ached because I was sitting on a board; my feet ached because a current of cold air swept along the floor in spite of the upper heat. The programme was very poor—the adult part was crude and cheap, the children's part badly prepared and rendered. But it did come to an end—everything does, even a pie social. We came out and came home, getting here at 12. I've got myself a hot cup of "Oxo"[315] and now I'm going to bed.

Sunday, December 21, 1919

I was so tired last night I cried. Yesterday morning I got up tired. I had company coming for tea so I made cake and salad and did a hundred or so odd jobs. In the afternoon I went to the S.S. practice, came home, got supper, as Lily was busy with concert preparations—and then hur-

---

314   From "Ode on the Morning of Christ's Nativity" (1629) a poem by John Milton about the birth of Christ and the promise of redemption. At the birth of Christ, humanity's much-needed redemption had yet to take place: "But wisest Fate says No; / This must not yet be so; / The Babe yet lies in smiling infancy; / That on the bitter cross / Must redeem our loss."

315   "Oxo" beef stock cubes had been first produced in 1910, and popularized during the war.

ried back to the church and stayed there till eleven helping with the rehearsal. The children were noisy and silly—the grown-up performers seemed more anxious to get off into corners and hold hands than attend to practising. I felt like wringing their necks, as I smiled sweetly at them and suggested this or that. And these girls, mark you, are not young. Some of them are nearer 30 than 20 and all are old enough to have some sense. When I was a girl my chums and I had our good times, driving with and talking to the boys, and I admit we all flirted a little, but we did not make asses of ourselves in public, especially when we were supposed to be working. When I came here eight years ago the then set of young people were sensible, well-behaved boys and girls—at least, the majority of them were and they kept the rest in order. But they are married or gone—the generation in power at present seems to be devoid of sense, ambition, executive ability. Consequently I came home feeling worn-out, cheap, out of place, *declasse*, discouraged— and as aforesaid I cried. This morning I was so tired I could not go out to church. I rested all day as well as I could and tonight I feel more courage and a determination to see the wretched thing through since I have put my hand to the plough.

Another volume of my journal finished.[316] It covers less time than any of the others—less than four years. But in those four years have been crowded a lifetime of emotions. Since I began this journal the war has ended—Frede has died. I will begin a new volume with the bitter certainty that in it there will never be any Frede, save in my memories. It will record no footsteps of hers on my threshold, no laughter of hers at my fireside. The Gates of Life and Death have opened and shut between us—I on this side, she on that. Perhaps, when the night of the universe is over she and I will find each other again. But I want her now.

---

316 Here ends LMM's handwritten volume four.

JOURNAL

Vol. IV

L.M. Montgomery Macdonald

December 22nd, 1919 – August 26th, 1923

Monday, December 22, 1919
The Manse, Leaskdale, Ont.

Sometimes—fortunately—things we dread turn out to be quite pleasant. I have been dreading the S.S. concert at Zephyr tonight—especially the long cold drive there and back in the buggy. But it was not cold. Today was very mild and when Ewan and Chester and I left after supper we positively enjoyed our drive over. Owing to the skim of snow the night was not dark. The road was good, the trees and fields and groves pleasantly suggestive and eerie and elusive, as if full of elfish secrets. Chester chattered amusingly and I enjoyed the drive. The concert and Christmas tree was also nice. Chester recited, Ewan read and acted as Chairman. I gave two readings and also read the Cottar's Saturday Night[317] while it was shown in a series of tableaux—so I think the Macdonald family did its duty and quite deserved the nice fat goose which was hung on the tree for it. The first and only goose we have ever been given, as it happens!

The drive home was just as pleasant as the drive over. I was not tired—or rather my tiredness showed itself in a certain exaltation of feeling and imagination, such as I sometimes experience when I am really much fatigued. My drive home was a seven-mile-film of brilliant adventures of fancy.

Tuesday, Dec. 23, 1919
The Manse, Leaskdale

Thanks be, the S.S. concert is over. We had a fine night, a good crowd, and a programme that seemed to please. To me it seemed a two hours' nightmare for besides looking after Chester and Stuart I had to arrange dialogues and "run" tableaux and evolve order out of the chaos behind the scenes. And under all this ran a current of dull worry over Ewan who had seemed duller today than usual. So it was a very different evening from last evening and when it was over I gathered up my chattels, rounded up my boys, and came home through the thickly-falling snow, with a profound thankfulness that it was over.

Wednesday, Dec. 24, 1919

I was busy all day preparing for Christmas, with very little heart in it. I made pudding and doughnuts and thought of Frede incessantly.

---

317   Robert Burns' long poem from 1786, describing homely family life.

Tonight when I was dressing the Christmas tree for the boys I broke down and cried. It was the first Christmas since Chester was born that there was nothing for him from "Aunt Fred." I felt an unbearable sense of desolation. Frede, *where are you?* Three years ago tonight we were together—you were here in my home, a guest for the last time. I remember that when you went away I felt a strange loneliness and desolation such as I had never felt before when you went.

The other day when I was looking over some books in the parlor searching for a reading for a concert a Christmas card dropped out of one of them. It was from Frede and some verses were printed on it. Some lines struck to my heart with their poignancy.

One face *with unaltered friendship* fraught
And the friend of my dream was *you.*

"Unaltered friendship!" Oh, Frede! Yes, thank God, you never saw anything in my face but unaltered friendship—or I in yours. *Will we ever meet again?* I would give all I possess for an affirmative answer to that question. But there is *no* answer. We may wish—hope—believe— we can never *know.* But if I *knew* that I would see Frede again—talk with her—laugh with her—I would not care how many years must pass before the meeting came.

Thursday, Dec. 25, 1919
Leaskdale, Ont.

The saddest, dreariest Christmas I have ever spent is over. I am thankful. I got up in the bitter, cold, gray morning and—for Lily had gone home—got breakfast while the boys exulted over their tree. Then I cooked the dinner and had so much trouble over it, owing to a smoking stove and an oven that *wouldn't* get hot that my nerves went to pieces. It was two before we had dinner and four o'clock before I got the dishes washed. By this time one of my headaches was fully underway and I had to take an aspirin tablet and lie down. In an hour the aspirin had worked and the pain was gone, but I was exhausted physically and mentally. I had seen no living soul outside of my own family all day. The outer world was gray and cold. Ewan was dull and complained of his head. There was no mail—nothing to cheer, stimulate, or encourage. But it is over—my first Christmas with no Frede in the world. The children had a good time and that is the main thing with me now.

These headaches of mine have been periodic occurrences for the past twenty-three years. Up to the time I was twenty-one I never had a headache, save when I was catching some disease such as measles or scarlet fever. But after that winter in Bedeque I began to have them regularly. Their origin is nervous and was probably due to the rack of suppressed passion and suffering on which I was stretched that winter. I tried everything in the way of medicines and doctors to no avail. For ten years I suffered miserably from them, never getting any relief from the pain until, after hours of suffering, I vomited bile. Then it ceased and left me exhausted for a day. Worse almost even than the pain was the day of depression, languor and general nervous unrest which always preceded it.

About thirteen years ago I heard of aspirin and tried it. It worked like magic and since then I have not suffered overmuch as a tablet will almost always cure me speedily. But it is of no use to take it until the pain comes—the boring pain over the left brow. All the preliminary discomfort I must endure. Today would not have been so hard if my nervous misery had not robbed me of the strength to bear the worry and loneliness bravely.

Friday, Dec. 26, 1919
Leaskdale, Ont.

Today I felt unusually well. Always after my headaches I do—as if something that had been pressed down by pain had rebounded with redoubled energy. Mr. Fraser was here to tea and the bit of intellectual companionship resulting was just the stimulation I needed and gave me courage to carry on.[318] I won't cry myself to sleep tonight.

Sunday, Dec. 28, 1919

Ewan is none too well these days and I am never free from unrest concerning him. An outsider would not see much amiss. He sleeps well and does such work as is absolutely necessary. When we go out the stimulation of company makes him fairly cheerful for the time being. But I realize that he is far from being himself. He has no energy or ambition whatever and his fears and dreads are by no means absent. Of course, he is nothing like as bad as he was those first two weeks in December, but I am always afraid of a renewed attack.

Today in copying my old journal I came to the part dealing with my first month in Belmont and the doings of Fulton and Alf Simpson.[319]

---

318   Mr. Fraser was the Presbyterian minister in Uxbridge, whom LMM had described as "a clever fellow" (December 1, 1912). See also the entry for August 8, 1918, and April 12, 1921.

319   These events are described in LMM's 1896 journal. There were six children in the Simpson family, including Alf, Fulton, and Edwin (mentioned the next paragraph). LMM taught for a year in Belmont, Prince Edward Island. The teaching position she took had been vacated by Edwin Simpson (to whom she later became engaged; she eventually broke off the engagement). In Belmont, she boarded for a time at the Simpson house, which included Fulton and Alf.

Really they were an absurd pair—or rather Fulton was absurd. The two geese quarrelled over me and never spoke to each other all winter. Fulton never forgave me for not appreciating him. He turned against me and hated me as bitterly and unreasonably as he had loved me. Some years later he married a Miss Taylor—of St. Eleanor's I think. They have—or had at last reports—three daughters and are living at the old place in Belmont.

Alf has never married—not because he did not get his first love but solely, I am afraid, because nobody else would take him—nobody he wanted anyhow. His uncouth appearance was against him. Yet I always liked Alf—indeed, to be frank, I was quite a little bit taken with Alf that winter we went about together in Belmont. It did not go very deep—and as he was quite out of the question for anything serious I nipped it severely in the bud and no one, least of all Alf himself, ever suspected it.

I had always supposed that likely Alf thought bitterly enough of me, too. But a few years ago, just before Aunt Mary Lawson died, he was up to see her, and in speaking of me he told her that he had never met anyone in his life he liked as well as me. So he must think kindly of me. He lives with his mother at St. Eleanor's and the last report I heard of him was that all he was interested in was the piling up of money. Perhaps that may be the criticism of jealousy: or it may be true, all other aspirations having been thwarted and other passions starved.

Of Ed I never hear much. He seems to roam about a good deal. The last time I was home I heard Myrtle Webb saying that she thought the reason "Ed hadn't been more successful was that his conceit spoiled him. He could get a good church easily but couldn't hold it long."

His wife is a clever, talkative woman, quite a dab at public speaking. They have no children. This must be a disappointment to Ed. But he would never have had children, no matter whom he married, I believe. When I was engaged to Ed I did not know enough of men to realize what was lacking in him, but I know now that there *was* something lacking and I believe that was why, though I did not understand it, I felt such a mysterious repugnance to him.

Monday, Dec. 29, 1919
Leaskdale, Ontario

I finished Gibbon's *Decline and Fall* this evening. It is the third time I have read it, but the first since my marriage. I hardly think I shall ever find time to read it again. It is a monumental piece of work. I know of no historian so coldly impersonal as Gibbon. He seems more like a machine recording history than anything else I can think of. This makes for the proper impartiality; but it is also largely accountable for what, after all, must be called the monotony of his style. Almost the only portions of his history in which we get a glimpse of Gibbon himself—the intellect behind the machine—are in his famous chapters on Christianity and—such a coupling!—his sprinkling of sly, spicy, smutty stories. Naturally these—the chapters, I mean—are therefore the most interesting part of the work, since only personality makes anything interesting. As for the aforesaid scandalous little anecdotes—well they haven't a Puritan flavor—but now and then a *little* risque seasoning is agreeable! But it is a seasoning easy to overdo and an overdose is nauseating. Gibbon doesn't overdo but his smirk, as he pens a choice tidbit, rather gives the effect of a Satyr leering suddenly around the columns of Karnak.[320]

---

320   Located along the Nile river, some 2.5 km (1.5 miles) north of Luxor, is the Karnak Temple Complex, constructed between 2055 BCE ad 100 AD. A satyr, from Greek mythology, is part man, part wild creature (often depicted with an erection).

1920

Sunday, Jan. 4, 19<u>20</u>
The Manse, Leaskdale, Ont.

This finishes a week of bitter and unbroken cold—zero at the best, 20 and 22 below at the worst.[321] I could count on my two hands the hours I have been really warm this week out of bed. Our house is miserably cold; we have poor coal this year and can't ever get the best out of it because our flue needs cleaning so badly and smokes vilely. I tried to get Ewan to clean it in November but the apathy of his malady was on him and I couldn't get him to do it. But it *must* be done soon for we can't go on living like this. I am sitting here by the dining room table with a thick sweater on and an oil heater burning beside me and my feet are like ice. I really haven't suffered so from cold since my winter at Frasers' in Belmont.[322]

Ewan has seemed rather better this week. Out in company he is quite cheerful. But at home he is very dull and certainly not a stimulating companion. I cling to the hope that when spring comes he may get well again as he did the year he was in Glasgow.[323] But sometimes the dread possesses me that his melancholia has become settled and I ask myself dully if I can face years of this kind of life.

Tuesday we drove to Uxbridge in the cold and then out to tea at Jas. Mustards'. Wednesday and Thursday evenings we also had to spend out and in no case was the pleasure of the evening among dull people great enough to compensate for the cold drives and late hours. Besides, though Ewan is quite cheerful when out most of the times he is occasionally *distrait*[324] and shows by his vague remarks how little attention he has really been paying to the conversation, and this wears terribly

---

321   Canada used the Fahrenheit temperature until March 31, 1975, when, as part of an overall "metrication" program, the Celsius scale came into use. A temperature of –22°F is the equivalent of –7.6°C.

322   In 1896–97, LMM had boarded with the Fraser family in Belmont, Prince Edward Island, where she worked as a teacher. In an entry of November 14, 1896, she described "a piercing wind that goes through this crazy old house as if it were made of paper, for not one of the doors or windows will shut squarely or tight."

323   In October 1906, Ewan Macdonald—then a moderately successful young Presbyterian minister—had departed Prince Edward Island for additional schooling at the prestigious Trinity College Seminary in Glasgow, Scotland. Upon arrival in Scotland, however, it appears that he began to suffer from some kind of mental illness, what at the time would likely have been called "religious melancholia." He returned to Canada in March 1907. There are no records of Ewan completing any work at all in Scotland. (For more information on Ewan Macdonald and mental illness, see Mary Henley Rubio's 2008 biography, *Lucy Maud Montgomery: The Gift of Wings*.)

324   French for "distracted."

on my nerves, so that when I reach home I am woefully tired physically and bedraggled in soul.

I had only two days in this week on which I could do any work on my book.

Friday morning we started out in the forenoon for a day's visiting at Zephyr. It was intensely cold with a bitter penetrating wind blowing from the northwest, right in our teeth. I never drove out on a worse day. But I was not cold myself. I had put on sweaters and coats and furs until I was a shapeless mass and I had a sizzling hot brick at my feet which kept me warm. So I buried my nose in my collar and forgot the outside world in a series of reflections upon this astounding new discovery of the nature of light made by Einstein which is going to utterly revolutionize most of the beliefs held by scientists for two hundred years.[325] It is a curious thing that this upsetting discovery should come just at a time when almost everything else that made up our old world is being upset, revolutionized, or torn to pieces. The result will probably be in the end a very wonderful era of development in everything.

But whether light be matter or vibration there was not enough of it coming from anywhere on Friday to warm up our planet—on our part of it at least—and when we finished our drive of eight miles I was beginning to get so cold that I could not have detached myself from the material world around me much longer.

We had a good dinner—roast duck etc. etc. I have never been one of those who consider "a liking for a tasty bite" something to be rather ashamed of. Frankly, I'm very fond of a good table. I keep one myself and I like to sit down to one. It is an old Montgomery tradition and when I hear anyone say, "I don't care what I have to eat," I conclude that that individual is either lying, or is a pale anaemic creature of very little use and no charm or force in the world. And I have mostly found that this conclusion was borne out by the facts of the case. So, though I would certainly not have driven to Zephyr on such a day for that, or any dinner alone, still, since I had to go, the "savory meat" was a bit of compensation which I welcomed very cordially.

We went to another house to supper. Then Ewan went to a business meeting of the Guild but I had reached my limit. I was tired out with making endless small talk on harmless and incombustible subjects and with taking off and putting on overshoes, overstockings, hat, veil, muf-

---

325   Theoretical physicist Albert Einstein (1879–1955) had published his theory of general relativity in 1911. His theory calculated that light from another star should be bent by the gravity from our sun, a prediction confirmed during a solar eclipse in May 1919. In November of that year a "revolution in science" was announced.

fler, extra underskirt, sweater, suit coat, fur coat, two pair of gloves
and a muff. So I hied me to Lily Shier's where I lay on the sofa till ten,
resting and silent. At ten we left for home. The wind was in our backs
which made every difference; my brick was beautifully hot; we drove
though a fantastic fairy world where moonlight was shining through a
very thin skim of cloud and the fine, floating mist of snow falling from
it. As Ewan had relapsed into quietude I again went roaming in an ideal
life of adventure and brilliancy and the drive home was a pleasure.

I did not go out today. I have had a strenuous week and another still
more strenuous is ahead of me. So I resolved to stay home and rest up
a bit.

It is 1920. 1919 has gone—the most terrible year of my life—the
year of Frede's going—the year in which I discovered that my husband
was subject to recurrent constitutional melancholia. I hailed its dawn
gladly. The war was over—I looked forward to a year of peace and old
time pleasure and freedom from gnawing care. But what a dreadful
year it has been almost from the first! So I shrink from 1920. I think I
will never again welcome in a New Year with gladness or anticipation.

Monday, Jan. 5, 1920
The Manse, Leaskdale

This morning it was 23 below zero. I spent the forenoon making eats
for a meeting of the Guild executive here tomorrow night. This evening
Lily and I and the boys went to a "shower" at Alec Leask's, held for
Ada Marquis, one of our girls who is to be married Wednesday. Ewan
had to go to Zephyr and, as Stuart could not walk home in the snow I
had to wait until everybody was ready to go before I could get a chance
home. It was long after twelve and I was bored to tears and envious of
Chester and Stuart who had fallen asleep—and then had to be waked
up and dressed, limp and cranky. I'm home now, have got them tucked
up in bed and come to my journal for a bit of companionship while I'm
waiting for the water to get hot for my faithful bottle—without which
the mistress of Leaskdale manse would have been found several times
this winter frozen all stiff and stark.

Speaking of that, however, I hope for better things after this. This
afternoon, driven to desperation, Lily and I went to work, took down
the kitchen pipe and burned the chimney out with newspapers and
coal oil. It was a long process and very vile in the early stages when the
smoke poured out at every crevice and filled the house with gloom and
vile odors. But in the end we got it done. Then, while the place still

reeked and I was a sight for gods and men with soot and grime the door bell rang and I had to go, for Lily was wrestling with the problem of the spare room where soot had fallen on bed and carpet. The caller was a "stylish" Christmas visitor who had been sojourning in Leaskdale and was the last person I expected or desired to see just then. But I dressed my smutty features in a smile and took her into the parlor where I talked to her as if I had no other thought on earth. When I finally shut the door behind her, I muttered a profane "Good riddance." But when Lily rekindled the fire it burned gloriously with a heart gladdening draft— and so once more we fare forward.

Chester, by the way, is undergoing the pangs of his first love affair— at the mature age of 7 1/2. A few weeks ago he informed me that he had "picked out a girl to marry" when he grew up, adding in strict secrecy that she was "V. Harrison"—the full name, I presume, being too sacred to desecrate by utterance. Since then he had alternated between hopefulness and spasms of despair lest the said V. Harrison prefer Douglas Madill after all. One day he informed me with sparkling eyes that she had called him "My dear little Chester." Another day he confided to Stuart that he just couldn't help winking at Velma whenever he looked at her. But today he sighed to me that he was afraid Douglas would get her. "I suppose I didn't tell her soon enough," he concluded mournfully.

As for the said Velma, to my eyes—but then perhaps I'm jaundiced!— she is a coarse featured, rather bold little girl, aged ten, quite devoid of charm or beauty. But kissing goes by favor and evidently Chester finds her desirable extremely.

Chester and Stuart are occupied these days poring over their Christmas books. Stuart as yet cons only pictures but Chester is quite a remarkable reader for his age. Indeed, he reads too much, I fear. I am anxious lest he injure his eyes. I had to put a decisive stop to his reading in bed. If I let him he would read there until ten o'clock—as he did one evening when I had company. I supposed he had been asleep for hours and was horrified to discover him at ten lost in the adventures of Peter Rabbit and Bobby Coon and Ol' Mistah Buzzard.[326]

Both the boys seem to have inherited my good memory. I am glad of this. I had been afraid that they might "take after" Ewan in this. His memory is very poor—abnormally so indeed. This has been a serious drawback to him in every relation of life, especially in his profession

---

326   *The Tale of Peter Rabbit* (1901) by Beatrix Potter; *The Adventure of Bobby Coon* (1918) by Thornton W. Burgess.

and in society. Nothing that he reads seems to stick in his memory at all, so that, as far as any enrichment of intellect or life goes, he might just as well not have read it. But Chester and Stuart seem to remember everything easily and long.

Tuesday, Jan. 6, 1920
Leaskdale, Ont.

Much milder—our burning chimney must have loosened things up. This was what I call a scrambling day—a constant endeavor to "catch up." I had to go to Uxbridge this afternoon and have a tooth filled—then home to get ready for the Guild executive meeting at night. I always have it here—it is my annual entertainment of the Guild. Its personnel varies from year to year, old ones dropping out, new ones coming in. We drew up the year's programme and I served lunch. Ewan was not well and I was secretly worried and anxious.

Wednesday, Jan. 7, 1920

All day I worked hard getting ready a supper for Ada Marquis and her husband, who came here at five this evening to be married. Ordinarily of course I don't get tea for the couples who come here to be married. But Ada has always been a particular friend of mine and there were other reasons why I wanted to give her a nice little send off. So I made salad and cake and biscuits etc. and fixed up a pretty table with pink-shaded candles etc. and all went off well—on the surface. But Ewan was very miserable all day and especially so this afternoon, restless and gloomy. He hasn't had such a bad attack for a long time. This evening, after I had helped Lily wash and put away all the dishes I broke down and cried. But tears never seem to relieve me now. They only give me a throbbing headache.

Thursday, Jan. 8, 1920
The Manse, Leaskdale, Ont.

Last night Ewan wakened at four and didn't sleep again. I was filled with terror lest another bad attack was brewing. But he has been better today than yesterday—no spasms of weakness or unrest. I worked all day catching up with a hundred things left undone in the rush of the past few days. This evening I could sit quietly down and write letters and read a bit—a welcome change.

Friday, Jan. 9, 1920

Very cold and gray again. But Ewan is better. His attacks do not seem to last long now—perhaps they are gradually wearing off. But at nightfall I felt dull and tired and weary of life. I would have liked to put on a pretty frivolous dress and go somewhere to a dinner party. That would have restored the morale of the army! Instead, I waited up until everyone was in bed and the furnace banked up for the night and then I put on the oldest, ugliest things I had, went down on my marrow bones and painted the dining room floor. It had grown so scandalously mangy from the boy's sparables that I couldn't stand it another day. I've got it done and Daff shut in the cellar so that he can't track it up. So now for bed.

Tonight when I put the boys to bed Chester said eagerly, "Are you going to read us a chapter of *Hiawatha* tonight, mother?"[327] Ever since he was two I have always read to him when I put him to bed—just the Peter Rabbit series etc. But lately I have been reading selections from the poets. *Hiawatha* seemed wonderful to me when I was a child. I revelled in it and never tired of it. I haven't read it for many years and I confess it seems rather poor and thin now. But Chester seems to find it full of charm and it is wonderful how much he understands of it and how he loves it.

Monday, Jan. 12, 1920
Leaskdale, Ont.

Mr. Forbes, our missionary, came yesterday, and today he and Ewan were away all day visiting. I must frankly say that it was a decided relief to have Ewan away for a day, where I know he has congenial company. It is rather hard on me to see him moping around the house *all* the time, feeling that he is not interested in anything and that the unavoidable noise of the cooped-up boys worries him. It is bad for my own sore nerves that have grown so sensitive in this long stretch of bitter gray sunless days, with no stimulation or comradeship, that there are times when I feel I *must* break loose and get away from it all for a time—out and away somewhere, where I can draw a free breath.

But tonight after I finished a busy day's work, and got the boys off to bed I had a blessed little treat. I got Daff, a bag of nuts and candy, and one of the most interesting novels I have ever read—*The Secret*

---

327   *The Song of Hiawatha* (1855) by Henry Wadsworth Longfellow was a poetic narration about the adventures of Ojibwe warrior Hiawatha.

Orchard.[328] I got into the parlor, which is at present our cheerfullest and warmest room and ate and read and cuddled old Daff for two golden hours.

Tuesday, Jan. 13, 1920
The Manse, Leaskdale

A missionary meeting this afternoon and one of Stella's letters full of growls and complaints spoilt today. I led the meeting and tried to put a little life and inspiration into the programme but the sight of that circle of stolid, fat, uninteresting, narrow old dames would have put out any poor little fire of my kindling. They just sucked all the animation out of my soul.

But tonight I read Tarkington's *Seventeen*[329] and laughed as I haven't laughed for years over a book. It isn't a very subtle book—it has no great literary charm and it verges on caricature. But it *is* so excruciatingly funny and the laughter it gave me a boon. It flooded my drab soul with a rosy light and entirely headed off the fit of nervous crying with which I had expected to end the day.

Wednesday, Jan. 14, 1920
Leaskdale, Ont.

After a few days of comparative mildness today was extremely cold again, so life hardened up also. I wrote for two hours this morning with a very cramped hand, then spent the rest of the day doing a hundred little odd jobs, the culminating effect of which was a dull depressed feeling of not really having accomplished anything. I wanted to have a quiet evening of reading but instead had to muffle up and plod up to the church through snow and dark and frost to read a paper for the Guild. Owing to the bad night very few were out and the whole performance seemed like a millstone around my neck. But it is over—and I am going to have an hour of reading.

Friday, Jan. 16, 1920

About this time two years ago we had a terrible three days of bitter cold. With the exception of those three days today has been the coldest I ever endured in my life.

---

328   *The Secret Orchard* (1908), by Agnes and Egerton Castle.

329   Booth Tarkington's humorous novel, *Seventeen: A Tale of Youth and Summer Time and the Baxter Family Especially William*, was first published in periodical form in 1914; in 1916 it was published as a novel.

Yesterday was very frosty and the house was not comfortable. But I managed to work a couple of hours at Book 10 in the forenoon. In the afternoon we went to Zephyr a-visiting. Although so cold that my lashes froze it was calm and bright, so the drive over was not so bad, thanks to furs, a brick and so many clothes that I felt like a Dutchwoman. The folks we visited were fairly nice, too, had a good warm house and a good supper. Ewan seemed better than he has been for a long time. After supper we went to Guild. Partly owing to the bitter night, partly to the fact of a carnival at the rink, and partly I daresay to the fact that a family in the village has developed smallpox, only four were there besides ourselves. However, we had Guild and then started home. My brick was cold and the drive home through the white and iron night was not pleasant. How many of those miserable drives we have had home from Zephyr in the past eight years! I detest that merciless road with its never-ending hills. But we got over them and when we came to Quigley's Hill I was only rather chilly and not positively cold. Quigley's Hill is what "David's Hill" in Cavendish used to be—a place that fills up on the least excuse of a drift. It was badly filled up last night and the road was very sidelong. All at once we went over and landed in a snowbank. Luckily our mare halted and we got up but then she got into soft snow and it was some time before Ewan could get her through it to the road. It was lucky everything was not smashed up. By the time we got in again I was ready to cry with cold hands and feet, and, what was far worse, Ewan's heart began to act badly, as a result of his plunging in the deep snow. I was distracted with anxiety but by the time we got home he was all right again. We got in, I got a hot drink for both, a hot water bottle and presently we were in bed, comfortable and warm. But this morning—Lord, how I hated to get out. It was dark—it was cold—my muscles ached from the cramped drive. But up I got—got dressed—got the boys dressed—and got down. But I got *not* warm. In spite of a good furnace fire the house has been barn-like all day. Our oil heater is out of whack so we could not supplement the furnace by it. My feet were cold and I developed chilblains.[330] Chilblains are not romantic. The heroines in novels never have them. But they are cussed things for torment. For three hours tonight I "suffered the tortures of the damned" as Stell is so fond of repeating. But I got the boys tucked up in bed, and

---

330   Chilblains are an uncomfortable, itchy inflammation of small blood vessels near the surface of the skin that arise as a response to exposure to cold air. They usually take the form of red patches and blisters.

there they are sound asleep and cosy and rosy, the darling little creatures. I could fall upon them and eat them.

Ewan and I are in the parlor now. It has got comfy at last. Daff is
asleep on his pet rocker. My chilblains have ceased from troubling. A
north-east snow storm is howling outside. I fear we are going to be
blocked up. But we have a roof over us, a house not colder than most
barns, and plenty to eat. We might be worse off. Let us be cheerful and
apply Nyal's Mentholatum.[331]

Sunday, Jan. 18, 1920
The Manse, Leaskdale

Zero again. Went not
forth as it was too cold
to take Stuart out and
it was Lily's turn to go. I
finished copying Volume
One of my journal today.
I have found it an inter-
esting task. Writing it,
much more than reading
it, brought back all the
past very vividly. I seemed

Corner of Parlor

to be living it over again as I wrote it day by day. The next volume will
not be so pleasant—at least the first part of it, for it deals with my engagement to Edwin Simpson.[332] I heartily dislike the thought of "re-living" that, even in illusion.

Sunday, Jan. 25, 1920

A year ago this morning at sunrise Frede Campbell died! For one year
I have lived—or rather existed—without her. So I suppose I can go on
existing indefinitely as far as that is concerned. I wonder if it will ever
be any easier to live without her. I do not think that in this past year
there has been a waking hour when I have not thought of Frede—not
a day when there has not been at some moment or other a pang of

---

331 A medicinal preparation containing mint oil used for skin complaints.

332 LMM had been engaged to her cousin Edwin Simpson in 1897. She found that she did not
love him and broke off the engagement in 1898.

remembrance that pierced to the marrow.

> If I should live your epitaph to write
> Naught would I say but, "I, too, died that night."

That stray couplet, read lately in a magazine contest, comes into my mind whenever I think of Frede, as also another in the same contest,

> If I should live your epitaph to write
> I'd pen no more than this "True friend, good-night,
> And when I, too, have slept if first you wake,
> Bid me good-morrow for our old love's sake."

This day last year I was tied to the stake all day—racked with a torture of anguish so unbearable that it seemed as if life itself must be crushed in that brief struggle. Today, in place of the keen torture was one long, heavy, throbbing ache of longing and loneliness and *emptiness*.

But I feel a dull thankfulness that the year is ended. I shall no longer be pricked by the recurring thought—and it was no mean pang—"This time last year Frede was alive"—"this day last year I had a letter from Frede." and so the contrast between past and present will not be so strongly emphasized.

Today was bitterly cold—32 below zero. It has been cold all the week—never above zero and mostly much below.

Wednesday, Jan. 28, 1920
Leaskdale, Ont.

Yesterday was that rare thing this January—a mild, pleasant day. I drove to Uxbridge in the afternoon and underwent the torture of the drill—that is to say I had a tooth filled. I have always found the drill an abominable business—it never hurt me badly yet but I always feel that it is *going to the next minute* and the nerve strain is just as bad as if it did. Since I had the flu I really cannot endure it. It is an agony in ludicrous disproportion to the cause. I felt as exhausted last night as if I had been through a week of illness.

Today was bitter cold again. Drove to Zephyr, spent afternoon visiting and read a paper on Burns before the Guild.[333] Then ensued another unpleasant drive home but I managed to displace some of the discomfort by repeating as many of Bobby's poems to myself as I could remember and visualizing them.

---

333   Robert Burns (1759 – 21 July 1796), Scottish poet and lyricist.

Arriving home I found a letter from Cam. Opening, I saw that it had been written on Jan. 25th—and I thought, "He has written me on the anniversary of Frede's death knowing what a bitter day it would be for me." I thought it sympathetic and thoughtful and my heart softened to him.

Well! Perhaps he did remember the significance of the date but there was nothing in the letter to indicate it. Frede's name was not mentioned—nothing in connection with her or her death or life was mentioned or suggested. There was absolutely nothing in the letter but an obscure farrago about his work which I really could make nothing of—or Ewan either. He is certainly an odd character—and past my solving—probably because there is really nothing to solve.

Last night I was copying the entry in my old journal concerned with my visit to Alberton in the June of 1897 and the incident of the runaway horse.[334] I recall it very clearly. It is possible that it had more disastrous results than were immediately apparent.

Dan Montgomery—"Cousin Dan"—one evening took his daughter Nettie and me out for a drive. Nettie was a pretty girl and a nice one, but in the opinion of those who knew her best she had always been somewhat abnormal. Certainly for a year or two she had been quite hypochondriacal, loving to detail all her aches and woes, most of which had no real existence.

This evening Dan began racing with a couple of young sparks who came up beside us with their trotter. The race was very close. Men and horses became wildly excited. It was in the dusk. Nettie and I were terrified and implored her father to stop but he was temporarily bereft of reason in a mad determination not to let the others pass him. Suddenly I sensed that his horse had escaped from his control and was running away. A moment later our off-wheel struck a cow which was standing placidly across the wheel track. The next second I felt the buggy going over and believed we were being thrown out directly under the flying hoofs of the other horse just behind us.

A moment later I was picking myself dazedly up, covered with dust, with torn and dishevelled dress. A little distance away Cousin Dan was helping Nettie up and distractedly demanding to know if she were hurt. I remember how keenly I suddenly felt that there was nobody there to care or ask if I were hurt. I did not blame cousin Dan for rushing to Nettie first—it was the right and natural thing for her father to do—but it did make me feel all at once desperately lonely and forsaken—a feel-

---

334   This event is described in a long retrospective entry of June 30, 1897 (in which LMM also describe her ill-fated engagement to Edwin Simpson); see also note 330, page 233.

ing that was probably intensified by the shock my nerves had received.

Nettie was not hurt apparently save for a slight skin cut on her cheek. It was very slight—did not even leave a scar. The buggy wheel which had come in contact with the cow was lying shattered on the road, the buggy itself was jammed between the fence and a tree a few yards further on, horse and cow were nowhere to be seen. Later on it transpired that the horse had gone home to his stable. As for the cow, we never saw or heard of it again, so perhaps it was scared into the fourth dimension.

Cousin Dan, Nettie and I limped home and went to bed. Nettie said indignantly to me, "what if father has marked me for life by his crazy racing with those boys." The little wound left no scar, however, but the next fall poor Nettie began to develop very markedly the abnormal characteristics which ran their course into absolute insanity. She has been practically insane ever since, with occasional lucid intervals which grow rarer as she grows older. Her friends were inclined to attribute it all to that unfortunate upset which they said affected her nerves. It may have hastened the onset of the malady but I do not think it produced it. It was bound to come anyway, sooner or later. Nettie's mother is a sister of Uncle John Campbell and there is undoubtedly a little taint in the family. Their father developed dipsomania[335] at fifty. Uncle John C. was quite insane during the last year of his life. In Stella it has developed into hypochondria, falsehood, and abnormal self love. In some of the others it only showed its presence in utter lack of self control of passions and appetites. Poor Nettie has been the only one in which it produced absolute insanity early in life. Her existence has been a tragedy—for herself and for the unfortunate parents and sisters who have suffered with her.

Saturday, Jan. 31, 1920
Leaskdale, Ont.

This has been a *damnable* day. Bitter cold—20 below zero—and a sharp east wind blowing; a gray, wintery world; chilly house, worry over some matters connected with the Page Co. and this book of old stories they are bringing out—and a persistent dull headache which even aspirin did not relieve. The headache made everything else harder to bear, for it prevented me from indulging in my usual solace of imaginary adventures.

This power of mine has been all that has saved me many times in

---

335 Dipsomania is a now-outdated term describing the symptoms associated with alcohol misuse.

my life from absolute break-down. I can imagine things so vividly that it seems to me almost exactly the same as if I were *living* them, and it has the same, or largely the same, stimulating physical effect on me as the real adventures would have—I really thrill and glow and delight and exult—and so I have always been able to escape from "intolerable reality" and save my nerves by a double life. It is a power for which many a time I have been profoundly thankful; but when I have a head-ache, or any too-insistent worry, I lose it—I can still imagine things in an intellectual way, so I might compose a story but I can't *live* them, and so I get no good effects from them—no antidote to the numbing grayness and monotonous discomfort.

Had two letters, one from Stell, and the other from some unknown, sixteen-year-old worshipper who addresses me as "Dear Wonder-per-son." The letter, full of girlish enthusiasm and hero-worship, was a pleasant antidote to Stell's usual compound of growls and egotistic complaints about trifles.

January goes out tonight. It has been the coldest January on record in Ontario. I think there were no more than three days when the mercury was above zero. And Arthur Mustard on the side road has been quite positive that we would have a thaw *yet*. "I've never seen a Janu-ary without a thaw and I've seen hundreds of them!" he averred. But he has seen a thawless one at last.

There is one bright spot in all this gloom—Ewan has been *much* better these last two weeks. He seems almost well except that he has occasional spasms of headache—or rather of the nervous discomfort in his head which it is convenient to call by that name. It is possible that he will soon be entirely well again. I must hope it, at least.

This evening I was looking over an old blank book in which I used to copy little quotations and epigrams that took my fancy. Some of them are really very good; this, for instance:—

"In that curious compound, the feminine character, it may easily happen that the flavor is unpleasant in spite of excellent ingredients."[336]

Most true—and just as true of masculine as feminine I think. How many excellent men and women I know, most excellent and good and moral people, in whom the flavor is unpleasant—or, which I think is re-ally worse still, in whom there is no flavor at all. And some quite wicked folks have a delightful flavor. Who was responsible for the mistakes in mixing, pray? Did the cook nod?

Another one appeals to me on days such as this:—

"A solid blow has in itself the elements of its rebound; it arouses the

---

336   From George Eliot's novel, *The Mill on the Floss* (1860).

antagonism of the life on which it falls; its relief is the relief of combat. But a hundred little needles pricking at us—what is to be done with them? We cannot so much as *gasp* because they *are* such little needles."[337]

"Examine your words well and you will find that even when you have no motive to be false it is a very hard thing to say the exact truth, even about your own immediate feelings—much harder than to say something fine about them which is *not* the exact truth."

Exactly so. George Eliot had a way of saying things uncomfortably true.[338]

Kipling's verse,

Twelve hundred million men are spread
About this earth—and I and you
Wonder when you and I are dead
What will those luckless millions do![339]

touches one of the secret, unacknowledged convictions of human nature. Yes, we really all think if we would admit it, that the world cannot possibly get on without us.

Oliver Wendell Holmes says a lot of wise things.

"A woman would rather talk with a man than an angel any day."[340]

Of course she would! Why not? For one thing, she wouldn't know what to say to an angel. She couldn't talk the gossip of heaven and it is inconceivable that he would be interested in that of earth—or even in tidings of new discoveries and uplift movements. For myself, I am sure I should be extremely uncomfortable with an angel. But I have not yet found anything much pleasanter than talking with the right kind of a man—except—but I won't write it. My descendants might be shocked.

"There is a genius for religion just as there is for painting and sculpture,"[341] says Holmes.

Exactly again; and there is no more reason in blaming a man for not being religious than there would be in blaming him for not being a great painter. The truly religious person—I am not referring to much so-called religion—has, I believe a source of comfort not easily, if at all, rivalled by any other source.

---

337   From American writer and spiritualist Elizabeth Stuart Phelps' *The Gates Ajar; Or, A Glimpse into Heaven* (1870).

338   George Eliot (1819–80) was the pen name of novelist and poet Mary Ann Evans, a favourite of LMM. The quote above is from her novel *Adam Bede* (1859).

339   From Kipling's poem "The Last Department" (published in his collection *Departmental Ditties and Ballads and Barrack-Room Ballads* [1919]).

340   From "The Poet at the Breakfast Table" (1872) one of a series of essays first published in *The Atlantic Monthly* by Oliver Wendell Holmes (1809–94).

341   From "The Poet at the Breakfast Table" (see note 340 above).

I think we are much too narrow in our definition of a religious person. A religious person, in my conception of the term, is an individual who has a close and deep and abiding sense of contact with and communion with God. But what is God? Has He not many aspects? Is not Beauty one of them? And may not a person—such as myself, for instance—whose love of beauty amounts to passionate worship, who finds comfort and help and rapture and courage and satisfaction in a wonderful sunset, or starry waters, or a wood-blossom, or the sleek, ineffable curves of a drowsy cat, or the dance and glow of an open fire—may not such a person be as truly religious as one who finds God in some other manifestation of His personality. But Mrs. Grundy says, "No, you must go to church every Sunday and believe, or pretend you believe, in certain man-made dogmas and consign every one to hell who doesn't agree with you and then you'll be religious."[342]

"It is not everybody" says Charlotte Bronte, "even among our respected friends and esteemed acquaintances, whom we like to have near us, whom we like to watch us, to wait on us, to approach us with the proximity of a nurse to a patient."[343]

No, not everybody—very, very few. No wonder the gods of old always veiled themselves from humanity. And what torture it is to have people come too near us—physically, mentally, socially—who don't belong to our household of faith.

Barrie says many good things. Here is one of his which has always appealed especially to me.

"The keenness with which she felt necessitated the garment of reserve which they who did not need it for themselves considered pride."[344]

No one ever said anything truer than that. If we feel very keenly we *have* to wrap our feelings from sight. To betray them, blood-red and raw, would be indecent. The world despises you if you show it your feelings—and hates you if you don't!

Another chunk of philosophy from Anthony Hope is,

"It is easy to be too hard on life; one should make a habit of reflecting occasionally out of what very unpromising materials happiness can be manufactured."[345]

'Zackly. When we are young we think we can never be happy un-

---

342   "Mrs. Grundy" is a figurative name, popular in British literature, personifying staid, priggish attitudes and excessive fear of offending respectability.

343   From Chapter 17, "La Terrasse," of Charlotte Brontë's 1853 novel, *Villette.*

344   From J.M. Barrie's 1888 novel, *When a Man's Single: A Tale of Literary Life.*

345   From Chapter 18, "William Adolphus Hits the Mark," in Anthony Hope's 1899 novel, *The King's Mirror.* ("William Adolphus" is also the name of a cat in LMM's short story, "The Quarantine at Alexander Abraham's.")

less we have all the wonderful things we dream of. But as we go along in life we discover that we can make a very tolerable happiness out of very inferior substitutes—out of mere shreds and patches indeed, sometimes—always supposing the kitchen range doesn't smoke and the mercury go more than ten below zero.

"Our natures own predilections and antipathies alike strange. There are people from whom we secretly shrink, whom we would personally avoid, though reason confesses they are good people. There are others with faults evident enough beside whom we live in content, as if the air about them did us good."[346]

Bronte again. She was a wonderful psychologist. But she only put into those clear words what we have all found and realized—and what none of us can explain. "As if the air about them did us good." Oh, excellent comparison! I wonder if, in verity, people don't give off subtle exhalations of personality which affect their atmosphere. There is a girl in our church against whom I can say nothing—against whom nobody can say anything; yet I am uncomfortable in a room if that girl is in it and want to get out if possible. She has a stronger effect on me in this way than anyone I have ever encountered—and I have met at least a round half dozen to whom I have felt this apparently causeless and certainly inexplicable antipathy.

"There are those who from a fortunate want of perception are called sensible."[347]

Right again, Anthony Hope! Don't we all know them?

"Life," says "Ouida" in one of her novels, "never gives two opposite sets of gifts to the same recipient: it never bestows both the king's dominion and the peasant's peace."[348]

Amen! One cannot have imagination and the gift of wings, along with the placidity and contentment of those who creep on the earth's solid surface and never open their eyes on aught but material things. But the gift of wings is better than placidity and contentment after all.

In Olive Schreiner's *African Farm*[349]—which long ago was one of my wonder books—is a very fine and unforgettable paragraph on love:—

"There are different species of love that go under the same name. There is a love that begins in the head and goes down to the heart and

---

346   From Chapter 17, "La Terrasse," of Charlotte Brontë's 1853 novel, *Villette*.

347   From Chapter 25, "A Smack of Repetition," in English novelist Anthony Hope's *The King's Mirror* (1899).

348   "Ouida" was the pen name of English novelist Maria Louise Ramé. This quotation is from Chapter 44 of her 1885 novel *Othmar*.

349   South African novelist Olive Schreiner's *The Story of an African Farm* (1885) had been an early favourite of LMM's.

grows slowly; but it lasts till death and asks less than it gives. There is another love that blots out wisdom, that is sweet with the sweetness of life and bitter with the bitterness of death lasting for an hour. *But it is worth* having *lived a whole life for that hour*.

There are as many kinds of love as there are flowers; everlastings that never wither; speedwells that wait for the wind to fan them out of life; blood-red mountain lilies that pour their voluptuous sweetness out for one day and lie in the dust at night. There is no flower that has the charm of all—the speedwell's purity, the everlasting's strength, the mountain-lily's warmth; but who knows whether there is no love that holds all—friendship, passion, worship?"

Yes, I think there must be a love which embraces them all—but it is rarer than a blue diamond. Most of us have to content ourselves with far less. I have loved different men in vastly different ways; but I have never loved any man with the whole force of my nature—with passion and friendship and worship. They have all been present repeatedly but never altogether in any of my loves. Perhaps it is as well, for such a love, in spite of its rapture and wonder and happiness, would make a woman an absolute slave, and if the man so loved—the *Master*—were not something very little lower than the angels I think the result, in one way or another, would be disastrous for the woman.

And yet—such a love might be worth disaster. One would always have its memory at least. My own love for Herman Leard,[350] though so incomplete, is a memory beside which all the rest of life seems gray and dowdy—a memory which I would not barter for anything save the lives of my children and the return of Frede.

So there you are! Who knows?

"There is much that is humorous in life as well as much that is holy; and healing virtue lies in laughter as well as in prayers and tears," says Ellen Thorneycroft Fowler.[351]

Yea, thank God. Laughter is one of three great gifts of the gods. It is the secret of the supremacy of the Anglo-Saxon race. They know how to laugh properly. No other nation does. Russia never knew how—that is why she is a welter of red anarchy today. The Oriental nations have no sense of humor—and so they are dark and wicked and subtle and fatalistic. But Britain and the New World can laugh—and so they conquer. When a man or a nation forgets how to laugh there is an end of strength and usefulness.

---

350 The year she taught in Lower Bedeque (1897–98), LMM boarded with the Leard family. She fell in love with Herman Leard, a son of the family. The affair is described in a long entry of April 8, 1898

351 From *Concerning Isabel Carnaby* (1898), a novel by Ellen Thorneycroft Fowler.

Ruskin says,

"Taste is not only a part and index of morality—it is the *only* morality. The first and last and closest trial question to any living creature is 'What do you like?' Tell me what you *like* and I'll tell you what you *are*."[352]

Well, let us see. What do I like?

I like my own children and all nice, fat, clean babies anywhere. I like *all* kinds of books if they're well written whether they are religious or philosophical or sentimental or cynical or humorous or exaggerated or indecent. I like writing books myself. I like cats and horses and some dogs. I like curling breakers, woods and mountains and stars and trees and flowers. I like nicely furnished houses. I like good Victrola records and the music of the violin. I like pretty china and glass and old heirloom things. I like a cosy bed and a tight hot water bottle. I like to be kissed by the right kind of a man. I like jewels and pretty clothes. I like doing fancy work and I like cooking and I like eating the nice things other people cook. I like motoring and driving and walking. I like a systematic life with occasional dashings over the traces. I like open fires and moonlit nights. I like nice chatty letters. I like compliments. I like to see a person I dislike snubbed. I like my own looks when my hair is dressed a certain way. I like a snack at bed time. I like going out to dinner. I like helping other people and I like to be very independent of help myself. I like sunsets and pictures and sea bathing. I like keeping a journal. I like reading old letters. I like housecleaning—I *do*! I like entertaining the race of Joseph. I like day-dreaming. I like going to concerts, good movies and plays. I like—or used to like before I wedded a minister—dancing and playing whist. I like reading the Bible—most of it. (I like the folk-lore of Genesis and the drama of the Exodus and the gorgeous furnishings of the tabernacle and the doings of the kings and the good maledictions of the Psalms and the warm imagery of the Song of Solomon and the cynicism of Ecclesiastes and the worldly wisdom of the Proverbs and the idyll of Ruth and the blazing fire of the prophets and the wonders of Jesus' teaching and the poetry of Revelations.) I like listening to good sermons. I like gardening. I like good spruce gum. I like my husband. I like people to like me. I like a good joke. I like rainy days. I like old homesteads. I like people who agree with me. I like chocolate caramels and Brazil nuts. I like—or liked in pre-prohibition days—Miss Oxtoby's dandelion wine. I like perfumes. I like a little gossip with carefully selected people. I like shopping at Eaton's.[353]

---

352   From John Ruskin's essay "Traffic" (published in his 1819 collection, *The Crown of Wild Olive & The Cestus of Aglaia*).

353   Founded in 1869 by Timothy Eaton, Eaton's was one Canada's largest department store.

There now, Ruskin, tell me what I am.
A bitter little bit of magazine verse is "Amen."

Some day the dawn will fail to break,
Inert and cold the sun will lie,
And God will smile along the sky
That one world's heart has ceased to ache.
And say, "That cosmic butterfly
I always fancied my mistake.

Is this world really "God's mistake?" Verily, at times we are almost driven to think so. Or is it just that we are living in "the dark of the universe"—and that after the passage of millenniums, many or few, the light will return and souls that are incarnate then will live in the day of the universe as we live now in its night? When that time comes our earth will be a burnt-out, forgotten planet: but other worlds will be coming into being to bear other races. What else can be the meaning of our racial memories of a far-past "Golden Age"—an unshadowed Eden—or the persistent instinct of something good yet to come? "Man never *is* but always *to be* blest." But in that far-off dayspring of the universe *we*, who sigh and suffer and long in the darkness—darkness now dense, now moonlit—will not have any being as *we*. We may exist in numberless new incarnations; but those new personalities will have no remembrance of the old. For *us* then it seems to me there is nothing but to make the best of it and fight against our night with the little fires and tapers of hopes and creeds and dreams and visions. They are as a flickering lantern to the sun. But a lantern keeps us from stumbling hopelessly in the darkness and gives one enough light to travel by with a fair degree of safety. The teachings of all our wise men are the little stars in our night; and by them it is possible to shape our course until the Golden Age comes round again. The material universe is created after the system of circles and therefore it is only reasonable to believe that the spiritual one is, too, and that through endless duration cycles of light and darkness will alternate, as do the Ormuzd and Ahrimanes of the old Persian creed.[354]

Tuesday, Feb. 3, 1920

In copying my old journal tonight I found the following passage. Writing of having drifted away from old beliefs I said, "I have not yet formulated any working belief to replace those I have lost."

Since those days I *have* formulated a belief—or rather one has

354   Mythical figures from the spirituality of ancient Zoroastrianism.

seemed to take shape within my mind slowly and relentlessly as experience and comparison and reflection have forced me to certain conclusions. I *know* quite clearly what I believe but I have never yet reduced it to black and white. Let me see if I can do so now.

I believe in a God who is good and beautiful and just—but *not* omnipotent. It is idle to ask me to believe in a God who is *both* good and omnipotent. Given the conditions of history and life the two things are irreconcilable. To believe that God is omnipotent but *not* purely good— well, it would solve a good many puzzling mysteries. Nevertheless, it is a belief that the human soul instinctively shrinks from. Well, then, I believe in God who is good but not omnipotent. I also believe in a Principle of Evil, equal to God in power—at least, at present—opposing hideousness to His beauty, evil to His good, tyranny to His justice, darkness to His light. I believe that an infinite ceaseless struggle goes on between them, victory now inclining to the one, now to the other. So far, my creed is the old Persian creed of the eternal conflict between Ahrimanes and Ormuzd. But I did not take it over from the Persian. My own mind has compelled me to it, as the only belief that is in rational agreement with the universe as we know it.

I believe that if we range ourselves on the side of good the result will be of benefit to ourselves in this life and, if our spirit survives bodily death, as in some form I feel sure it will, in all succeeding lives; conversely, if we yield to or do evil the results will be disastrous to us. And I admit the possibility of our efforts aiding to bring about sooner the ultimate victory of good.

That victory will come—perhaps not in the time of our universe— perhaps not for the duration of many such universes—but eventually evil, which is destructive, will be conquered by good and remain in subjection for age-long duration. Perhaps forever; and perhaps all eternity devoid of *all* evil would be tiresome even to God, who, like us, may find in struggle a greater delight than in achievement—a greater delight in contest with his peers than in unquestioned supremacy over vanquished foes. Perhaps alternate light and darkness—the alternate waxing and waning of evil must follow each other through the unnumbered, the innumerable eons of Eternity, even as night and day follow each other in our little system.

This is my creed, it explains all which would otherwise puzzle me hopelessly; it satisfies me and comforts me.

Orthodox Christianity says reproachfully, "Would you do away with my hope of heaven?" The hope of heaven is too dearly balanced by the fear of hell and the one thing implies the other. I believe in neither; but

I believe that *life* goes on and on endlessly in incarnation after incarnation, co-existent with God, and Anti-god, rejoicing, suffering, as good or evil wins the upper hand. To me, such an anticipation is infinitely more attractive than the dull effortless, savorless existence pictured to us as the heaven of rest and reward. Rest! It is a good thing; but one does not want an eternity of it. All we ask rest for is to gain fresh strength for renewed effort. Reward! Even in this life reward once tasted, soon loses its flavor. Our best reward is the joy of the struggle.

Saturday, Feb. 14, 1920

This has been a week when, as far as my personal bit of life goes, Ahrimanes has been in the ascendent. On Wednesday Ewan came down with his old foe, neuritis, in back and shoulder, and has been lying helpless in bed ever since, unable to move an inch without agony. Wednesday and Thursday I was very miserable myself with a slight attack of flu. Yesterday was a really dreadful day. Lily and Chester came down with flu. I was hardly able to drag around, do the work, and wait on the sick and helpless. Fortunately Mr. Warner did the outside work, feeding horse and hens etc. so I did not have to go out. It was a bitter-cold, dull-gray day spitting snow. So was today. I got no sleep last night with Chester and tonight Stuart is taking the flu. I am worried constantly over the Page affair, I am ill and tired. I have spent four lonely desolate evenings when I think I would have gone quite crazy if it had not been for old Daffy, who cuddled up to me and purred, "Take a brace. We've weathered many a storm together and we'll weather this one." Really, the cat was no end of a comfort to me. I would get a nurse to help out if only one could be got. But such a creature is unobtainable owing to the prevalence of flu everywhere. Half the people in the congregation are down with it.

I had a letter from Mr. Rollins today but I have not yet opened it. I shall leave it till tomorrow. If I can get some sleep tonight I shall not be so nervous and so easily upset and shall be in better shape to face whatever news or opinion it contains.

The Page matter is briefly this: George Page told me in 1919 that they did not have copies of the 1912 versions. In December last he wrote me, giving me notice according to our agreement, that they were going to publish the stories in 1920 and informed me that they had "found" their copies of the 1912 versions after all and would use them. I instantly saw that I had been tricked. They had those stories all the time—I know that now perfectly well—but did not dare to tell me so because they knew I would not let them use them without my revision.

Now they claim the contract gives them the right to use these stories.

I did not want these stories to be used for two reasons. In the first place Anne is mentioned in two or three of them, and this will be a violation of my agreement with Stokes; in the second place there was a good deal of material in those versions which did not appear in the original magazine stories. When Page sent these stories back to me I used this extra material in my following books; and now to have a volume of stories come out apparently repeating this material will make me ridiculous. So I put the matter into Mr. Rollins' hands and will bring suit if necessary to prevent the Pages from publishing that book from any MSS except the MSS I authorized. What scoundrels they are!

Sunday, Feb. 22, 1920

I sent for the doctor for Stuart last Sunday for I was afraid the child was developing pneumonia. But he is better and I think we are all improved. Lily and Chester are up. Ewan's neuritis is better but he is very dull and depressed. The weather has been exceedingly cold and Mr. Rollins writes me that Page refuses to be good—which means that they are going ahead with the book. I feel very draggy but have sought to while away the dismal hours by reading Prescott's *Conquest of Mexico*.[355] Cortez was a wonder of determination and "grit." But to what end?

I am blue and disheartened.

On Friday I went in to Toronto and saw *Anne* on the screen at the Regent. It was a pretty little play well photographed but I think it I hadn't already known it was from my book, that I would never have recognized it. The landscape and folks were "New England," never P.E. Island. Mary Miles Minter was a sweet, sugary heroine utterly unlike my gingery Anne.[356] "Matthew" was a dear but totally unlike the "Matthew" of the book. "Marilla" was a commonplace female who says "*Ain't*," instead of the dour, rigid *lady* of my conception. A skunk and an American flag were introduced—both equally unknown in P.E. Island. I could have shrieked with rage over the latter. Such crass, blatant Yankeeism!

The play has had an enormous success and I don't get a cent from it!! Well, I wish the Pages joy of it.

---

355   American historian William Hickling Prescott's (1796–1859) *The History of the Conquest of Mexico* (1843).

356   Mary Miles Minter (1902–84) had starred in many silent films by the time she played "Anne" at age 17.

I came home yesterday morning and was nearly frozen. Rollins writes advising me to take no action until the book is really published. I would prefer to go ahead at once and settle the question of their right or no right.

Monday, Feb. 23, 1920
The Manse, Leaskdale, Ont.

Yesterday and today have been really dreadful. East wind—snow—dull, lifeless, gray, bitter cold. Can't get furnace to burn so house is not comfortable. I am worried over many things. Lily doesn't seem to be getting over the effects of the flu and her terrible cough in the evening and at night alarms me. Ewan is very dull and moody. Then this Page affair—altogether I am dreadfully upset and nervous. This afternoon I couldn't even work—couldn't take an interest in anything. And I feel so horribly *alone*. I have *no one* to go to for help and sympathy. Ewan is apathetic towards everything but his own worrying delusion. I am haunted by a fear that his condition will grow worse in spring and be as it was last year. Lately I am beginning to feel that life is *at last* too hard for me. These past six hard years of constant toil and worry, added to the crushing blow of Frede's going, have broken down my courage.

Wednesday, Feb. 25, 1920
Leaskdale, Ont.

Not much improvement anywhere. This journal is a melancholy record these days. But I must have *some* outlet or I could not bear patiently things as they are.

Ewan went to Toronto yesterday for a few days. Perhaps the change will do him good and help him. Our bitter cold continues. I have never known such a continuance of severe cold in my life. It would not be so bad if we could keep the house passably warm but our coal is so poor we cannot. We have used up all our good coal. I have felt torpid and lifeless and *stale* all day. Everything seems hapless and jarring.

This evening I was copying the part of my old journal concerning my life in Bedeque and my love for Herman Leard. Even when I merely *read* that it always brings it back with terrible vividness. But *writing* it makes me feel that I am again *living* it and I love him as madly as ever and long for him as sickeningly. This mood couldn't get such a hold on me if I were not lonely and worried. But one has to escape now and then from a miserable present into either the past or the future. And just now I cannot find any escape in thought of the future.

Friday, Feb. 27, 1920
The Manse, Leaskdale

Rose betimes and got my fires on in furnace and range because all had gone out in the night. Lily and I between us have had to "run" the furnace this winter because Ewan has gone to bed at 8 and stayed in bed till 11 or 12 next morning all winter. His strange indifference to his duties as man of the house is one of the symptoms of his malady. Lily seems better today but can't do anything yet. I managed a chapter of Book Ten and got on fairly well.

I had a letter today from a man in the U.S. who felt it laid upon him to write and tell me that he had been dreaming "Patrick Grayfur" was alive, said P.G. being the cat in "The Story Girl." Also a letter from some pathetic ten-year-old in New York who implores me to send her my photo because she lies awake after she goes to bed wondering what I look like. Well, if she had a picture of me in my old dress, wrestling with the furnace this morning, "cussing" ashes and clinkers—if not aloud, in my heart—she would die of disillusionment. However, I shall send her a reprint of my last photo in which I sit rapt in inspiration—apparently—at my desk, with pen in hand, in gown of lace and silk with hair just-so—Amen. A quite passable looking woman, of no kin whatever to the dusty, ash-covered Cinderella of the furnace cellar.

Wednesday, March 3, 1920

Cold keeps. Ewan is home and seems much better. Lily is slowly improving. I suppose we shall get through somehow. But "getting through" is not living. I go through the days now, dreading a 'phone ring, because I am expecting a wire any day saying that *Further Chronicles of Avonlea* is published. And if that happens I am in for another lawsuit—for I will not let the Page Co. put a trick like that over on me and get away with it scot-free. Yet I loathe the thought and whenever the 'phone rings I turn cold with apprehension. The other day it rang and when I answered it the station agent at Uxbridge said, "A wire for you." "Yes," I said, steeled for the worst. "It's from Charlottetown," he said—and I almost dropped the receiver in my relief. But it is a miserable condition to live in—this constant wearing suspense.

Tonight I finished copying that part of my journal dealing with Herman Leard. It is a relief. I will not be further tortured by the upleaping of fires that have long seemed only white-ashes.

Monday, Mar. 8, 1920
The Manse, Leaskdale, Ont.

Another abominable day of bitter cold, high wind, and balky furnace.
The house was literally freezing cold all day. Water froze if spilled on
the kitchen floor. I could not write. Ewan's arm and back are bothering
him again, too.

Chester is reading the Jungle Books now and revelling in them.[357]
He is a wonderful reader for his age—reads too much, I fear. But the
cold is so intense he can not go out much and has to have something
besides play to put time in. I have made a practice of reading a story to
him every night after he went to bed since he was a tiny tot and he has
always loved it. He is especially interested just now in Shere Khan and
Mowgli's[358] adventure with the monkeys.

My dear little boys! It is only my love for them that gives me strength
and courage to fight on. I want them to have a happy childhood and a
happy and useful manhood.

Friday, March 12, 1920

At last the iron winter has broken. For the first time we have had a
thaw—and a tremendous one. The cellar has been full of water all day
and one of the results is that the furnace went out. Luckily the day was
so mild that it isn't so great a matter. But it has been a dismal day and
Ewan is dull and headachy again after seeming almost normal for a
week.

Something I was copying in my old journal made me think of Pensie
Macneill tonight.[359] Poor Pensie! We were such chums in those dear
childish days. I thought she acted strangely to me at the time of her
marriage and after she went to New Glasgow I did not see her often.
She died about eight years after her marriage of tuberculosis, having
literally worked herself to death. The summer before she died I talked
with her at her old home where they were having a family reunion of
children and grandchildren. I spoke to her about her looking so thin
and advised her to take things easier and give herself a chance. "Oh,
Maud, my life is broken," she said pitifully. I went to see her one evening shortly before her death and we talked over all our old merry
times. She did not then know she would not recover but I knew it and

---

357 Rudyard Kipling's *The Jungle Book* (1894).

358 Characters from Kipling's *The Jungle Book*.

359 A cousin and childhood friend from Cavendish. See note 262, page 180.

the knowledge made our evening a rather ghastly farce to me.
"Friend after friend departs."[360]

Sunday, March 14, 1920
Leaskdale, Ont.

Two more hard days—today especially so. Yesterday the house was so
cold I could not write. A letter came from Mr. Rollins. I knew there was
fateful news in it of some kind and dared not open it till bed-time, lest
it unfit me for work. After I had had my final "rassle" with the furnace
I read it. It contained a copy of a letter to Mr. Rollins from Mr. Nay,
Page's lawyer, stating that the Page Co. would use the 1912 versions
and fight the matter out. I had expected nothing else but the certainty
was a blow. I could not sleep all night and today has been very hard for
me. Ewan seems not so well again and made a mess of preaching. I feel
pessimistic and discouraged, but a good cry tonight has helped a bit.
Tears generally relieve. It is when I am too worried to cry that I have
the hardest times. Well, well, cheer up. "Even this will pass away." The
lane *must* turn sometimes—but it has been a long one indeed.

Monday, Mar. 15, 1920
The Manse, Leaskdale, Ont.

Some questions Chester asked me today reminded me that in our class
at Prince of Wales College one day, the question of being able to move
the ear by voluntary action of the muscles came up. The professor said
that animals all possessed it but human beings, as a general thing, had
lost it. Then he had all the members of the class try it. Out of the big
roomful were only two who could "waggle" their ears—myself and a
Trainor or Kelly scion of Irish blood. I can still do it quite easily. Am I
then a case of atavism? It is a disgrace or a gift to be able to wiggle your
ears by their own muscles? Anyhow, it doesn't seem of much use to
me. I don't suppose I could paralyse Page's lawyer by suddenly shaking
my ears at him!

Sunday March 21, 1920
Leaskdale, Ont.

Things are brightening a little. The winter is over. Ewan has been better this past week than he has been since October. Today for the first

---

360   The title of a poem by Scottish-born poet James Montgomery (1771–1854).

time since Christmas we have had a good church service with a comfortable temperature and a good attendance. A letter from Mr. Rollins this week was quite reassuring. But, win or lose, I hate the thought of that lawsuit.

Friday, April 8, 1920

There is no longer any doubt—or hope. Page has published the book from the 1912 versions. I have wired to Rollins to proceed. I feel I am foolish—I fear my chance of winning is not good, considering the unscrupulous character of the men I have to deal with. They will swear to any lie they safely can. I will likely lose and throw away a lot of money. But there is *something* in me that *will not* remain inactive under injustice and trickery and to satisfy that I am driven to this. Besides, the Page Co. need a lesson. They have traded for years on the average woman's fear of litigation and the fact that very few authors can afford to go to law with them, especially when they can't expect to get money out of the result. They have done the most outrageous things to poor authors who can't afford to seek redress. I want to teach them a lesson, even if I can't obtain my rights. But I hate the thought of it all. Fortunately it will not take long—not more than a day or two, Mr. Rollins says. So the agony will be short if sharp. Really, the worst aspect of the case to me is that I will have to come into the presence of Louis and George Page again. I despise them so—I shrink from their atmosphere as from pollution. It is painful to think of them—how much more to be in the same room with them. But I can surely endure it for a day or so.

Saturday, April 10, 1920

Page sent me a copy of the book today—*Further Chronicles of Avonlea*. It is got up to resemble the *Anne* books in every way and is an evident attempt to palm it off on the public as an *Anne* book. They have put a red-haired girl on the cover as appears on all the *Anne* books—another evasion of the terms of our agreement. But everything is so skillfully done that it will be very hard—impossible, I fear,—to bring it home to them. They have also mangled one of the stories by crude interpolations, in one of which a character is made to do an absurd and impossible thing. This reflects on my literary skill. But what else could one expect of such a firm? I was a fool ever to let them have the stories in the first place. I did it to oblige them—and this is the result.

Saturday, Apr. 17, 1920
Leaskdale, Ont.

Last Tuesday I went to Toronto and stayed till tonight. I had a busy week of shopping etc. but had some pleasant hours, too, which were sadly needed after this dreary winter. But when I got on the train to come home tonight I was very sad and depressed—I could hardly account for the latter. But for the first time since I came to Leaskdale I dreaded the thought of going home. My presentiment proved true. When I reached Uxbridge and Ewan met me I saw at once that another attack of his malady was upon him. He was gloomy and dull and has had several days of headache and nights of sleeplessness, and had seemingly gone to pieces worse than at any time since last November. I was too tired to bear up and cried silently all the way home through the raw dark night over the rough roads. I *can't* go on like this.

Monday, April 19, 1920

We think we can't—but we can because we have to. Ewan seems slightly better but moody still. Stuart was sick all last night and I was up with the poor darling. Mr. Rollins sent me the bill of complaint for our suit. It sounds very plausible. But will the Judge think so?

Friday, Apr. 23, 1920
The Manse, Leaskdale, Ont.

It is one o'clock. I have been up all the evening writing business letters, after a busy day of papering Chester's room. Ewan was very poorly up to yesterday but seems much better since. Probably the crisis of this attack is over. But I suppose others will follow.

The Old House.

    I had a letter from Cavendish today in which the writer said that Uncle John was tearing down the old house.[361] It gave me a nasty pang. Yet it might as well be—it was falling into ruin. Yet—that dear, old, beloved spot—my old room—to go into nothingness! It cannot be

---

361   After her Grandfather Macneill's death in 1898, LMM had lived with her grandmother Macneill until her grandmother's death in 1911. In the late 1980s the foundations of this house were restored by Uncle John Franklin's grandson, John Macneill, allowing visitors to see the site where the house once stood.

helped—it is foolish to feel it—but it hurt someway—just as it would hurt to see the body of one we loved destroyed though the soul be gone. But is not life one pang after pang?

Friday, April 30, 1920

A very good sample of my days this spring. Lily and I house-cleaned two rooms. Then I scrubbed another carpet, made a pair of curtains, put the boys to bed, and then sat up till twelve writing business letters. But the day was fine and spring is here—only clouded as every spring has been since 1914 by some kind of bitter worry. I wonder if I shall ever again have a spring free from it. I have almost begun to entertain "a fixed idea" that I never will.

Sunday, May 2, 1920
Leaskdale, Ont.

There is nothing to say about today except that it was fine and cold, that I went to church, and that I am going to bed now at nine o'clock for the sake of getting warm.

Tuesday, May 4, 1920

Today I wrote a chapter of my book, house cleaned, and attended the W.M.S. Had a very nice letter from an English school teacher about my books. Tonight I spent an hour copying my old journal. Something in it reminded me of old post-office doings in Cavendish. There is no post-office there now—naught but post-office boxes strung whitely along the roadsides. Much more convenient, no doubt. Yet I think something is lost in the way of friendliness. At least, I was always glad that we kept the post-office—even apart from the assistance it was to me in sending away—and getting back!!!—MSS. in secrecy. Hardly anyone would ever have come to the house if we had not had the post-office. As it was, in the evenings, especially the winter evenings, the neighbors would come in for the mail and stay to talk politics and news with Grandfather and each other around the old kitchen. Occasionally, too, a boy friend, who would never have dared to come otherwise, ventured to linger for an hour or so and chat to me. Pensie and Amanda used to come on summer nights and furnish an excuse for me to get out for a walk, "going a piece with them"—"down the church hill" and up "as far as David's gate" with Amanda, or "down to Will Laird's gate" with Pensie.

Wednesday, May 5, 1920

A letter from Stella today tells me that she is pregnant. Now for months of wildly complaining letters!

The Old Kitchen

But I'm sorry it has happened. Stella is not young and it may go hardly with her. In spite of everything it would make a big blank in my life if Stell should go utterly out of it. This will be a dull worry all summer now. Well, what is life but worry—my life anyhow? I've never been free from it since I was twenty—never will be free from it again I suppose. If it is not one thing it's another. The only thing to do, I suppose, is to "carry on" and play the game.

Sunday, May 9, 1920
Leaskdale, Ont.

Have been reading Byron's *Life*.[362] Don't like the man as well as I like his poetry—for I *do* like Byron's poetry very much. It thrills some chords in my being as no other poet can do. Byron is out of fashion—but he is immortal for all that. Passion is always immortal and he touched too poignantly all its notes, of spirit as well as sense, ever to be forgotten. But his letters make a disagreeable impression on me. They give me a sense of unreality and posing. And his life—what a series of tragedies it was! For himself and the women entangled in it. He was a being of storm-cloud and lightning flash—beautiful, ruinous, transient.

Friday, May 14, 1920

Had a wire from Rollins today, saying that the case will come up May 20. So I must even hie me to Boston. Fortunately I won't have to stay long. Rollins says the case won't take more than a couple of days. I would hate to have to be long away from home and my dear boys.

Ewan is not very well lately. His head troubles him and his sleep is restless. He plans to go down home for the month of June. Perhaps it will help him—but I have dreary hopelessness of that. What a horrible malady melancholia is! It is far worse, both for the victim and those connected with him than any organic illness—its maddening suspen-

---

362   Most likely Ethel C. Mayne's *Life of Byron* (1912).

sions—its sudden returns just as one faintly begins to hope that it has gone for good—its terrible power of cutting its victim off from the kindly intimacies and wholesome activities of life, of blotting out ambition and interest and sympathy!

Well, it must be endured. And there is no one to help me endure it—the friend who could have given me courage is gone—life is gray and colorless around me—a monotonous succession of routine days with the soul gone out of them.

Patience!

Nearly eight

Thursday, May 20, 1920
East Braintree, Mass.

I left home last Monday and reached Braintree on Tuesday night. Yesterday I conferred with Mr. Rollins and today our case opened. I was in the witness stand most of the day. Page's regular lawyer, Mr. Nay, could not—or would not—take the case and they have a Mr. French[363]—a very able fellow and a "trick" lawyer. I don't think he found me so easy a subject to handle as he seemed jauntily to expect at first. I dislike the man: he is a cad: Judge Fox called him down very sharply once for something he said to me. But he rouses a combative instinct in me—and that is well. I can fight well when I am goaded to it. From today's developments I rather fear the case will take some days longer than we thought. But if I get home by June 1st it will not matter. I am tired tonight—a nervous tiredness that will not let me rest.

Friday, May 21, 1920

The case goes over to a Master. Mr. Rollins gave George Page a drilling today. They have suppressed a certain letter of mine which George Page swears was destroyed at my request—an absolute lie. The suppression will not do them any good, no matter how they camouflage it.

Bungalow at Braintree.

---

363   Asa Palmer French was the lawyer representing the Pages.

Saturday, May 22, 1920

This being Saturday there was no court. So I went into Boston in a pouring rain to lunch with Alma Macneill. Then we went to a movie. Had a good time inside. But outside! The streets of Boston in a pouring rain are quite unthinkable.

Tuesday, May 25, 1920
East Braintree, Mass.

Had a tedious day in court. Yesterday Rollins was cross-examining George Page all day but as French "objected" to almost every question and the two wrangled it out to the Master nothing got very much "for-rarder." George Page told a few more lies. I used to think he was not quite so conscienceless as Louis but I find I was mistaken. When court closed I went out to Concord Square and spent the night with Alma Macneill. Had a nice time but under it all felt the strain of worry. Also, a recalcitrant tooth had begun to bother me.

Our case did not go on today as the Master had to have the day off for some reason or other. So I came home and spent the day nursing a bad cold, a bad tooth and a bad worry.

Wednesday, May 26, 1920
East Braintree, Mass.

Had a rather bad night. Wakened with headache, took aspirin, and finally slept again; but felt very tired this morning and certainly not in any mood for fighting with wild beasts at Ephesus.[364] Yet, having got up early (I have to get up at six to catch the only train from East Braintree that will take me in in time for court) and made the trip in. I was disgusted to find that Mr. Mellen, the Master, was sick and could not sit on the case today. So here we are hung up again. We can not possibly get through now before June 1.

Friday, May 28, 1920
East Braintree, Mass.

I have heard of "the maddening delays of the law." Now I am experiencing them. Yesterday morning I wakened at four o'clock and threshed the case over in my mind till six—as if that would do any good. But I

---

364   From 1 Corinthians 15.32: "If after the manner of men I have fought with beasts at Ephesus, what advantageth it me, if the dead rise not? Let us eat and drink; for tomorrow we die."

cannot help it and occasionally an idea of some importance crops up in the welter of my thoughts.

I went in yesterday and found that Mr. Mellen was still ill and no likelihood of the case going on this week. The delay is getting on my nerves. I can't eat at all and am beginning not to sleep. Today Flora and I went to Malden to visit some friends. At first I enjoyed myself but as the day wore on the undercurrent of worry became an overcurrent. I talked and laughed automatically and argued the case over in my mind continually. I couldn't eat the banquet our hostess provided and felt badly because this disappointed her. Oh, Lord, *why* can't people let us eat or not eat, as we choose or need, instead of vexing themselves and us over it. My tooth, too, has bothered me all day and I fear ulceration.

Saturday, May 29, 1920

A cold, long, lonely day. I am in bad shape, worried and unhappy. Got terribly nervous as night came on. I dread next week and can't help thinking of the case. It is becoming a sort of obsession with me. And I get so homesick for Chester and Stuart, dear little fellows. I have nothing here to divert my thoughts in any way—no books, no real company. Flora is a dear kind soul whose dearness and kindness hasn't a spark of interest mixed up with it, and Amos is an unmitigated bore. Well, "even this will pass away."

Tuesday, June 1, 1920
East Braintree, Mass.

Went to Boston today—but nothing doing. It is very depressing. Ewan will be leaving for his vacation today and the boys will be alone with Lily. She will look after them well but she will tyrannize over them and antagonize them and make their little lives unhappy.

The stenographer had sent Mr. Rollins a copy of my evidence under Judge Fox and I had the novel experience of reading it over. It sounded to me as if somebody else must have given it. But it was very satisfactory. French didn't trip me up in spite of his "trick" questions. This afternoon I went out to visit the Geo. Ritchies[365] and spent the rest of the day with them. Had a nice time—on the surface. George is

---

365   Lucy Ritchie was LMM's cousin (she was the daughter of Uncle John Montgomery and Aunt Emily Macneill). She had married George Ritchie and lived in Roslindale, a suburb of Boston.

an intelligent fellow and one enjoys talking to him—but he is such a rampant socialist and parlor Bolshevist that it is a little hard to have patience with him. I came home finally and walked up the hill from the station through the moonlit woods. They were full of subtle beauties and allurements but though I perceived them I did not enjoy them. I am wretchedly homesick and upset. Found a 'phone here from Rollins telling me not to go in tomorrow—so no hope yet of getting on.

Wednesday, June 2, 1920
East Braintree, Mass.

Couldn't sleep till late and wakened early. Had a very hot, intolerable day but tooth is better so I begin to hope I'll escape ulceration. An ulcerating tooth and a lawsuit together is a very bad blend. Rollins 'phoned at one that they must get a new Master as Mr. Mellen[366] cannot go on with the case. This means heaven knows how much more delay. I felt almost despairing. But I read and crocheted alternately the rest of the day. I have got a set of Maupassant's[367] works from Mr. Dobson. One wearies of his "eternal triangle" but in some respects his style is very wonderful. But he is obsessed by sex and cannot write about anything else.

The moonlit woods

This evening I am very upset and nervous. I feel a childish, impatient desire to be *free from worry* after such a continuance of it. I'm just a baby tonight, that is exactly what I am. Only I'm doing all my howling and kicking and squirming inwardly. Outwardly I smile and talk to Flora on the weather and to Amos about future punishment—a theme on which he seems to like discoursing. Future punishment, indeed! I am more concerned with present punishment. God knows we are all punished enough in this life for our misdeeds. Only—it seems to me that it is *weakness* that is punished—not *wickedness*. The weak suffer—the strong go free. The Pages are the

366   George Henry Mellen (b. 1850) was the Master first assigned to the case.

367   Henri René Albert Guy de Maupassant (1850–93), French writer best-known for his short stories in the naturalist tradition.

scamps in this affair—they have cheated and lied right through—yet they are not worrying over the case I'm ready to wager—never think of it except academically. I know I am foolish to do so either. After all, no matter how the suit goes, the consequences will not be very dreadful. But I cannot help it. It is the uncertainty of when I am to get home that is worst. And the whole business is so distasteful to me—French re-acts upon me as a rattlesnake would. I hate and fear him.

Tuesday, June 3, 1920
East Braintree, Mass.

Went into Boston. Rather better news. A Mr. Sampson has been appointed Master.[368] We are all to begin tomorrow and Rollins thinks we may finish in six days. But I am dubious. I feel as if I were caught and held by some huge, slimy octopus and that all struggles and attempts to escape are futile. This thing will go on forever.

Friday, June 4, 1920
East Braintree, Mass.

Went in as usual. I am sick of that train ride and loathe the sight of East Braintree station. Court opened again today. Master Sampson seems to be a nice gentlemanly man but I have an idea that he is rather narrow and literal. George Page was in the chair all day and Rollins screwed some rather important admissions out of him. I have had no word from home for several days and I have a half frantic feeling about the children.

Besides I keep worrying over the days when French will begin to cross-examine me again. There is no reason why I should worry. I have nothing to tell but the truth. But in this case so much—everything in fact—depends on mere memory. And it is so hard to recall exactly everything that happened in those long negotiations of 1919, just as and when it happened.

Much of the misery of my life—just as much of the pleasure—has been caused by my habit of living everything over beforehand. It is never half as bad—or half as delightful—when it really, comes. When I finally find myself in the chair with French glaring insultingly at me I know I shan't mind it at all, my spirit will flash up at his challenge and I shall thrust and parry vigorously. But this knowledge never seems to help me much beforehand. I feel just now as if I *couldn't* face next week.

---

368   Harry LeBaron Sampson (1878–1971), a partner at the law firm Hutchins and Wheeler.

Monday, June 7, 1920
East Braintree, Mass.

I have had to take veronal these last few nights to get any sleep at all but such sleep is very unsatisfactory. We had only a morning session of the court today as the Master had to be absent in

East Braintree Station

afternoon. George Page admitted a certain important allegation of mine in his evidence. Nevertheless, I felt blue until, as we left the courtroom, Rollins astonished me by saying, "I think we've won our case. I was afraid we couldn't get Page to admit that."

Rollins should know—but it seems to me that we are very far short yet of having established our case. The Page defence is yet to come and Rollins doesn't even yet know their capacity for lying as I do. Nevertheless his opinion cheered me up and I came home in a better mood and pleased Flora vastly by being able to eat some supper. It is three weeks since I left home—and it seems three years.

Tuesday, June 8, 1920
East Braintree, Mass.

I slept well last night for which praise be. But today was unsatisfactory. Most of the time was wasted by French and Rollins wrangling over the admissibility of certain questions and it did not seem as if we made any progress at all. Rollins is depressed again,—thinks "the Master's mind doesn't get his—Rollins'—ideas." I worked hard all my spare time today tabulating certain statements for evidence. When I came home I found a card from Lily saying that Ewan had not gone away after all. This worried me. I had spoiled Ewan's vacation—and he needed it so badly. I felt as if I couldn't endure this on top of all my other worry so I fled to my room and had a good howl.

Thursday, June 10, 1920

Yesterday George Page swore to some rather dreadful lies. How can he? I used to think Louis was the champion liar of the firm but George can equal him. Today I had to go on stand and Mr. Rollins examined me. In a way I dread his examination worse than French for of course *he* doesn't arouse my fighting instincts and I am so afraid of getting mixed up in my many recollections of 1912 and 1919 and all the different revisions and MSS. of those wretched stories. Yet Rollins says I am an excellent witness and make a good impression on the court. That may be—but I always leave the stand feeling that I have made an incredible ass of myself and smeared everything up. Then when I get Miss Dowd's typed report and read it over it seems quite unbelievable that those clear-cut and definite statements can be mine.

So I came home, tired, worried, miserable, unable to eat or think of anything but myself in the chair tortured and badgered by French—disgraced—put to shame—all especially absurd. I know he cannot do it—but still I am obsessed with a sort of hypnotic terror that he can.

Will I *ever* get home? That peaceful, vine-hung manse and green, maple-shadowed lawn seem an unattainable heaven just now—something I'll never see again. The truth is, I'm very far from normal just now and as a result I have lost every particle of my sense of proportion. This case looms up before me in grotesque exaggeration, shutting out everything else from my view. I *know* this—but I cannot *feel* it—and consequently I am obsessed.

Friday, June 11, 1920

Had to take veronal again last night. I hate taking it but I cannot face the ordeal of the day without some sleep. I spent today in the chair examined by Mr. Rollins. French raged and uttered vain things but we

"That peaceful, vine hung manse."

got our evidence in. Mr. Rollins' persistency and imperturbability are things of wonder to me. I never saw anything like his poise. Nothing disturbs it—he never shows the slightest impatience or irritation, even when French is acting in a fashion that would aggravate a bronze Buddha. When, after a long wrangle, the Master decides against him, Mr. Rollins, instead of striding madly about the room, as does French, bows and says suavely, "Very good. I'll try again," and proceeds to ask the very same question in a different form, until finally French is wearied out and the Master appears to think, "I may as well save time by letting that question in, since this man will keep on until he does get it in somehow." In this respect Mr. Rollins is admirable. But in other respects I fear he is hardly a match for French. He has not as good a memory for one thing and cannot anticipate and prepare for the moves of our opponents as does French. It is certainly all amazingly interesting—this battle of wits—and if I were not the toad under the harrow I should enjoy it. But as it is I am conscious only of the torture.

After court closed Mr. Rollins said, "I think we have them on the run," but I feel he is too sanguine.

I lunched today on a glass of milk because it could be easily swallowed. The heat and crowds in the South Station were dreadful tonight and I had to wait a long time for a train. Got so homesick and *children sick* that I could scarcely endure it.

Sunday, June 13, 1920
East Braintree, Mass.

Friday night I slept well and on Saturday I went to Roslindale for a week-end with the Ritchies. I enjoyed the day and an evening spent discussing religion and social problems with George. But today was miserable. I was in a simply intolerable condition of mind. My nerves are all raw, and I feel imprisoned—hounded—tortured. Reason tells me that there is no need for me to feel so but reason is powerless before a nervous breakdown. This evening I could no longer control my nervousness and had to walk the floor for an hour. I do not think I have ever felt more wretched. But I have hardly slept or eaten for three weeks and have been so worried about Ewan and the children that I'm down and out. I know from Ewan's letters—what *isn't* in them—that he is not well and I am exhausted by the dread that he will become what he was last summer.

Monday, June 14, 1920

After a veronal sleep I went to Boston and was cross-examined by French all day. As per usual, when fairly "up against it" I could fight well—without nervousness or fear. I came home exhausted but not so worried and spent the evening reading Maupassant. I wonder if he believed that there was *one* decent woman in the world. Well, he died insane—so his point of view on life is not to be taken too seriously.

Wednesday, June 16, 1920
East Braintree, Mass.

Court did not sit yesterday—another delay—so I slept well, and went into Boston through this damp, muggy morning, going as usual down that pretty, lovable little woodland path to whose appeal I cannot respond. French cross-examined me all day and got nothing for his pains. Mr. Rollins says he never saw a better witness than I am. He is blue, however, because he thinks we won't get much in the way of damages. I don't care a hoot whether we do or not. I want to get an injunction against that book and teach Page a lesson in square dealing. But I see no prospect of the case being concluded this week and I came home frightfully depressed over the prospect, or rather the no-prospect of getting home. Guess I'll never get there. For the rest of my life I must get up at 6, trot down through the woods to that East Braintree station, go to Boston court-house and be put to the question by French. At least that is exactly the way I feel.

Friday, June 18, 1920

Yesterday was a public holiday so there was no court, but I had to go to Boston to mail an important letter as the p.o. here was closed. On return found a wire from Ewan saying that all were well, not to worry etc. But I felt very restless and near absolute collapse. Had veronal sleep last night and went to Boston this morning in a pouring rain. French grilled me all day but didn't advance much. Rollins says he went back. Those three grave lawyers and myself wrangled all day over the question of the exact color of "Anne's" hair and the definition of "Titian red."[369] Ye gods, it was funny! The big table was snowed under with literature and prints to prove or disprove. Years ago, when I sat down in

---

369   Titian (Tiziano Vecellio in Italian, c.1488–1576) was an artist famous among other things for voluptuous, red-haired women. "Titian red" would most commonly describe hair that is brownish-orange in colour. Anne's hair is described as "Titian" when she gives a recitation at the White Sands Hotel. LMM's 1919 contract with Page had stated that "No Picture of 'Anne Shirley' ... shall appear in or on said proposed book." However, the cover of *Further Chronicles of Avonlea* did feature a red-haired girl.'"

that old kitchen at Cavendish, that rainy spring evening, and dowered "Anne" with red hair, I did not dream that a day would come when it would be fought over like this in a court room. It would be deliciously amusing—if it were not so beastly horrible. French was determined to prove that Titian hair was dark red and that I knew it was dark red. I didn't. I always supposed Titian-red was a sort of flame-red and I stuck to it through all his badgering. Rollins dug up an encyclopedia in which Titian hair was defined as a "bright golden auburn" and the Master said it had always been his impression that Titian hair was the hue of burnished copper! And so on!

The *raison-d'etre* of all this is the red-headed girl's picture on the cover of the book.

Mr. Rollins and I went to see the big Ringling circus[370] tonight—I having never seen a circus. It was worth seeing—though having seen it I don't fancy I'll ever want to see another. The animals were good. There was a magnificent Bengal tiger pacing restlessly and endlessly up and down.

I know exactly how the poor brute felt!

Saturday, June 19, 1920
East Braintree, Mass.

Slept fairly well and slept again on the lounge in the den this afternoon and dreamed I was home, kissing my dear little children. I woke up longing for them and feeling as if I *must* see them. Do all women feel like this when they are absent from their children?

Sunday, June 20, 1920

A very long tedious day. Haven't felt well at all. Feel that I *cannot* go through another week of this. But I have to. Every night I feel "I *cannot* face tomorrow"—and every morning I pluck up a certain amount of desperate courage and fight the day through.

Five weeks ago tonight I was motoring home from Sunderland with Ewan and thinking, "It will be all over a week from tonight." And now it is no nearer being over than it was then apparently.

---

370   In 1919, several established circus groups from across the United States merged to form the "Ringling Bros. and Barnum & Bailey Combined Shows."

Tuesday, June 22, 1920

All day yesterday and the forenoon of today I was on the stand. Then my torture was intermitted for a time and Mr. McClelland took the chair, having come down to witness in my behalf in the matter of damages. Louis Page came into court for the first time—to hear what Mac. would say I presume.

When we left the court a deputy served a writ upon me to the effect that the Page Co. meant to sue me in September! As there is nothing else they can sue me about it must be for "false and malicious litigation" in the present suit. Rollins says they can do nothing and as I have had plenty of experience of their empty threats in the past it does not really worry me. They want to frighten me if possible into a compromise. They shall not do it. I'll fight them all the more determinedly for such a contemptible proceeding. Rollins seems to be amazed that "a reputable lawyer like French" would do such a thing. But it is my opinion that there is very little French would not do if he thought he could get away with it.

Nevertheless, the incident has added a little more to my discomfort. There is always the possibility that Louis Page, who is the most vindictive man on earth, will go to any extreme, even if he knows he goes to certain defeat, in order to inflict worry and vexation upon me.

I lived on "milk shakes" all day. I've forgotten what it is like to feel the slightest desire for food.

Wednesday, June 23, 1920
East Braintree, Mass.

Even veronal could not make me sleep past three last night. When I went in Mr. Rollins said, "I have been thinking over the matter and I think I can promise you you won't have any serious trouble."

"Anyhow," I said, "I am not going to let them bluff me into surrender." "You are a good fighter," said Rollins. "After a summons like that you came here this morning looking as pink and pretty as if you hadn't a care in the world."

You see, I don't tell Mr. R. of my sleepless nights and nervous unrest. But I'm *not* a good fighter—or I wouldn't feel so. I'm only a good bluffer. I sailed into the court-room, bowed coolly to French, flashed a gay smile and "good-morning" at the Master, laughed and jested aside with Miss Dowd. French and the Pages did not find me flattened out, if they expected it.

McClelland was cross-examined this morning and French made

mince-meat of him. I have been wondering why Rollins persisted in regarding me as "a splendid witness" until I saw a solid, middle-aged business man like McClelland go all to pieces under cross-examination. I feel he has done our cause more harm than good. It was Rollins' idea to send for him. I had a feeling against it somehow but gave in. It would, I believe, been better if I hadn't. The court did not sit this afternoon.

Thursday, June 24, 1920

Had a good cry last night and as a result slept well. Nothing like a good howl for calming distracted nerves. Mr. Morrow came on from New York today and testified. French could not rattle or brow-beat *him*. In the afternoon I went on the stand again. French tried to trap me twice with two inordinately long and involved questions, the meaning of which was fearfully hard to follow. But I saw the trap and avoided it. That man is a fiend. Nevertheless, he is the right sort of a lawyer to have if you want to win. I do not really think Rollins is a match for him.

I continue to feel worried and depressed—though only about not being able to get home. I have ceased to care whether the case is lost or won. My whole summer is spoiled—and Ewan's, too, which is worse. I had planned to spend August on the Island but I'll have to give that up. After having wasted all this time down here I can't go away again—supposing I ever *do* get home.

Friday, June 25, 1920
East Braintree, Mass.

I was again on the stand all day. Hitherto I have kept my temper amid all French's grilling but today he made such an insulting remark that I flared out in anger. "I will not allow you to make such a statement to me, Mr. French," I flashed out at him. And Mr. French, realizing, I suppose, that he had gone too far, muttered a sort of apology and dropped the subject. Rollins says the Master flashed a quiet smile of enjoyment at him during this passage at arms. French isn't popular with other lawyers and they rather enjoy his discomfiture. Rollins was pleased as Punch today over some change in the Master's point of view which he had discovered. I am not enough of a lawyer to grasp its significance and should not have considered it worth getting excited about. But I came home tired completely out. Those hateful, crowded streets—that hateful South Station! I fear my *morale* is giving way completely. Soon

I won't even be able to "bluff." The thing that I can't bear is the wretched uncertainty of how long I must be here. If I only *knew*—if I could only say, "I must endure to a certain date"—I *could* endure it.

Saturday, June 26, 1920
30 Dobson Road, East Braintree, Mass.

This has been the hardest day yet. These holidays are the hardest because they don't advance me any and I have nothing to do. I help Flora with the work but there is so little to do in this well-planned bungalow. Then I am idle for I have nothing now even to read, having finally finished with Maupassant. I did not enjoy him—I enjoy nothing—but he served to drug the hours to a certain extent.

Monday, June 28, 1920
East Braintree, Mass.

Yesterday and today were two very bad days—for the court did not sit today. Yesterday was so bad that I realized that I was just on the verge of a nervous breakdown. So this morning I walked to Weymouth to consult a doctor. He gave me bromide tablets[371] for nerves and appetite tablets. So far they haven't helped at all. I am restless, homesick, discouraged. I was weighed today and weigh only 110 pounds—a loss of eight since I left home.

Tuesday, June 29, 1920

Got through today by help of bromides. Mrs. Hayden and Mrs. Stone were here—friends of Flora. The latter is a thin, Christian Science[372] lady, wearing three necklaces, who asked me dreamily if I "ever worked against mental trouble?"

I did not ask her to explain the process!

I wonder what effect the Christian Science methods would have on French! Let me see. Evil does not exist—French is evil—therefore French does not exist!

What could be clearer?

I think it would be fun to see Mrs. Stone in the witness box, cross-examined by French. No, it is cruelty to animals even to think about it.

---

371   Bromide compounds were used as over-the-counter sedatives and headache remedies.

372   Christian Science was a religious movement developed in nineteenth-century New England by Mary Baker Eddy, focusing on the healing aspect of Christianity.

Wednesday, June 30, 1920
East Braintree, Mass.

At last my acutest martyrdom is over. Today French finished cross-examining me and Rollins closed our case for the present. The defence opens tomorrow. I want to go home but Rollins thinks it is of extreme importance that I should hear the evidence for the defence. So I must stay a few more days longer. Then I suppose I'll be able to get home—but I don't believe it.

July 1, Thursday 1920

French opened his defence today, with three witnesses. One of them told two point-blank lies. But we have no means of *proving* them lies and Rollins regards it as "dangerous testimony" unless we can break it down in cross examination and seemed blue. The witness swore that I *was told in his presence* during the 1919 negotiations that Page had found most of the 1912 versions but not all. This is an absolute falsehood. George Page told me distinctly that all they had were newspaper copies. I remember, too, though I did not catch the significance at the time, that he made the statement when and where nobody but myself could hear him.

I came home blue, and worried all the evening. I am in such a bad state that, in spite of my wild longing to be home, I have at the same time an odd feeling of *dread of going home*—of having to take up my routine duties again while feeling quite unfit to cope with them.

Friday, July 2, 1920
East Braintree, Mass.

Rollins was flat this morning—so flat that he said he did not believe it would be profitable to fight the case longer and suggested we ask for a compromise. I vetoed this flatly. I told him I did not care whether we lost the suit or not. I would fight it to the end and pay the piper cheerfully rather than humble myself to the Page Co. So Rollins acquiesced and we went up to the court-room. He crossed the witness, with the result that the latter went to pieces, floundered helplessly, and "couldn't remember certainly" about anything—couldn't say anything more than that it was "probable" I had been told Page had the 1912 stories. So, Rollins says his testimony will not be so damaging after all and is quite encouraged again. He also extracted another bit of important evidence from another witness. Louis Page was in the chair in the afternoon and told a few lies too many for he contradicted George flatly on some rather significant points. I simply cannot understand how even he could sit there before me and tell the atrocious lies he did.

Monday, July 5, 1920
East Braintree, Mass.

Have had a hard three days of nervous unrest, tortured by "fixed ideas" on which reason has no effect. Besides it has been cold and wet and lonely. But this week *must* finish it. The testimony of the defence will be in then and I shall not wait for the lawyers' pleadings.

Tuesday, July 6, 1920

Court sat this afternoon and Louis P. reeled off a few more perjuries. Mr. Rollins says I can go home on Friday. I don't believe it. I shall have to stay here forever beyond any doubt!

Wednesday, July 7, 1920

I couldn't sleep till late last night but for the first time since coming here my thoughts were pleasant and normal—and what a delightful sensation it was! I slept till it was time to get up and went to Boston feeling a *faint enjoyment* of external things once more. Louis Page was in the stand today again and Rollins thinks he got some important things out of him.

There will be only one day more of it for me. I am afraid to believe this—for fear something happens again to prevent it—and *that* would break me all into little bits. I should "vanish, leaving not a rack behind."[373]

This is dear little Chester's eighth birthday—and I am away again. Last year Ewan and I were both away. I got him a little wrist watch for a present.

Thursday, July 8, 1920
East Braintree, Mass.

I felt *afraid* of today and literally trembled with dread as I went to the court-room, lest something happen that I could not get away. Louis

---

373   From lines 148–158 in 4.1 of Shakespeare's *The Tempest*: "And like the baseless fabric of this vision, / The cloud-capp'd tow'rs, the gorgeous palaces, / The solemn temples, the great globe itself, / Yea, all which it inherit, shall dissolve, / And, like this insubstantial pageant faded, / Leave not a rack behind."

Page was in the stand and we were treated to an odd outburst. Evidently I am not the only one who has "nerves." When Mr. Rollins was questioning him he stood somewhat near Louis. All at once the latter bounded to his feet, his face suffused with passion, and exclaimed,

"Mr. Rollins will you have the goodness to stand further away from me. Your personality is so offensive to me that I cannot endure to have you standing so near me!"

The whole scene was peculiar. I have become convinced that Louis Page's mind is not sound. I would not be surprised to hear at anytime that he had become quite insane. He is certainly not normal.

The matter of "Anne's" red hair came up again and was re-threshed.

Rollins was greatly encouraged by today's developments. But I have made up my mind that the suit is lost and I am not going to think about it any more. All I want is to get home to my children.

When four o'clock came Louis Page and Brother George and their precious French went out, and as their backs disappeared I breathed a fervent prayer that I might never see their faces again.

I came back to Flora's, feeling that I had scrambled out of Hell, though the reek of the pit was still upon me. I came up the little path through the woods and found it sweet and friendly and alluring. This evening I spent happily packing up and preparing to go home. I have a strange, dream-like sensation that I am going back to a place I lived many years ago. It would not surprise me at all if I found on getting home that Chester and Stuart were grown up!!

Saturday, July 10, 1920
The Manse, Leaskdale, Ont.

On Friday morning I actually felt a little hungry! Left Boston at ten, having first weighed myself in the North Station and found I was down to 110. Isn't that too bad—a whole fourteen pounds when I have none too much of this too, too solid flesh to lose at any time? But the only wonder is that there is any flesh at all left.

I had a passable day, caught the Toronto train in Montreal and reached Toronto this morning. I could not get out home, so shopped a little and walked about but felt rather hunted and rotten. All my neurasthenic ideas returned and I couldn't shake them off. Ewan met me tonight at Uxbridge. Says he has been fairly well through June but for the past few days has had a return of his headaches, gloomy ideas, and sleepless nights. So my home-coming was not a very cheerful one. I spent the evening unpacking and reading letters. My dear boys were so glad to see me back.

Saturday, July 17, 1920
The Manse, Leaskdale

Home Again

I have had a rather hard week but I seem to be improving slowly and the neurasthenic worries and dreads that have tortured me seem to be gradually losing their hold as I get more rested. I was not able to sleep the first part of the week but last night I had a good normal sleep. For a few days after coming home I could not keep from crying all the time and everything worried me. Ewan, too, has been poorly, but now he seems to be over the crisis of this attack. What troubles me most is that I cannot write and that book is only about one third done. How am I going to finish it by September? If I could get able to resume work on it I would be all right, because what is keeping me upset now is the fear that I won't be able to write it. So I go around in a "vicious circle."

My appetite is improving, however, and if Ewan keeps on improving also I ought soon to become a rational creature again.

"Blessings on thee, barefoot boys!"

Saturday, July 24, 1920
Leaskdale, Ont.

The first few days of this week were hard. I seemed to be as neurasthenic as ever and Ewan was miserable again. Then—I just suddenly got well and have been so ever since. I don't worry about the case—I eat and sleep well—and today I wrote a chapter of my book and found that I could get on all right. When I discovered that all other worries ducked under cover and I am my own woman again.

Thursday night just when Ewan and I were both feeling very rotten, Captain Smith motored in and in no time had us both cheered up. There seems to be something infectiously healthful about his person-ality—you simply *catch* optimism from him. He stayed all night and we had a very pleasant evening. He and his family are living at Whitby now, so we can be neighborly, as it is only 30 miles away.

Copying my old journal tonight I was reminded of Henry MacLure.[374] Poor Henry! He died in 1910. Bessie did not take his death hardly and has since re-married. Not that I blame her for doing that—it was only her conduct after his death that disgusted me. She did not stay long in Cavendish and I have lost track of her of late years. She was a su-perficially agreeable companion and she and I were friendly while she was there. We had lots of fun together and she always amused and in-terested me—not the least when she was telling me sentimentally that Henry had never loved anybody but her!!

Well, perhaps he didn't!

Monday, July 26, 1920
The Manse, Leaskdale

I am keeping well. And I seem to feel so deeply now the peace and rest of my home after that hideous strain in Boston. It is like heaven. Ewan seems well and in fairly good spirits. Last night he remarked that he felt better than he had for a long time.

Had a charming letter today from some Miss O'Connell of Washing-

[Capt Smith]

374 Henry McLure (1872–1910), from North Rustico, had unsuccessfully pursued LMM's af-fections: "Henry McLure ... has been driving me about this summer, although he clearly un-derstands that he can have nothing, now or ever, but friendship. He is a crude young farmer of Rustico, whose best point is the possession of a dandy gee-gee and I neither like nor dislike him. He is nil—but convenient" (October 8, 1899). McLure married Bessie Schurman in 1907.

ton, D.C.—who vows she isn't a Sein Feiner[375]—telling me that her father at 85, a retired U.S. army officer, enjoys my books so much and is at present afraid that he won't live long enough to read the next one! I suppose uncharitable people would say the poor old gentleman is in his dotage! But I prefer to think otherwise and feel happy in such a compliment.

I had another letter from a little U.S. girl, asking the old, old question, "Is Anne a real girl?" I must have been asked that literally a thousand times since *Green Gables* was published.

Sunday, Aug. 1, 1920
Leaskdale, Ont.

On Thursday Ewan and I motored to Toronto. We didn't get on as smoothly as that sentence might indicate. We left home at 5 a.m. hoping to be in by 8 and have a good day's shopping. About 6 o'clock just as we got to Goodwood, one of our springs broke and we had to stay there till twelve o'clock before we could get it fixed! At such times I yearn for a reliable old nag and buggy. But after all a car is a mighty good thing and adds hugely to the pleasures of life. What a pity pleasure and happiness are two entirely different things!

We brought Laura and Pat and Mac out with us for a fortnight's visit.[376] I have gained 3 lbs. since coming home so am evidently on the up-grade.

Laura told me an item of gossip tonight which at first made me inclined to rage and utter vain things. Then my sense of humor got the upper hand and I laughed instead. She and Bertie once met Aunt Hattie[377] at some social function in Vancouver and the lady gushingly informed them that *she* was the inspiration of "Anne"!!!

This is atrociously funny. Aunt Hattie, that cold, shallow, childish, selfish, hopelessly uninteresting woman, whom I have always detested and who alternately snubbed and ignored me during her few visits to Cavendish during my childhood and girlhood, the "inspiration" of "Anne"!! I cannot imagine two beings more hopelessly different in every respect. Poor Aunt Hattie! Her vanity was always patent and egregious but I should scarcely have supposed that even she could imagine

---

375   Sein Féin, a political party founded in 1905 in Ireland (the term translates from Irish as "ourselves"), associated with Irish independence.

376   Laura MacIntyre Aylesworth was the daughter of Mary Montgomery McIntyre (LMM's father's sister). She lived with her family in Toronto.

377   Aunt Hattie was the wife of LMM's Uncle Chester Macneill, who lived in Vancouver, BC.

Pat, Chester, Mac, Stuart, Ruth Cook.

that she was Anne.

Ewan has been miserable enough these past three days.

A Group of Visitors.

Monday, August 15, 1920
The Manse, Leaskdale, Ont.

Laura and family went away today after a very pleasant visit. Laura and I had a good time. Mac is a dear little fellow and was beloved of Chester and Stuart, but Miss Pat is an *enfante terrible* and my hand has yearned to spank her with no uncertain spanks. I was truly thankful to see the last of her and her freaks and tantrums.

I have had an exceedingly strenuous fortnight of visiting and being visited, picnics, barn-raisings, funerals, missionary meetings and guilds. Now I hope to settle down to quietness and peace and get in some good work on my book. I am at the twenty-eighth chapter now and ten more will finish it, I hope. I loath writing against time like this.

It seems to me that my life nowadays is simply one mad rush to overtake work that "must be done" in a dozen different departments of existence and that I never "catch up," leaving me with a sense of breathlessness and failure that is depressing. I cook and sew and mend and train my children and write novels and endless letters, and run three societies and make innumerable parish visits and garden, and advise and can berries and encourage Ewan and entertain endless callers and shop and plan menus and take snapshots—all mixed up together pretty much as enumerated, with countless interruptions thrown in, and undercurrents of worry over several things running all the time. Sometimes I feel quite desperate. I get up at seven and generally work until twelve at night. Then usually my sleep is broken by E's unrest or some little need of the children. I think something must change—or bust! Well, once my book is done I *will* take a little rest.

Laura and I

[Children in Water]

Sunday, Aug. 22, 1920
The Manse, Leaskdale, Ont.

Last Saturday morning, while I was writing in the parlor Lily came in and said that Daffy was over at Mrs. Leask's *dying*. I tore madly over and up to their barley field where my heart was nearly broken to see my dear old pet lying limply on the stubble. I thought he was already dead but when I gathered his chilling body up in my arms he opened his eyes and mewed faintly. I thought he had been poisoned but when I got him

[Daffy]

home I discovered that he had been shot—accidently by some ground-hog hunter, no doubt, as there is nobody round here who would do it purposely. He lived for two hours while the children and I hung over him in an agony of tears. Then he died. There are not many human beings who are mourned more sincerely than he was. To me it was a real tragedy—the last *living* link with the old life was gone. Daffy was not a cat—he was a *person*, and had more individuality than seven out of ten human beings. He was fourteen years old last spring—the age limit for cats. But, except for a little slowness in

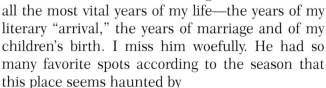

the matter of a jump, he showed no sign of age and would, I feel sure, have lived for several years yet if he had not been thus done to death. He was with me through all the most vital years of my life—the years of my literary "arrival," the years of marriage and of my children's birth. I miss him woefully. He had so many favorite spots according to the season that this place seems haunted by him. Everywhere I look I see Daff. When I came home from Zephyr the other night there was no big gray cat waiting for me on the back platform and running nimbly before me to the door, as Daff always did. I could not keep the tears back as I came in alone. I have had him so long I cannot realize that he is dead. We buried him behind the asparagus plot on the lawn—old Daff, with his plumy tail, his distinctive markings, his

wild glowing eyes—my old companion of days and nights of long ago, my faithful furry comrade through the many lonely evenings of the past two years. I feel a sense of desolation and loneliness. Ewan says, "Get another cat." I don't want another cat. No cat can ever again

be to me what Daff was. One day when Laura was here I showed her the snapshots of Frede, Miss Ferguson, and Daff, taken together on the walk and I said "Only Daff is alive now of the three." *Now* they

are all gone—those three who were here that happy summer day eight years ago. Frede loved old Daff so—I think I loved him doubly for her sake.

> He was a cat—
> take him for all in all
> We shall not look
> upon his like again.[378]

Good-bye, Daffy, old friend.

---

378 A rewording of lines 186–87 from *Hamlet* 1.2: "He was a man. Take him for all in all. / I shall not look upon his like again."

I am writing furiously at my book these days and getting on pretty well.

Stuart came to me today and announced that he had "made a poem." When I asked what it was he responded,

"Who did that?

It was Oxtoby's cat."

Well, it rhymes, anyway. Stuart has not begun with *vers libre*. May he never finish with it. *Vers libre* aggravates me beyond my powers of expression.

I feel
Very much
Like taking
Its unholy perpetrators
By the hair
Of their heads
(If they have any hair)
And dragging them around
The yard
A few times,
And then cutting them
Into small, irregular pieces
And burying them
In the depths of the blue sea
They are without form
And void,
Or at least
The stuff they produce
Is.
They are too lazy
To hunt up rhymes,
And that
Is all
That is the matter with them.

Monday, Aug. 23, 1920
The Manse, Leaskdale

I had a letter from Mrs. Estey today.[379] We have got into touch again through a letter which her daughter Maud—now Mrs. Dr. Mahoney

---

379   LMM had boarded with Mrs Ada Estey and her husband during her year teaching in Bideford, Prince Edward Island, in 1894–95. (In an entry of January 27, 1911, she writes that "the notable incident of the liniment cake—when I was teaching in Bideford Mrs. Estey flavored a layer cake with anodyne liniment just as it happened in the story. Never shall I forget the taste of that cake.") This event inspired a famous incident in *Anne of Green Gables*.

of St. John, N.B.—wrote me in the summer. It is over twenty years since I heard from her and over twenty five since I saw her. She is coming to Toronto in September and will visit me. I feel pleasantly excited over it. How odd that life should double back on itself like this! It somehow gives me an uncanny feeling. I suppose Mrs. Estey will be much changed. She was a very pretty woman when I knew her—rosey, brown-eyed, satin haired. Mr. Estey has been dead five years.

Tuesday, Aug. 24, 1920

Today I wrote the last chapter of *Rilla of Ingleside*. I don't like the title. It is the choice of my publishers. I wanted to call it *Rilla-My-Rilla* or at least *Rilla Blythe*. The book is fairly good. It is the last of the *Anne* series. I am done with *Anne* forever—I swear it as a dark and deadly vow. I want to create a new heroine now—she is already in embryo in my mind—she has been christened for years. Her name is "Emily." She has black hair and purplish gray eyes. I want to tell folks about *her*.

And I want—oh, I want to write—something entirely different from anything I have written yet. I am becoming classed as a "writer for young people" and that only. I want to write a book dealing with grownup creatures—a psychological study of one human being's life. I have the plot of it already matured in my mind. The name of the book is to be "Priest Pond." If I had only time to go to work on it—time and leisure. But I haven't as yet. The boys are too young—there are too many insistent duties calling me—I can't give up my profitable "series" until I have enough money salted down to give the boys a fair start in life—for my "real" novel will not likely be a "best seller."

Saturday, August 28, 1920
Leaskdale, Ont.

Ewan has been very miserable this past week—sleeps badly and is depressed and dull. I have been tired and worried and found it hard to work but grind away doggedly.

Yesterday morning we motored to Whitby to visit the Edwin Smiths, who are living there now. It was a lovely day and as Ewan seemed pretty well I enjoyed the drive down. But once there his headache and melancholy returned and spoiled the day for us both. Mrs. Smith is a nice matronly person but not especially stimulating. I liked her, however.

Friday, Sept. 17, 1920
The Manse, Leaskdale

Lily has been away for two weeks on her vacation, consequently I have been very busy. Ewan has been quite miserable all the time.

On Wednesday afternoon we motored to Mt. Albert where I read a paper before the Women's Institute there. It was a perfect afternoon and in the evening we motored into Toronto. Ewan seemed very well again in one of the sudden improvements of his strange malady and I enjoyed the drive keenly. We took the boys with us, in order that they might visit the Riverdale "Zoo"[380]—a long-promised treat. Their chatter behind us increased the pleasure of the drive—it was so naive and interesting and funny. They are great companions for each other and get along very nicely for the most part, in spite of the fact that they are so markedly different in almost every respect.

We came home last night. Found a letter from Rollins in which he says French asked him if it would be all right to file the declaration in the new suit later. Rollins says he thinks we may conclude from this that "French's case" is not of much importance. Well, I'll hope so. I've ceased to worry over it anyhow. It seems to me that I have reached the limit of my power to worry and am getting numb.

Monday, October 18, 1920

How can a month have slipped away so fast? Last night the autumn stars were especially brilliant. I often think of Emerson's passage about the stars. "If the stars should appear only one night in a thousand years how men would believe and adore and preserve for many generations the remembrance of the city of God that had been shown."[381] How true! But because it is a common sight most people never notice them at all. It always fascinates me to gaze on the stars—"the poetry of heaven," as Byron called them.[382]

In September I had a letter from Mr. Rollins in which he said French had filed a declaration of suit for "malicious litigation," but added that I need not worry as he was tolerably sure it would never come to anything. That remains to be seen. I know what the vindictiveness of Louis Page is.

We have had a wonderful autumn—more like summer than autumn. I do not remember anything like it—warm golden days and summer-like nights.

---

380   The municipally operated farm now known as Riverdale Farm was originally purchased in 1856. The plan was to reconstruct the land as a new park and industrial farm, to be maintained by inmates at the Don Jail. The 162-hectare park opened in 1890 on top of a garbage and manure landfill. By 1902, the zoo included pheasants, two ocelots, a male camel, a dromedary, a bull buffalo, six pens of monkeys, a Siberian bear, lions, and a hippo.

381   From Ralph Waldo Emerson's essay, *Nature* (1836).

382   From Canto 3 of Byron's *Childe Harold's Pilgrimage* (1812–18).

Thursday, Oct. 21, 1920

Mrs. Estey came Tuesday evening and stayed until this evening. We had a delightful time together. Except to grow stouter she has changed very little and is as nice and jolly as ever. We talked over all the old Bideford days and doings and people until they seemed to *be* again.

Thursday, Dec. 2, 1920
The Manse, Leaskdale

I left home on Tuesday Nov. 3 for P.E. Island, having decided to run down for a brief visit to see poor Aunt Annie. I reached Breadalbane on Friday night which I spent with the Stirlings.[383] Margaret and I sat up and talked most of the night, having a very hilarious time as of old. The next day I motored down to Park Corner.

It was in some ways a very painful experience. To be there without Frede or Stella—to know that Frede would never be there again. I felt like a ghost, revisiting a world I had once lived in, with no fellow-ghost to keep me company. There was *nothing* of the old life left, except Aunt Annie. The house is full of youngsters who call me "Aunt Maud" and look at my diamond rings and my silks and laces as I used long ago to look at those of the city aunts who came to visit us in Cavendish. To them I am a somewhat fascinating mysterious outsider from an unknown world—*not* anyone who belongs to Park Corner.

Oddly enough I found that Irving Howatt[384] was also home on a visit to his parents. He is not much changed. I was tempted once or twice to say to him, "How is it that you are not to be my cousin after all, Irv?" But I concluded it was better to let sleeping dogs lie. So Stell's name was not mentioned between us. But I daresay Irv has a case, too. The fault was not all on his side.

Mrs Estey and I.

I had a nice visit in some ways. Aunt Annie's pathetic pleasure made me feel it was worth while to have gone. And I had the *first rest* I have had since I was married, for it is the first time I have been

---

383   Margaret Ross Stirling was a Cavendish friend, wife of the Reverend John Stirling. Reverend Stirling had presided over the marriage of Ewan and LMM.

384   Irving Howatt was an early romantic interest in Park Corner; LMM's cousin Stella was engaged to him for 15 years.

away from home for more than a few days when I did not have either the children, or else some acute worry. I went to bed early—alas, there was no Frede to sit up and laugh with—in the cosy little bedroom off the

sitting room and slept late and ate apples and drank cream. It did me "heaps" of good.

On Saturday, Nov. 12 Ern Webb came over for me.[385] He had a bit of interesting news for me. Ches Clark[386] was home.

Ches has never

Breadalbane Manse

Park Corner.

---

385   Ernest Webb, of Cavendish, had married Myrtle Macneill in 1905.

386   Chesley Clark was the son of Jane and Darnley Clark, neighbours in Cavendish. His siblings were Wilbur (mentioned in the next paragraph), Maggie, and Fred.

been home since he first went west twenty-three years ago. As we passed the forge we met Ches and Wilbur there. At first glance I thought I would never have recognized Ches had I met him casually. He seemed changed incredibly from the slender, handsome lad I remembered. He has grown very fat and it does not become him. To tell truth, he looked a little bloated—as if he had drunk something besides water quite frequently. His good looks had vanished.

Ches.

I stayed with Myrtle until Sunday evening and had a very nice time. It seemed very strange to be in Cavendish in November again. On Saturday afternoon I went back through Lover's Lane—snowy and chill and beautiful as I had not seen it since that last winter in the old home.

In the evening I went to Alec's and stayed there till Tuesday morning—and certainly I had a good time. Almost everybody I wanted to see came to see me.

Ches and his wife came—the latter a very jolly lady, a good ten years older than Ches. He and I had a vivid chat—over old school days and "Literary nights." Ches and I were never "beaux" at any time but we were always rather good chums and had lots of fun together in the old

years—surface fun, for Ches was very superficial. The appended photo flatters him, or was taken before he got so fat, but it is very good of his wife.

Tuesday morning Alec brought me over to Park Corner. We stopped at the Geddie Memorial Church and I went in to see Frede's grave. There it was and on her stone the line,

After life's fitful fever she sleeps well.[387]

When I die I want the same quotation on mine.

Yes, she sleeps well. The "fitful fever" is over for *her*—not yet for *me!*

I turned away from that cold grave in its shroud of snow. Frede was not *there*.

Last Saturday I went to Breadalbane again and spent Sunday with the Stirlings. When I reached home I found both Chester and Stuart down with whooping cough *and* chicken-pox. Fortunately they are not very bad with either.

Saturday, Dec. 4, 1920
Leaskdale, Ont.

Tonight when I was reading a story to my small sons in their bed Chester suddenly exclaimed,

"Mother, there is something in your voice like the thrush's song."

What a nice little compliment for eight-years-old to pay!

Ewan seems pretty well now and has been so for quite a while. After last fall's experience I dare not believe the improvement can be permanent. Yet he certainly is better than he has been since last fall.

Saturday, Dec. 11, 1920
The Manse, Leaskdale

Have just returned from Chatham,[388] whither I went on Wednesday to give readings from my books to the Women's Canadian Club there. I had a delightful time and met some very nice people. When I rose from my seat on the platform to begin my readings the whole large audience rose to its feet. The tribute thrilled me—and yet it all seemed as unreal as such demonstrations always seem to me. At heart I am still the snubbed little girl of years ago who was constantly made to feel by all the grown-up denizens of her small world that she was of no importance whatever to any living creature. The impression made on me

---

387   *Macbeth* 3.2, lines 19–23. LMM mentions this quote several times in connection with Frede's passing.

388   Chatham is in south-western Ontario, near the north shore of Lake Erie.

then can never be effaced—I can never lose my "inferiority complex." That little girl can never believe in the reality of any demonstration in her honour. Well, perhaps it is just as well. Likely it is very effective in keeping me from *developing symptoms* of *swelled head*.

Monday, Dec. 13, 1920
Leaskdale, Ont.

I began writing again today after a holiday of two months. I have begun to collect material for my *Emily* books and I also want to do a few short stories and some verse. Poetry was my first love in literature and my deepest. I enjoy writing it more than anything else.

Today I finish reading Mrs. Asquith's autobiography.[389] No wonder it has set English society by the ears. I don't see how she dared. But the book is *real* and so is very intriguing and interesting. But there is nothing vital in it. I doubt if it will live when the generation it castigates or betrays has passed away.

Mrs. Asquith's analysis of herself has been much commented on by reviewers. Some praise it highly. Others say it is not so frank and thorough as it claims to be. I agree with the latter. I do not believe any human being can—or would if he could—make a thorough and absolutely frank analysis of himself or herself. Even if one could be sufficiently detached to be able to do it one wouldn't. There are some faults that we all are willing to acknowledge; some that the frank ones among us will acknowledge and *some* faults—I believe in *everyone*—which nothing would induce us to admit. I do not think one person in a thousand sees or knows his own real faults—and perhaps his own virtues. But the thousandth *has* the power of *getting outside* himself and *looking on* at himself as at another person, and he *does* know himself in weakness and strength.

I believe I have such a power myself. But I could not, even in these diaries which no eye but mine ever sees, write frankly down what I discern in myself. However, I will go as far as I can and endeavor to do what Mrs. Asquith has endeavored to do—describe and analyze myself. It will be amusing and interesting.

---

389   Socialite Margot Asquith, Countess of Oxford and Asquith (1864–1945), was married from 1894 until 1928 to H.H. Asquith (who served from 1908 to 1916 as the Prime Minister of Britain). Her *An Autobiography* (1920) described a range of personalities in her life as well as her experience during the war years.

I will begin with myself physically. I am of medium height—about five feet five inches, but somehow usually impress people as being small—probably because I am delicate featured and have been, until lately, very slight. My feet are quite large in proportion to my size—I wear number fours—but they are said to be "perfectly shaped" and I have a high instep and a good ankle. My figure has generally been described as "neat." I hate the term but I believe it is true. Lately I have been filling out and getting plump. My hands are exceedingly small. I wear a 5 3/4 glove but could wear 5 1/2. If my hands were plump they would be very pretty, but they are too thin for beauty, especially when I am cold. *Then* they are absolutely scrawny. When I am comfortably warm they look plumper and being white and soft have sometimes been complimented. But they are not pretty hands. I use them a good deal in conversation and I believe my gestures are animated and graceful. I have pretty, well-turned delicately made wrists but my arms and elbows are too thin.

My hair was golden-brown in childhood but turned very dark brown when I grew up. It has quite a few gray hairs in it now but not yet enough to destroy the dark effect. It has always been very long—quite to my knees—and thick, although in late years influenza and maternity have thinned it somewhat. It is absolutely straight but has been noted for its gloss. When it is dressed properly my head looks very well-shaped.

My complexion has always been good, though at times rather pale. When I am excited I flush up, sometimes even to crimson. My skin is very soft and fine and when I was a girl my nose was freckled. My forehead is too high but I have good arched eyebrows. My eyes are not beautiful in color, being a grayish blue, but the lashes are long, the expression good. By artificial light the pupils always dilate and people who meet me then go away and assert that I have dark eyes. It is a family peculiarity. Bertie and Laura MacIntyre have it, too. My lids when down-dropped are pretty, and so I have always passed as having beautiful eyes which I really have not. I have been accused of "making play" with my eyes but I never do this consciously.

My nose, viewed from the front is not bad, looking quite straight, but in profile it is poor, being crooked. My cheek bones are high and my cheeks slightly hollow. My teeth are very poor, being crowded, crooked and rather yellow. I do not show them very much, except when I laugh. Then I show my upper gum—very unbecomingly. I have a very small mouth—the smallest mouth I ever saw. It is red, pretty, and "sweet" but I do not like it and would have preferred a larger one. My chin is small and pointed. It does not recede but it is rather a weak chin. My ears are quite good.

And what of the general effect of all these features? Well, it varies tremendously. When I have my hair dressed becomingly, drawn low over my forehead, and am excited enough about something to redden my cheeks and darken my eyes I candidly state that I believe I am a very pretty woman and have been told so times without number. On the other hand when my hair is combed off my forehead, plain and straight I am not even good-looking. Now a really pretty woman is one who looks pretty at all times. So I am not really pretty. I only *look* pretty when I am properly "done." Old rose and salmon, pinks, creams, and yellows become me in colors and I look well in black, brown and navy. Some people think the photograph on the first page of this journal is very like me. Others prefer the one appended herewith. No one has ever yet been wholly satisfied with any photo of mine but all agree that one taken years ago, with my hands clasped under my chin was the most like me of all I have ever had "taken."

My enemies accuse me of being "fond of dress." The charge is perfectly true. I am very fond of pretty dresses, hats and jewels and cannot enjoy myself if I do not feel well-dressed. I don't like to be in any company where anyone is better dressed. I do not feel happy when I am *alone* if I am not prettily dressed. I am especially fond of lace, pearls and diamonds.

I am not bad-tempered and never go into rages but I am inclined to be impatient when people or things don't "measure up" to my ideals and then I say sharp things—which I am immediately sorry for and worry over afterwards. I am easily hurt by my friends and am not as wholly indifferent to what those outside my circle think and say of me as I would like to be. I am not easily offended but when I am I never forgive. I withdraw myself with a cold dignity and avoid the offender contemptuously henceforth. I would never seek to inflict revenge on anyone who had injured me but I do not feel sorry when fate does it. I am entirely free from deceit and it hurts me to pretend to anything. I hate ructions and disturbances and I go too far and yield too much to avoid such things. I would never knowingly hurt a friend's feelings. I am very loyal in my real loves and friendships and very intense and passionate—too much so. I am too extreme in all my feelings. The

pleasures of sense make a very strong appeal to me but have always been kept in check by a certain fastidiousness of choice in me and by the fact that it is only one man in a thousand who has any appeal for me. I have strong will and a determined ambition. I am very persevering. I believe I am naturally truthful but I can tell a lie without worrying over it when people meddle in what isn't their business. I am distrustful of people and suspicious of their motives. Externals make too deep an impression on me and have too great an influence over me. I am jealous in so far that I cannot bear to have anyone I love love another better than me but I am not jealous in regard to other matters. In thought I am independent and would be so in action if it did not injure anyone dear to me. I am energetic and systematic. I am inclined to worry too much over certain things. I am keenly sensitive to all forms of beauty. Ugliness inflicts anguish on me. I have a keen sense of humor and am a fairly good conversationalist with certain people. With others I am dumb. I am reserved to the world, but very frank and open to real intimates. I can hide my real thoughts, feelings, and opinions very skilfully when I want to. Perhaps this is why there are so many different opinions of me floating about. I like the admiration of men. I like luxury and leisure, though my ambition has always spurred me to hard toil and unceasing activity. I dislike change and am very conservative. Yet I am not bound by conventions. I am physically a great coward, intellectually quite fearless; morally about half and half. I am petty and small in some ways and quite big and generous in other ways. I am very impatient of any control.

I walk where my own nature be leading,
It vexes me to choose another guide.[390]

I am not vain or conceited but I am very proud. I am too much given to acting on impulse and I attach too much importance to unimportant things. I have a keen sense of justice, both in regard to myself and to other people. I want to "play fair" but I want others to play fair, too. And I want to win the game. I have no self confidence and have always been greatly hampered by this. I am very healthy in body and mind. I have a very vivid imagination which has been a great blessing and also a great curse. I dread physical pain terribly, yet when it comes I seem to bear it tolerably well. I can see quite clearly into people—or *feel* quite

---

390   From Emily Brontë's poem "Often Rebuked" (published in a collection 1846): "I'll walk where my own nature would be leading: / It vexes me to choose another guide: / Where the gray flocks in ferny glens are feeding; / Where the wild wind blows on the mountain side."

clearly, since my understanding of them seems to be more of intuition than of mind. My feelings are very easily touched by the distress or suffering of others. I hate to inflict suffering on others, yet when I am keenly annoyed I can say very cruel things. I like to rule—to be "boss," yet not enough to fight for it. I have a remarkable memory but as for reasoning power—I don't know. I was a dunce in geometry, a star in algebra, fairly good in arithmetic. I am a good sewer and a good cook. I want to do everything *well* or not do it at all. I am lacking in equanimity and moderation. I am generally in a turmoil of some kind of feeling— joy, sorrow, worry—and I am inclined to go to extremes in everything though maturity has toned this down somewhat or rather controlled it to some extent. I can't haggle over bargains. Mr. Rollins said I was a good business woman but I am not. That is, I am theoretically, because I can see clearly but I lack some stamina or backbone necessary to standing out for what I see. I think my "inferiority complex" is to blame for this. The idea at the back seems to be that my merchandise can't really amount to much and I ought to be thankful to take what people give for it. In childhood I had very deep religious instincts but I do not seem to possess them now. I am not in the least spiritual—that is, in the ordinary meaning of that word. I am a good, intelligent and patient nurse in sickness, except when anything offends my stomach and then I am useless. But I do not like nursing. I am tolerant of almost anything except deceit, deliberate cruelty, and bad manners. I have better manners in company than I have at home.

Well, that is all I can think of now except a few things which I know quite well of myself but which nothing would induce me to admit. I wonder how this analysis would compare with one which an *unprejudiced* person who knew me for many years would write. But that, I suppose, is a comparison which will never be made.

Sunday, Dec. 26, 1920
The Manse, Leaskdale

Christmas is over—that is well. This past week has been bad. Ewan has had another bad attack—the worst since August—with all the symptoms present in full force. He spent most of this week in bed, declaring that he was "a guilty man" etc. But he is better again, though very dull and depressed still. So Christmas was a poor sort of affair. But I felt well myself and the children had a good time which is the main thing now. Christmas can never again mean much to me since Frede has gone.

Monday, Dec. 27, 1920

This morning a wire came from Lowry Keller saying that Stella had a son the day before Xmas. I am much relieved as I had been feeling very anxious about her. I hope her child will make a difference in her outlook on life generally and divert some of her monstrous egotism into other channels. Her letters this past year have been awful.

The baby is named Ewan Campbell. When Stell was here last fall she and Ewan made a crazy compact that the "first boy" was to be called after him. Stella did not then expect she would ever have any children but the unexpected has happened and she has kept her "agreement."

Wednesday, Dec. 29, 1920
Leaskdale, Ont.

Ewan was very bad all day. Poor fellow, his trouble is a terrible one. Physical illness is nothing to it. We had a wedding here today, too—a young couple came to be married. I decorated the parlor with plants but hadn't the heart to serve coffee and cake as I sometimes do.

I found a picture of Cavendish Pond in a magazine today—mistakingly labelled "Lake of Shining Waters." It is not but I love it as well. And looking at it I can see much more than is in the picture—the sand dunes and the old Watch Tower to the left—Amanda's home beyond

[Cavendish Pond]

the central group of trees, the woods of Lover's Lane to the left and the glorious old gulf beyond. That little field dotted with stooks is on Hamilton MacNeill's farm—Amanda and I used to walk through it on summer evenings of long ago on our way to the shore. To look at it all gives a terrible tug to my heart-strings—for my youth is lurking there somewhere in those green fields and secretive woods.

1921

Sunday Jan. 16, 1921
The Manse, Leaskdale

This has been a busy, typical average week. For my own amusement I jotted down in my note-book a detailed account of my doings throughout the whole week. I will copy it here. My descendents may read it with interest and my great-great-grandchildren may use it as a peg on which to hang compassionate opinions as to what country ministers' wives did back in the old-fashioned days a century ago!

Last Monday morning I rose at 7.30 and dressed by lamplight—a thing I always hate to do. There always seems to me something dismal about getting up before daylight. Luckily, with the lengthening days there will soon be an end of this. And luckily also the house was warm. We have good coal at present—and so we have had no real winter yet. So it is a heartening difference from last winter—that most hideous winter of all my winters here.

Having dressed and got Chester up and dressed—a more strenuous proceeding still—I went downstairs and prepared his school lunch and after breakfast got him off to school. He is, I think, getting on pretty well at school and likes it pretty well—better than I did at his age. He has quite a long distance to walk and the school is small and the teacher a very commonplace young girl. But at his age this does not so greatly matter. He is an inveterate reader and reads far more mature books than I did at eight years. And he has more books than I had when I was eighteen—a whole bookcase full. I have given him a good many and Mr. McClelland very generously sends him many new volumes. Stuart and he read together and learn the poems that take their fancy, and then spout them at all times and seasons until we are sick and tired of them. At present they are at Drummond's *Leetle Bateese*, quite undaunted by its dialect, and they say it very well.[391] I have to answer about

Chester's School

---

391 "Leetle Batise" is a poem by Irish-Canadian William Henry Drummond (1854–1907), popular for his humorous dialect poems. "Little Bateese" was from his collection, *The Habitant and*

On Chester's road to school

a thousand questions per day in regard to every subject concerning this world and the next.

Chester having gone, I washed the breakfast dishes as I always do every wash day. Then I gave Stuart his writing lesson. He reads so well, having practically picked it up by himself, that I no longer give him reading lessons. Then I "tidied up" all over the house, arranged the books in Chester's bookcase, mended a torn cushion, and sewed for half an hour at an underskirt I am making—a false economy of the "penny-wise-pound-foolish" kind. It would pay me much better financially to put the time on my writing. But there are some things in me, inborn and confirmed by long years of necessary, careful economy lang syne;[392] and one of them is an inveterate hankering not to waste anything. I had a good, full, old-fashioned skirt of shantung silk[393] with embroidered design. As a skirt I could no longer wear it but the material was excellent and I could not resist the urge to make use of it.

Then I got the vegetables ready for dinner and dressed for visiting. After dinner we drove to Uxbridge where I did a lot of shopping and then dropped into the Hypatia Club for half an hour. I enjoyed this. I am a member of that club but rarely can get down to its meetings. After leaving Uxbridge we went to John Taylor's for tea and spent a rather dull evening, which I improved by crocheting at a strip for an afghan. I get considerable fancy work done during these pastoral visitations. Fancy work is something I never touch at home now. I am, as always, very fond of it and it reconciles me to the many deadly tedious evenings I have to spend thus. Nevertheless I grudge them. It would be so delightful if I could have the time thus wasted for reading or a little recreation. For it *is* wasted. Nobody is done any good to. The vanity of the family so visited is appeased or flattered—*they* have not been overlooked by "the minister and his wife." That is all. Why then do we go—or why do I go? Well, my reason is this. If I did not go they would be rather "sore" and they would visit it on Ewan as well as on me. They

---

other French-Canadian Poems (1898).

392   Scottish for long ago.

393   A midweight silk weave traditionally from Shandong province, China.

would begin to find fault with him and the end would be that he would either be unhappy here, or have to leave. Now, Ewan is not the type of minister who finds it easy to get a new congregation that would suit as well as this. He always makes good as a pastor, once he is settled, but to get settled is a different matter—thanks to the absurd and abominable system the Presbyterian church has for settling its ministers! How I hate the thought, either of his getting discontented here, or of his having to go somewhere we might not like to go. So in order to do all I can to prevent this I visit as much as I can to keep them in good humor and pleased with their slaves of the manse.

When I came home from the Taylor's at 10.30 I had a bad half hour of rebellion over certain things. Then I recovered my self-control and went to bed at 11.

Tuesday—early rising as per usual and Chester's lunch made ready. Then, with due, housewifely care I took a batch of hams out of my pickle barrel and put a fresh batch in—neither a romantic nor a tragic proceeding. But I am fond of ham and one cannot live on tragedy and romance, so somebody must do the pickling. Then I put away the purchases of the preceding day and shut myself up in the parlor to write for two hours. Then I put the house in order and dressed. After dinner I walked up the hill to Mrs. Jas. Blanchard's where the W.M.S. met. When it was over I came home, mended for half an hour, wrote a little, helped Chester with his home work, taught Stuart a recitation for Guild and gave him a lesson. After supper I wrote a paper for Guild on "The Duty of Saying Pleasant Things," wrote letters to Clara and Bertie, copied my old journal until 9. Then read Grote's *History of Greece* until bedtime.[394] Wednesday morning: Rose at 7.30. Got ready Chester's lunch and tidied house. Then I made a crockful of brine for pickling tongues and wrote two hours. After which I did mending, sewed for an hour, copied journal, wrote a letter and dressed.

At supper we had a domestic laugh. Lily was having a squabble with Stuart—she has "a poor way" with children—and finally said pettishly, "Well, I'll leave you to your mother. She'll have to straighten out your manners." Whereupon Chester, who always sides with Stuart when the latter counters Lily, remarked gravely "I think my own manners have a *slight curve.*"

After supper I put the boys to bed, read to them as usual, then went to Guild and read my paper. The work in the Guild is not as pleasant as

---

394   British historian George Grote's (1794–1871) major work A *History of Greece, From the Earliest Period to the Close of the Generation Contemporary with Alexander the Great* (1846–56). LMM recorded reading A *History of Greece* in an entry of January 10, 1914.

Stuart and girl chum

it was in our first years here. Then we had quite a fine class of young people in their twenties. They had considerable initiative and helped us a good bit. These have all married or gone. The Guild we have now is composed of young people in their teens and they seem unusually giddy and entirely lacking in aspiration. I don't decry young folks for wanting and having a good time. But they seem to care for nothing else. I can't discern any germ of anything else in the lot we have now. And there is not to be found the two or three superior ones who sometimes leaven a whole society. They all seem to be on a dead level of dullness and vapidity. I came home at 9.30 more or less discouraged, and put a lot of old hens, which Lily had killed and dressed, into a tubful of salt and water to be ready for the next day's canning. Then I read Mrs. Browning's[395] poems for half an hour and had an anguish of my own special brand for a time, too.

Thursday:—Rise at 7.30. Chester's lunch and house as usual. Then Lily and I spent the forenoon cutting up the aforesaid old hens and packing the pieces into glass sealers. After which I sorted out my linen closet, mended several things, made a saucepanful of cranberry sauce, and cleaned the fragments of meat off the boiled hen carcases, out of which the fragments I concocted a very nice "jellied chicken" mould for supper. I spent the afternoon in attending to the canning of the hens, thus transmogrifying them into "canned *chicken*"—and prepared all the ingredients necessary for a big fruit cake; hemmed a pair of pillowslips, gave Stuart a lesson, copied old journal, sent a batch of MSS away to be typed, and then read from 9 to 10.30 in Mrs. Wharton's *The House of Mirth.*[396] "And so, to bed."

Friday:—Rise and make rise; C's lunch; Hang up hams for drying, tidy house, compound fruit cake, bake it in afternoon with gratifying success. Then I did a lot of odd jobs, wrote up the minutes of the W.M.S., sewed half an hour, gave Stuart lesson, wrote a letter, copied journal, read half an hour, put boys to bed, read to them, and then,

---

395   Elizabeth Barrett Browning (1806–61) was a favourite of LMM's.

396   *The House of Mirth* (1905) by Edith Wharton (1862–1937).

everybody being out of the way, I painted the library door which has needed it for some time. I was through at 8.30 and rested from my labors and read till bedtime.

Saturday I could sleep blissfully till ten to eight and there was no small boy's lunch to prepare. I put my fruit cake away, turned my hams and tongues, wrote two hours, got lunch for Ewan who was going away, washed a bunch of embroidered doilies, and dressed. After dinner went to Mission Band. Got home at four, peeled a tongue I had previously boiled, ironed doilies, sorted out a trunk of stuff upstairs, entertained a caller, got the children to bed, blacked the family shoes, wrote a letter, wrote in journal, and read rest of evening—what little "rest" remained.

This morning we slept till 8.30. Lily was away—it was stormy—Chester had a headache. So I thought I could brave public opinion by staying home all day. I did, and wrote letters and read and got the meals. So endeth the week. I am done as I always am these winter evenings. Ewan is rarely home. Since his illness he seems not to care, or be able, to read much, as he used to do, and generally goes out to visit someone in the village. If he is home he goes to bed. So I sit alone, not even having old Daffy for company now—alone with books and dreams. For I dream still—I must or die—dream back into the past and live life as I might have lived it—had Fate been kinder. I cannot dream of the future now—I dare not.

Today I was glancing over my volume of verse and read my old poem "The Choice," written some twenty years ago. Certainly the wishes I expressed in it—whether I was sincere in making them—I *think* I was— or whether I was merely working out a good literary idea—have been granted me. Life did not come to me "in pale guise and ashen"—I *have* "sounded the deeps and reached the highest passion"—"wan peace, uncoloured days" have been no portion of mine. Life, as I begged her to do, *has* "taken my heart and filled it brimmingly" with many a poignant brew of anguish and rapture.

Well, shall I say now with Swinburne,

> From too much love of living
> From hope and fear set free,
> We thank with brief thanksgiving
> Whatever gods there be,
> That no man lives forever,
> That dead men rise up never,
> That even the weariest river
> Winds somewhere safe to sea?[397]

---

397   From "The Garden of Proserpine" by Algernon Charles Swinburne (1837–1909).

"From too much love of living." Yes, that was meant for me. And to love living *too* much is a sin of presumption the gods do not pardon. They punish surely and terribly those who are guilty of it.

But I do not thank the Gods that dead men rise up never—nor do I believe it. Life is immortal and indestructible and reclothes itself in flesh through all the eons of eternity. And so can we not still dare to love living, even in pain and weariness?

Monday, Jan. 17, 1921
The Manse, Leaskdale

A hard day. In the first place I did not get much sleep last night partly owing to the tremendous wind that kept shutters and windows banging and rattling all night and partly to some physical discomfort, and got up feeling tired and nervous. In the second place, it was bitterly cold—the first real cold day we have had this winter and as a result the manse has been uncomfortable despite a good furnace fire and we have all been shivering and goose-fleshed. As Chester was not very well yesterday I thought it wisest not to let him go to school today. It was too cold for him and Stuart to go out. Usually they get on very well together but today—well I suppose the general chilliness got on their nerves as it did on older people's and they teased and squabbled and bickered, matters being complicated by the presence of little Ruth Cook who had been sent down here this afternoon because of the arrival of a new baby at her home. Even when the three children were on good terms, they made a frightful noise and got into one kind of mischief after another until my head ached. Finally Chester had to be punished. I had, as usual, to do all the disciplining myself. Ewan has never, since the boys were born, attempted to teach or train them in any respect, not even in the truths of his religion. Everything, from morals to manners, has been left to me. It was a bitter moment in my life when I

[Ruth Cook and Stuart]

was forced to accept the fact that *all* the responsibility for the teaching and training of my children was to fall on me. I accepted and make the best I can of the situation. But the lack of the training a wise and judicious father can give is a terrible want in a boy's education and one no mother can wholly supply. Ewan is very fond of his children but his only idea in connection with them seems to be romping with them when he is disposed for it. And he has done little even of that since his trouble began. There was a time when Chester and Stuart were babies and I was finding all rapture and sweetness in motherhood, that I hoped earnestly I would have more children, and was deeply disappointed that I did not. But these past two years I have been well satisfied that I have no more. Under different circumstances I would have liked at least six children if I could have had them—but not as matters are.

Then this was the day of the annual congregational meeting and as usual Ewan came home from it blue and discouraged. I do not know if Leaskdale is worse than other rural charges in this respect—probably not. But I do know that, since I came here, there has never been one cheerful, optimistic, encouraging annual meeting. I dread the day every year and especially now when Ewan is dull enough anyway.

And now, having got this all out of my system, I begin to feel a little less pessimistic. After all, our house is generally pretty comfortable; and Ewan is never stern or harsh or unjust with his children; and our boys are hearty, healthy little chaps with no very dreadful faults, as far as they have yet developed; and there has never been any friction in the congregation between people and minister or minister's wife. So things might be worse. But I shall take a hot water bottle to bed with me tonight!

Thursday, Jan. 20, 1921
The Manse, Leaskdale

There is nothing to write concerning today. It was just the ordinary one of ceaseless work. But I feel so lonely and sick at heart tonight that I come to my old journal for comforting, as many times of yore. There is no one else I can go to. I have no friend near me to help me in any way. And if I had I could not go to her and say, "My husband is in the throes of one of his attacks of recurrent melancholia. He has lain around the house all day, either gazing into space with a wild, haunted look in his eyes, his hair on end, his very features so changed as to make him look like a stranger to me, or chanting hymns from the hymnal in a singsong way that makes me feel like rushing out of the house and screaming, so intolerable it is to me in its childish futility and still more because of the state of mind it reveals in him." I cannot say this to *anyone*. No one must know, for Ewan's sake and the children's as well as my own, what his trouble is as long as I can keep it secret. It is fortunate that my present maid is a girl of very low intellectual calibre and consequently easily hoodwinked. If she were as bright as Mrs. Reid it would not be possible to hide from her the nature of Ewan's malady. But as it is, we can keep up the headache fiction without difficulty. Of course, poor Ewan has headaches but alas, that is only a small part of the terrible malady to which he is a helpless prey. I have lost hope now of his ever being any better. I can see nothing before either of us except a continuation of the wretched existence of the past few years; and tonight, as I am tired and nervous from a day of ceaseless and rather monotonous work I have no courage to face it and feel "down and out." Tomorrow, if I get a decent sleep tonight, I will be able to take up the burden again and drug myself with work till the pain of life seems bearable; but just now, if I were not writing here I should be shut up in a room by myself, crying wildly. This is a better way to work it off—as I used to do years ago down home in those terrible winter nights when endlessly recurring days of monotonous drudgery and hideous solitude had almost driven me to desperation. Things aren't so bad with me now as then—I am well and healthy, and seem capable of endless endurance without a break. But I am so lonely and starved for a little real companionship and sympathy, and at times, as tonight, I feel that I can't bear it.

Little Stuart has just been down in his nighty, with his beautiful rosy cheeks and his big shining blue eyes, to say his prayers at my knee. I don't put my boys to bed now. Until lately I have always done it. But now they are so "big" that they want to go up and "put themselves" to bed, and so I let them do it. But I gave it up with a pang. It always hurts me to give up any of the little duties that I have done for them since they were born. So it will go on for a few years until they go from me altogether—and I will be alone. But they still want me to go in after they are in bed and kiss them good night. *That* must never be omitted. Stuart used always to go through a certain little formula—"Good-night and good-bye and good-day and good-morning," which I had to repeat. Then, when I got to the stairs it was—"Do you love me?"—"Yes." "Do you like me?" "Yes." "Throw a kiss"—one thrown—"Throw a hug"—a dumb show of hugging. He has given this up now—outgrown it. But he throws his chubby arms around my neck and says, "You are the sweetest little mother in the world." *That's* worth something.

And when I go to bed I will slip into their room for a last good-night look at their rosy sleeping faces. Stuart looks like an angel when he is asleep.

Sunday, Jan. 23, 1921
Leaskdale, Ont.

Last night I read over a packet of Laura Pritchard's[398] old letters. I had to laugh a little over some of them, in which Laura poured out her affection for me. I read the first four pages of one of them aloud to Ewan

Two little dreamers.

and howled over his puzzled, half-jealous question, "What fellow ever wrote such stuff to you?" It *did* read exactly like the outpouring of a very badly smitten lover!

A stranger, reading those letters, would certainly form a very unjust idea of Laura's personality and character. He would be sure to think she was a gushing, sentimental girl, whose sole ideas were dress and beaux. Nothing could really be further from the truth. Laura was really a merry, sensible, hard-working and unselfish girl; and the most of her "flirtations," like the majority of my own, were little more than a few walks, drives, and dances, well sprinkled with badinage, with the young men we met casually in society for a few weeks or months.

Laura got through with her flirtation in due time and married Andrew Agnew. They have had a very happy life together. I have not heard from Laura since 1917. Then she had five children—three boys and two girls. Her oldest son was in France. When I was down in Chatham I met a lady whose old home was in P.A. She told me that the Agnew's had had business reverses and had gone to live in Saskatoon. I was very sorry to hear it. It must have been very hard for Laura to leave the lovely new home they had planned and built, and the town where she had lived all her life. But up to that time she had had a life of such happiness as few women have, I think and it seems it is not permitted to anyone to have sunshine from first to last. In some way or another we have to pay.

I would like very much to see Laura again. She was the most dearly loved friend of my teens. But I question if we could be to each other now what we once were. Laura, from her letters, does not seem

---

398   LMM had befriended Laura and Will Pritchard in her year living in Prince Albert, Saskatchewan, in 1890–91.

to have changed much. I have changed immeasurably. I could never now pour out to her all my thoughts and feelings as I once could. I have become too reserved to reveal my feelings to anyone. No, I don't think Laura would satisfy my demands on friendship now—not after having known Frede—not after having had my soul seared in sorrow and pain and passion for thirty years while Laura has walked only the hedged paths of happy, protected girlhood and wifehood. She would not know my language and I should have forgotten hers.

[Laura and Andrew Agnew]

Sunday, Jan. 30, 1921
Leaskdale, Ont.

In writing over my old diaries I have recently copied out the "Oliver Macneill" section—and I'm afraid I laughed a bit over it—or over the memory of the frantic Oliver.[399] He went back to Dakota when he found he couldn't get either me or Campsie. We corresponded occasionally that winter—Oliver used to send me a "much" of "poetry" he had composed himself—addressed to me and extremely sentimental. It was *not* "free verse"—*that* much could be said in its favor! Oliver could mostly find a rhyme whether it was a very suitable one or not! He also sent me a volume of poetry for Christmas—*not* his own—entitled, "To Thee Alone," and full of verses fairly reeking with sentimentality.

The next summer Oliver again visited the Island. We had a few more frantic scenes. I remember one in particular back in the woods near Lover's Lane when Oliver sat on the trunk of a fallen tree and declaimed bitterly, "I could *never, never* have believed that a woman could take such a hold on a man as you have taken on me." But I had quite recovered from the physical infatuation he had once cast over me

---

399   Oliver Macneill was a second cousin who lived in the United States, an early romantic interest. In an entry of September 21, 1909, LMM wrote, "Tonight I realized clearly that Oliver Macneill is one of those men of whom I have met a few in my life—men who, without being able to inspire in me one spark of real love or even admiration, yet have the power to kindle in me a devastating flame of the senses. I have a horror of feeling thus towards any man I cannot marry."

and he could not bind the spell again. So I laughed at him and advised him to marry Lucy McLure, a second cousin of mine and a willing damsel. I did my best to make the match—the only time I ever tried my hand at matchmaking—and I all but succeeded. I think I *would* have succeeded if only Lucy had had more hair! Her scanty tresses jarred so horribly on Oliver's sensibilities that eventually he decided against her and married Mabel Lea of Summerside—one of my old Belmont pupils, by the way. His Aunt, Mrs. Allan Fraser, made *that* match and Oliver decided to take Mabel because, so he told me, she reminded him a little of me!! I never heard from or about him after his marriage.

This part of my old journal was largely written under the blight of those dreadful attacks of neurasthenia from which I used to suffer in winter. I don't wonder at it—when I recall those ghastly months of loneliness and worry and solitude. I don't quite know how I escaped with my reason. Life is strenuous enough still and holds many baffling and perplexing problems yet; but at least I do not have to wrestle with such periods of nervous agony. What should have been the best years of my life were years of such ghastly, long-drawn-out loneliness and suffering as make me shudder in the recollection.

Tuesday, Jan. 25, 1921
Leaskdale, Ont.

Two years ago today Frede died. Two years ago! Bright, brave spirit, whither have you fared since you went out through the sunrise? Shall we meet again? Or shall we take up again "the fever called living" in new incarnations of flesh? There are some moods when this idea appeals to me more strongly than aught else. And there are other moods when I am afraid—afraid!

Tuesday, Feb. 1, 1921

This afternoon the W.M.S. met and I led. I am not President but I occasionally help the President out by leading. I am really Secretary of the Society. I do not like leading because it involves praying. I don't know what the society thinks of my prayers. I am sure Lizzie Oxtoby holds them in contempt. When Lizzie—who is one of the bitterest and most malignant old gossips on this planet!—prays in public, she pours out a perfect flood of glib platitudes and conventional phrases that have been in use for so many generations that they are worn absolutely smooth and slip off the tongue as unctuously as butter. Lizzie calls that praying.

I have no "gift" for public prayer. But at least I try to make some sincere requests, with real meaning in them.

This evening I was so lonely I couldn't work. As usual I was alone, Ewan being out. So I read over some of Nora Lefurgey's[400] old letters. Nora married Edmund Campbell about twelve years ago and as he is a civil engineer she has lived a rather roving life but one that suits her. We still exchange an occasional letter but as our interests have ceased to be mutual there is not a great deal of "pep" in our correspondence. But Nora was a clever girl and I never had any friend, except Frede, who was so thoroughly congenial. I remember that when Nora came to board at our place some one in New Glasgow who knew her when she taught there said, "Maud and Nora will never get on together. They are too different." Perhaps it was because we were so different that we did get on so beautifully and had such a satisfying friendship. If there was just *one* woman like Nora in this whole congregation!

Wednesday, Feb. 2, 1921
Leaskdale, Ont.

I have been writing a good deal of verse lately—some of it very good—for me. Poetry was my first love in literature. The H.C.L. drove me to prose but I have always liked poetry best. I touch a higher note in it than in my prose. I finished quite a long poem the other day—"The Bride Dreams"—and it is, of its kind, the best thing I've done.

Chester is beginning to learn to skate. I hope he gets on well. I have all my life longed to be able to skate but I never had any chance to learn when I was a girl. I am sure I should love to skate—and ride on horseback. Those were two of the things I always wanted muchly to do. It doesn't matter much now. But I want my children to learn these things while they are young enough to enjoy them.

Thursday, Feb. 3, 1921

We drove over to Zephyr tonight and had an awful and indescribable supper at a certain place where a young couple live. They are very ignorant and the cookery was quite unmentionable—and I'm sure it wasn't clean. Ewan baptized their baby afterwards; they have lived all their lives in a civilized community and neither of them appeared to know that a bowl of water is a necessary adjunct to a baptism. When I told them this delicately Mrs. Mother had to skip out to the kitchen and wash out a bowl! And Mr. Father stood up for the ceremony in

400   Nora Lefurgey (1880–1977), a teacher, boarded in Cavendish for a year in 1902 and became good friends with LMM. See also note 303, page 208.

overalls and shirt sleeves!

Then we went elsewhere and had a cottage prayer meeting. Ewan has seemed very well this past fortnight—quite cheerful and normal. But I suppose just as soon as I dare begin to hope that he has recovered another attack will come on.

Wednesday, Feb. 9, 1921
The Manse, Leaskdale, Ont.

As it did—On Monday Ewan complained of his head and yesterday and today he has been very gloomy and miserable. It is not, however, quite as bad an attack as the last one. And there is nothing for either of us to do but endure. Last night we had to go to tea as we had promised. I smiled and made talk and discussed clarified gossip and looked at uninteresting snap-shots of uninteresting people and gave expert opinion on two new quilts the ladies of the house had just finished and explained for the hundredth time what I was making, what an afghan was, what it was for, how many stripes I had to make, what color they are, and how they are to be joined together!

Thursday, Feb. 10, 1921

Ewan was poorly enough all the forenoon but seemed better the rest of the day. We went over to Zephyr, called on a stupid, snub-nosed little bride who seemed a bit squiffy that we hadn't called sooner, went further on and had tea with another bride who was nice and agreeable, stayed till 10.30, drove home over sloppy roads through a pitch dark night. I explained all about the afghan again!

Last night I sat down and computed the number of dollars I have made by my pen since that day in Halifax twenty-five years ago when I got my first check—five dollars for a story. The result totals up to about one hundred thousand dollars. Not such a bad total, considering the equipment I started out with—my pen and a knack of expression. If Pages had not been rogues I should have had at least fifty thousand more. But it's not so bad. It's a pity it doesn't mean happiness. But perhaps my children will reap the happiness from it that I cannot have. And perhaps they would be better off, and more ambitious and successful, if they had to scramble along and struggle as I did. That seems often to be the way in this mad world.

Friday, Feb. 11, 1921

Today I came across a very suggestive little verse in a magazine.

A Fancy

> Perhaps the little souls that float
> Beyond the bounds of space, remote,
> Await in dread the thing called Birth
> Whose finger beckons towards the earth,
> And each life-stricken fugitive
> Cries out "I do not want to live,"
> Aghast and shrinking even as I
> Protest "I do not want to die."

Well, I daresay we would feel that way about living if we knew we were going to be born!

Saturday, Feb. 12, 1921
The Manse, Leaskdale

I've had an exasperated afternoon—the result of a letter from Stell coolly demanding more money!!!

Last spring I loaned her $2,700.00 to buy a cotton ranch. She was going to make a fortune in cotton—very glowing reports—and would give me as security a joint note signed by her husband and his *brother*—said brother being a well-to-do man. They would pay me back in the fall plus interest etc. I had little faith in their success but I lent her the money for Aunt Annie's sake. She sent me a note signed by herself and her husband—worth the paper it was written on and no more, since neither of them has a cent. I was furious over such a trick but still I said nothing. They had a fair cotton crop but the bottom fell out of the market. They could not sell nor pay me any interest. Still I said nothing. Three weeks ago I had a curt cable from Stell, ordering me to send $350 to pay her hospital bills. I said "once more," for Auntie's sake, and said nothing. Today comes a letter demanding that I loan them several thousands more to enable them to hold on until "a big oil boom" makes their land worth "$1,000 per acre."!!!

Poor Stell is not in her right senses, that is all. As for me, the breaking point is reached at last. I am done with wasting money on her. She and her husband can go to work and earn money for their own financing. Counting the loans I have made Stell—not to mention the hundreds I've *given* her—and to her friends the *Howatts*[401] at her request,

---

401   Stella had been engaged to Irving Howatt for many years.

I have ten thousand dollars out, from which in eight years I have never received a cent of interest, and have very little hope of ever getting even the principal back, for the security is not good and none of them have anything behind them. Ten thousand is my limit to waste money. I have written Stell a letter which may bring her to her senses. She will be furious no doubt but I am past caring. The break had to come sometime—it may as well come before I waste any more money on her, the insolent, ungrateful spendthrift that she is.

Monday, Feb. 14, 1921
Leaskdale, Ont.

Today Ewan came to me in the library, put his arm about me, and told me I had brought a great deal of joy into his life and that I was "the dearest little wife in the world." Poor Ewan. His life is gloomy enough now in the shadow of his malady; but I am glad I have made him happy, apart from that. At least, I have not failed in everything, as in my dis-couraged moods I am sometimes inclined to think I have.

I finished a short story today—"The Tryst Of The White Lady"—a fanciful little thing.

Wednesday, Feb. 23, 1921
The Manse, Leaskdale

Have been very busy this past week—but when am I not busy? And I should be—and am—very thankful that I can be busy—that I can plan and dovetail and overtake things. Only at night I am just a little too tired.

Lately in copying old diaries I came to "the Grey Time," as Bertie McIntyre used to call it—and laughed again over the seance Earl Grey and I had on the McPhail w.c. steps.[402] There was a sequel to that con-fab which was amusing enough and which I don't think I ever wrote about in this journal. Three years later I was on the Island and came up from Uigg station[403] with Janetta McPhail—Dr. McPhail's sister who had been there that night. She said she had always wanted to see me to tell me about it. Thereupon she did tell me the tale as follows:—

When Earl Grey and I had disappeared that evening Mrs. McPhail

---

402   This is recounted in an entry of September 10, 1910. Albert Henry George Grey, 4th Earl Grey (1851–1917), had served as Governor General of Canada. Grey married Alice Holford in 1877.

403   Uigg, Prince Edward Island, is 31 km (20 miles) east of Charlottetown. The name is likely derived from Uig, a village on the Isle of Skye, Scotland; the word itself is thought to derive from Old Norse for bay or inlet.

went to Janetta in distress, saying that she was afraid the countess was upset about something, as she was walking restlessly up and down the veranda and would not join any of the various parties of sight-seers about the grounds. Janetta said, "Oh, don't worry, mother. Lady Grey must be bored, of course, and can't find much entertainment here. I'll go and ask her if she would like to lie down a few moments before dinner."

Accordingly Janetta went to the veranda where the Countess was striding fiercely about and said politely, "I am afraid your excellency is tired. Would you like to lie down etc."

"Her Excellency" paid no attention whatever to Janetta's question. But she halted before her, took her arm in a savage clutch, and demanded in an intense tone,

"How old a woman do you think Miss Montgomery is?"

Naturally, Janetta was flabbergasted by such a totally unlooked-for query. Moreover, she didn't know my age; but recollecting that I had been to P.W.C. shortly after one of her brothers had been there she made a guess at it and stammered out, "I think she must be about thirty-five."

"Oh," said the countess in a tragic tone, "I had hoped she was at least forty."

And with this she dropped Janetta's arm and resumed her agitated pacing on the veranda.

Poor Janetta did not know what to do. But to her intense relief the Earl and I now hove in sight on our way back. The countess saw us also and flew down the steps and through the orchard to meet us, while Janetta thankfully washed her hands of the matter.

I remembered that the Countess had met us in the orchard and had whisked the Earl off without even a glance at me. I thought it rather odd and very rude of her, but concluded that it was probably my ignorance of the way of the English aristocracy that led me to think it so. It certainly never occurred to me that her ladyship was jealous. *My* conscience was clear. *I* certainly hadn't been trying to "vamp" the earl. I don't think Earl Grey, with his bald head and his squirrel teeth, could have flirted if he had tried. He didn't try to flirt with me, at any rate.

I howled over Janetta's story and concluded that Lady Grey—who seemed older than the earl and was certainly no beauty—must be the victim of a morbid jealousy which tortured her whenever her husband paid any attention, even of the most harmless character, to another woman. Something I heard later on at Macdonald College confirmed this. Some person, speaking of Earl Grey laying a cornerstone somewhere, remarked. "The Countess wasn't with him." Another lady said,

"It's a wonder she would let him out of her sight that long." So evidently "Elsie" kept pretty strict tabs on friend husband and didn't approve of him decoying middle-aged authoresses to the steps of mysterious houses back of cherry orchards!

Saturday, Mar. 5, 1921
Leaskdale, Ont.

Most of last week I was busy reading the proofs of *Ingleside*. Also had a letter from some locality called "Myrtle Station" entreating me to go down and "give a missionary address" in their (Methodist) church on Easter Sunday evening!

I declined!

Monday I went in to Toronto and stayed till Thursday doing spring shopping. Came home Thursday night and had a drive home over terrible roads of frozen mud. I wonder if I shall ever be able to live near a station. The drive was further "en-wretched" for me by the fact that Ewan said a letter had come from Stokes complaining that *Ingleside* was "too gloomy," and wanting me to omit and tone down some of the shadows. *Also*, subtly intimating that I had not "taffied up" the U.S. enough in regard to the war—this last being the real fault, though they did not like to say so bluntly.

Well, I didn't and I won't! I wrote of Canada at war—not of the U.S. But I have felt worried by the matter. I do not like to feel that my publishers are dissatisfied with my book. Mac liked it—said it was a good story and would sell well. This last is what Stokes doubts—and he has made me doubt it.

But I had a nice letter from Mrs. Estey, stating that Dr. Logan of Acadia University,[404] recently lecturing in St. John, said that Canada had produced "one woman of genius"—that "L.M. Montgomery" in the opinion of eminent critics "equalled or surpassed Dickens in her depictions of child life and character."

Ha—hum! No, I'm not a genius but thank you all the same, Dr. Logan.

Mrs. Willis of Uxbridge writes me that they want me to give them an address at some cantata performance round Easter on "Jerusalem, Past, Present, and Future." I told Mrs. Willis I didn't know enough about the past or present of Jerusalem to be worth telling, and had no conceit of myself as a prophet.

---

404   John Daniel Logan (1869–1929) was a specialist in Canadian literature, with a particular interest in the Maritimes.

Tuesday, March 8, 1921
The Manse, Leaskdale

"Pat"

"Pat"

This morning our six months old gray kitten "Pat" got worried by a dog and was brought in by a tearful Stuart in what seemed a dying condition. I never saw an animal so nearly dead that didn't die. Its eyes were set and half glazed, its jaws were open, its breath almost non-existent. Yet it eventually recovered and by night was as lively as ever. I am glad for the boys' sake. They adore the little beast and would have been heart-broken if it had died. They take it up to bed with them every night and the thing goes to sleep between them—not curled up as a proper cat should curl, but lying stretched out like a person, its head on the pillow and its forepaws around Stuart's neck. I sneak in after they are asleep, pry poor Paddy out, and consign him to the cellar. Of course I wholly and sternly and remorselessly disapprove of cats sleeping in the bed with anybody! But when *I* was a child—and long after I had ceased to be a child—didn't I have my pet puss with me whenever I could smuggle it past the Powers That Ruled?

Saturday, March 12, 1921
Leaskdale, Ont.

Last night Ewan and I went down to a Hypatia Club in Uxbridge. The roads were undescribable and my courage almost failed me. But I wanted to go for two reasons—I thought it might do Ewan good, for he has been very dull all the week, and as I had not had any real social evening since my Chatham visit early in December I was hungry for a "function." So I got out my little-used evening dress and went. And we had an exceedingly nice time—almost nice enough to compensate for the roads.

Had a letter from Stell today—pretty squiffy. I was rather amused. I know she was literally boiling with rage. But I am the one person in the world she doesn't dare insult or quarrel with because she owes me so much money. So she dare not give way to it and it nearly kills her.

Clara writes me that Stella doesn't seem to have much love for her baby. I had thought as much from her letters. She only refers to the baby to complain of him. Stell really has no affection for anybody. Like all mentally unbalanced people she is completely centred on self. Poor creature. I had hoped that the child's coming might cure her of her neurasthenia and bring her back to normality. But it evidently has not done so—probably it came too late in life—and what is to become of her I don't know. The poor wretch who has married her has an awful life of it, so Clara says, and I can well believe it. He was wildly in love with her when he married her, completely duped by her surface jollity; but I fear he has had a rude awakening since. Poor Stell is a nightmare to us all. She is the most terrible example I have ever seen of what un-checked indulgence in bad temper and selfishness can bring a person to.

Sunday, March 13, 1921

Today I finished copying my Cavendish diary—and so seem to have come to "modern history" in my life. I have lived over those old years in thus writing them over—relived them more vividly and intensely than I have ever done in reading them. I am a little sorry that I have finished with them. The last thirteen years of my life there were certainly not happy years, and parts of them were violently unhappy. Yet there were many hours of happiness and sweetness in them, too,—the happiness of a loved work and success in that work, the happiness of wonderful communions with sea and field and wood—and I tasted this happiness again in writing over those years.

There are many different happinesses—and we never have them all at once—because that would be perfect happiness and that is some-thing the gods do not allow to mortals. We have some at one period of our lives and yet others at another. Perfect happiness I have never had—never will have. Yet there have been, after all—many wonderful and exquisite hours in my life.

Monday, Mar. 14, 1921
Leaskdale, Ont.

Early in February I got a letter from Laura Agnew[405]—the first for four years. She said she had been "thinking so much about me" of late that she felt impelled to write. The time of her so thinking must have

---

405 A friend from LMM's year in Prince Albert, Saskatchewan. See note 398, page 301.

been just the time I was reading over her letters and thinking so much about her every night before I went to sleep. So there is circumstantial evidence of "thought waves." They are living in Saskatoon now, having lost everything when Agnew Bros. failed. I think Laura feels very bitter over it and I do not blame her, for it was not her husband's fault, and it was hard to see everything go, including their beautiful new home, and have to start all over again in middle life with a young family dependent on them.

Today in glancing over a book picked up at random I found a card sent by Frede years ago. It bore the picture of a P.E. Island scene and on it Frede had written in her characteristic hand,

> But one thing lacks these banks of Rhine,
> Thy gentle hand to clasp in mine.[406]

I felt as if a knife had been struck through my heart. Oh, Frede!!

Friday, April 8, 1921
The Manse, Leaskdale, Ont.

We have had a very early spring. This week has been summer-warm; the grass is green and the leaves coming out. We have been exceedingly busy housecleaning and visiting. Ewan has been pretty well and life has been very stimulating and agreeable.

Tonight I finished Grote's *History of Greece*—twelve volumes. This is the second time I have read it through and I think it will be the last. I shall not be able to spare the time for it again. But I'm glad I've read it twice—though the reading of history always makes me feel somewhat cynical and very dubious as to the "uplift" moments of our time.

The winter is over. Compared with the previous winters of several years it has been much easier and pleasanter. It was not cold or stormy and no new anxiety or racking sorrow has come with it. Yet it was not very delightful. Ewan was miserable enough most of the time and Lily has been so cranky and impertinent that I found it hard to keep my patience with her. I did so because the girl is not really well. She is suffering from some ailment usually designated by the abominable name of "female trouble" and moreover she was "left" a year ago by a young man she wanted very badly. This has soured her and she is very unlike the cheerful and good-humored girl she was for the first two years. If I knew where I could get another girl I would let her go. But help is hard to get here and I can't do without help. So I have not blown Lily

---

406   From Canto 3 of Byron's *Childe Harold's Pilgrimage* (1812–18).

into little bits or sent her packing though almost every morning I have been strongly tempted to do both. I have been very good to Lily, as to all my maids, and have always considered her convenience and feelings before my own. I pay her good wages and always give her a nice present for any time I am away. So I feel that it is very ungrateful of her to act as she does. She is so hateful and cranky with the children too. She nags at them and "bosses" them from morning to night and never says a kind word to either of them. They are old enough now to resent this but not old enough to control their resentment and the result is that she is always fighting with them and then comes yowling to me like a big silly baby herself. They are average good children and would be all right if she had any sense in dealing with them. She is a good worker, a fair cook and used to be obliging; but she has neither "gumption" nor judgment. She is always in a mass of untidiness and has no "head" to plan her work. When she came here first she was willing to let me plan it for her and got on quite nicely; but now she resents this and as a result she has no method and is always "through-other."

Tuesday, April 12, 1921
The Manse, Leaskdale

There is nothing like perseverance. It must be all of twenty years since I wrote a screed of verse called "Premonitions." I've been sending it out at intervals all these years and getting it back. Today a magazine took it; the verses are trash but I've had many no better accepted long ago.

Today we went to Uxbridge to attend the induction of Mr. Bennie, the new minister. When I came here Mr. Fraser was minister in Uxbridge. He was a widower, with a small son and daughter, a middle-aged man, slightly lame, very clever and well-read.[407] We have always been good friends and he has often been here. I always enjoyed his visits. Despite his cleverness, he had no charm and he somehow

[Mr. Fraser and Uxbridge people]

---

407   James R. Fraser (b. 1867) was a widower with a daughter Margaret (born 1900) and Neil (born 1903). See also LMM's entries for August 8, 1918, and April 12, 1921.

mopped up all the conversation himself. He not only talked a great deal but he left his hearers with nothing to say. Yet I liked him very well and always liked to see him come. He was very much interested in Frede at one time but she did not respond and so nothing came of it. He has somehow been linked with our life here during the past nine years. But last fall he did a mean thing—mean from a professional point of view as well as a personal one.

He resigned from Uxbridge in the spring, but his resignation was not to take effect until the end of the year. This left him free to "candidate" when and where he wished. He preached in a great many vacancies but no call came. This was rather odd; but I suppose his lameness and widowerhood were rather against him.

Last fall the congregation of Columbus and Brooklyn became vacant. Ewan asked the moderator for a Sunday and was given the last one of the **leet. He preached, made a good impression, and it was reasonably certain that he would get the call. We were both pleased. It is not an easy thing for a settled minister to get away "to preach for a call." I have always felt satisfied in Leaskdale and never hankered for a change. But Ewan has not been contented here for some time, owing mainly to the unsatisfactory conditions in Zephyr. And as he was anxious to make a change I was very glad that we had the chance of going to a place we would like. There was a nice large manse and it was near Whitby. Besides, I have always had a feeling that if Ewan got a call to a place he liked he might get quite well. Looking back over his attacks I find that they have always come on suddenly when he was disappointed or homesick. Evidently his disappointment and loneliness were repressed into his subconscious mind and began playing tricks with his nerves, as psycho-analysis has recently discovered such things do. Two years ago Ewan preached in Pinkerton and Priceville. Priceville did not call him: Pinkerton wanted to but after being there he did not like it and declined. But all the same he was disappointed that his efforts had been fruitless and a few weeks later I am convinced that his suppressed disappointment brought on his last and worst attack. If he were now to get a call to a place he liked this old rankling disappointment might be rooted out and he would be perfectly well.

We had never thought of Fraser trying for Columbus and Brooklyn. It was not in his "class," being a straggling double rural charge. Besides, he knew Ewan was trying for it. But he wrote and asked the moderator for a day and when the moderator refused, saying that it was not a congregation he would really like, Fraser wrote again and *pleaded* for a Sunday. Alas, he got it.

From the time I heard Fraser was to preach there I lost all hope of Ewan getting the call. For Fraser can preach quite brilliantly when he likes. He got the call—and accepted it.

Ewan and I resented his behavior very keenly and we did not try to hide from him the fact that we thought he had behaved very meanly and unkindly towards us. As a result we parted very coolly. It hurt me a little and has left a bit of a soreness. As for Fraser, he felt *galled*. It hurt his pride woefully to be the rival of Ewan for a little country charge. The whole affair is one of those things that leave a bruise—as if our past friendship and social hours had all been stained and discolored by it.

As for the Bennies I don't think I shall find either of them at all congenial. I dislike him; and she is a pretty, dull girl.

I have been reading May Sinclair's *Mary Oliver* and *The Romantic*.[408] *Mary* is a strong gripping book without a particle of charm or atmosphere and defaced by some disagreeable mannerisms. Life can have neither charm nor atmosphere when you strip it to the bare bones. As for *The Romantic* it is a disagreeable, unnecessary piece of work, and it is hard to see just why anybody should have written it or wanted to write it—unless to show the difference—the unfathomable gulf—between the heroines of the Victorian age and the "heroines" of today. Certainly there is some difference between Amelia and Charlotte Redhead—even between Jane Eyre and Charlotte.[409] But at least Amelia was sweet and Jane Eyre vivid and womanly while Charlotte is something you wouldn't like to have around—and all Miss Sinclair's cleverness can't alter the fact.

Sunday, April 17, 1921
The Manse, Leaskdale

Yesterday was an abominable day—inside and out. Outdoors, it was bitterly cold, with an ice-storm—a return of winter entirely unexpected after the two weeks of summer we've had—weeks that have brought the leaves out and turned the fields green.

Inside matters were worse. Lily flew into an utterly unprovoked and unjustifiable tantrum this morning and was insolent and absurd. I felt

---

408   English poet and novelist May Sinclair (whose real name was Mary Amelia St Clair; 1863–1946) wrote over twenty books in her career, including novels and short stories. *Mary Oliver: A Life* (1919) was one of the first female Bildungsromane of the twentieth century; *The Romantic* (1920) was a fictionalized version of her own unsuccessful experience volunteering with an ambulance team in Belgium during the War.

409   *Jane Eyre* is the main character in Charlotte Brontë's 1847 novel by the same name.

that the time had come when she must be taught a lesson. I rebuked her sharply and ignored her absolutely for the rest of the day. It made me unhappy—I cannot bear to be "out" with anyone in the house with me. It poisons everything. But I held out resolutely for I knew if I thawed too soon she would not be taught the necessary lesson. I think she *has* learned it and will be careful for a time at least not to make a similar mistake. But these things blister my soul somehow.

Today was cold, with the world coated in ice—trees, ground, everything. We seem to have been pitchforked bodily back into winter.

Thursday, April 21, 1921
Leaskdale, Ont.

Today I carried about 1200 books out of the library into the parlor—preparatory to cleaning the room. This left me by nightfall feeling that the world was a wilderness of woe. But after I got the boys to bed I curled up on my own bed with a bag of chocolates and read *The Tiger In The House*[410] until I forgot all about the woes of the flesh. It's a very fascinating book, all about cats by a man who loves them. Some of it made my blood run cold.

Grandfather and Grandmother hated cats. I always loved them. Just where I got my fondness for them would be hard to say since my "forbears" on both sides, back to the third generation at least, detested them. But love them I did; and I was also convinced that it was very reprehensible in me to love them, since Grandfather and Grandmother condemned them so harshly, that I felt it was somehow a shameful thing to find pleasure in pussies. Nevertheless I went on loving them and love them to this day. Yet I have never been able quite to throw off a sort of apologetic attitude regarding my affection for them. I always say I like cats a little defiantly, as if I were adding in effect—"and I don't care if you do think it disgraceful."

As for those people who say they "like cats in their place" I know *all* about them from that one phrase!

Having had it so grained into me in youth that a love for cats betokened utter depravity and weakness of intellect, I was rather surprised and pleased to learn from *The Tiger In The House* how many eminent and admirable individuals of both sexes were lovers of puss—Petrarch, Mohammed, Cardinal Richelieu, Chateaubriand, Zola, Dr. Johnson,

---

410   American writer and photographer Carl Van Vechten's (1880–1964) *The Tiger in the House: A Cultural History of Cats* was published in 1922.

Dickens, Victor Hugo, Sir Walter Scott, Montaigne, Charlotte Bronte, Carlyle (I have a better opinion of Carlyle than I ever had before), Walter Pater, Andrew Lang, Edgar Allan Poe, Mark Twain, Sara Orne Jewett, Mary E. Wilkins and many more. Verily, 'tis no company to be ashamed of.

Pat

I miss Daffy this spring. When he died last summer I thought I could never care for another pussy. Yet, as Samuel Butler[411] says, I have "catted" again. I am becoming fond of the boys' *Paddy* and find pleasure in him. Yet he will never have the personality of Daff. Daffy never got over the Bubastis habit of godship. Pat is a nice puss but he has forgotten the worship of the Nile.

Sunday, May 1, 1921
Leaskdale, Ont.

Last Tuesday Ewan and I motored to Toronto. I spent Tuesday night with Laura. They are leaving Toronto and going to Trenton. I am sorry, for it has been such a jolly place to visit and Laura is the only creature of my own kin near me. On Wednesday I went to London and was the guest of Mrs. Dr. Hughes during my stay there. On Thursday I lunched with Mrs. MacGregor ("Marian Keith")[412] and Miss Wilson (Anison North), then had a motor drive round London which is a clean, pretty, tree-y town. Then I gave readings to the Canadian Club, got a bouquet of roses, went to the Girls' Ca-

"Marian Keith"

nadian Club in the evening and read to them and got another bouquet of roses. Then went to the home of Miss Grace Blackburn, a clever journalist, to meet the Woman's Press Club, and got another bouquet of daffodils and narcissus.

---

411   English author Samuel Butler (1835–1902).

412   Mary Esther Miller MacGregor (1876–1961), who wrote under the pen name "Marian Keith," was—like LMM—a prolific novelist who was also a Presbyterian minister's wife. She and her husband lived in many locations across Ontario, including 22 years at St. Andrew's Presbyterian Church in London.

I admit I enjoy these excursions very much. I am always treated beautifully and meet many clever and interesting women, besides seeing the different parts of the country.

That evening at the Press Club I happened to say of some book that I "always read it when I felt blue and despondent."

"Oh," said Miss Blackburn, "I do not believe you ever feel blue or despondent. You are too full of humor and philosophy."

I wonder what she would think if she could read some of the pages of this journal. But perhaps it may be accounted unto me for righteousness that I confine my blues to my journal and don't scatter them abroad in my household or community.

I came back to Toronto Friday, in a pouring rain, shopped all day Saturday and came home in the evening to find that Ewan had sold our Chevrolet car and bought a new Gray-Dort.[413] It's a very nice car.

Saturday, May 8, 1921
The Manse, Leaskdale

Cleaned house all week and are through all but kitchen—for which I'm glad. House-cleaning has been unpleasant this year owing to Lily's grouchiness, and doubly hard because of her inability to systematize her work, or let me systematize it for her.

Friday was a lovely day. Captain Smith called and I went down with him to Whitby. We motored through a spring world of young leaf and blossom and had a wonderful drive. In the evening I gave a programme of readings to the girls in the Ladies' College and there was a little reception afterwards and we all had a very nice time.

Capt. Smith

Ewan and the boys came down this morning for me and we motored home, to find Lily crankier than ever and full of complaints. I can't decide whether the girl is really sick or not. By times I think she is; but she is always able to go out on the road or to a dance, no matter how much she has complained through the day, so I believe her malady is mainly nervous, induced by her secret bitterness

---

413   Gray-Dort was one of the early cars manufactured in Canada, founded when Robert Gray secured rights from Flint, Michigan, producer Dort Motor Co. The company folded in 1923, having manufactured some 26,000 automobiles.

and disappointment.

I have been reading Scott's *Betrothed*[414] this week. It is one of his poorest novels. But I was struck by his immeasurable superiority to the novel-writers of today— even those who are acclaimed as the strongest

[Ontario Ladies' College, Whitby, Ont., Canada]

and most virile. Compared to Scott they seem like a feverish nightmare of unrest and chaos. To go from them to him is to go to sanity and breadth and perspective. The novel-writers of today have no perspective. They will spend pages describing a character's passing emotion of lust and greed—as if lust and greed were something uncommon, instead of being passions we all experience more or less all through our mature lives.

Stuart and Chester were gathering trilliums today and brought me big bunches of them. Stuart is especially thoughtful about bringing me posies. He is very fond of flowers. Chester does not care much for them I think.

Wednesday, May 11, 1921
The Manse, Leaskdale

Captain Smith was here tonight. Our plans for summer vacation have assumed a definite form. We have decided to motor down East and the Smiths are going too in their car. I am not very enthusiastic about it. It is a long distance to motor and I think I will be frightfully tired. I can imagine an auto trip being very delightful under certain conditions but these conditions will all be absent in this case.

Had a letter from Stokes today re my new book-series. I suggested calling it *The New Moon Series*, making the first book *Emily of New Moon*. They like the idea but want "a more attractive name than Em-

---

414   Walter Scott's 1825 novel The *Betrothed*, set during the reign of Henry II.

ily." I have written them my ultimatum on this. "Emily" is a quaint, delightful name, and hasn't been worn threadbare in recent fiction as almost every other name has. Besides, my heroine *is* Emily, just as Anne was Anne. She has been "Emily" for the past ten years during which time I have been carrying her in my mind, waiting for the time when I could put her into a book. She has "grown" just as "Anne" did and so ought to be just as well-beloved. And "Emily" she shall remain.

Monday, May 16, 1921
Leaskdale, Ont.

Ewan has had another attack. He has been pretty well ever since early in April. He has not been so well since that interval in the fall of 1919. Once more, in spite of past experience, I let myself hope that his recovery was permanent. But he is very bad just at present—restless and melancholy. I seem to have grown *hardened* to it and don't worry over it quite as much as I used to. But my heart sinks at the idea of a third summer like the last two. Our trip down East will be no pleasure to either of us if he is like he was last summer, poor fellow. What an awful curse melancholia is to all concerned! I cringe sometimes with the fear that Chester or Stuart may inherit the tendency—especially the former, who resembles his father very strongly in physical appearance. He is subject to occasional headaches and this worries me. But they seem to be connected with his stomach and to be more like my sick headaches. They disappear after he vomits. So very likely they indicate nothing worse than some digestive disturbance. Yet I will always have my little secret dread.

I had a letter from Stell today—the first cheerful epistle for many moons. She is out of her troubles—or fancies she is. The U.S. Gov't is going to lend money to the soldiers to give them a start, so Lowry and she expect to get a loan, repay me, and make a fortune out of the rest. I shall be very glad if it is so; but I'll wait until I see the cash before rejoicing. Stell has been going to do wonders so many times. Poor old Stell! But she's one of the "old gang"—and there are not so many of us left.

Wednesday, May 18, 1921
The Manse, Leaskdale

I wonder if I shall ever again have a pleasant spring. Since 1914 I have not known one. Every spring of the war was an anguish of suspense and worry; and when the war was over Ewan's malady has darkened every spring since. Poor fellow, he is good and kind and never did wilful harm or wrong to anyone in his life. Yet he is most miserable. Yes, it is weakness that suffers in this world—not wickedness.

But I suppose I am inclined to take the gloomiest view of everything tonight, for this has been a hard day. Ewan could not sleep at all last night and has been very bad all day—nearly as bad as any attack yet I think. Then Lily was exceedingly cranky all day—for no reason at all that I could see—except that the cistern pump was acting badly, which was nobody's fault and inconvenienced us all as much as it did her.

Ewan and I went to Quaker Hill manse for tea, as we had promised to. The Millers are bores, I was physically wretched with a cold in the head and Ewan was so dull that everything dragged. Then we came home and went to Guild. The subject tonight was a literary one—"Masterpieces of Poetry." I had arranged a good programme but Lord ha' mercy! How those masterpieces were murdered by the readers thereof. It was agony to sit and listen. What are the public schools of Ontario about that they turn out such readers? The meaning of the poems was wholly lost and not a creature there was any the better or wiser in any way for them.

I came home alone through a night of magic spring moonlight and sought refuge from unhappy realities and vexations in imagining something very wonderful and delightful and impossible. It kept me from ending up my day with a fit of tears and I'll go to bed now and sleep.

Tuesday, May 31, 1921
The Manse, Leaskdale

We have had some very hot and muggy weather. Last week Ewan was very miserable but he seems better again now. Tonight was cool and I had a very happy evening—one of the kind I delight in. I spent it on the lawn setting out my geranium bed. It was clear and cool, with a beautiful sunset behind the trees. Stuart and Chester were delightedly mowing the lawn which they consider great fun. Neighbors passed by and called greetings over the gate. Ewan strolled about and seemed fairly cheerful. It was so delightful that I wondered what I would have to pay for it.

Thursday, June 16, 1921

We had a terrible accident last Sunday. It might have been a thousand-fold worse. I am thankful we escaped as we did. But it was horrible—horrible. This is the first day I have felt at all like myself.

We went to Zephyr last Sunday afternoon—Ewan, the boys and I. After service Mrs. Jake Meyers asked us to go there to tea and she and her little girl got in behind with Stuart and me. Ewan and Chester were in the front seat. We stopped at the garage for gas. After we pulled out from the tank Ewan turned to cut the corner. Then I looked up and saw a car in the middle of the road and going very fast—Marshall Pickering's car, as it turned out. I said to Ewan "Look out for that car" but it seems he did not hear me. Neither did he see the car, although it was right in front of us and only a few yards away. *He turned northwest across the road in front of the oncoming car*, meaning to turn up the side road.

Why he did such a thing without looking to see if the road was clear is inexplicable, unless—unless—oh, I fear that his mind was so fastened on the one gloomy idea of his melancholy dread that he was not thinking about anything else. Too late he saw the other car. There was one awful moment when I saw that a collision was inevitable and felt that it was impossible to escape without someone being killed. Then the cars crashed together.

What saved us was the fact that we were still on low gear and going very slow. The whole thing was like a nightmare. There was a tremendous crash, the sound of breaking glass—screams—then the cars were still. I said, "Thank God, nobody is killed." Then I sat there in a curious kind of numbness. Our new car was badly done up—the Pickering car was worse—Mrs. Pickering was being taken out her face bleeding from a cut on the windshield—which looked very bad though it afterwards turned out to be very slight—and yet all that I was worrying over was how Mrs. Meyers and her little girl were to get home!

The sight of the blood on Mrs. Pickering's face broke up this abnormal calm. I began to cry and shake. Mrs. Law took me up to her house and I stayed there an hour and cried all the time—just nervous crying that I couldn't stop. Mr. Law brought us home and I went to bed and stayed there for two days unable to eat or sleep.

The damage done our car has been fixed up—axle straightened, new fender and lamp post put on. But the affair has left me very nervous and I fear has spoiled my summer. I can't go in the car again without fear of another accident. For if Ewan did not see that car simply because of his obsession the same thing or worse may happen again.

Of course Marshall Pickering was equally to blame. He is notorious as a speeder and road-hog. If he had been on his own side of the road as he should have been—since according to his own admission he saw our car in plenty of time to turn out—nothing would have happened.

We would have crossed to the sideroad behind him. But when I recall that moment when, as it seemed to me, Ewan turned our car deliberately across before that other car in plain sight—oh, I thought he had gone violently insane at last and was taking us all to destruction with him.

I am sick of the talk it has made. Everywhere we go we have to talk of it and explain. A hundred exaggerated reports have gone abroad concerning it. This is the third nasty automobile accident I have been in and I feel as if I had had enough.

Sunday, July 3, 1921
Leaskale, Ont.

The last two weeks of June were dreadfully hot. I have been very busy. All the boys' clothes had to be got in order for our trip. I weeded the garden for the fourth time from one end to the other. We had men here putting a cement floor in the garage. Stuart ran a rusty nail in his foot and was laid up for three days. There was a Sunday School picnic. I had cherries and strawberries to preserve. Lily has been in a vile temper most of the time—and the heat day and night has been dreadful. Nevertheless, I have felt well and cheerful also, since Ewan has been pretty well. We leave tomorrow night on our long drive. Goodness knows how we'll get along. Chester and Stuart are wild with delight and anticipation. Nothing clouds their horizon, thanks be. I hope we'll strike a cooler zone erelong.

Yesterday I finished reading Dr. Prince's *Dissociation of a Personality*.[415] It is one of the most fascinating, extraordinary and illuminating books I have ever read. Today I began to read *Human Personality and Its Survival of Bodily Death*.[416] I am intensely interested in these psychical subjects.

I hate to leave my garden. It is just coming into bloom and is the first good garden I have had for three years since it was neither washed out nor given over to weeds because of my absence. I shall miss all its best. Lily is supposed to keep it weeded but goodness knows whether she will or not. She was in a terrible temper yesterday forenoon but is quite amiable today.

---

415   American physician and neurologist Morton Henry Prince (1854–1929) had written about a case of "abnormal psychology" of a female patient named Christine Beauchamp in his 1906 study, *The Dissociation of a Personality*.

416   Frederic William Henry Myers's (1843–1901) *Human Personality and Its Survival of Bodily Death*.

Thursday, Aug. 11, 1921
The Manse, Leaskdale

We got home last Friday after what was, on the whole, a disappointing trip—at least, to me. There were a few odd hours and days of enjoyment in it but not enough to make up for the many that were downright miserable. It seemed to me that almost every day brought something that spoiled it; I was very tired and never seemed to get really rested; and the obligation we were under to be back by a certain date compelled us to "make" so many miles per day and so spoiled our pleasure to a great extent.

Monday July 4th, was exceedingly hot and exceedingly busy. I packed, put the house in order and made all the final arrangements. After tea we motored to Whitby and spent the night at Capt. Smith's. Rev. Alonzo Smith and his wife were also there, as they were going along too. They are very nice folks and we enjoyed their companionship on the way down muchly. We left at ten the next morning and reached

[Travelling group]

Kingston at nine. It had been a dreadful day of heat—in mid-afternoon it was 103 in the shade. As long as we were moving the breeze kept us cool but it was necessary to have the windshield open and as a result we were literally gray with dust. We passed through Trenton where Laura and Ralph[417] are living now and called to see them. Laura had a delicious lunch ready for us and we had a pleasant hour. We got our supper along the road, making tea on my little camp stove and picnicking on the grass. It was a good bit of bother, especially on the hot days, but it was also very jolly and offered the only chance for social intercourse on the way. We had lots of fun over our gypsy meals.

When we reached Kingston[418] everybody was tired, dirty—and cross.

417　That is, Laura McIntyre Aylsworth and her husband Ralph. Trenton is on the north shore of Lake Ontario.

418　Located on the eastern end of Lake Ontario, some 100 km (60 miles) east of Trenton.

By the time I had got the children bathed and to bed I was too tired to sleep myself. And Ewan had one of his sleepless nights and tossed and groaned so that all chance of sleep fled for me. At two I took a veronal tablet but veronal sleep is a poor sort of substitute for the real article.

We left at seven, crossing the St. Lawrence to Watertown, N.Y.[419] The heat continued. Ewan was dull and rather morose—at least out of tune with everything. The boys—who certainly did enjoy the trip and so justified it—asked a million questions more or less. We motored till eleven that night. Our lights were bad—the road crowded—I was very nervous. We stopped at a tourist hotel in the Berkshires[420]—Big Nose Inn. I got a fair sleep in what was left of the night, for a cool breeze blew in from the big hill behind the house and Ewan had another room. Thursday, July 7, was a roasting day

Breakfast on the Road

but an interesting one. We climbed the Berkshire range and coasted for twenty miles down "Jacob's Ladder."[421] We reached Springfield[422] at night but it was so hot that I slept poorly again.

Friday morning we left at eight and had our breakfast on the road. When we reached Boston the Smith party went to their friends and we went on to Braintree. I was almost exhausted when we got to Flora's but a cool lovely breeze blew up in the evening and I looked forward to a good sleep and a pleasant, restful visit. It was not to be. East Braintree is certainly a place of evil omen for me. Nothing good can come out of it.

To begin with, that night there happened the worst electric storm that has been known in New England since 1837. I never saw anything like it. Sleep was impossible. The house next to Aunt Flora's was struck. One could have read by the incessant glare of the lightning, and the crash of thunder was continuous. It lasted all night and rained at intervals all day Saturday.

Aunt Flora's

Saturday forenoon I washed out our laundry. After dinner Ewan said he was going to take the car to a garage for over-hauling and the boys wanted to go with him. I ought not to have let them go—I knew well enough that Ewan, when getting anything done to the car, pays no attention to anything else. But Flora was going, too—the garage was just at the foot of the hill, and I was woefully tired and wanted to get a little rest that afternoon if it were possible. So I let them go.

About an hour or so later I went to the street door and to my amazement found Stuart there, playing with a neighbor's boy. I asked him where Chester was and he said, "Oh, just down the hill." I supposed Chester had stayed with his father at the garage and thought no more about it. The afternoon went by—it began to rain heavily again and thunder growled ominously. Just before six I heard the car and the next minute Ewan and Flora rushed in, demanding,

"Are the boys here?"

I stared at them in amazement.

"Stuart is here," I said. "Where is Chester?"

They gasped out a tale that almost made my heart stop. Not finding the garage at the foot of the hill up to requirements, they had gone to Quincy,[423] two and a half miles away. While there they had suddenly missed the children. Search proved fruitless. They had been searching frantically for an hour, then had come home in desperation.

We hastened to question Stuart. His tale was as follows:—

He and Chester had grown tired waiting round the garage and wanted to come home. They had told their father so, and started. Ewan had not heard or noticed them. The extraordinary thing is that those two boys, one only nine and the other not yet six, *did* find their way home over two and a half miles of thronged and twisted city streets which

---

423   A Massachusetts town south of Boston.

they had only traversed once and that in a car. They got to the street at the foot of the hill and here Chester made his first mistake and went on round a curve of the East Weymouth road. Stuart was lagging behind and turned up the right street and came home, thinking Chester would soon be after him.

This was all. *Where was Chester?* It was growing dark and beginning to pour in torrents. I was nearly crazy. I could do nothing—except walk the floor! Taking one time with another I must have walked a hundred miles on the floor of that Braintree bungalow.

Amos, who was nettled over the bother of it all, vexed because his supper was delayed, and who has no liking for nor patience with children, remarked sharply that Chester ought to be whipped within an inch of his life. I retorted that such would be a sufficient punishment if Chester had set fire to the house. Flora was upset because her heart is weak. Ewan was distracted—though the real trouble pulled him out of his melancholy rut of brooding over unpardonable sins for the time being, so that he was quite well for a week.

The police of Braintree, Quincy and Weymouth were notified. The East Braintree men organized themselves into a posse to comb the streets. Ewan went to a small store below the hill and found that Chester had been seen passing it, apparently on the way back to Quincy, about half an hour before. When I heard this I said,

"If Chester found his way home from Quincy he is not lost. I know what has happened. When he looked back and saw that Stuart was not in sight he would go back to look for him and not finding him would think he was lost. He would be afraid to come home without Stuart. He is looking for Stuart and won't come home without him."

Ewan decided to go back to Quincy and see if he could find Chester on the road. Back he went—I walked the floor. Half an hour passed— it was pitch dark—it was pouring rain. I pictured my poor little son, lost, terrified, broken-hearted over Stuart, wandering about in strange streets, not knowing where to go. For Chester is such an odd, independent little chap that he would never stop anybody and ask to be shown the road home.

Then Ewan returned—*with Chester*. The poor child had gone all the way back to the Quincy garage to get his father to come and find Stuart. The garage man at once 'phoned the police station and a policeman came and took him over.

I was so thankful I cried; but that night I couldn't sleep again after the worry and excitement. I had seen Chester, in imagination, crushed beneath the wheels of a motor car.

We left next day after dinner, met the Smiths at the State House and set out for Portland.[424] That afternoon was delightful—one of the few times when I really enjoyed the journey. It was deliciously cool and gray; the road was splendid and much of it was along the New England coast where the Atlantic waves were rolling in in great gray misty breakers.

But our luck did not last. Just at dark, when we were about six miles from Portland it began to rain heavily—and our lights went out! Ewan had to get out and put a new fuse in. I had to get out and hold the flashlight. I got soaked to the skin and arrived at Portland with ruined hat and clothes, very disgruntled.

The next day went fairly well until we reached Belfast. Then we got separated from the Smiths and passed them owing to their taking a wrong road. We had to make a long detour over a terrible mountain road. Fortunately, we *did* get over it, crossed Bucksport Ferry, and an hour later got to Ellsworth[425]—and found no sign of the Smiths. And then our car broke down! Some of the interior mechanism connected with the clutch had been broken on that dreadful road. There we had to stay. The Smith party turned up.

[Group witthh cars]

We refused to let them wait for us, as they could not help us and it would only worry us to feel we were holding them up, too. So, in the end they went on. We had to stay there nearly two days. It was a dull little town and the time seemed endless. But at last at two o'clock Wednesday, we got away and had a pleasant drive to St. Stephen's, New Brunswick,[426] which we reached a little after eight Wednesday evening. We found out that the last boat left Cape Tormentine[427] for the Island at 7.30 o'clock P.M. and Ewan said he believed we could catch it if I could be ready to start at 5.30. I *was* ready. We left in a fog cold enough to freeze the marrow. We had an *awful* road to St. John.[428] Most of it was under construction and we *wallowed* through miles of gravel and had constant trouble with

---

424   Portland, the largest city in Maine, on the Atlantic seaboard.

425   Villages on Penobscot Bay, north of Portland.

426   Canadian border town, across the St. Croix river from Maine.

427   Location in south-east New Brunswick, Cape Tormentine was the point from which ferries departed across the Northumberland Strait to Prince Edward Island.

428   St John, New Brunswick, on the north shore of the Bay of Fundy.

our clutch. From St. John on the road was quite good and we literally tore across New Brunswick. It grew very hot and terribly dusty. Chester developed a headache. But on we rushed. We reached Sackville[429] at seven and discovered we had a punctured tire! I was so tired that I was really pleased.

I went to the hotel and asked for a room with a bath. The clerk did not *say* but he *looked* "You need it." I certainly did. Never in my life did I look so disreputable. My hair was hanging in strings around my neck and I was gray with dust from head to foot. But I got my bath room. I got Chester bathed and dosed and put to bed—then Stuart—then myself. I got a good sleep—there was a nice rain in the night—and the world was quite a different place in the morning.

Breadalbane Manse

We had a delightful run down to the Cape. It was cool and dustless and pleasant. When we got to Point Borden we motored up to Breadalbane.[430] The roads—the dear old red roads—were very bad after the recent rain; but they were the Island roads, green-bordered, vivid, and lovely. We got to Breadalbane manse at dusk and had a delicious supper and a pleasant evening. But my night was disturbed for it was Stuart's turn to be sick.

Next morning we went to Ch'town where I am a hopeless stranger now. In the evening we went out to Kinross and stayed with Christie[431] until Wednesday morning. Then we came up to town. I had dinner with Fannie Wise at their Brighton cottage, spent the afternoon with Ida McEachern—Mrs. George Sutherland—my old P.W.C. chum; then we went out to Winsloe and had tea with Mary Campbell.[432] I have not

429   Sackville, New Brunswick, located on the border with Nova Scotia.

430   Breadalbane is a village in Prince Edward Island where the Macdonald's friend John Stirling was minister; his wife Margaret Ross Stirling was a long-time friend of LMM's.

431   Christie Macdonald McLeod, one of Ewan's sisters, lived in Kinross, in Queens County, Prince Edward Island.

432   Mary Campbell (by this time Mary Beaton, whose daughter was named Maud) was a third cousin who had also been LMM's roommate at Prince of Wales College.

seen Mary for eight years. They have moved to Winsloe, since then and have a very nice place. Mary looks old—thin and pale and gray. She has not had a very happy life I think. Maud Beaton is eighteen, very tall, and quite nice-looking, though not pretty, and a nice girl.

We had a dear drive up to Alec Macneill's that evening over the old "town road" I knew so well in childhood. It was cool, and a gray mist came in from the sea on the wings of the north easter. When we got to Alec's and I went up to put the children to bed the same north easter was keening around the eaves and down below on the shore was the boom of the surf. How I loved that sonorous old music—how I loved that windy, dark-gray night on the old north shore.

We stayed till Friday night at Alec's and at Myrtle's till Sunday night. There were pleasant things in those four days but we had too many people to visit and we all got tired and disgruntled. We had some good hours at Alec's. May cooked us the most gorgeous meals and we sat and talked and laughed over them—really, they were the pleasantest parts

[Lover's Lane]

of our stay. We saw changes everywhere—in people and places. It hurts. But I suppose if there were never any change there would be no progress. And we would probably in time get bored with the everlasting sameness. Just the same—it *does* hurt.

Next morning I walked through Lover's Lane. Alas—alas! Lover's Lane has grown old. That I should have to say it! It hurt— oh, how it hurt. It is three years since I saw it in summer and it had changed more in those three years than in all the years of my remembrance. So many of the trees have died. And all the spruces which were young and green a few years ago have grown so tall that their lower boughs along the lane are dead. The woods around it are growing thin, too. I suppose the dry summer has also robbed it of some beauty there was no growth of fern or waving grass to cloak the bareness. I came back—and I did not go again.

We went over to Park Corner Sunday night and stayed there

[Webb family of Cavendish]

until Thursday. I had a rest and many pleasant hours. But, as everywhere else on the Island, there was an undercurrent of worry and misery because of Ewan's malady. His melancholy and restlessness returned soon after we got to the

Group of Children

Island and clouded all our time there. In company he generally brightened up and talked with some cheerfulness; but I knew that all the time he was troubled with that wretched obsession of guilt and punishment. The only time he seemed free from it was when we were in the car. The necessity of concentrating his mind on the business of driving banished for a time his haunting spectre of worry and his headaches ceased.

Oh, how I missed Frede at Park Corner! The last summer I was

On birch tree

there she was, too. Somehow, I missed her even more than last fall. She seemed to belong to Park Corner in summer time. Oh, Frede, dear old comrade, whither have you strayed? Do you still *know*—and understand?

Aunt Annie is wonderfully smart and energetic. Dan[433] is almost grown up. He is smart, too, and seems to be taking an interest in the place. Chester and Stuart had a glorious time at Park Corner. They "ring in" with their cousins and enjoy playing with them. They "got on" very well with the Webb children but never seemed to have very much fun with them. Now the house and yard are ringing with shouts and laughter from morning to night—just as they rang years ago for other children!

---

433   Donald (LMM always referred to him as "Dan") was the son of LMM's cousin George Campbell (Frede's brother George, who had passed away during the influenza epidemic in 1918).

Thursday, July 28, we went to Breadalbane and stayed all night with the Stirlings. We left at six the next morning and had a lovely drive to Borden. I hated to leave the Island—somehow I had a nasty feeling that it would be long ere I saw it again. I have learned to shrink from these presentiments. Too many of them have come true.

We met Capt. and Mrs. Smith at Sackville. Alonzo and Mrs. A. did not go back with them. We got to St. John that night and stayed with Dr. and Mrs. Mahoney—the latter being "little Maudie Estey" of the old Bideford days. She is anything but little now—a big, fat, "sonsy" woman of 160 lbs. I couldn't see any resemblance to the little pale, fairylike maiden of long ago. Mrs. Estey was there, too, and we had a gay evening. Next day we motored up the St. John river to Woodstock where I arrived sinfully tired, partly because of bad roads, partly because of constant worry over the car, which didn't act right, partly too, because Ewan was morose and contrary. This is a phase of his malady, of course, and it spoiled all pleasure in the day for me.

Things were better next day. It was cool and pleasant and most of our road was through the wonderful pine woods of Maine. I never tired of them. We reached Bangor[434] that night. I was tired but did not get much sleep as Ewan had a bad night of sleeplessness and kept prowling around the room. I dozed fitfully and felt almost as tired out at starting as when we had stopped.

Next day we made Bridgeton and the next Burlington.[435] The road was very fine. We crossed the Green Mts.[436] through the famous Crawford Notch and it was very fine. Also the Bretton Woods and Poland Springs were lovely.[437] Wednesday we had a nasty day. There were several delays and as we wanted very much to get across the St. Lawrence that night we tore madly along—far too fast for enjoyment. In the forenoon we crossed an arm of Lake Champlain where the scenery was the finest we saw anywhere. But we missed the last ferry after all and had to stay in Morristown[438] until Thursday morning. Then we crossed and motored from Brockville to Whitby. It was a nightmare of a day—hot and dusty, a good deal of bad road, and several occurrences very trying to the nerves. But we got to Whitby, got cleaned up, dressed, and had a pleasant evening.

---

434 Bangor, in north-central Maine, is located on the Penobscot river.

435 Bridgeton, Maine, near the Vermont border; Burlington is on the east shore of Lake Champlain.

436 A mountain range in Vermont.

437 Crawford North, Bretton Woods, and Poland Springs are New England tourist attractions

438 Morristown, Vermont, across the St Lawrence from Brockville, Ontario.

Friday morning we came home. I was thankful to get here and get back to work after my disappointing trip. Lily was here—didn't seem overjoyed to see us. I suppose she didn't like the idea of getting down to work under a mistress again. Perhaps that is natural enough but she need not have vented it on us. I am not responsible for the fact that she has to work out. I give her good wages and much consideration. She is treated like one of the family. So I thought I hardly deserved my cool reception. As for poor Chester, he wasn't out of the car before she began heckling him and she did not speak a kind word either to him or Stuart. She has not been quite so cranky since we came back, however, but even more untidy, "feckless" and gadding. Her work is never done on time or completely. Something is always at loose ends—everything in a muddle. When she first came she was willing to let me plan out the work but now she resents this and rather than have her in a temper I let her alone. But the result is a fearful muddle as a rule.

I was ill for three days after getting home with stomach and bowel trouble. Since then I've got settled down again. In the evenings I have been copying my old journal of the summer of Chester's birth. It hurt me. I was so happy then. Frede was here and I had my dear little chubby baby and Ewan was well. Those two years after Chester's birth were the happiest of my life. After that the war came and the loss of dear "little Hugh"; and when the war was over Frede died and life changed forever; and then Ewan's malady came upon him and all happiness left my life. I do not suppose it will ever return. Sometimes Ewan is so much better that I almost think he is as he used to be. But as I wrote over that old journal I realized how unlike his old self he is, even in the days when his trouble grows lighter. It is only in contrast with his dark days that he seems well.

Wednesday, Aug. 17, 1921
Leaskdale, Ont.

This has been a miserable sort of day, so I come to my old journal to get it out of my system. I really feel blue and discouraged. It poured rain all day. Ewan was terribly miserable. Lily was cranky. Then I had a letter from Mr. Rollins with a copy of the Master's report which was on the whole decidedly adverse. I never expected anything else, after the false statements sworn to by the Pages, yet the injustice of it all hurt me. Of course the Judge has to pronounce on the case yet but it is not at all likely he will reverse the Master's findings.[439] Rollins sent another bill for $3,000. Six thousand so far thrown away for nothing. And the end is not yet.

One cheering item in his letter, however, was that the Page suit against me[440] was dismissed August 11th on the ground that it was illegal. French threatens to carry it to the Supreme Court. I suppose he does not like to rest under the imputation of doing an illegal thing.

Yes, I'm blue!

Thursday, Aug. 18, 1921
The Manse, Leaskdale

I had a bad night—couldn't sleep. But I feel a bit pluckier today, though I couldn't settle down to writing. Had a letter from McClelland. He is going to give *Rilla* to Hodder and Stoughton in England, Constable not having "measured up." [441] I hate changing publishers like this.

Hattie Harrison and her mother were here to tea tonight. The mother is a very sweet and quite brainy little old lady whom I have always liked. When I went up to the spare-room with her she put her arms around me and said,

"Mrs. Macdonald, you have done a great deal for our little church."

I was touched and pleased—and surprised. For in all the ten years I have been here and hard as I have worked in all the societies no living soul has ever said to me a word of similar appreciation. It has often hurt—but among other deeper pangs did not seem worth noticing.

"And you always seem so bright and happy that it heartens us up to see you," she went on.

Happy! With my heart wrung as it is! With a constant ache of loneliness in my being. With no one to help me guide and train and control my sons! With my husband at that very moment lying on his bed, gazing at the ceiling and worrying over having committed the unpardonable sin! Well, I must be a good actress. I wonder how many other women I know, who seem "bright and happy," have likewise a closet full of skeletons. Plenty of them, I daresay.

Yet today was not wholly unpleasant. After the Harrisons went away

439   "The Master" refers to a judicial expert hired to give an adjudication in LMM's case against her former publisher, L.C. Page & Co. (See her entry of February 14, 1920.).

440   In May 1920 the Pages had opened a suit against LMM for "malicious litigation," following the two lawsuits she had brought against them. Asa Palmer French was the lawyer representing the Pages.

441   Hodder and Stoughton, a London publishing house, had brought out the British edition of *Rilla of Ingleside* in 1921. Constable had published *Anne's House of Dreams* in 1917.

I coaxed Ewan to go out for a little drive to call on some sick people. As always when in the car he brightened up and was better. It was a perfect evening—clear, sunset-lit and cool, with a big lucent "harvest moon" floating over the golden fields. For a little while I forgot care and enjoyed it.

Saturday, Aug. 20, 1921
The Manse, Leaskdale

This morning I wrote the first chapter of my new book—*Emily of New Moon*. It ought to be good. "Emily" is a dear little soul and I have some good experiences waiting for her. And it is such a relief to be done of the "Anne gang." I had gone so stale on them.

This evening was pleasant. Ewan has been much better this week and we motored over to Sonya[442] to call on the Masons, picking up Rev. McDonald of Wick and his daughter. We found a little ice-cream social on over there and had a very nice time.

Saturday, Sept. 3, 1921

Rilla of Ingleside came today—my eleventh book! It looks very well. I don't suppose it will be much of a success, for the public are said to be sick of anything connected with the war. But at least I did my best to reflect the life we lived in Canada during those four years. It is dedicated to Frede's memory. I wish she could have read it. It is the first one I have written with a purpose.

Cover design of Rilla

This past week has been very busy. Ewan has been better and as a consequence everything has been easier. It is so much easier to plan and organize when my mind is free from worry.

Sunday, Sept. 11, 1921
Leaskdale, Ont.

Another busy week, with much strain. It has been unseasonably hot for September—hot as many Julys. Monday was a muggy day. Ewan and I

---

442 A small village 18 km (11 miles) east of Leaskdale. (Wick is on the way from Leaskdale, about 7 km/4.5 miles west of Sonya.)

went to Cannington[443] and had dinner with the Kennedys. In the evening we went to Woodville to the opening services of the new church there. The programme didn't begin till nine and continued till twelve. We didn't get home till nearly two. Mr. Fraser came with us—the first time he has been here since he left Uxbridge. I made no difference and he appeared to make none; but I shall never feel the same to him again. He behaved contemptibly in that matter.

I got the men a lunch and we got to bed at three. Got up early as

[Chester]

Fraser had to be taken to Uxbridge. Chester began school again. There is a new teacher—I hope she will be better than the former. All the teachers they ever get here are inexperienced girls of sixteen or seventeen. Yet they are paid a thousand dollars a year. I taught school for $180 a year plus $10—"supplement." Well, "the world do move"—also prices.

On Wednesday Miss Mitchell came to address the W.M.S. at Zephyr and was here all night. Mr. Curtiss of Uxbridge came up to give a talk to the Guild and I got lunch for him after it—and then had the only pleasant thing this week—an hour's chat with intelligent people as we sat over our cake and cocoa.

Thursday was a hard day. I had a nasty cold in my head, Ewan developed the opening symptoms of another attack of melancholia and I felt blue and discouraged, also a little worried over Chester's operation on the morrow.

Friday Dr. Shier came up and removed Chester's tonsils. When Chester was three years old Dr. Shier told me he had enlarged tonsils. But he was too young then to have them removed and as Ewan was much opposed to the operation nothing has been done. They have never seemed to trouble him—he never has sore throats or anything like that. But lately the increasing frequency of his headaches has led me to wonder if his diseased tonsils might be causing it. Shier said not, but thought the operation should be performed as one side of his throat was almost closed. So I prevailed on Ewan to consent and it was done on Friday morning. I stood by and watched it—which shows how

---

443   A small village about 26 km (16 miles) north-west of Leaskdale.

much my nerves have improved since two years ago when Chester had to have chloroform for his eye. Well, they have—thanks to vitamines.[444] Ewan tried to watch, but broke down, cried, and started a headache. Chester was found to have some adenoids also. Miss Payne, the nurse, stayed till yesterday morning. Chester was plucky and patient. His stomach was not settled until yesterday at noon. Today he is up and about, eating as usual. I am glad it is over.

Ewan has been very bad yesterday and today—the worst attack this summer. Last year and year before he had had attacks in September and then he was very well for a couple of months. I hope it will be so this year—that hope is all that keeps me up.

Tonight I am alone. The boys are in bed. I feel lonely and depressed. I am sitting in the dining room. Outside in the September darkness the crickets are chirping. It is close and muggy. I wish somebody would come in and make me laugh. But there is nobody to come in. There isn't a single interesting person in this village—not one who makes you feel better just because of a chat. I really never saw such a collection of stupid, uninteresting people. They know nothing but gossip and malicious gossip at that. They are all old or elderly, not only in body but in mind—old maids or retired farmers and farmeresses. When I am feeling normal I suffer them gladly and find some amusement in their very stupidity but when I'm below par I'd like to blow them all up with gunpowder.

Saturday, October 1, 1921
The Manse, Leaskdale

I have had a fortnight so quiet and orderly that it has seemed uncanny. On September 17th Lily went away for her fortnight's vacation and the next day Ewan left for a motor trip to Warsaw[445] to visit his brother Angus. Monro of Cannington went with him. The boys and I were left alone.

The first thing I did was to put everything in complete order, especially the kitchen and pantry—which under Lily's regime are commonly in awful disorder. I keep the rest of the house fairly tidy but I haven't time for the kitchen and if I had Lily would resent it. But by Monday night everything was in order. Then I mapped out my work on a system

---

444   "Vitamines" were a new term at this time; in 1921 three had been isolated: anti-scorbutic C, water-soluble B, and fat-soluble A. (Names and understanding of the bio-activity of various have changed over time.)

445   Angus Cameron Macdondald (1865–1944), Ewan's brother, was a prominent physician in Warsaw, a town in central Indiana. He had established the first hospital there.

and followed it. As a result it was all done early every day leaving me from three o'clock free. There was no "visiting" to do—or endure—I went nowhere—nobody came. I could read or sew or dream. And I've had a glorious two weeks of it. It was lovely to have no alien about—and a cranky alien at that. I can't do without a maid—but I wish I could. But at least I've had two good weeks without one. Lily at present is laid up with tonsillitis and can't come back for another week. It is such a full week that I must have help, so I've got a young girl to come and help out.

Ewan returned Thursday. He had a good trip and seems very well. He has been well every fall for awhile so probably it will be the same way this year. It is a relief to have him well even for a few weeks. And what a relief it must be for him to be free from that torturing fear of "eternal damnation." I do not think normal people, who are not the victims of such a delusion, can have any real idea of the full horror of it.

I am keeping one eye on my writing and the other on the filling for my lemon pie. Which reminds me of a compliment I got last Sunday—an Englishman's compliment and such as only an Englishman could pay. We had Dr. Schofield supplying last Sunday—a medical missionary from Korea—a clever tactless man who certainly isn't afraid of man or devil. He seemed to have the Englishman's customary contempt of crude colonials, but when he had eaten his section of lemon pie at dinner he said,

"Well, *at least*, you certainly do know how to make lemon pie."

The italics are mine!

I remember that the only compliment Uncle Leander ever paid me in his life was to say that my lemon pies couldn't be beat. Who says that the way to a man's heart *isn't* through his stomach. I might have talked with the tongues of men and angels—I didn't—and it would not have extorted approval from Dr. Schofield. But the pie did the trick.

Stuart and Chester were delightfully good those two weeks. Ordinarily Lily rags them so unceasingly that she keeps the poor little monkeys cross and contrary. But they've been lovely. Chester has picked up finely since his operation and is getting rosy and plump again. Stuart is always rosy and plump and adorable. I never saw a sweeter child. He has never from birth given me a moment's care or worry.

Several mornings the two little chaps sneaked down and had the breakfast table set when I came down. Stuart generally set the dinner table for me—and did it beautifully, too.

The reviews of *Rilla* are beginning to come in. So far they are good.

Monday, October 3, 1921
The Manse, Leaskdale

Had my semi-annual report from Stokes today, dealing with sales of *House of Dreams* and *Rainbow Valley*. It's the poorest one I ever got— probably owing to the extreme financial depression in the States, print- ers' strikes etc. I shall not find it any too easy to get through the winter without drawing on my capital. That three thousand I had to send Rollins would have made a good deal of difference to me if I could have kept it. Well, I never cry over spilt milk; and if I can get along until spring when the *Rilla* reports come in I ought to come through all right.

I had a letter from poor Aunt Annie today full of complaints and groans. I wonder what the Campbell family would do without me to un- load their miseries on. I don't mind Aunt Annie doing it. She is old and overworked and *has* a hard time of it. If it is any solace to her to pour out her woes to me she is welcome to do it and I am ready to give what aid and sympathy I can. But Stella and Clara do the same. I never get a letter from either of them which is not full of complaints and grum- bles. Yet they are young women with no more worries and troubles than I have or than most people have. And I *do* get tired, amid all my own troubles and anxieties, of their endless shrieks of despair.

But Park Corner was very good to me long ago. So for "old sake's sake" I must try to keep the Park Corner folks now. What good times we did have. How that old house used to ring with laughter! I shut my eyes and see it—trim, snug, prosperous looking, with the great grove of maple and beeches behind it and the big orchard in front. Uncle John was so proud of his orchard. He was never happier than when working in it. And the blossoms of it in springtime! Oh me!

Friday, Oct. 7, 1921

This is Stuart's birthday; he is six years old today—six beautiful years. And every year seems to make him smarter and more lovable. And it is not because he is my own child that I think him so. Chester is my own and first-born and exceedingly dear and precious to me. Yet I see qualities in him that may interfere seriously not only with his success in life but with his happiness and the happiness of those he lives with. He has some very engaging qualities but there is the same curious little streak of contrariness in him that there is in Ewan. He may outgrow this—I hope he will; but its presence has always made him an exceed- ingly difficult child to train, especially in the more superficial aspects of existence—table manners, social observances etc. Stuart, on the other hand is not only easily taught but seems to possess the social graces as a natural endowment. It "comes natural" to him to be courteous and polite and engaging. In the detestable slang of the day he is "a good mixer." Chester is not. Perhaps it is not an unmixed blessing for Stuart. He will be as easily influenced for evil as for good. Chester is, perhaps in this respect, the less likely to be swayed by others. But he is a blunt reserved little fellow while Stuart, with his angel face and joyous pervasive smile, is the friend of all the world.

Stuart, too, is a quite wonderful worker and always has been. He is a most industrious little mortal. Chester doesn't like work; he is a bookworm; but Stuart eats it. Today he went over to Richard Oxtoby's and picked potatoes the whole day, coming joyfully home at night with fifty cents which Mr. Oxtoby had given him and which I have no doubt he fully earned.

He possesses a weird liking for the medicine known as "Emulsion of Cod Liver Oil"—which most people take when they have to and not otherwise. I have been giving a bottle of it to Chester to build him up after his operation and Stuart always pleads for some, too, but has been refused, as he did not need it. This morning he said, gravely and earnestly, lifting his large brilliant blue eyes to me,

"Mother dear, since this is my birthday can't I have a dose of emulsion as a *special treat?*"

He got it!

Six years old! I have no baby now.

Tuesday, October 18, 1921
Leaskdale, Ont.

Lily has been back for a week. Her throat isn't very well yet, but that doesn't prevent her from going out every evening, fine or wet. However, she has been much better tempered. I think she had imagined that I would put up with everything because I could not get other help. But now that she has found out that I can fall back on Elsie at a pinch she has decided that it will be safer to be amiable.

A small village like this, is, I think, the pettiest place in the world. The "retired" folk have little to do except "keep tabs" on their neighbors. And they are all devouringly curious as to what goes on in "the manse"—curious about details that it would never enter into my head to think of. They even count the mats that we hang out on the backyard fence on sweeping day—count them and tell their neighbors about them. They know the exact moment our washing is hung out, the number of pieces, and everything else that is done in our back yard. As to what goes on indoors, where they can't see, I fear their agony of curiosity about it will shorten their lives.

Ewan has been very dull of late—seems to take no interest in anything. I dread the winter.

Chester came to me the other day and said he wanted to read *Green Gables*. He has lately been awakening to a realization that he has an author for a mother. So he is poring over it now and seems to find it fairly interesting—though I think in his soul he prefers *Granny Fox* and *The Cockhouse at Fellsgarth*[446] which is natural enough.

I have finished reading McCarthy's *History of our Own Times*.[447] I have read it many times since I was a child of 12, when I read it first. Then and now I found it fascinating. McCarthy had a style almost equal to Macaulay and most of his opinions have stood pretty well the test of time. I doubt if I shall ever have time to read the book again—there are too many new ones coming out all the time which I want to read. Yet an old book has something for me which no new book can ever have—for at every reading the memories and atmosphere of other readings come back and I am reading old years as well as an old book.

Friday, October 21, 1921
Leaskdale, Ont.

The weather this October has been an atrocious mixture of rain and wind. I have finished the ninth chapter of *Emily*. I should have more finished, considering the weeks I have been at it, but it is very hard to get all the time I should. However, I feel pretty well satisfied with the quality. I think *Emily* will be a good bit of work.

A little incident that happened this evening in connection with Stuart reminded me, by the law of association, of a long unthought-of happening of my early childhood. I was about five or six and grandma was teaching me a spelling lesson. I don't remember the lesson—I don't remember what I did that annoyed her—but I *do* remember the punishment she made me undergo and the humiliation and anger and disgust with which it filled me to the core of my soul. Grandma "meant well" of course but she did a terrible thing. She made me kneel down on the floor before her and pray to God to forgive me for being such a bad

---

446   Two popular boys' novels by English writer Talbot Baines Reed (1852–93).

447   Irish writer and politician Justin McCarthy's (1830–1912) *History of Our Own Times* (vols i–iv published 1879–80, vol. v published 1897) recounts the history of Queen Victoria's reign, from her accession to her diamond jubilee (that is, from 1837 to 1887). On "Macaulay," mentioned in the next sentence, see note 15, page 5.

girl—that is, she made me utter the words with my lips.[448] There was of course nothing of *real* prayer in them—for I only uttered them because I was compelled to do so, sorely against my will, and with a soul filled with humiliation, impotent anger, and a queer sense of degradation as if something in me was outraged. And truly something was—something sacred and inalienable. It was a dreadful thing for her—for anyone—to do. To force a human soul to utter words of prayer when it was not in a fit state to do so—when stormy rebellion and bitterness filled it. Grandmother never realized what she had done but she filled me with a lasting sense of disgust with and hatred for prayer and religion—what she called prayer and religion at least. It never left me. From that day I loathed it. It was not until I grew old enough to think for myself and began to realize that real prayer—real religion—was something very different from pattering formulas and going blindly through certain meaningless ceremonies that I escaped from the influence of that day. And indeed I never fully escaped from it. My conscious mind cast it off at the bidding of reason; but that subconscious mind over which we have little, if any, control, retained it—retains it still. To this day, the humiliation of that hour manifests itself in a *feeling* which lurks under all the beliefs and conclusions of my reason, that "religion" and all connected with it was something which—like sex—one had to have but was ashamed of for all that.

I suppose I am like most people in being a helpless victim to impressions made in early years. Perhaps I am more helpless than some owing to the exceeding sharpness and depth of the impressions made on a somewhat unusually sensitive nature. But in that same subconscious mind I carry an irrational detestation of "being a Christian."

When I was a child a certain Mr. Secord travelled over the Island as a Bible Society Colporteur.[449] He came around about twice a year and I always hailed his arrival with delight since it generally meant a new volume of *Talmage's Sermons* and perhaps a *Pansy* Book or something similar where the so-called religion was sugar-coated with an interesting story. But for Mr. Secord himself I felt no enthusiasm. He was a thin, anaemic individual with a straggling pointed beard and pale, indeterminate eyes.

One evening in late November he arrived at twilight, chilled to the bone. He sat hunched up in front of the kitchen stove, trying to get warm and evidently bent on sowing good seed in season and out of season, for he said to me, as I stood in the corner by the stove, watching

448 An incident in *Emily of New Moon*—which LMM was composing at this time—recalls this episode, with Emily almost forced to kneel before an angry teacher.
449 A bookseller hired to sell Bibles.

him curiously, in his thin, squeaky voice,

"Little girl, isn't it nice to be a Christian?"

I looked at him—at his shivering form, his pinched blue face, his claw-like hands spread over the stove, and I thought that *he* was a Christian and that I certainly didn't want to be one! I have never been able really to divorce the two ideas that were so incongruously wedded at that moment. To this day, a *Christian* really means to me, *not* an individual who is trying to carry the ideas and ideals of Jesus into the practical life of community and state, as my reason tells me—but a creature like "old Secord"—and I can't separate myself from the deeply-rooted idea of repugnance to the *name* "Christian," born in me by that unlucky incident.

Another thing that I dislike is the *name* "Jesus" itself. I do not know exactly why—at least, I cannot recall any such specific cause as the Secord one to account for my feeling about it. I believe it was because I used to hear it howled forth so frequently in absurd, meaningless "gospel hymns" by unctuous evangelists and revivalists. Perhaps because the name itself, like so many of the Hebrew names, was disagreeable to me. Until I learned to think of the man, apart from the name. I felt repulsion towards both. Eventually I did accomplish this and came into my heritage for love and reverence for that unique and wonderful Personality with its lofty aspirations, its pure conceptions of truth, its radical scorn for outworn conventions and laws. I never call him "Jesus" but always Christ, though I know the latter is a title and not a name. But to me it seems a beautiful word with none of the obscurely disagreeable suggestions of "Jesus."

I wish I could protect my children against false and ugly conceptions of these matters. I try to do so. But in dealing with children who "blurt out" things, I have to be careful for Ewan's sake. And they have to go to Sunday School where they are taught by a couple of crude, ignorant old women who never had an original thought in their lives and who would think anyone who didn't believe in the literal existence of Adam and Eve and a talking snake as an infidel of deepest dye.

Stuart was learning his catechism question the other evening, "Why did God make all things?"; the answer being, "For his own glory."

This has always seemed to me an abominable libel on God—seeming to present him in the light of a monstrous egotist. I resolved to dare the Leaskdale grundyites for once, and I said to Stuart,

"That is not how that question should be answered. God made all things for the love and pleasure of creating them—of doing good work—of bringing beauty into existence."

That seems to me a very much higher conception of God's creation than the other.

Monday, October 24, 1921
Leaskdale, Ont.

"To him that hath shall be given."[450] Recently I sent a short story of 5000 words to a New York Magazine and it sent me $270 for it. In other years I wrote dozens of stories every bit as good and some really much better for $30 apiece—and thought myself lucky to get that. Even for the best short story I ever wrote—when it was published in *Chronicles of Avonlea* a reviewer said it was "one of the finest short stories in the world"—I got only a hundred.

Yet after all it was not really for the story they paid the price but for the name, and that name was won by the long toil of the obscure years—a toil that blossoms now.

We have been housecleaning lately and doing a hundred other things. I work from seven to eleven with hand or head and sometimes both. Yet I never feel worse than nominally tired and then I sleep like a top and waken fresh as paint. This to me is quite wonderful, who for years felt tired half the time. I am as fat as a seal, rosy as an apple, and fuller of "ginger," "pep" and "vim" than I ever was since I was twenty. There is no very deep-seated reason for this—instead a very prosaic one indeed—*yeast cakes*.

One of the recent discoveries of science is *vitamines*. Yeast cakes are full of them. For over a year I've been taking a yeast cake every day—and this is the result. It aggravates me to think of how much I might have been spared if I had known this years ago. I always had good health; but I felt, much of the time, horribly *tired* in body and soul. I never feel that way now, even amid all the hard work and worry of my present life. I really feel as if I had been reborn. It is delightful to feel so. I believe if I had known of yeast cake magic I should have escaped many of those terrible months in the winter after Grandfather's death. Our winter diet, I realize now, was sadly lacking in "vitamines." It is not only an army that moves on its stomach!

Tuesday, Nov. 1, 1921
Leaskdale, Ont.

I have been having a dreadful week of it. Ewan has had one of the worst attacks of his malady he has ever had—by far the worst this year. It came on last Wednesday and increased in intensity until yesterday.

---

450 Matthew 13:12. "For whosoever hath, to him shall be given, and he shall have more abundance: but whosoever hath not, from him shall be taken away even that he hath."

When he came home from church on Sunday he said to me, "I was preaching to the people today—and they should be preaching to me."

I said,

"Would you call it rational if a minister who was delirious with the delusions of typhoid fever should say that he was not fit to preach to his people?"

"No."

"Well, then, can't you see that it is just as irrational for you, in the delusions of your malady to imagine the same thing?" But, no, he couldn't see it. Poor Ewan, in these attacks, doesn't believe that he *has* any malady.

"I am perfectly well; but I am outcast from God. *That* is my trouble. You do not sympathize with me."

That is Ewan's attitude. Because I cannot believe that he is a lost soul I have "no sympathy." Dr. Garrick told me I must not argue with him on the subject but that, on the other hand, I must be careful not to say anything that would confirm it. I never do. And yet, so well do I know a certain ingrained contrariness in Ewan's personality which has always seemed to drive him into opposition to any opinion held or expressed by other people, that I verily believe that if I were to agree with him and say bluntly, "Yes, I *do* think you are lost and that there is no hope for you," that very quality of his would assert itself and oppose me, to the auto-banishment of his obsession. But I dare not make the experiment.

He slept better last night and seemed more restful today, though dull. Tonight he was lying on the bed in our room after supper, and I was brushing my hair, when he said suddenly,

"Maud, there are times when I am afraid of myself."

I knew too well what he meant but I said,

"What do you mean?"

He said, "I am afraid of what I may do."

I said,

"My dear, put your meaning into plain blunt words. It will help you to do so—it will take it out of your mind. Do you mean suicide or anything like that?"

He nodded. I felt aghast but I took his hand and said earnestly, "Ewan, promise me that you will *never* do anything like that."

He said,

"Oh, I won't do it—I am too much of a coward."

I feel sick at heart. During the first summer of his melancholia I knew he was tortured by such thoughts but I did not think they had troubled him since. Oh, *can* I go on like this, with no one to advise or share the burden? I have been living on the hope that he would have a normal interval this fall again—but we are not to have even that short respite. Oh, religious melancholy is a hideous thing. A man who is physically ill is still the same man: but a man in Ewan's case is *not*. Ewan seems to me like an absolute stranger in these attacks. He is no more like the man I married than—he is *not* the man I married. An altogether different personality is there—and a personality which is repulsive and abhorrent to me. And yet to this personality I must be a wife. It is horrible—it is indecent—it should not be. I feel degraded and unclean.

Sunday, Nov. 6, 1921
Leaskdale, Ont.

On Thursday we motored in a pouring rain to Whitby and had tea with friends. I gave an evening of readings in the Methodist church—a horrible place from an acoustic point of view, with an abominable echo. Then we stayed all night with Captain Smith and next morning went to Bowmanville[451] and stayed with friends there until yesterday. Ewan was not keen about going but, as usual, the outing did him good and he is much better again.

Thursday, Nov. 17, 1921
The Manse, Leaskdale

The weather has been mild but abominably messy. I have been very busy, and have sat up till twelve or one every night writing letters and publicity articles for the Canadian Book Week[452] which begins Saturday. I am going into Toronto for it. Ewan is much better and seems fairly normal but I take anxiety with me. And yet I want to get away for just a few days and have a sort of *change of tribulation*—use a different set of nerve cells.

Friday, Nov. 18, 1921
2 Nina Ave., Toronto

It used to be an old family joke that "Maud always takes rain when she goes." It really does seem so. I came in today and it has poured all the time. Mary and I went to the Authors' Association Dinner in honor of

---

451   Bowmanville is located some 75 km (47 miles) east of Toronto.
452   Sponsored by the Canadian Authors' Association in 1921 to promote Canadian books.

Nellie McClung at the Arts and Letters Club tonight.[453] There were about 80 there and I had a seat at the head table next the president and guest of honor—which didn't make a very poor menu taste any better. But the evening was enjoyable and I met heaps of clever people. Basil King[454] was on my left. I haven't seen him since that evening of the reception at his home eleven years ago in Cambridge. Nellie is a handsome woman in a stunning dress, glib of tongue. She made a speech full of obvious platitudes and amusing little stories which made everyone laugh and deluded us into thinking it was quite a fine thing— until we began to think it over. And she told one story, as happening to herself which is a hoary old jokes-column chestnut. *Why* will people do things like that? There is sure to be one person in the audience who will know its genesis.

Basil King made an excellent speech, full of good ideas, with no superfluities or frills or gallery plays.

Old James S. Hughes[455] was there and told me, *Anne* was "the finest piece of literature we had in Canada." This may be an absurd statement but at least he meant it for he is a terribly outspoken old fellow and pays no idle compliments.

Saturday, Nov. 19, 1921
Toronto, Ont.

Still rainy. This afternoon Mary and I went to hear Basil King speak in the auditorium in the Robert Simpson Co. store.[456] Then we went to the big reception given by the Press Club to the Authors' Association. A horrible mob! Twelve hundred people packed together—nothing much to eat. But I met Jen Fraser,[457] Frede's old Macdonald crony who is in Toronto now, organizing the Commissariat of the Bell Telephone. We had never met before but seemed old friends because of hearing so much about each other from Frede. Jen seemed to bring Frede back to me—I felt that she *must* be there too—and the feeling was so compounded of pain and sweetness that I did not know whether to smile

---

453 The Canadian Authors' Association was founded in 1921 by prominent writers of the day, including Stephen Leacock and B.K. Sandwell, with the goal of lobbying for the protection of authors and the promotion Canadian books. Writer and feminist Nellie McClung (1873–1951) published nine novels between 1908 and 1931.

454 Writer and former clergyman William Benjamin Basil King (1859–1928) shared with LMM an interest in spirituality.

455 James Laughlin Hughes (1846–1935), Toronto-based writer, poet, and essayist.

456 Canadian department Simpsons had been founded in 1858.

457 Jen Fraser is in the picture with Frede on page 119.

or cry—and finally cried, there in that swarming mob where I felt like
a maggot in a swarm of inane maggots—at least they seemed inane in
that personality smothering mass—coming and going and repeating
endlessly, "I love your books"—"Was 'Anne' a real girl?"— — — — —
— — . etc. etc.

Mary and Norman and I went to Hart House[458] tonight to see the
Community players of Montreal[459] put on a couple of plays. I enjoyed
them. Good amateur acting is always enjoyable, all the more so from
the absence of stage mannerisms and too-great skill. There is more
reality about it. And some of the actors were very good. The final shriek
of one of them—"Oh, not Siberia, mother!" was so realistic that it
haunted me all night.

Monday, Nov. 21, 1921
2 Nina Ave., Toronto

The weather has cleared up. I shopped all the morning, since my family must eat and be clothed. Then I had lunch with Jen Fraser at Simpsons—with Cam's doings and peculiarities for sauce. Jen's opinion of
him is the same as mine. She says the only excuse for his behavior is
the possibility that the war affected his mind in some way. She did not
know him before his marriage, so couldn't tell me if he were always
like that. She says he was running around with all sorts of girls last
summer. Well, Frede has gone beyond it—and those of us who loved
her—who *love* her——.

Jen told me a little story of Frede so characteristic of her that I
must record it here. When Jen and Frede first met at Macdonald Frede
looked at her across the room and said briefly,

"Maritime."

"Yes," said Jen.

"Presbyterian?"

"Yes."

"Shake," said Frede. "They're the only decent things to be!"

In the afternoon I went to Jarvis St. Collegiate[460] and read and talk-

<hr>

458   Established in 1919, Hart House was one of the earliest student centres in North America.
The Hart House theatre opened the same year, and soon became a leader in the Canadian "Little
Theatre" movement of the 1920s and 1930s.

459   The Montreal Players were then considered one of Canada's most successful groups
emerging from the Little Theatre Movement.

460   Toronto's Jarvis St. Collegiate (now Jarvis Collegiate Institute) is the second oldest school
in Ontario. Dr Archibald MacMurchy—the father of LMM's friend Marjory MacMurchy and doctor Helen MacMurchy—had been principal from 1873 to 1899.

ed to an audience of about 800 girls. I enjoyed it. They were so eager, so appreciative, so enthusiastic. I felt at one with them from the start. I autographed about a hundred books and cards and then went to an I.O.D.E. meeting[461] in Parkdale, gave a reading, answered innumerable questions, met some charming women and some very foolish ones. Came home to dinner, then went to Victoria College[462] and spent a very dull evening listening to a couple of literary papers by erudite authors who could not stoop to be interesting as well as erudite.

The thing *has* been done—but they didn't do it. I nearly fell asleep. But at least the evening was restful!

Tuesday, Nov. 22, 1921

A full day—full of something at least. This morning I went to Moulton College[463] and gave a reading and a brief talk to the girls thereof, writing a hundred autographs afterwards. I shopped the rest of the forenoon and after lunch went with Mary to see *Quo Vadis*[464] on the screen. I don't know why I keep on going to see my favorite books screened. The result is always a disappointment. And yet I suppose I will keep on doing it whenever the chance comes my way. At 4.30 I went to give readings in the auditorium of the Simpson store. I had a bumper audience. The room was packed and half as many more couldn't get in. It was not an easy place to read in—the acoustic properties were poor and the noises of the street outside disturbed me. I was told my audience heard me well, however. After it came the usual autographing and handshaking. Two men came up to me and asked me to speak next Sunday at the Dunn Avenue Methodist Sunday School.[465] At first I refused: but they would not take no for an answer. They stood there and pleaded, holding up the line and keeping everything at a standstill, so finally I said yes to get rid of them. I couldn't give readings on Sunday to a Sunday School—I hadn't a thing to talk on to such an audience. The whole thing worried me until after dinner tonight when it suddenly occurred to me that I could give a talk on "The Bible as Literature."

An amusing coincidence happened in the store today. I passed two

---

461   The Imperial Order of the Daughters of the Empire was founded in 1900 to provide support to Canadians going overseas to fight in South Africa.

462   Victoria College had been founded in 1836 as a Methodist college of University of Toronto.

463   Moulton Ladies' College was founded in 1888 as a preparatory school for girls.

464   A silent movie based on the life of Jesus, after the 1895 novel by Polish writer Henryk Sienkiewicz (*Quo Vadis: A Narrative of the Time of Nero*).

465   Dunn Avenue Methodist Church was built in 1889–90 on the south-east corner of Dunn Avenue and King Street in Toronto. (It was demolished in 1970.)

women at a counter, evidently women of refinement and culture, and as I went by I heard one say, evidently *apropos* of some person they had been discussing, "Oh, she has a *perfectly wonderful* husband." About half an hour later I was going down in an elevator and two women, evidently of a very different class, were talking behind me and one said emphatically,

"Gosh, but she's got a swell man."

The colonel's lady and Judy O'Grady![466]

Wednesday, Nov. 23, 1921
Toronto, Ont.

Last night I went to bed very tired, and should have gone right to sleep like a sensible person. But frequently I am not a sensible person. I let myself begin thinking out my address to that Sunday School and got so interested in it that sleepiness fled and I kept at it until two o'clock when I had it complete in my mind. But I felt quite differently at 7.30 this morning when I had to crawl out in the chill of the gray dawn.

I went to Oakwood[467] where I gave readings to an audience of 1300 boys and girls. I felt rather nervous for I had never read to boys before and did not know if I could appeal to them. I gave the story of *Dog Monday* from *Rilla*, arranged to form a continued reading and my audience seemed to like it very much. I autographed 91 books. In the afternoon I went to the School of Commerce[468] to read to the High School girls of Toronto. I had a very enthusiastic audience of about 1500. Before I began to read they gave me a magnificent basket of big white and pale pink "'mums" in the "name of the girls of Toronto," which was very sweet of them. Afterwards I was nearly mobbed by a sea of girls wanting autographs. They nearly smothered me. I wrote about 400 autographs in half an hour. I was so tired that evening that everything seemed vanity and schoolgirls the vainest things of all.

Thursday, Nov. 24, 1921
2 Nina Ave., Toronto

Today I got a letter from Mr. Douglas of the Carnegie Library, Vancouver,[469] which warmed and illumined the whole day. He says of *Rilla*;

---

466   From Rudyard Kipling's poem "The Ladies."

467   Located in north-western Toronto, this is collegiate was founded in 1907.

468   The High School of Commerce and Finance (now the Central Toronto Academy) was founded in 1916.

469   Now Carnegie Community Centre in downtown Vancouver, this was the city's main

"You have written a very wonderful book—a book that will live, I think, when most of the ephemeral literature of the time will be forgotten. You have visualized the soul of the Canadian people in the war; you have given a true picture of what we went through during five long years of agony, and you have lighted up the canvas with gleams of humor which no other living writer could have excelled . . . The storm and stress of home life during those anxious days have never received audible expression, except in your wonderful book."

I was especially pleased with this because that is exactly what I tried to do in my book and this is the first competent testimony that I had succeeded.

Mary gave an At Home for me today—the usual thing. One guest was interesting to me—Mrs. Rochester who came to Prince Albert as a bride with her young husband thirty years ago. I knew her well then but have never seen her since. She has changed beyond recognition. Naturally there would be a change between the bride of about twenty and the woman of fifty. But she looks so much older than that, with her white hair and shrivelled face. Two of her sons were killed in the war and a third has been an invalid ever since. Probably that is the reason of her aged appearance.

This evening Norman and Mary and I went to see "Biff-Bing-Bang."[470] It was incredibly funny and well done, and I laughed as I haven't laughed for years. The female parts were all played by men and three of them were the most stunning beauties I ever beheld. When I read that in the days of Shakespeare the parts of women on the stage were all played by men I used to think that the result must be ludicrous and unpleasing. But I think so no longer. The ladies of "Biff-Bing-Bang" were wonderful creations, with their snowy shoulders, jewelled breasts and rose bloom cheeks. The only thing that gave them away was their thick ankles!

I am fogging up with an abominable cold.

Friday, Nov. 25, 1921
Toronto, Ont.

Shopped all the morning and picked up an adorable Chessy-cat brass knocker for my bedroom door at Ryries.[471] I was delighted over my find

---

public library (it was one of the 2,509 Carnegie libraries built between 1883 and 1929 by Scottish-American businessman Andrew Carnegie).

470   *Biff, Bing, Bang!* was a 1921 musical directed by Ivor E. Ayre.

471   The Ryrie Building, located at 229 Yonge Street on the north-east corner of Shuter Street

for it had an interest for me entirely apart from its own quaint charm. In the summer of 1918 when Frede and I were at Park Corner she showed me with great delight a chessy-cat knocker exactly like this one which Cam had picked up in England and sent her. We laughed and gloated over it and I told her to put it out of sight lest I be tempted to poison her tea for the chance of falling heir to it! Frede howled and declared she would lock it up instanter.

The next time I saw it was in her room at Macdonald after her death. I packed it away with Cam's things, crying my heart out. Yet I would have liked to have had the thing—it was so expressive of Frede— the very spirit of all our old jokes and traditions was in it. It was impossible to look at the grin on the face of that cat without a responsive grin. When Cam was here I admit I did give him a hint—for I thought Frede would have liked me to have had that knocker. I told him how we had laughed together over it and how quaint and wholly delightful I thought it. But he did not say, as I thought he might have, "Would you like to have it, Maud?" So today I was much pleased to find an exactly similar cat at Ryries among some English brasses they had imported for Xmas. I shall put it on my room door. I have been trying to train Chester and Stuart always to rap on my door before entering; but they have been so long used to rushing in in baby days that they find it hard to remember. I think they will get into the habit now for they will want to rap with the chessy for the fun of it. And every time I see it I will see Frede, too, with her laughing face and pleased eyes, and she will not seem altogether gone from me.

This afternoon I went to Hamilton to autograph books in the Cloke bookstore[472] there. Mr. Ford of Mac's went with me and saw to everything and I had a nice time.

Saturday, Nov. 26, 1921
Toronto, Ont.

I am beginning to get desperately homesick for the children. Hitherto I have been so drugged by the rapid succession of the crowded days that I haven't really thought of home at all. But now the effects of the drug

---

and Yonge Street in Toronto, had been constructed in several stages between 1891 and 1921. A "Chessy-cat" knocker would recall the smiling "Cheshire cat" in Lewis Carroll's *Alice in Wonderland* (1865).

472   Cloke & Son Stationery store was a business in downtown Hamilton until the 1990s, specializing in postcards, booklets, business paper, and other printed material.

have worn off and last night my hunger for Stuart and Chester seemed absolutely physical in its intensity. I could not sleep for thinking of them and longing for them—my darling little boys!

Today Mr. Stewart gave a luncheon for me at the National.[473] Mrs. Stewart and Mr. and Mrs. Brady were also there and we had a jolly time. Mr. Mac is over in England at present. After luncheon I went to Sherbourne House[474] and gave readings to a mob of school teachers who may have been very nice individually but were bores *en masse*. The crowd was almost suffocating and I was thankful when I got away.

Sunday, Nov. 28, 1921
2 Nina Ave., Toronto

This afternoon I spoke to the Dunn Ave. Methodist Church Sunday School for half an hour. It is really the first "honest-to-goodness" speech I ever made in my life—for when I have "spoken" before I have read my speech or had notes. I was nervous before I began but forgot it and found myself enjoying it. As 600 S.S. pupils, half of them boys of all ages, kept perfect order they must have found it fairly interesting. If I had had the proper training in early life I think I could have made a fairly good speaker. But it is too late now and I don't want to bother with it anyway. I have one work to do and have no time to take up another. Besides, the country is lousy with amateur speakers.

Tuesday, Nov. 29, 1921
The Manse, Leaskdale

Yesterday I was one of the guests at a Business Womens' Club[475] luncheon. My fellow guest was Mrs. Pankhurst of suffragette fame—the redoubtable "Emmeline" in the flesh.[476] As I looked at her I could not see the smasher of London windows and the hunger striker forcibly fed in Holloway jail. She had a sweet, tired, gentle face—looked like some

---

473   The National Club on Bay Street in Toronto was a private men's club, founded in 1874.

474   Sherbourne House on Sherbourne Street in Toronto was a club for young professional women.

475   The Canadian Women's Business Club on Yonge Street in Toronto had been founded in 1920.

476   British activist Emmeline Pankhurst (1858–1928) had led the movement for women's voting rights before the war. Charged with property damage in 1912, Pankhurst was incarcerated in Holloway Prison, London; she staged hunger strikes, and suffered force-feeding. At the outbreak of the war, Pankhurst (along with other "political prisoners") were released.

Presbyterian elder's wife in a country village who had done nothing more strenuous in her life than putting up with the elder and running the W.M.S.

After the luncheon Mary and I dressed and went to the Press Club reception of Lady Byng.[477] It was a pleasant affair. Lady B. is not handsome. She has an enormous nose, but fine eyes, and is rather stately in appearance. I liked her. She was jolly and democratic—which is a new thing in vice-reines. She is a novelist also, having written two novels. They are readable books of the kind almost any clever English woman seems able to turn out.

Tonight I came home—a little fearful of what might await me. But Ewan met me in pretty good spirits and after a dull, dark drive home which seemed intolerably slow after our car we got here and I had my darling boys again.

Thursday, Dec. 1, 1921
Leaskdale, Ont.

This dull foggy day was *not* enlivened by a letter from poor Aunt Annie full of woes and complaints. She told me all over again everything in her last letter and then some. At the end she wound up by entreating me not to "tell Clara or Stella anything of this because it would worry them."

Of course, it does not matter about worrying me!

But poor old Aunty *has* a hard time of it—and will have it harder I fear. She is getting too much like grandma for her own good. The crop was not good this year and I think she is pretty hard up for a little ready cash. I must send her a check for Christmas. It will not occur to Stella or Clara to do anything of the sort.

I must "hoe in" now. Christmas is in the air and I have no preparations made. I shall have to do some planning and hustling. Fortunately Lily is a changed creature. All last year she was almost unbearable with crankiness and bad temper. But ever since she came back after her tonsillitis she has been like her old self—good-tempered, obliging and respectful. I can't account for it. Perhaps her nerves are better. In any case, I am very thankful for last winter she was really intolerable.

---

477   Evelyn Byng (1870–1949) was the wife of Baron Byng of Vimy (Governor General of Canada from 1921 to 1926). Lady Byng had published several novels.

Wednesday, Dec. 7, 1921
The Manse, Leaskdale

Yesterday was election day. I have not been able to get up the slightest excitement about it.[478] There does not seem to be any vital difference between the parties. In our riding there was no Liberal Candidate— only a Conservative and a "U.F.O." I have no use for the U.F.O's in general and the candidate here in particular. He is an ignorant boor. So I voted for the Conservative because he is a fine fellow. But I "lost my vote" for Halbert went in after all. But the Liberals are in at Ottawa. I was, however, much more excited over the *Globe* announcement that "the peace treaty" between Ireland and England had been signed at last.[479] Lloyd George has pulled it off. That little Welshman is a wonder. As for the Irish, I predict fun. They have been fighting England for 700 years. Now they will fight each other—for fight they must.

Tuesday, Dec. 13, 1921
Leaskdale, Ont.

Last night I got back from a trip to Cleveland, Ohio where I went at Stokes' request to attend a reception in the book dep't of the Halle Bros. big store. I had good weather and a good time.

I reached Cleveland at 6.30 on Friday evening and was met by Miss Hutchinson, head of the Book Dep't, and young Mr. Stokes who took us, with Mr. Claggett of Lippincott's, to dinner at the Carlton Terrace, a high-class cabaret where we "dined" from seven to twelve, listened to "jazz" music and watched the modern dances concerning which there are such skirls of wrath in the magazines of the period. I hardly wondered. I have always liked dancing, but truth to tell, some of the couples I saw there (*not* all—the majority really danced unobjection-ably) reminded me of Byron's biting line,

---

478 The December 1921 election brought the Liberal party, including William Lyon Mackenzie King, into power in Canada. The "U.F.O." party, described in the next sentence, refer to the United Farmers of Ontario, the provincial branch of the United Farmers movement. Robert Henry Halbert, the first president of the U.F.O., had been elected Member of Parliament for the riding of South Ontario in 1919, and was re-elected in 1921.

479 David Lloyd George (1863–1945), Prime Minister of Britain since 1916. In Ireland he campaigned for a Dominion Home Rule, a similar political structure to Canada. Lloyd George had been born to Welsh-speaking parents and grew up speaking Welsh (he lived in both England and Wales, following changing family fortunes). Coming from a family that had seen its share of hard times, Lloyd George positioned himself as a champion of working people when he came to power.

"Nor leave much mystery for the nuptial night."[480]

However, I enjoyed the evening as a variety. Soft and mellow light, delicious food, agreeable music—"jazz" may "appeal to the baser passions" perhaps, but I liked it although I had not expected to like it—and most of all, conversation with intellectual and cultured people were very delightful.

Saturday Miss Hutchinson and I went to Luncheon at a Women's Club where I spoke, giving P.E. Island a good boost—and then I spent the afternoon in the store talking to customers and autographing endless books. Miss H. and I then dined together and went to a movie. I left for home at 11.30 and arrived in Toronto Sunday morning. Got home yesternight to find Ewan very blue and miserable again. I am glad my journeyings are over for a while.

Had a letter today from "Pastor Felix."[481] He tells me that Nate lost one of his sons last year from a gun accident and felt it very deeply. What a horrible thing!

Thursday, Dec. 22, 1921
The Manse, Leaskdale

Ewan has been very dull this past week. I fear another bad attack is coming on.

This afternoon Miss Rundle had her "school concert" and Xmas tree—which here takes the place of the old "exam" down home. So I went and saw my small man among his mates—and he was the rosiest, sturdiest, healthiest-looking of them all.

Saturday, Dec. 24, 1921

We celebrated Christmas today—and it was quite a pleasant one after all. I say "after all" for until this morning I did not expect it would be pleasant. Ewan seemed very miserable yesterday. I was busy all day making preparations for Christmas and for the concert at night. Among other things I made our customary Christmas pudding—the delicious old Park Corner "Lemon Bread Pudding"—and cried as I made it, for it reminded me so of Frede. I always made it for her. She loved it—and

---

480   From Byron's long poem, *English Bards and Scotch Reviewers: A Satire* (1809).

481   Methodist clergyman Arthur John Lockhart (1850–1926), the uncle of one of LMM's Cavendish friends Nathan Lockhart, had published *The Papers of Pastor Felix* (1903) as well as several books of verse, including *The Masque of Minstrels, and Other Pieces* (with Burton Wellesley Lockhart; 1887) and *The Isle of Song: A Dream of Arcadia and Other Poems, 1870–1918* (1918).

never got at Macdonald any pudding so deliciously extravagant in eggs. I generally made it on the day I expected her. Oh, the change! Will I ever be able to think of her without this pain and longing. Frede, it is five years since that last Christmas of ours together in 1916. Oh, we little dreamed then it was our last. Frede—Frede.

Our S.S. concert came off at night. Stuart recited "Just Afore Christmas"[482] splendidly. He was the best number on the programme. He has inherited my knack of elocution with a frank, charming roguishness of delivery which I never possessed, so he carried his audience along with him and enjoyed himself as much as they did.

When we came home I got the boys to bed. Then I stayed up till one dressing up the tree. Last year Ewan kept putting off getting the tree till it was too late. A storm came up the day before Christmas and he could not get it. This year I was determined to have one, so I began early and kept at him until he got one in good time. It looked very pretty when I got through. But I had bought a "railroad" for the boys in Toronto and wanted to put it together to have it ready. But I could *not* get it to work. I tried for an hour and a half, got all tired out, and went to bed too weary to sleep and thoroughly down and out. I lay there for hours and *everything* was absurdly black. Ewan would *never* be better—everything I tried to do was a failure—Chester and Stuart would be unhappy failures—and so on and so on. Nothing good could come out of the Nazareth of my future. That was at three o'clock. Then I fell asleep. And even three hours' sleep made the world over for me. The boys were delighted with the tree and their gifts. That perverse railroad worked without a hitch. Lily—whose people do not celebrate till Monday—was here, so for the first time since 1916 I was not alone and did not have to spend the most of the day cooking meals and cleaning up. The boys had good fun and I had a glorious "read," Mr. McClelland having sent us his usual generous parcel of books. Ewan, too, seemed much better today—the first Christmas day since 1918 that he was at all well.

Thursday, Dec. 29, 1921
The Manse, Leaskdale

For the eleventh time I entertained the Guild executive tonight. I have done so every Xmas week since I came. The personnel of the Guild has wholly changed. We had a nice time tonight. For the first time for

---

482   Probably "Jest 'Fore Christmas" by American poet and children's writer Eugene Field (1850–95), a humorous poem written in the voice of a young boy.

three years Ewan happened to feel well on this occasion and enjoyed it all, instead of trying to slip away and indulge his broodings alone as formerly.

I took a couple of flashlights[483] of the crowd, gave them a tip top lunch, and we got out a good guild programme. Reading something in today's paper about Miss Agnes MacPhail, the first woman to be elected to the Dominion Parliament,[484] reminded me of one of the "dream lives" I was fond of living when I was a child. I have lived a great many "dream" lives—I live them yet. But this was a great favorite. In it I was "Lady Trevanion" and a member of the British House of Commons to boot. Also a famous novelist. There was a "Lord Trevanion" but he was a very nebulous personage and didn't cut much ice. One of the

[The Guild Executive]

[The Guild Executive]

favorite scenes in this dream was when another M.P. made a contemptuous reference to me as a *woman*. A thousand times have I bounded to my feet and burst into a vehement speech in my own defence. This speech was not original. I took "Pitt's Reply to Walpole"[485] and hurled

---

483   That is, photographs using an early version of a flash (in this case, the "flash lamp" involved blowing magnesium powder through a small flame).

484   Agnes Macphail (1890–1954) was the first woman in Canada to be elected to parliament, serving from 1921 to 1940. After that she was member of the Legislative Assembly of Ontario, representing the Toronto riding of York East.

485   William Pitt, 1st Earl of Chatham (1708–78) was a British statesman and Prime Minister.

it at my sneerer—only of course in the dream it *was* original—changed to suit the circumstance.

"Sir, the atrocious crime of being a *woman* which the honorable gentleman has, with such spirit and decency charged upon me, I shall attempt neither to palliate nor deny but shall content myself with wishing that I may be one of those whose follies cease with their *sex* and not one of that number who are ignorant in spite of *manhood* and experience."

Here I was always interrupted by thunders of applause. And nobody ever again dared to sneer at "Lady Trevanion."[486]

My, what fun I got out of that!—hundreds of nights when my small body was cuddled between the blankets in that old P.E.I. farmhouse!

The time of the South African war I began living a dream life in South Africa—and have lived it to this day. Side by side with my real life the current has flowed on. An idealized *Cecil Rhodes* has shared it with me in various plots and developments some widely differing from the other.

Chester is reading *Midshipman Easy*[487] and finds it very enthralling. I can recall how delightedly I revelled in it when a child and how I laughed over Jack's green silk petticoat banner. By the law of association this reminds me of the green silk petticoat I am at present making for myself—out of my mother's wedding dress.

My mother was married in the fashionable taffeta silk of the time. And the silk was the brightest, vividest green imaginable! When I was a child the dress hung on the wall of the north room. It was made with the full crinoline skirt of the '74's, the sloping shoulders and large, loose sleeves, trimmed with green satin bands and green silk fringe. I would give much if I had that dress today just as it was. It would be a valuable heirloom. But grandma was always saying that when I grew up it was to be made over for me. I was too young then to realize how much better it would be to keep it as it was, and I rather looked forward to the time when I could wear it. When I was about fourteen Grandmother ripped it to pieces and discarded everything but the sleeves and

---

Pitt was a fierce critic of the government of Robert Walpole; following an altercation in Parliament with Walpole in 1741, Walpole accused Pitt of being too young and inexperienced to grasp a complex political problem. Pitt's response was reported to writer Samuel Johnson, who composed the version of it that became famous. LMM knew the Johnson version of the speech; a similar passage is found in *Emily of New Moon* (1923).

486   This name may derive from Edgar Allen Poe's character, Lady Rowena Trevanian, a character in his 1838 short story "Ligeia."

487   Frederick Marryat's novel for boys, *Mr Midshipman Easy* (1836); Marryat was a retired Royal Navy Captain.

skirt breadths. Then these were rolled up and stowed away to await the day when they should be made up for me. That day never came. When I was old enough to wear silk dresses the fashion of silks had changed. I was secretly aghast at the idea of appearing out in that brilliant green silk—so I never said anything about it and Grandmother appeared to forget it. As the years went by I cherished a design of having the dress made up with a black lace overdress to tone it down or something of the sort. But somehow the years came and went and I never did it. When I came here I brought the rolls of silk with me and they have lain in my trunk ever since. Not long ago, I decided to make a couple of silk petticoats out of it. There was really nothing else it could be used for now and while I would have loved to have and keep the whole dress these fragments of it mean nothing to anybody.

The petticoats are going to be very pretty. The silk must have been a wonderful stuff. It is 48 years old but there is never a sign of cut about it. It is as soft and glossy as ever. Last night I tried the petticoat on—and as I did so I thought of how, forty-eight years ago, the beautiful young Clara Macneill must have tried it on, too—her wedding dress. It would become her fair beauty. It made her seem a little real to me for the moment. It is very seldom mother has seemed *real* to me. If she were alive she would be sixty-eight—quite an old woman. I wonder if she would be proud of her daughter's success. I suppose my life would have been absolutely different if she had lived—perhaps a happier life. How I wish I could remember her as she was in her young womanhood. I have not even a good picture of her. Grandmother and Grandfather never talked of her—Aunt Annie and Aunt Emily never talked of her. It was only by casual remarks dropped here and there that I picked up any idea of her. I know nothing of her childhood—her girlhood—except that she was thought very beautiful—a tall, fair girl— and had a great many admirers. William Clark was always supposed to have gone insane and hanged himself because she did not care for him. I never heard her parents or her brothers and sisters talk of her in their family gatherings. Yet she must have been a gay, lively, mischievous little lass. I have an old daguerreotype taken of her when she was twelve. She looks sad in it. I think she was always "fey"—that people always felt she was not to live very long. Yet she was not considered delicate. She caught cold after I was born, when she was run down from nursing me, and developed consumption very rapidly. She was not ill very long. I fear her death was hastened by worry. Father had failed as a merchant in Clifton, owing to the extravagance and dissipation of his partner, Duncan McIntyre[488]—and things were very hard for mother. I am afraid she must have been not unwilling to die. But I *know* nothing—I have never heard *anything* of what she thought or felt after her illness came on. Did she grieve to leave me? Does she live yet? Will I ever see her? Will we be anything to each other if I do? Somehow, I have an odd feeling that mother is *very near* me as I write. *Does* human personality survive death? And is it possible that when we *think* of our dead it summons them irresistibly to us? Oh, we *know* nothing. We are lost in the blackest ignorance of *everything* we *should* know—we stumble blindly in the night of the universe and the dawn of a new day will not be in the lifetime of our planet!

Mother, I can see you on your bridal night, flushed and lovely and radiant in your flowing green silk dress, with its point lace collar, in the old parlor in Cavendish. Father stands beside you, a handsome young man of thirty-two—handsome, in spite of fine, dark, side-whiskers! For to the taste of the '70's side whiskers were the hallmark of a handsome man. And, if one could tolerate whiskers at all, side whiskers were the best kind. They certainly became father. I always liked them much better than the full beard he afterwards wore. It is the *name* that is against them. "Side-whiskers"—could anything sound more ridiculous? Romance and sentiment wither away beside such a name. Yet father and mother were a handsome couple and mother was doubtless a radiantly happy bride in that green silk dress.

I have not even a letter of mother's—no scrap of her writing save one or two copied poems in an old album—nothing that would savor of her personality to me. I would give anything if mother had only thought of writing a letter to *me* before she died and giving it to someone to keep for me until I was grown-up. Failing that, I wish I had a letter she had written to anybody. There would be something of *herself* in it. I have a letter written *to* her, which I treasure, but nothing *from* her.

I will paste a little scrap of her wedding dress here.

[scrap of gren fabric appended here]

---

488   Duncan McIntyre was the husband of LMM's Aunt Mary Montgomery (sister of Hugh Montgomery, LMM's father). Duncan McIntyre was the father of LMM's cousins, Cuthbert, Harry, Laura, and Beatrice.

Acknowledgements

As with *L.M. Montgomery's Complete Journals: The Ontario Years, 1911–1917*, the list of people to thank for this volume is a long one. It begins with the first generation of L.M. Montgomery scholars: Mary Henley Rubio, Elizabeth Hillman Waterston, Elizabeth Rollins Epper-ly, Father Francis W. Bolger, Gabriella Åhmansson, and the late Rea Wilmshurst. (To give an idea of span in my own lifetime: Mary Rubio is my mother and began working on Montgomery when I was a teen-ager; my own daughter, who has had some involvement in all this, is now 13.) The wonderful research by Mary Beth Cavert for The Shining Scroll (among other sources) has been indispensable. Bernadeta Milewski gave me some invaluable help. There is not space to mention help from many others, including Lisa Bode, Lesley Clement, Ben Lefebvre, Jenny Litster, Kate Macdonald, and Emily Woods.

And where would Montgomery scholarship be without the archivists at the University of Guelph's Montgomery Collection?

I am grateful for the help of an "army" of historians, military and otherwise, who helped me with the annotations.

Special thanks to Allan McGillivray, David Hepper, Elaine Crawford, Jennie Macneill.

Index

Index of Photographs

My little lads 33

The Manse 34

All very good friends 34

Mud Pies 35

At George R' 36

Geo R's House 36

The school road 37

As it used to be 37

The old front orchard 38

Alec Macneill's 38

"Two of a kind" 39

"The barefoot boy" 39

Park Corner, PEI 42

Stuart, Alec and I 44

Ham and Chester 44

"Off for a first ride in a car" 46

Aunt Emily's 46

The old trees at the gate 47

x The north veranda 47

The Maple Grove 49

A barrow-full. Jim, Chester, Stuart, Amy and Georgie 51

The big hall window 58

Carl 61

Aunt Annie and I on the Anderson lawn 64

Aunt Annie 66

The parlor 66

Stuart 67

Chester and two chums 67

The old house 71

The sitting room 71

The old spruces down by the road 73

Across the pond 73

Corner of Parlor 82

Daffy 82

My old room 84

Lover's Lane 86

The bungalow at Braintree 88

Christie Montgomery Viles and cousins at Braintree 92

Chester and Stuart 92

Frede 93

The entrance gates with Boys' Building beyond 97

Miss Hill 97

X. Infirmary of Macdonald College 98

X. The Apartment 99

Frede under the Park Corner birches 103

Lecturers in Household Science 104

Frede with quote Sonny Punch 105

Sleighing in Mount-Royal Park Montreal 108

Margaret MacFarlane 109

Frede in 1902

School of Household Science, Class 1912 115

Frede and two others 116

Frede and two others 116

A Macdonald group 117

Groups at Macdonald College 117

Groups at Macdonald College 117

Frede's Diploma 118

"The cat who walked by herself" 119

Mrs F.C. MacFarlane, late Demonstrator to Homemaker's Clubs 119

Frede and Jen Fraser in greenhouse 119

Frede and Dan 120   Frede and Miss Fer-   Frede's Artwork   Frede's Artwork
                        guson 121

Frede's Artwork   Frede's Artwork   Frede's Artwork   Frede's Artwork

Frede's Artwork   Frede's Artwork   Frede's Artwork   Frede 123

Frede 123   Chester and Queen   Queen 130   Cameron 139
                        129

A Road to School 143   C's school 143   Off to School 143   Miss Ferguson 143

Daffy 144

Ewan, Chester, Stuart, Mr. and Mrs. Dodds?147

Uxbridge 151

The bungalow on the hill 157

The little wood path 158

East Braintree Station 158

The Woods on the Hill 169

Dobson House 170

Tiger 174

"In the Thousand Islands. St. Lawrence River, Canada" 175

Stuart 175

Stuart 187

Hugh Mustard's House 187

Captain Smith and Ewan 191

Red. Edwin Smith, M.A.

Mrs. Dodds 193

Geo. R's Place 199

Stella 194

Wm. C. Macneill's 201

Cavendish Churchyard 201

Brock St. E., Ux-
bridge 208

Making the best of
it 211

The Manse

LMM

Corner of Parlor 233

The Old House 252

The Old Kitchen 254

Nearly eight 255

Bungalow at Brain-
tree 255

The moonlit woods
258

East Braintree Sta-
tion 260

"That peaceful, vine
hung manse" 261

Home Again 271

"Blessings on thee,
barefoot boys!" 271

Capt Smith

Pat, Chester, Mac,
Stuart, Ruth Cook
274

A Group of Visitors
274

A Group of Visitors
274

A Group of Visitors
274

Laura and I 275